The most
amazing places
to visit in
Britain

The most amazing places to visit in Britain

Published by
The Reader's Digest Association Limited
London • New York • Sydney • Montreal

Contents

Introduction

Britain is amazing, as full of wonder as it was when the Roman legions landed in Kent, the Vikings settled in the Orkneys and the industrial pioneers of the midlands set steam engines, furnaces and power looms into frenzied activity. Take a good look around.

Nowhere in the world is there such a concentration of natural beauty, rich history, vibrant culture and incredible examples of human inventiveness, folly or fancy. In *The Most Amazing Places to Visit in Britain* you will discover the unexpected – the grave of the last jester in England or the Scottish mausoleum with a 15 second echo – and see the familiar cast in a new light: the world's oldest grape vine at Hampton Court Palace or perhaps fossilised seashells at the top of Mount Snowdon. But this is not just a book about landscape and the past. Modern wonders, such as the Eden Project and the London Eye, are as important to what makes Britain so fascinating as the medieval stained glass of Canterbury Cathedral or Edinburgh's Royal Mile. By scouring all parts of Britain, from the Shetlands to the Scilly Isles, we have found 1000 amazing places where you may see or learn something to make your jaw drop.

Britain in sections

The Most Amazing Places to Visit in Britain is intended to be a voyage of discovery, with surprises at every turn. The structure is simple, but here are a few pointers.

Britain is divided into 10 regions (see right), each of which is introduced by a map showing the location of the amazing places. English regions are divided into counties, which appear in alphabetical order – so, South of England starts with Bedfordshire, followed by Berkshire and so on. County boundaries are clearly marked on each English map.

Traditional English county boundaries are followed, ignoring the smaller administrative units introduced in recent years. For example, Bath appears under Somerset, rather than Bath and North East Somerset.

Wales and Scotland are divided into two and four sections respectively – see the regional maps. Northern Ireland is one self-contained region. The Channel Islands appear as an inset map on the West Country plan.

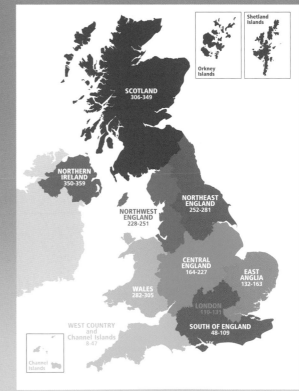

Shetland Islands

Orkney Islands

SCOTLAND
306-349

NORTHERN
IRELAND
350-359

NORTHWEST
ENGLAND
228-251

NORTHEAST
ENGLAND
252-281

CENTRAL
ENGLAND
164-227

EAST
ANGLIA
132-163

WALES
282-305

LONDON
110-131

WEST COUNTRY
and
Channel Islands
8-47

SOUTH OF ENGLAND
48-109

Channel
Islands

Finding your way

Amazing places are numbered, not named, on the regional maps, starting at **1** in each county – or section if it is a Welsh or Scottish region – and follow a rough geographical progression across or around an area. The numbers relate to keys that appear spread-by-spread throughout the book. Each spread of entries displays the county name or, for Wales and Scotland, the section name as shown on a regional map.

1 You can use the regional maps to locate places. For example, if you are looking at the regional map for the West Country – pages 8-9 – and want to know what entry **6** is, turn to the Cornwall section – pages 11-19 – and on page 12 you will find **6** in the key, which shows you that the place is St Michael's Mount.

2 You can use the key numbers on each spread of entries to locate places on a regional map. For example, if you are looking at page 258 in the South Wales section and want to pinpoint where Dinas Island is, look in the key to find its number, **4**, then turn to the regional map for Wales on pages 246-7 and find **4** in the South Wales section of the map.

3 There are more than 50 features in the book, most of which include a number of amazing places based on a particular theme, such as Dorset hill-forts, or location – Ironbridge Gorge, for instance. In each feature the amazing places are highlighted in the text in bold type, and given a number, which appears on the appropriate regional map, but in a different colour to that of the main entries – see the key on each regional map. Where there is more than one feature in a section, the numbering runs consecutively from one to the next. For example, in South Wales the feature numbers **1** to **5** cover five amazing islands on pages 260-1 and the numbers **6** to **7** denote two Victorian Gothic castles on pages 264-5. Where the feature is based on one location – such as Conwy, on page 254 – one number only is used in the feature and on the map.

▶ Directions and other details

At the end of each entry there are simple directions for finding the place, and a guide to opening details, which may be subject to seasonal alteration – it is always worth checking on this before you set out. Where details are complex, or if any kind of special arrangement is involved – for instance, booking a guided tour or a ferry – then a telephone number is given. Many churches and most areas of open country covered in this book are always accessible. Where this is not the case it is stated in the details.

In features, the details appear either collectively at the beginning or within the text after each place.

The following heritage or conservation organisations are noted in the details:
EH English Heritage
www.english-heritage.org.uk
NT National Trust **www.nationaltrust.org.uk**
Cadw Welsh Historic Monuments
('cadw' is a Welsh word meaning 'to keep')
www.cadw.wales.gov.uk
HS Historic Scotland
www.historic-scotland.gov.uk
NTS National Trust for Scotland **www.nts.org.uk**
SNH Scottish Natural Heritage **www.snh.org.uk**
MNH Manx National Heritage **www.gov.im/mnh**
RSPB Royal Society for the Protection of Birds
www.rspb.org.uk

West Country
and Channel Islands

England dips a toe into the Atlantic on a peninsula filled with legends of mermaids and ancient kings, where valleys creep below the edges of windswept moors and granite-walled harbours shelter in the lee of tumbling headlands.

5 Ilfracombe
3
6
2 Barnstaple
4
Bideford
2 3
A39
A386
A377
24
Bude
DEVON
20-26
Okehampton
A30
20 19
18
Launceston
A39
A30
23
24 A386
21
Tavistock
20
21
5
6 4
16
17
6 4
Liskeard
A38
2
CORNWALL
11-19
Plymouth A38
Newquay
A30
14
12
13
St Austell
A390
7
15
Truro
1
St Ives 1
A30
2
3
5
11
6
Penzance
6
A394
Falmouth
8
4
Helston
4 5
9
10
13

Bodmin Moor

Dartmoor National Park

Padstow
23
22
A39
Bodmin

Isles of Scilly
3 Tresco
St Mary's
4

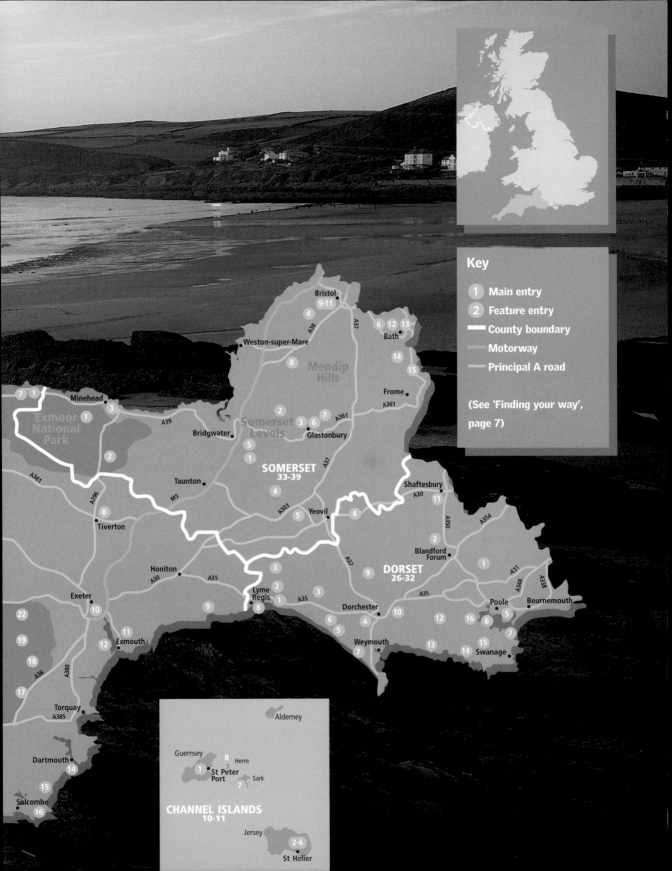

(See 'Finding your way', page 7)

Key

1 Main entry
2 Feature entry
— County boundary
— Motorway
— Principal A road

Bristol
9-11
Bath
6 12 13
14
15
Weston-super-Mare
Mendip Hills
Frome
A361
Minehead
Exmoor National Park
Bridgwater
Somerset Levels
Glastonbury
SOMERSET
33-39
Taunton
Shaftesbury
A30
Tiverton
Yeovil
A303
Blandford Forum
Honiton
A30
A35
DORSET
26-32
Exeter
Lyme Regis
A35
Dorchester
Poole
Bournemouth
Exmouth
Weymouth
Swanage
Torquay
A385
Dartmouth
Salcombe

A39
A37
A38
A396
A361
A38
A380
M5
A37
A350
A354
A348
A338
A31

CHANNEL ISLANDS
10-11

Alderney
Guernsey
St Peter Port
Herm
Sark
Jersey
St Helier
2-6

CHANNEL ISLANDS

1 The Little Chapel 2 Mont Orgueil Castle 3 La Hougue Bie 4 The Glass Church

5 Jersey War Tunnels 6 Jersey Zoo 7 Sark 8 Shell Beach, Herm

The Little Chapel

The 'world's smallest church', decorated with broken china

With room inside for only one priest and a congregation of up to three or four, the Little Chapel is said to be the smallest church in the world at 6 x 3m (20 x 10ft).

It stands in the grounds of a former Roman Catholic college and was begun in 1913 by a Frenchman, Brother Deodat Antoine, who decorated the interior and exterior with shells and pieces of broken china. When sunshine floods through the windows, the walls glitter in a multicoloured mosaic.

Since Brother Deodat's death in 1951, a grotto – modelled on Lourdes – and the stations of the cross have been added. Contributions of broken china are still sent to Guernsey from all over the world.
▶ *Guernsey, Les Vauxbelets. Signed from Guernsey airport-St Peter Port road. Daily.*

Mont Orgueil Castle

Invader-proof fortification

The Channel Islands' most dramatic building was constructed in the 13th century to guard Jersey against attacks from France – which is visible from its ramparts, towering 100m (328ft) above the sea. The maze of gateways, towers and immense walls that make up Mont Orgueil Castle fell to invaders just once, in 1461, and then only because of a treacherous governor.
▶ *Jersey. 4 miles E of St Helier. Daily summer; Fri-Mon winter.*

La Hougue Bie

A place to remember prehistoric Jersey islanders and slave labourers

Local legend says that a fiery dragon lived on La Hougue Bie and the French knight who rescued the people of Jersey by slaying the fearsome beast was buried in the site's 12m (40ft) high mini-mountain. In fact, the conical-shaped mound of earth and rubble covers one of the finest surviving Neolithic passage graves in Europe.

Visitors can still walk – or, rather, creep – along the low 10m (33ft) long passage leading to the tomb chamber. The skill of its builders about 5800 years ago was extraordinary: the passage is aligned to the equinoxes, the temperature within the tomb remains constant whatever the season, and the great capstones of up to 20 tonnes covering the grave are a solid foundation for the mound built over the site.

A former German command bunker close by, used during the occupation of Jersey in 1940-5, has been reconstructed as a memorial to thousands of slave workers transported to the Channel Islands during the war.
▶ *Jersey. Rue des Trot, 3 miles E of St Helier. Apr-Oct.*

The Glass Church

A fragile Art Deco masterpiece

Enter the outwardly plain and simple 19th-century St Matthew's Church in the St Helier suburb of Millbrook and you may not believe your eyes. 'The Glass Church' contains a spectacular collection of art deco Lalique glass – a 1930s bequest from a parishioner. The Parisian glass worker René Lalique came out of retirement to design the church's doors, windows, altar cross, decorative motifs, ceiling lights and the world's only glass font, which lend the church's interior an ethereal glow.
▶ *Jersey. W of St Helier, on St Aubin's Road.*

Jersey War Tunnels

Chilling reminders of wartime island occupation

Between 1941 and 1945 slave workers built two huge underground hospitals on Jersey and Guernsey, carving them out of solid rock to make them safe from land or air attack.

As part of the 'Captive Island' exhibition that tells the story of the German occupation of the island during World War II, 2 miles of chambers and corridors of the Jersey hospital, the operating theatre, telephone exchange, boiler room and storeman's office have been re-created. The everyday horrors and hardships of wartime life on Jersey are also recalled in sound and pictures, and by recipes for such unappetising staples as acorn coffee and bramble tea.
▶ *Jersey. 3 miles W of St Helier. Daily mid Feb-Dec.*

Jersey Zoo

Vital conservation work in the zoo that Gerald Durrell built

Plenty of people retire to the largely tax-free Channel Islands, but when the author and naturalist Gerald Durrell moved to a former manor house in the north of Jersey in 1959 he had a serious project in mind: he wanted to set up a zoo devoted to conservation work.

The zoo at Les Augrès Manor is more than a tourist attraction – it carries out a vital role in the preservation and breeding of some of the world's rarest animals. Here, in 12ha (30 acres) of landscaped grounds and gardens, visitors can meet gorillas, Sumatran orang-utans, tamarins and lemurs, black macaques, and birds seldom seen in the wild, such as the Asian white-eared pheasant and the Mauritius pink pigeon.
▶ *Jersey. Les Augrès Manor, Trinity, 4 miles N of St Helier. Daily.*

Sark

Feudal island stuck in a time warp

Helicopters, cars and even pigeons are banned from Sark, the fourth largest of the Channel Islands, which is reachable only by sea. It is the smallest state in Europe, with a population of about 500, 'ruled' by a hereditary seigneur who exercises a surprising range of feudal rights – he can, for instance, confine wrongdoers to the two-man jail, one of the smallest in the world.

For a spectacular walk, take a horse-drawn taxi or hired bicycle to the precipitous path known as La Coupee: a 90m (295ft) long sliver of rock, only 4m (13ft) wide in places, which links Sark with the peninsula of Little Sark.
▶ *Daily ferries in summer from St Peter Port, Guernsey.*

Shell Beach, Herm

A touch of the tropics

On a tiny island 3 miles from Guernsey is the Channel Islands' most beautiful beach. From afar the ½ mile long strip appears to be of golden sand, but close to you see that it is made up of billions of broken shells. Complete shells, prized by collectors, have washed up here from as far as the Caribbean, carried by the Gulf Stream.
▶ *Daily ferries in summer to Herm from St Peter Port, Guernsey.*

St Ives

Cornwall's vibrant artists' colony

Is it the wonderful clear light, the golden beach setting or the crowds of free-spending visitors that attract artists to St Ives like bees to nectar? In this charming, haphazard town you can find art at every level from amateur daubs on waterfront easels to modern masterpieces. At the **Barbara Hepworth Museum** on Barnoon Hill, the house, studio and garden that belonged to the sculptor (1903-75) are crammed with examples of her work. The **Bernard Leach Pottery**, founded by Leach in 1920 at Higher Stennack on the outskirts of the town, is now a museum. His workshop and kiln shed are used to show the practices and skills of one of Britain's foremost potters. In a spectacular position overlooking Porthmeor Beach, the **Tate St Ives**, opened in 1993, exhibits modern art in imaginatively designed spaces, some illuminated with the brilliant light that streams in from the sky and sea.
▶ *Barbara Hepworth Museum and Sculpture Garden, Barnoon Hill; daily Mar-Oct, Tues-Sun Nov-Feb. Tate St Ives, Porthmeor Beach; daily Mar-Oct, Tues-Sun Nov-Feb.*

Zennor

A village steeped in stories

Legends lie thick on granite-built Zennor. It is said the villagers once planted a hedge round a visiting cuckoo, to hide the changing seasons – they believed that if the bird left, springtime would be lost. There is the tale of the giant who built Zennor Quoit, the Neolithic tomb outside the village: if the stones are ever moved, he will bring them together again.

Then there is the legend of the mermaid who came to church with a long dress hiding her fish's tail so she could hear the singing of Matthew Trewhella, the squire's golden-voiced son. She lured him to her under-sea grotto – on summer nights you may hear their duets. You can also see the mermaid – a saucy-looking girl with long hair and a prominent belly-button, holding her comb and mirror. She was carved into a bench-end in St Senara's Church 600 years ago.
▶ *4 miles W of St Ives, on B3306.*

WEST COUNTRY

CORNWALL

3 Tresco 4 Porthcurno 5 Chysauster Ancient Village 6 St Michael's Mount

7 Wheal Coates 8 Pendennis Castle

Tresco

Paradise on a windswept island

A riot of exotic plants smothers the centre of Tresco. Yet when Augustus Smith, a banker, bought the Isles of Scilly, 28 miles off Land's End, in 1834, the little archipelago was at the nadir of its fortunes, its piloting and fishing livelihoods in ruins, its population emigrating. Smith transformed the fortunes of the isles by ruling like a king, establishing a tough regime and expelling any who disagreed with his methods.

Round the ruins of Tresco's abbey, founded in the 10th century, Smith and his successors created a glorious subtropical garden. Today, well over 5000 species flourish here, a spectacle of fertility utterly at odds with the island's natural weatherbeaten moorland.

Seek out also the 'Valhalla' section of Tresco Abbey Gardens for its magnificent collection of nautical figureheads – a poignant reminder that the treacherous seas around the islands has made this the shipwreck capital of the world.
▶ *Access by helicopter, plane or boat. Contact Isles of Scilly Tourist Board, St Mary's, Tel 01720 422536. Tresco Abbey Gardens daily.*

Porthcurno

The nerve centre of Empire and Britain's most spectacular theatre

Go to the beach in Porthcurno Cove after stormy weather and you may see cables emerging from the sea, uncovered by shifting sands. An obelisk marks the spot where in 1870 the pioneer telegraph cables linking Britain with India came ashore, the beginning of Porthcurno's vital 100–year role in telegraph communication all over the world. At the **Porthcurno Telegraph Museum**, in secret wartime communications bunkers beside the old Eastern Telegraph Company building, the full story is told through vintage telegraphic equipment in gleaming mahogany and brass, sections of giant seawater-proofed cable, and posters and maps.

The nearby cliffs hold what looks like an ancient Greek amphitheatre, a monument to the determination of local woman Rowena Cade. She began the **Minack Theatre** in 1931, building much of it herself. Its precipitous location with far views over Porthcurno Bay give the Minack's audience the most inspiring theatrical backdrop in Britain.
▶ *Signed off B3315 Penzance-Land's End road. Museum daily Easter-Oct, Sun-Mon Nov-Easter; Tel 01736 810966. Minack Theatre, Tel 01736 810181 for information.*

Chysauster Ancient Village

The way our Iron Age ancestors lived

High on a bleak down stands a remarkable Iron Age settlement – the eight houses of Chysauster, four on either side of a short street, each with its tiny courtyard and garden. The houses were occupied from around the 1st century BC, and abandoned some 300 years later. Apart from the loss of the thatched roofs, they have deteriorated remarkably little in nearly two millennia.
▶ *4 miles N of Penzance, off B3311 Penzance-St Ives road. EH. Daily.*

St Michael's Mount

Drama and romance in a high-piled castle on a rocky island

The breathtaking views of the craggy peak of St Michael's Mount (right), with its Tudor fortress and 14th-century priory church perched at the summit, draw you from the beach at Marazion. Cross the causeway on foot at low tide, or take the ferry if the sea is up; then climb the slopes through banks of subtropical trees and exotic flowering plants, warmed by the close proximity of the sea and sheltered in their landward-facing position, up to the castle with its armoury, museum and superbly elegant Blue Drawing Room.

The first church on the Mount was built after the Archangel Michael miraculously appeared there in AD 495. Shortly after the Norman invasion of Britain the island was granted to the abbey of Mont St Michel in France – the two sites are remarkably alike. The monks built a Benedictine Abbey on the peak. Later Henry VIII made it a coastal fortress, and in the mid 17th century the St Aubin family converted the whole place into a fabulous extravaganza of a dwelling.
▶ *Off Marazion (A394); on foot via causeway at low tide, or ferry (summer only) at high tide. NT. Sun-Fri Apr-Oct (Nov-Mar guided tours only, Tel 01736 710507).*

Wheal Coates

Gaunt and dramatic remains of a once-thriving Cornish industry

Perched on the cliff edge overlooking a wonderful sweep of north Cornwall coastline, the gaunt ruin of Wheal Coates's 19th-century pumping-engine house points a finger of chimney skywards. The Cornish tin industry, active from the pre-Christian era and bedrock of the economy of the west half of the county from medieval times onwards, perished in the 1980s from lack of investment and the effects of foreign competition. Its demise left the landscape dotted with bleak ruins, notably the tall church-like structures built to house the beam engines that pumped the mines dry.

Around Wheal Coates you will find more traces of the 'wheal' or works – scars stained with tin ore, old shafts, the base of a great horizontal pumping engine in the shadow of the chimney. But it is that tall stone chimney with its brick top, forever smokeless, and the silent shed ruin beside it, that form the most poignant memorial to the death of Cornwall's toughest occupation.
▶ *On South West Coast Path, ¼ mile N of Chapel Porth car park (Chapel Porth signed from B3277 on southern outskirts of St Agnes).*

Pendennis Castle

A Tudor fort that defied Oliver Cromwell's might

Strikingly outlined against sky and sea on a rocky headland, Pendennis outstares its sister stronghold of St Mawes Castle across the entrance to the great natural harbour of Carrick Roads. Henry VIII built the forts in 1544-6 to keep the French out of Falmouth and the harbour, and Pendennis Castle proved strong enough to withstand Sir Thomas Fairfax's besieging Parliamentarian army for five months a century later. The defending Royalist commander, Sir John Arundell, was allowed to march his men out with drums and flags and the full honours of war.
▶ *Pendennis Head, 1 mile SE of Falmouth. EH. Daily.*

DRAMA AND ROMANCE IN A HIGH-PILED CASTLE ON A ROCKY ISLAND

ST MICHAEL'S MOUNT

CORNWALL

THE CORNISH ALPS

Halliggye Fogou

Moody, murky and mysterious

By the light of a torch – or better still, a
flickering candle to enhance the eerie
atmosphere – you stumble along a cold, stone-
lined passage under the earth. Thick granite rocks
form the walls, and flat stone slabs shape the roof
from which spiders have hung white silk bags of
eggs. Many fogous – subterranean chambers such
as this one at Halliggye – were constructed
during the Iron Age some 2000 years ago. Did
their builders use them to store food, to hide
from their enemies, or as a setting for long-
forgotten rituals? You can take your pick of
explanations, as no one knows.
▶ *Trelowarren estate, signed from B3293 near Garras
off A3083. EH. Daily Apr-Oct.*

Goonhilly Downs

Spaceman meets ancient man on a rugged heath

Vast white satellite dishes rise from empty
heathland on skeletal gantries to scan the skies
for messages from space. In the distance, the huge
spindly arms of wind generators chop the air,
sucking power from the sea wind. Such
endeavour would have seemed pure magic to the
long-ago people who raised the standing stones
and buried their dead on Goonhilly Downs.

At **Goonhilly Earth Station**, the world's largest
satellite station, you can watch – and have a hand
in – the tracking of communications satellites
that are able to pinpoint your house from space
or follow the movements of galaxies. Then walk
across **Goonhilly Downs**, a Site of Special Scientific
Interest, among great drifts of Cornish heathers,
orchids and lousewort, over the rough heathland
(the warmest spot in Britain), where larks sing
and hen harriers glide, to find the prehistoric
standing stone known as the Dry Tree. The hut
circles and round burial mounds of ancient
cultures – Bronze Age and Iron Age, spanning
some 2000 years – lie all around. Raising your
eyes from these to the futuristic shapes of the
skyline dishes, you can see alien worlds collide.
▶ *On B3293 between St Keverne and Helston
(off A3083 Helston-Lizard). Goonhilly Earth Station
daily Feb-Dec. Goonhilly Downs daily.
Tel 0800 679 593 for details.*

St Just in Roseland

A sub-tropical churchyard, the prettiest in Cornwall

'There is a degree of beauty that flies so high
that no net of words or no snare of colour can
hope to capture it, and of that order is the beauty
of St Just in Roseland…I would like to know if
there is in the whole of England a churchyard
more beautiful than this.' H.V. Morton, *In Search
of England* (1927).

Since the travel writer H.V. Morton fell in
love with St Just in Roseland in the 1920s, its
beauty has not diminished. The botanist John
Treseder planted the steeply sloping churchyard
of 13th-century St Just's Church with specimen
trees and shrubs he brought back from Australia
in 1897. The view today, looking down over
bamboo, palms and cedars, rhododendrons and
camellias, magnolia and fuchsia to the wide
waters of Carrick Roads, is as spectacularly
exotic as ever.
▶ *2 miles N of St Mawes off A3078.*

Roche Chapel

Follow a restless soul in its desperate search for sanctuary

The unquiet spirit of John Tregeagle, a dishonest
17th-century steward, is condemned for eternity
to empty Dozmary Pool on Bodmin Moor with
a leaky limpet shell. When it can bear no more,

Tregeagle's spirit, pursued by shrieking demons, flees to seek shelter in the ruined early 15th-century chapel perched on Roche rocks five leagues off. If you climb the ladder to the bleak granite chapel on a stormy day with a gale blowing, you may hear those howling devils for yourself.
▶ *Beside road to Bugle, off B3274 on S edge of Roche village (off A30 Bodmin-Truro road).*

Eden Project
Green arrivals from another planet

The domes of the Eden Project bubble from the floor of the disused 50m (164ft) deep claypit at Bodelva, near St Blazey, like an alien life-form. The whole enterprise is the idea of Tim Smit – the man behind The Lost Gardens of Heligan (see page 18) – and is a triumph of architecture and engineering. Hundreds of clear hexagonal foil panels, each strong enough to bear the weight of someone standing on it, are supported on a honeycomb latticework of steel.

Inside, the domes are even more exciting: vast spaces – the biggest dome is 110m (361ft) across and 55m (180ft) high – containing a botanical wonderland. The largest of the two groups of domes, the Humid Tropics Biome, is the world's biggest greenhouse. In here, a waterfall's swirling spray hangs in the hot, humid atmosphere, and moisture drips from the lush foliage of balsa, mahogany and teak trees, orchids and bamboo.

Inside the second cluster of domes, the Warm Temperate Biome, the environment of regions like the Mediterranean, California and southern Africa is reproduced – a drier place heady with the scent of herbs and orange and lemon trees. The educational centre, known as The Core, has been designed to reflect the principles of plant growth.
▶ *2½ miles NE of St Austell off A390 Lostwithiel road. Daily.*

The Cornish Alps
Over the moor to a moonscape made by man

For the holidaymakers who stream into Cornwall on the A30, there is always a jolt of surprise at that first sight of the china clay workings from the long straight to Fraddon and Indian Queens. Like peaks covered with grubby snow, they rear above the Goss moor in small-scale imitation of the Alps.

Turn off the main road, through Roche or St Dennis, to discover lanes that snake through 'passes' between these giant spoil heaps and look down on the milky water of flooded pits. This barren landscape is the product of more than 200 years of quarrying a material used in items as diverse as fertilisers and face powder, porcelain and plasterboard.
▶ *In a 4 mile band N of St Austell, traversed by B3274 and B3279.*

WEST COUNTRY

CORNWALL

Polperro

Downhill rush to a smugglers' haven tucked in a fold of cliffs

Of all picturesquely photogenic Cornish fishing villages, Polperro wears the crown. The road through the village twists this way and that, forced down a narrow defile between whitewashed houses clinging to any foothold on the steep sides of the coombe.

The diminutive harbour, squeezed between 125m (410ft) high cliffs, reflects the tall Georgian fishermen's houses lining its walls. They were built three-storeys high so that nets could be stored (and contraband stashed) below the living spaces.

▶ *4 miles W of Looe on A387.*

Cotehele

Self-sufficiency in grand Tudor style

Above a wooded slope on the Tamar river, and largely untouched by time, stands Cornwall's loveliest Tudor house, its granite buildings grouped around two courtyards. Inside, rooms are fitted out with their original furniture. Some rooms are hung with delicate medieval tapestries, never submitted to artificial light – visit on a fine day to see them at their best.

After treading softly through the house, visit the grounds. Paths lead down the landscaped slopes to the working Cotehele Mill, a riverfront quarry, and a restored Tamar sailing barge and warehouses. It all evokes a sense of what it must have been like to live at a time when almost every need would have been met from the estate.

▶ *8 miles SW of Tavistock off A390. NT. House / mill daily, except Fri, Mar-Oct. Mill also Fri, Jul–Aug. Grounds daily.*

The Hurlers and the Cheesewring

Stone formations wrapped in legend

Folklore says that the Hurlers – three stone circles, two still standing, the other toppled – get their name from men turned to stone for being impious enough to play the ancient Celtic game of hurling on the Sabbath. Archaeologists say that the circles were erected some time between 2200 BC and 1400 BC, although their function is shrouded in mystery. One theory is that the circles were a huge stellar timepiece, with the season identified by the alignment of the stones with the stars.

Close by on this bleak southern edge of Bodmin Moor stands the Cheesewring, a 9m (30ft) high granite tor, said to have resulted from a weightlifting contest between saints and giants. In reality, it is a natural feature, formed by wind and water erosion. It gets its name from a cider-maker's 'cheese': a block of apples packed in straw and then put through a press.

▶ *5 miles N of Liskeard off B3254 Launceston road at Upton Cross. EH (Hurlers). Daily.*

Tamar Otter Sanctuary

Non-stop show for spectators

The sanctuary at North Petherwin in the little valley of Bolsbridge Water, appropriately enough a tribute of the River Ottery, is a grand place to get close to these sleek, intelligent creatures. Here you can observe otters more closely than in the wild because they have no fear; in fact, their feeding, playing and dazzling swimming antics suggest they enjoy an audience. Thanks to the breeding-and-release programmes of sanctuaries like this, otters are making a comeback in Britain.

▶ *5 miles NW of Launceston off B3254 Bude road. Daily Apr-Oct.*

The 'Auk Walk'

A lofty bird sanctuary

An accessible cliff-top path from Trevalga leads to one of nature's most beguiling sights. Here, from April to mid July, puffins come ashore to breed. Take binoculars to study their clown-like faces with bright red and yellow beaks and furious, whirring flight. These birds like to breed in burrows, which they dig in grassy slopes on inaccessible cliffs – and they find the perfect location in the offshore rock stacks of Long Island and Short Island. Their cousins, guillemots and razorbills, smartly jacketed in black and white, nest here too. Turn off the B3263 to park near Trevalga church. Follow signs to the South West Coastal Path (¼ mile) and bear left to walk parallel with the stacks.

▶ *2 miles NE of Tintagel on B3263.*

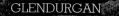

Botanical wonders shade Cornish coves

Victorian plant collectors introduce an exotic touch to the valleys of Britain's mild far southwest

1 **The Lost Gardens of Heligan** ▶ *2 miles NW of Mevagissey, off B3273 St Austell road. Daily all year.*

2 **Lanhydrock** ▶ *3 miles S of Bodmin, off B3269. NT. Garden daily all year.*

3 **Trelissick** ▶ *6 miles S of Truro, off B3289 King Harry Ferry road. NT. Daily all year.*

4 **Trebah** ▶ *Nr Mawnan Smith, 5 miles S of Falmouth. Daily.*

5 **Glendurgan** ▶ *Nr Mawnan Smith, 5 miles S of Falmouth. NT. Tues-Sat and bank hol Mon Feb-Oct.*

6 **Trengwainton** ▶ *3 miles W of Penzance, off A3071 St Just road. NT. Sun-Thur Feb-Oct.*

It is easy to feel disorientated in The Jungle and Lost Valley. Filtered sunlight slants through a high canopy of palm and tree fern fronds, illuminating the boardwalk with soft beams of light. Bird calls and the hum of insects sound through tall stands of bamboo. Purple, scarlet, yellow and white blossoms explode among thickets of rhododendrons. And everywhere there is water: it drips through the foliage, rushes along spillways, dissolves into veils of spray as it plummets over waterfalls, and rises as steam in the humid air. At any moment, you feel a jaguar might lunge into this subtropical valley. Instead, when the luxuriant growth parts it reveals a view of the picturesque port of Mevagissey, for these are **The Lost Gardens of Heligan** – where a sheltered valley dips to a Gulf Stream-warmed sea, creating ideal conditions for exotic plants usually found much farther south.

Restored to its former glory

For landowners inspired by the exploits of Victorian plant collectors, the wooded ravines at Heligan and similar places were heaven-sent spots where seeds brought back from strange lands could grow into botanical wonders.

At Heligan, the wonders came to a halt with the outbreak of the First World War, when its small army of more than 20 gardeners marched off to join the bigger one in France. For the next 76 years the gardens lay forgotten, slowly choking under a thicket of brambles and wild growth. Then, in 1990, Tim Smit and John Nelson hacked their way in and began to bring the gardens painstakingly and thrillingly back to life. The walled gardens with their citrus and melon houses were restored, the manure-heated pineapple beds made productive once more, and the tree ferns rescued from suffocation by encroaching wilderness.

Heligan shares the limelight with a dozen or more wonderful gardens strung along the Cornish peninsula. At **Lanhydrock**, for example, the mild coastal climate slips up the valley of the River Fowey, bringing frost-free winters to slopes where creamy-blossomed camellias and magnolias flower in quick succession. Farther west, the gardens at **Trelissick** look down the wide sweep of Carrick Roads to the open waters of Falmouth Bay. South along the coast two spectacular valley gardens, **Trebah** and **Glendurgan**, tumble down to the Helford river, the latter's massed conifers and knobbly old tulip trees rising above a splendid cherry laurel maze (above), planted in 1833. Mild sea air off Mount's Bay encourages exotic trees and shrubs to grow in the complex of walled gardens at **Trengwainton**, including rhododendrons grown from seed brought from Burma and Assam in the 1920s.

WEST COUNTRY

CORNWALL

Tintagel Castle

Romantic cliff-top ruins and a tale of deceitful seduction

Visit Tintagel during a howling gale, or on a dark winter's evening with the sunset bursting through storm clouds, to sense the romance of the place. It is not so much the 12th-century castle ruins that entrance visitors as their cliff-top location, and the wild legend that goes with them. It is said that the wicked Welsh king Uther Pendragon persuaded the wizard Merlin to disguise him so that he could pay a nocturnal visit to his enemy's wife, the beautiful – but gullible – Ygerna. That night the couple conceived Arthur, the future king, in the castle on the cliffs.

▶ *Signed off B3263 between Boscastle and St Teath. EH. Daily.*

Delabole Slate Quarry

A commercial quarry that has mined slate since medieval times

Visiting England's oldest working slate quarry is a much quieter affair since miners stopped using dynamite to extract the slate. It is thought that the quarry, which is now half a mile long, a quarter of a mile wide and 400ft deep, has been in use for around 1000 years. Certainly the pits which were in use during the reign of Elizabeth I were known to be exporting slate to countries as far away as the Netherlands. Take a tour of the enormous pit, watch 600 tonne slate blocks being sawed and see how the final products are hand crafted.

▶ *1 mile S of Delabole off B3314. Mon-Fri May-Aug, except bank hols. By appointment only at other times, Tel 01840 212242.*

St Enodoc, Daymer Bay

The church that was saved from the sand

All you see of St Enodoc, until you are right on top of it, is the crooked spire, for the Norman church lies sunken in a grassy sand dune. By 1863 it was half full of sand and the vicar had to be lowered through the roof to hold the annual service that justified the church being kept open. It was renovated and restored in 1864. John Betjeman, the late Poet Laureate, spent idyllic childhood holidays nearby and grew to love St Enodoc. His grave is marked by an elaborately carved slate stone in the churchyard.

▶ *Park at Daymer Bay, 5 miles N of Bodieve, signed from B3314. Walk ¾ mile S along coastal path to reach church.*

Polzeath Beach and The Rumps

A Cornish headland haunted by the spirit of Iron Age man

Long, narrow and crouched between rocky headlands, Polzeath Beach attracts rollers that crash in from the open sea. When the surf is up, wet-suited figures ride the fast waves. The South West Coastal Path leads north from the beach to Iron Age ditches and ramparts on The Rumps, a craggy promontory with extensive views over the Camel Estuary. On this bare, storm-blown outpost, thrust into the Atlantic, stood circular wooden huts whose inhabitants wove wool, fished, grew grain and possibly traded wine and pottery with Mediterranean cultures.

The 6 mile stretch of coast running east from Rumps Point to Port Quin is spectacular even by north Cornwall's high standards, and best appreciated by following the coastal path.
▶ *Polzeath, 5 miles N of Wadebridge, signed from B3314. The Rumps headland, 2 miles N on South West Coastal Path from Polzeath.*

Morwenstow

Home to a most eccentric parson

Robert Hawker was an unconventional country priest. He wore fishermen's seaboots, wrote poetry, smoked opium and pinched babies at baptism to make them yell the Devil out. Once he dressed as a mermaid to give his parishioners something to talk about. While contemptuous of convention, he was a good-hearted man who did his best to feed, clothe and educate the local fisherfolk. Hawker also 'Christianised' the pagan harvest festival by incorporating it into a church service.

At the remote village of Morwenstow you can visit the Norman Church of St Morwenna where Hawker preached – there is a stained-glass window to his memory. Alongside is the vicarage built by him: each chimney is a model of one of his favourite church towers. On the cliffs south of the church, a footpath leads to the little hut 'Pass'n Hawker' built from wreck timbers. He used to retreat to it and write poetry enhanced by opium fumes.
▶ *7 miles N of Bude, signed off A39.*

POLZEATH BEACH

DEVON

Lundy Island

A heavenly experience of island life

In the 19th century, the island of Lundy, then ruled by the Heaven family, was known as the 'Kingdom of Heaven'. That is not a bad description, even today, for a 3½ mile slip of grass-topped granite entirely free from the rush and roar of mechanised life. Instead, there are mighty cliffs and jungly paths, seals and puffins, starfish and orchids, wild goats and peregrine falcons.

Bronze Age subsistence farmers, medieval monks and pirates have come and gone as settlers and owners. The island was in decline when the National Trust bought it in 1969, leasing it to the Landmark Trust. Now you can visit for a day or longer to walk the 7 miles of soaring cliffs, admire the island's sika deer and soay sheep, spot dolphins and sharks, and repair to the Marisco Tavern to eat roast goat and drink Old Light Bitter.
▶ *11 miles off Hartland Point, in Bristol Channel. NT. Crossings from Bideford and Ilfracombe, Tel 01271 863636.*

Hartland Point and Quay

Towering cliffs pounded by the force of wild Atlantic waves

Visit Hartland Point on a stormy winter's day and you experience nature at its most elemental, as huge Atlantic waves burst thunderously up the dark 100m (328ft) high cliffs. Devon's coast turns south here, and wind and sea seem to hit the land at double strength. Countless seafarers have been lost and ships destroyed on this 20 mile stretch of coast, punctuated with treacherous rocky bays.

Two miles south of the point is the harbour of Hartland Quay, built in a crevice of the cliffs and partly financed by canny West Country adventurers, including Walter Raleigh and Francis Drake. By the late 18th century Hartland Quay was prosperous, sending out local grain, malt and wool, and receiving imports of building materials and fertilisers. The harbour closed to commercial traffic after storm damage in 1893. Today, the old harbourmaster's house is a hotel and a great place from which to watch the storm waves in comfort.
▶ *Hartland Point, 6 miles W of Clovelly off A39. Hartland Quay, 6 miles W of A39 via Hartland village.*

Clovelly

Picturesque village with a sea view

Whitewashed cottages with hanging baskets and flowery gardens spill down steeply towards the sea along Clovelly's car-free cobbled street. There are just two kinds of transport here: sleds for goods and donkeys for people.

The harbour with its two-tiered stone wall was built in Tudor times, and was the only safe haven along this stretch of coast. Christine Hamlyn, owner of the Clovelly estate from 1884 to 1936, insisted on high standards: there should be no beach booths, electricity cables, garish advertisements or untidy front gardens. It remains unspoilt today – take your camera.
▶ *On B3237, 2 miles N of A39 between Bude and Bideford.*

Braunton Burrows

A deserted sandy beach and wild flowers make a morning paradise

Imagine strolling through 4 miles of sand dunes carpeted with wild flowers, down to a pristine beach where not another footprint has preceded yours. The pleasure awaits you on a pre-breakfast ramble at Braunton Burrows. Salt-tolerant plants, including crinkly green sea kale and powder-blue sea holly, yellow horned poppy, purple sea lavender and the brilliant royal blue spikes of viper's bugloss, thrive here. If you set off early enough, you will reach the white beach of Saunton Sands in time to share it with rabbits, plovers and peregrine falcons.
▶ *SW of Braunton, where B3231 meets A361.*

St Nicholas's Chapel, Ilfracombe

Lighting the way home

High above Ilfracombe harbour stands a 14th-century chapel built of dark local stone. It is a sombre building in rain, but a high-perched landmark under cloudless skies. For the past 500 years a light has shone in the chapel – dedicated to St Nicholas, patron saint of seafarers – to warn passing ships off this dangerous coast, and to guide the town's fishing boats home. The chapel has been used as a church, a lighthouse, a practice room for the town band and a home for a family of 16.
▶ *On Lantern Hill, Ilfracombe Harbour. Daily May-Oct, except in bad weather.*

Arlington Court

Creative spirit discovered in captivity

Miniature ships, exquisitely made from scraps of bone, ivory and horsehair, are found among a larger collection of model ships at Arlington Court. They were crafted with great ingenuity by French prisoners of the Napoleonic Wars, who found a way to liberate their artistic skills during those years of boredom and frustration.

The ships are just one part of the exuberant hotchpotch of items acquired by Rosalie Chichester (1865-1949), a traveller and collector, who lived all her life at Arlington Court. She filled the Georgian house with thousands of souvenirs from her journeys.
▶ *6 miles N of Barnstaple, signed from A39. NT. Daily, except Sat, mid Mar-Oct.*

Lynton and Lynmouth

A tale of heroic determination and an engrossing museum

Situated on the coast, the harbour village of Lynmouth has had its fair share of dramatic moments in its history. The most heroic being the 'overland launch' of the Lynmouth lifeboat, *Louisa*, to rescue the drifting and helpless cargo ship *Forrest Hall* in a ferocious gale in January 1899. Mountainous onshore seas prevented a launch at Lynmouth, so coxswain Jack Crowcombe, his crew, village men and horses hauled the *Louisa* up the steepest hill in Devon, across the storm-lashed moors and down to more sheltered Porlock, 13 miles away.

Five hundred feet above Lynmouth, its sister village of Lynton perches in a saddle of ground. Here you will find one of the oddest and most appealing small museums in the West Country – the Lyn & Exmoor Museum. The collection contains everything from an otter trap to a peat plough, from a homemade barometer to a 100-year-old jar of bottled gooseberries. The way to get between Lynmouth and Lynton, known as Little Switzerland by the Victorians, is on the ingenious funicular railway, which opened in 1890. The two cars each have a counterbalancing water tank that is filled at the top of the hill and emptied at the foot.
▶ *18 miles W of Minehead on A39 Barnstaple road. Lyn & Exmoor Museum, Market St, Mon-Fri, Sun pm, Apr-Oct.*

Knightshayes Court

Mr Burges' gothic fantasty

William Burges, an eccentric Victorian architect who was given to striding around with a parrot on his shoulder, was the man to employ if you wanted bizarre and highly coloured Gothic designs in your house. Burges had just started on his most celebrated project, the refurbishing of Cardiff Castle (see page 264), when Sir John Heathcote-Amory engaged him in 1869 to let his imagination rip on Knightshayes. The results can be seen in smoking rooms, boudoirs and drawing rooms dripping with over-the-top stucco and gilt.

The gardens at Knightshayes are as famous as the house, with topiary clipped in the shape of peacocks and medieval battlements, and a succession of individual areas where the plants are grouped for characteristics such as fragrance, colour and foliage.
▶ *2 miles N of Tiverton off A396 Bampton road. NT. Daily, except Fri, mid Mar-Oct.*

Seaton Tramway

A rattling good ride for canoodlers

Diminutive vintage tramcars rattle through the fields along the estuary of the River Axe, an incongruous but endearing sight in the East Devon countryside. Brightly painted and immaculately maintained by volunteers, the Seaton Tramway brings a smile of pure pleasure to the faces of passengers, even those too young to remember what it was like to spoon with a sweetheart while 'riding on top of the cars'.
▶ *Terminus, Harbour Road, Seaton. Daily Apr-Oct; Sat and Sun Nov-Dec.*

Exeter Cathedral

Lift a lid on the medieval mind

Raise the wooden seats in Exeter cathedral's choir stalls and you are in for a shock. Devilish creatures rise up, all bulging eyes, unsheathed claws and dilated nostrils. These 13th-century carvings decorate what are probably the oldest misericords in Britain – those convenient supports against which the monks could prop themselves during long services. But while a medieval God could contemplate them taking the weight off their feet, a glance to the side provided a constant reminder of the consequences of relaxing their mental vigilance. There, in the woodcarvers' art, were all the horrors that Hell had in store for those who let sinful thoughts enter their heads.
▶ *Exeter city centre.*

WEST COUNTRY

Landscapes to stir the imagination

Best-selling novelists and writers of extraordinary guidebooks have found inspiration in Devon's high country

1 Lank Combe **2** Tarka Trail **3** Ox's Cross **4** Foxtor Mires **5** Bellever Tor **6** Vixen Tor

It is not surprising that the two great wildernesses of Exmoor and Dartmoor should have nurtured wordsmiths down the years. Exmoor has all the airy uplands, sunlit coasts and secret combes anyone with a romantic turn of mind could wish for. Dour granite Dartmoor, so prone to mists and moody weather, seems made for Gothic adventure and dark drama.

The most famous Exmoor novel is *Lorna Doone*, written by the teacher and poet R.D. Blackmore, and published in 1869. The hidden combes south of Oare, where Blackmore's grandfather was rector, fascinated the writer from an early age, and it was here that he set his tale of love between honest John Ridd and the beautiful Lorna. You can visit St Mary's Church in Oare (the village, just over the Somerset border, is signposted off the A39 between Porlock and Lynton) where the villainous Carver Doone shot Lorna on her wedding day, and follow a footpath south along Badgworthy Water to the waterslide at the entrance to **Lank Combe**, where John Ridd first met her. Lank Combe, or possibly nearby Hoccombe Combe, is also the likely model for Doone Valley, hideout of the murderous clan. On the way back, look out for the riverside memorial to the novelist.

Furry riverside hero and a hellish hound

Exmoor's other great novel, *Tarka the Otter*, a tale of the life, journeyings and death of a wild creature, was the masterpiece of Henry Williamson, who retreated to Exmoor in 1921 to nurse mental trauma brought on by four years in the trenches during the First World War. The book, which was published in 1928, won the Hawthornden Prize and made his name. But it did not bring Williamson peace of mind; he remained a difficult, driven man to the end of his days.

The course of Tarka's wanderings around Exmoor, including the scene of his hunt and death on the Torridge estuary, can be followed along the **Tarka Trail**, a 180 mile, figure-of-eight footpath based on Barnstaple. At the crossroads in **Ox's Cross**, just north of Georgeham, you see the wooden hut Williamson built as a writing retreat.

One Dartmoor novel stands above the rest – the 1901-2 Sherlock Holmes tale *The Hound of the Baskervilles*, by Sir Arthur Conan Doyle. Boosted by many film and television adaptations, this tale of murder, madness and mystery has lost none of its dread appeal. Though Holmes and Watson take centre stage as they pursue wicked conman Jack Stapleton and his devilish dog, it is Dartmoor that fires the imagination – its creeping fogs, granite tors, prehistoric huts and ghastly 'Grimpen Mire' bog, which swallows the villain at the end. The mire was probably based on **Foxtor Mires**, 2 miles southeast of Princetown, whose gloomy prison appears in the book under its own name, as do **Bellever Tor** (off B3212 at Postbridge) and **Vixen Tor** (off B3357 at Merrivale). You can also puzzle over the identity of Baskerville Hall and dastardly Stapleton's Merripit House, possibly Nun's Cross Cottage, near Foxtor.

Perhaps the quirkiest guide to the moor is *A Book of Dartmoor*, written in 1900 by Sabine Baring-Gould, rector of Lewtrenchard – a village on the moor's margin – and provider of the words for the hymn 'Onward Christian Soldiers'. In it he dissects prehistoric sites, recounts legends, spouts history and reels off anecdotes galore.

BELLEVER TOR

DEVON

11 A la Ronde 12 Starcross Atmospheric Railway Pumping House

13 Burgh Island 14 Bayard's Cove

A la Ronde

The Parminter cousins and their cutely crazy, many-sided house

In the late 18th century it was fashionable to while away a year taking the Grand Tour through Europe. Spinster cousins Jane and Mary Parminter spent ten years over theirs, and returned with some funny foreign notions. Inspired by the shape of the octagonal basilica of San Vitale, in Ravenna, Italy, they created A la Ronde.

The fantastical structure consists of a central octagon 11m (35ft) high, from each side of which two rooms fan out to create a 16-sided folly. Chief attraction is the Shell Gallery, with its frieze of feathers, seaweed, sand, stones, pottery fragments and seashells – a work so fragile that viewing is by a video link.

▶ *2 miles N of Exmouth on A376 Exeter road. NT. Sat-Wed mid Mar-Oct.*

Starcross Atmospheric Railway Pumping House

The great Isambard Kingdom Brunel is vanquished by rats

The plain-looking building with the tower next to the Exe estuary scarcely looks like a monument to one of engineering's most noble failures – but this is the sole surviving pumping house of Isambard Kingdom Brunel's ill-fated Atmospheric Railway. The Victorian Age's most flamboyant and successful engineer was trying to establish vacuum power as a cheap and reliable means of rail transport. A string of pumping houses, each 3 miles from its neighbour, sucked air out of one section of pipe laid between rails and pumped it into the next, so propelling a piston with a train attached.

Trials between Exeter and Newton Abbot went well, but there was a problem: how to seal the slot in the pipe through which a bar ran connecting the piston to the locomotive. Brunel's solution was a leather valve greased with tallow. Unfortunately, rats ate both, and what the rodents did not consume fell victim to rain and the salt estuary winds. In 1848 the project was abandoned, having cost investors more than half a million pounds. Nowadays, the pumping house is home to a sailing club.

▶ *8 miles S of Exeter on A379 at Starcross.*

Burgh Island

Take the tractor to an Art Deco haunt of the 1930s glitterati

At low water, it is a splashy walk over the sands to rocky Burgh Island. If the tide is high you will have to take the ferry, which doubles as a tractor. The big tyres make easy work of the crossing, a strip of sand covered by shallow tides twice a day. An Art Deco seventh heaven awaits in the curves, colour schemes and natural rock swimming pool of the Burgh Island Hotel, built by the millionaire Archibald Nettlefold in 1929. In the bar you can take cocktails where Agatha Christie, Noël Coward and the Duke of Windsor once supped.

For more earthy surroundings, try the Pilchard Inn near the shore. Smugglers, fishermen and sailors have drunk here over the course of more than 600 years.

▶ *Foot crossing at low tide from Bigbury-on-Sea, end of B3392, off A379, 6 miles NW of Kingsbridge. Hotel tractor at high tide, Tel 01548 810514.*

Bayard's Cove

Quay with a foot in the New World

Visit Bayard's Cove on a misty early morning with no one about and you can almost believe that you have stepped back in time. Here in the old seaport town of Dartmouth are sailing ships, cobbled quays and the handsome 18th-century houses built for sea captains and merchants, all reflected in the water under a green wooded cliff.

Bayard's Cove has a stake in both English and American history. It was here that the Pilgrim Fathers, on their way to forge a fresh life free from religious intolerance, put in for repairs in summer 1620 after a stormy voyage from Southampton in two ships. Shortly they were on their way to Plymouth, where the leaky *Speedwell* was abandoned and 102 pioneers, including 36 Puritan refugees, crammed into *Mayflower* for the hazardous crossing of the Atlantic to a new world.

▶ *Dartmouth (A379), on S waterfront.*

WEST COUNTRY

DEVON

Slapton Beach D-Day Memorial

An American disaster in Devon

A dumpy little Sherman tank, rusted and encrusted from 40 years on the seabed, makes a strange sight in the Torcross car park. It was dredged up from the bay off Slapton Beach in 1984 and is now a memorial to one of the biggest and most carefully concealed training disasters of the Second World War.

On the night of April 26, 1944, American forces were preparing to land on Slapton Beach as part of Exercise Tiger, a huge D-Day rehearsal. By chance, nine German torpedo boats arrived on the scene. They sank two landing craft and damaged another, killing 639 men. There followed a frantic hunt for the bodies of ten American officers, who held vital information about the planned landings. Miraculously, the searchers found all ten, and the D-Day secret was kept from the Germans.

▶ *Torcross, 8 miles S of Dartmouth on A379.*

Hallsands

A village left to the mercy of the sea

A few crumbling doorways and walls cling to a rock shelf under the cliffs near the headland of Start Point. Poignant in their ruin, vulnerable to every storm-driven wave, they are all that remain of the fishing village of Hallsands.

It was a decision by distant authority that condemned the settlement. Between 1897 and 1901 half a million tonnes of shingle were dredged from the sea floor here for dock construction work at Keyham, near Plymouth, 25 miles away. With its protective shingle bank gone, Hallsands bore the full brunt of the sea. A savage storm in January 1917 put paid to the village; the fisher families barely escaped with their lives, some having to climb the cliffs in pitch darkness to reach safety. No one returned to the ruined houses. They have been slowly yielding themselves to the sea ever since.

▶ *1½ miles N of Start Point, S of Torcross on A379 Dartmouth-Kingsbridge road.*

Buckfast Abbey

The church that 20th-century monks built with their own hands

On first sight the grey and gold tower and blue limestone walls of Buckfast Abbey look as if they must have been standing among their Devon fields and woods for at least 700 years. But this lovely church is less than a century old, part of a monastery abandoned in 1539 but re-founded in 1882 by a French order.

An exhibition tells the extraordinary story of how a handful of monks, learning on the job, created the abbey through their own labour between 1907 and 1938. Gorgeous floor mosaics in polished marble and granite, wood carvings and stained glass were all made by the Buckfast monks. You can admire their handiwork in small things, too, as you taste the tonic wine and honey they make and sell in their abbey produce shop.

▶ *Signed in Buckfastleigh, off A38, 20 miles S of Exeter. Church daily (except for services); shops daily. Tel 01364 645500 for information.*

Hay Tor Granite Tramway

A moorland railway that carried the building blocks of London

Tucked away in the shadow of Haytor Rocks is one of Dartmoor's strangest features – a railway made of stone. The trackway, sidings and points of the Hay Tor Granite Tramway were all cut from the granite that the line was built to carry. After the line opened with celebration and high hopes in 1820, Hay Tor granite was pulled by horses seven miles to the Stover canal at Teigngrace, then shipped by barge up the Teign estuary to Teignmouth, and finally taken in coasters to London. By this route went stone for the building of the National Gallery and the British Museum, and for the reconstruction of London Bridge. Rising costs and falling demand put an end to the tramway in 1858. Since then the old line has lain open to wind and weather, a monument to 19th-century Devon ingenuity and endeavour.

▶ *Haytor Rocks signed off B3387, 5 miles W of Bovey Tracey (A38).*

Grimspound

Discover the remnants of a Bronze Age community on Dartmoor

A winter visit to one of the circular Bronze Age huts of Grimspound makes it easy to visualise the smoky darkness, hunger and shivering cold endured by the hundred or so people who carved out short, hard lives here in around 2000 BC.

Within the 3m (10ft) thick walls of the circular enclosure are the remains of 24 stone-built huts. Their conical thatched or turf roofs are long gone, but many still retain their cooking pits and turf fire hearths, some with low earth and stone platforms for sitting or sleeping on. The doorway tunnels face away from the wind and weather, but imagination tells you how grim Grimspound must have been on a snowy, blowy night 4000 years ago.
▶ *6 miles SW of Moretonhampstead, off B3212. EH. Daily.*

Postbridge Clapper Bridge

Narrow stone crossing is a lasting monument to medieval ingenuity

It is hard to believe that the narrow span of the old clapper bridge at Postbridge carried all Dartmoor traffic over the River Dart for 500 years. Only when the present road bridge was built in the late 18th century did the clapper pass into retirement. It owes its long life to the skills of bridge-builders who used four granite slabs, 4½m (15ft) long and weighing 8 tonnes each, in its construction, and sheathed its slender piers in granite cladding as protection against the rushing waters of the Dart. Local legend suggests that the Postbridge Clapper is a prehistoric structure, but it is medieval and thought to date from the 13th century.
▶ *Postbridge, on B3212 Moretonhampstead-Two Bridges road.*

Wistman's Wood

Weirdly twisted dwarf trees cloaked in lichen and legend

Walk up the track to Wistman's Wood in a Dartmoor mist, and you may well think you are seeing things – a gathering of little old men, bent and bearded, scheming together among the mossy boulders. That impression might have given the wood its name. A 'wistman' or wise man is the local title for a wizard, someone with mystical powers.

Wistman's Wood is a fragment of ancient oak forest growing 400m (1300ft) above sea level – a higher altitude than oak trees generally tolerate. The trees are stunted by their exposed position and poor stony ground so that the tallest is less than 5m (16ft) high, an eighth of the size of normal oaks. The area is a National Nature Reserve, and visitors are asked not to walk in among the trees.
▶ *2 miles N of Two Bridges off B3212.*

Castle Drogo

When a man's house is a castle

Hanging on a craggy spur of rock 274m (900ft) above the wooded gorge of the River Teign, Castle Drogo is the stuff of fairytales. The situation is remarkable, as was the dream of tea magnate Julius Drewe – to build the last great castle in England. He engaged Edwin Lutyens, architect of the Viceroy's House in New Delhi, who realised Drewe's dream in solid granite from 1911 to 1930. Lutyens kept everything simple, and allowed the grandeur of the location to speak for itself. The exterior is sombre – a model of restrained good taste, which extends to the interior's plain stone walls and quietly sumptuous furnishings with just a hint of Art Nouveau.
▶ *14 miles W of Exeter, signed from A382 and A30. NT. Castle and garden daily, except Tues, mid Mar-Oct; Sat and Sun early Mar and Dec.*

Lydford Gorge

An exciting gorge path, where robbers once waylaid travellers

One of Devon's most thrilling round walks passes through Lydford's 1½ mile gorge. Start high in the woods, looking down the narrow cleft to the River Lyd, then turn back at river level onto the slippery path past the Devil's Cauldron and the 30m (100ft) White Lady waterfall. As you traverse the gorge, spare a thought for the 17th-century travellers who trod this path in fear of their lives. The wild, red-headed Gubbins clan would emerge from their Gorge hideouts to rob and murder anyone found on their patch.
▶ *7 miles N of Tavistock, signed from A386 at Dartmoor Inn. NT.*

DEVON

Brentor church

A prime position for contemplating the wonder of creation

There's no mistaking St Michael's Church at Brentor — it stands in dramatic silhouette on a granite outcrop. The elevated position of the 12th-century church on a naked peak top, rearing 30m (100ft) above the surrounding fields, is breathtaking.

The path up to the peak can be tricky to find on misty days — rough weather and an ominous atmosphere seem to cling to the tor. Locals recount how a Tavistock curate had to ply labourers with large quantities of whisky before they would agree to build a new track to the church.

▶ *1 mile SW of North Brentor, beside minor road — signed from A386 at Mary Tavy. Daily.*

DORSET

Golden Cap

Discover Britain's Jurassic Park in the South Coast's highest cliff

If asked to name the highest cliff along the English Channel, most people would probably say Beachy Head. In fact, it is Golden Cap, a 191m (627ft) slumped giant that glows in the low light of dawn and sunset, and dominates the wide sweep of Lyme Bay. From the South West Coast Path on the summit, the views extend across Lyme Bay to Portland Bill and westwards all the way to Start Point. Inland, the rugged heights of Dartmoor can be seen.

This is Britain's Jurassic Park — the crumbling sandstone cliffs are stuffed with fossils from the age of the dinosaurs. It was at nearby Lyme Regis in 1811 that 11-year-old Mary Anning found the first fossilised remains of an ichthyosaur — a huge aquatic reptile looking like a cross between a dolphin and a crocodile. Casual beachcombers are more likely to find the coiled remains of ammonites (prehistoric molluscs), ranging from the size of a 5p coin up to that of a car tyre.

▶ *1 mile S of A35 Bridport-Lyme Regis road at Chideock. NT.*

A PRIME POSITION FOR CONTEMPLATING THE WONDER OF CREATION
BRENTOR CHURCH

Whitchurch Canonicorum

The touching story of a saint

There's an ecclesiastical feel to the Latinised name of the village – a clue to the saintly secret contained in its church. This richly carved Norman and Early English building is dedicated to St Wite, said to have been a woman with healing powers who was murdered by Vikings in the 8th century. Her plain stone shrine, which has a top made of Purbeck marble – a kind of limestone – is pierced by three oval holes, through which pilgrims could thrust injured limbs and touch her bones.
▶ *N of A35 4½ miles W of Bridport.*

Marshwood Vale

Where a screaming skull disturbs the Wessex pastoral

The best place to view the classic slice of rural Wessex that is Marshwood Vale is from the top of Pilsdon Pen – at 277m (909ft), the highest point in Dorset. From the ramparts of the hill-fort encircling the summit, you can look south across rumpled meadows where wild daffodils bloom in spring to the sea. Below, in the maze of sunken lanes at the foot of the scarp, lies Bettiscombe Manor, a private residence that is reputed to contain the skull of a black slave, which screams if removed from the house.
▶ *2 miles SW of Broadwindsor, on B3164.*

Sherborne

Where puffing Sir Walter was put out

The great Elizabethan Sir Walter Raleigh – soldier-hero, writer and courtier – built Sherborne Castle in 1594. There is a stone seat in the grounds where the man credited with introducing tobacco to England was fond of enjoying a quiet smoke. It was while puffing on his pipe, the story goes, that he was dowsed with ale by an anxious servant who thought his master was on fire.

At the heart of Sherborne itself lies the abbey, a masterpiece of the Perpendicular style. Its best feature is the fabulous fan-vaulted ceiling, which can be viewed in an ingenious mirror-trolley, so avoiding a crick in the neck.
▶ *Castle ½ mile SE town centre; castle and gardens Tues-Thur, Sat (pm castle), Sun, and bank hol Mon Apr-Oct. Abbey in town centre; daily.*

Abbotsbury

A magnet for mute swans and star-crossed spinsters

Little remains of the 11th-century Benedictine Abbey from which this village takes its name. It was swept away by Henry VIII in the 1530s. But much of the monks' buttressed tithe barn – 84m (275ft) long and thatched with local reed – has survived. So has their swannery on the Fleet. Hundreds of mute swans breed here, and May is the time to see their fluffy cygnets. St Catherine's Chapel, built in the 14th century, is dedicated to the patron saint of spinsters. To find a husband, locals once said, just leave a pin in one of its pillars.
▶ *6 miles NW of Weymouth on B3157 Bridport road. Swannery daily mid Mar-Oct.*

Littlebredy

Village cricket under the Downs

This quiet hamlet takes its name from the little River Bride, which rises in an artificial lake beside Bride Head House. House, church and cottages lie in a deep bowl framed by tall beech trees and the rolling skyline of the Dorset downs, creating a fine backdrop to one of England's most idyllic cricket greens. It is a perfect place to watch a match on a summer's afternoon, as the breeze turns the weather vane on the tiny wooden pavilion.
▶ *S of A35, 8 miles E of Bridport.*

Chesil Bank

Nature's giant stone-grading machine

For students of geography, it is the classic example of 'longshore drift' – a narrow spit, backed by the brackish waters of the Fleet, where waves, current, backwash and prevailing winds constantly combine to sift and shift the 18 miles of shingle from west to east. The result is extraordinary: an arrangement of stones that gradually increase in size as the bank runs eastward. Near Bridport the shingle is known as pea gravel; at Portland, 15 miles away, the pebbles are the size of large potatoes.
▶ *1 mile W of B3157, between Portland and Abbotsbury.*

MIGHTY BULWARK
BRAVING THE WAVES
THE COBB, LYME REGIS

DORSET

8 The Cobb, Lyme Regis 9 Cerne Abbas Giant

The Cobb, Lyme Regis
Mighty bulwark braving the waves

Of all man-made sights on the Dorset coast, none equals The Cobb. For more than 700 years the huge walls of this breakwater have withstood the prevailing south-westerly gales. Like an elephant's trunk, it curls protectively around Lyme harbour, which sent two ships to fight the Armada in 1588, and from end to end it is steeped in literary associations. To descend Granny's Teeth – a flight of steps protruding from The Cobb's inner wall – is to follow Louisa Musgrove in Jane Austen's novel, *Persuasion*. The end of The Cobb is where Meryl Streep stood in a memorable image from the 1980 film version of *The French Lieutenant's Woman*, the novel by the local author John Fowles.
▶ *Off A3052 in Lyme Regis.*

Cerne Abbas Giant
Herculean figure cut in the turf

Most chalk hill figures are simple outlines. The Cerne Abbas Giant is different. Not only does he have a face, nipples and ribs, but he is also shamelessly showing off his manhood. Who he is meant to be and how long his 54m (180ft) frame has stood watch on the downland slope above the village from which he takes his name – brandishing a great club as well as his virility at all-comers – is a mystery. The best guess is that he represents the Roman god Hercules, whose image on coins and statues he resembles, and may date from the 2nd century AD, when the Emperor Commodus, flushed by his conquest of the Scots, added 'Hercules Romanus' to his other titles.
▶ *½ mile N of Cerne Abbas off A352 Sherborne road. NT.*

Mighty Iron Age castles in the air

They fell to Rome in quick order, but the sheer scale of Dorset's hill-forts still has the power to astonish

1 Badbury Rings ▶ *4 miles SE of Blandford Forum on B3082 Wimborne Minster road.*

2 Hod Hill ▶ *1 mile W of Iwerne Courtney on A350 Blandford Forum-Shaftesbury road.*

3 Eggardon Hill ▶ *10 miles W of Dorchester, off A35 to Bridport on minor road to Powerstock.*

4 Maiden Castle ▶ *2 miles SW of Dorchester, off A354 Weymouth road. EH.*

MAIDEN CASTLE

On display in Dorchester's County Museum is the skeleton of a warrior who died defending the hill-fort of Maiden Castle against the Romans, the head of the fatal arrow still lodged in his backbone.

The crucial battle took place in AD 43, after the Emperor Claudius ordered the Second Augusta Legion to crush the Durotriges. One by one the tribe's strongholds fell, and at Maiden Castle the dead were buried in what could be Britain's earliest war cemetery. It was here in the 1930s that excavations uncovered their remains, including those of the unknown warrior in the museum.

The brooding hill-forts that dominate Dorset's downland skylines are the most enduring monuments of Iron Age Britain. Built between the 6th and the 1st centuries BC, they often stand on earlier Bronze Age and Stone Age defence works. By the time of the Roman invasion, they were sophisticated fortresses: the only way in was along a winding passage guarded by sturdy timber gates, between ramparts reinforced with timber baulks and crowned with wooden palisades, from which defenders could hurl down slingshot and javelins.

Westwards along the road of empire

Today, these great earthworks – which enclose areas from as small as 1ha (2½ acres) to the 115ha (284 acres) of Bindon Hill, near Lulworth Cove (see page 30) – are the haunt of rabbits and skylarks. Yet the rippling grassy banks of places such as **Badbury Rings** are hugely atmospheric. Badbury is the likely location of Mount Badon, where King Arthur, said to haunt the hill-top wood in the guise of a raven, defeated the Saxons in 518. A few miles north is **Hod Hill**, where the Durotriges' slingshots proved no match for the legion's ballista bolts. After its capture, the Romans built a fort of their own on the spot, sprawling across 4ha (10 acres), with barracks and stables for 700 infantry and cavalry. The occupiers built roads too, and it is on the Roman road west from Dorchester that **Eggardon Hill** lies. At this spot, geology adds to the drama of the ancient fortifications; as the old military road reaches the end of the ramparts, it plunges off the airy tops of the southern chalklands towards the first combes of the West Country.

But it is **Maiden Castle**, where the museum's Iron Age warrior met his death, that is Dorset's, and Britain's, most impressive hill-fort. Here, the ramparts and ditches, at one point eight defensive lines deep, extend for 2 miles around the hill.

DORSET

Hardy's Cottage

Deep in the heart of the writer's Wessex

A stroll through beech woods brings you to the birthplace of Thomas Hardy, the great Victorian writer. Inside, everything is much as it was in Hardy's day, including the bedroom in which he was thrown aside as dead at his birth. Fortunately for English literature he was saved by the nurse, who exclaimed to the doctor, 'Dead? Stop a minute. He's alive enough, sure.' Whereupon the infant Hardy was revived. Events after his death, in 1928, were unusual, too: before the body was cremated and the ashes taken to Poets' Corner in Westminster Abbey, the writer's heart was removed – to be buried in **Stinsford churchyard**, a mile or so away in the direction of Dorchester (the Casterbridge of his novels).
▶ *6 miles E of Dorchester off A35 Bournemouth road. NT. Sun-Thur Apr-Oct.*

Shaftesbury

Hill-top stronghold of the Saxon king

Alfred the Great founded Shaftesbury, attracted by the steep, commanding ridge on which the town stands. The best place from which to see the steep fall to the south is from the top of Gold Hill, whose curving cobbled street is one of the most photographed scenes in Dorset. On one side, the roof ridges of a row of cottages descend in high steps; on the other stands the buttressed wall of Alfred the Great's abbey, where his daughter, Aethelgifu, was the first abbess, and where King Canute died in 1035. There is a small museum alongside the abbey ruins.
▶ *Abbey ruins and museum daily Apr-Oct.*

Bovington Tank Museum

Military muscle packing a heavy punch

Allow plenty of time for Bovington. A day would not be too long to spend looking at the world's finest collection of armoured fighting vehicles, and watching action displays. In all, the museum contains more than 300 exhibits from 28 countries, from battle-scarred veterans of the two world wars to battered Iraqi tanks captured during Operation Desert Storm in the 1991 Gulf War.
▶ *2 miles N of Wool off A352 Wareham-Dorchester road. Daily. Tel 01929 405096 for details of special events.*

Lulworth Cove

An emerald gem set in a clasp of cliffs with their own butterfly

Do not let the popularity of this celebrated beauty spot put you off: the almost-landlocked circular cove, scalloped out of towering chalk cliffs and filled with a clear emerald sea, is a scene of breathtaking drama. The finest view is from above, where the coastal footpath curls eastward around the lip of the cove towards the Fossil Forest – hollowed stumps of cycads (primitive trees resembling tree ferns) that grew in the age of dinosaurs. The 'forest' lies on the Army's gunnery ranges, so you should not proceed if a red flag is flying.

Follow the path in the opposite direction and more geological wonders are revealed. First, **Stair Hole**, a tide-washed chasm of crumpled strata, up-ended when a violent Earth created the Alps. Next comes **Durdle Door**, where the sea has made a lofty natural arch in the headland. Look out too for the Lulworth skipper – a small, moth-like brown butterfly found only along this stretch of coast.
▶ *5 miles S of Wool, on B3071.*

Kimmeridge Bay

Dark cliffs filled with fossils and fashioned by trinket-makers

Between Broad Bench and Houns-tout Cliff the creamy Purbeck limestone gives way to sombre shale, with wave-worn, fossil-studded ledges running into the sea and a foreshore covered with slabs of rock. The Romans once fashioned this stone into jet-like jewellery, leaving 'coal money' – in reality the cores from the lathes used by turners – to puzzle future generations of beachcombers.

Kimmeridge Bay has been a marine nature reserve since 1978 – the first to be set up on the British mainland – and the shallows are alive with cushion starfish and wartlet anemones. On the cliffs above stands a 'nodding donkey', extracting oil from a field over 900m (nearly 3000ft) beneath Broad Bench, discovered in 1959.
▶ *4 miles SW of Corfe Castle, off minor road from Corfe to Lulworth. Reserve daily, Apr-Sept; also Oct-Mar – Tel 01929 481044 for details.*

Corfe Castle

Where the stones speak of regicide, imprisonment, torture and siege

Approaching from the north, or looking down from the Purbeck Hills, Corfe Castle's gaunt ruins can be seen from miles away – sticking out of the landscape like a shattered molar. An air of melancholic grandeur seems to cling to the place, growing palpable when you know a little of its violent history.

It was at Corfe, in 978, that Edward the Martyr was murdered by his stepmother, Elfreda, clearing the way for her son Ethelred the Unready to seize the English throne. The hugely unpopular King John turned Corfe into one of the mightiest castles in the realm, an impregnable fortress – and maximum-security prison for his niece Eleanor, and 25 of her knights, 22 of whom were starved to death here. In the Civil War, Lady Mary Bankes, wife of Charles I's Lord Chief Justice, led resistance to one of the longest sieges of the conflict, earning the admiration of the attacking Parliamentary troops, who confined retribution to demolishing the walls.

▶ *4 miles S of Wareham, on A351 Swanage road. NT. Daily all year.*

St Martin's, Wareham

Lawrence of Arabia remembered

Set in the county's finest Saxon church, on top of a wall originally built by Alfred the Great to hold back the Vikings, is a wonderfully sympathetic effigy of Lawrence of Arabia. A cottage at nearby Clouds Hill was his retreat for 12 years until his death after a motorbike accident in 1935. The figure, sculpted out of Purbeck marble, the hard local limestone, by Eric Kennington, was intended for Westminster Abbey but was presented to St Martin's by Lawrence's brother in 1939. It depicts the enigmatic desert hero of the campaign against the Turks in familiar Arab dress, scimitar-shaped dagger in hand, his head resting on a camel saddle, his favourite books at his side.

▶ *8 miles W of Poole on A351 Swanage road. N of town centre. Daily Easter-Oct or obtain key from 35 North Street (A.F. Joy).*

Havens for wildlife on a harbour's shores

Fur, feather and scale find sanctuary among the reserves of Poole's great inlet

5 Brownsea Island ▶ *Daily Mar-Oct. Access at other times by arrangement, Tel 01202 707744. NT.*

6 Arne RSPB Reserve ▶ *Daily.*

7 Studland and Godlingston Heath NNR ▶ *Daily. NT.*

Over most of England native red squirrels (above) have been displaced by their larger American cousin, the grey, introduced in the 19th century. But on **Brownsea Island** more than 80 reds thrive, safely marooned in the middle of Poole Harbour and protected by the island's status as a nature reserve.

The best time to take one of the island ferries from Poole Quay or Sandbanks to see these agile animals is September, when foraging is good. But there is more to the wildlife around Poole Harbour than red squirrels. On the west side of the inlet, towards the landward end of this second-biggest natural harbour in the world, lies the **Arne RSPB Reserve**, a haven for nightjars and Dartford warblers. At the seaward end, running south from the harbour mouth, are the heaths and dunes of **Studland and Godlingston Heath National Nature Reserve** – home to Britain's rarest reptiles, the smooth snake and sand lizard.

SOMERSET

1 Dunkery Beacon 2 Wimbleball Lake 3 Dunster

Dunkery Beacon

Views to distant horizons and reminders of an ancient past

When the Spanish Armada was spotted in the Channel approaches in 1588, a huge bonfire lit here called the yeomen of surrounding shires to arms. At 520m (1706ft), Dunkery Beacon is the highest point on Exmoor: a heathery spot with one of the best West Country views, across sweeps of moorland to the Bristol Channel and the Somerset Levels below. On a clear day, the hills of south Wales are visible.

Yet the beacon is two worlds: the one of far horizons, and a closer one offering glimpses of a time when the tops were clothed in oak forest. Remnants of this forest survive along the coombs in places like nearby Horner Wood, from which skittish red deer venture.

▶ *Near Luccombe, S of A39 Minehead-Lynton road or W of A396 Tiverton-Dunster road.*

Wimbleball Lake

A tribute to the genius of artifice in hand with nature

This reservoir is a triumphant marriage of civil engineering and natural wilderness. From the road bridge across the northern end of the lake, or from Haddon Hill, to the south, you can marvel at landscape architect Dame Sylvia Crowe's achievement: an expanse of sky-reflecting water which seems essential to the scene, but dates from just 1980.

From the B3190 on Haddon Hill, there is a high view along the length of Wimbleball Lake, while at the opposite, northern, end of the reservoir, the path into the nature reserve offers a contrasting water-level vista.

▶ *S of B3224 Bishop's Lydeard-Wheddon Cross road.*

Dunster

Where the stage is set for a Norman warlord to come riding by

Stand on one of Dunster's cobbled pavements and it is easy to imagine the 13th-century warlord Reynold de Mohun and his retinue clattering by. For this is a medieval village that comes with all the requisite extras – a jumble of 15th-century cottages, monastic dovecote, packhorse bridge and Yarn Market, beneath the roof of which Tudor merchants once haggled. Over all loom the battlements of the castle – a symbol of power in the distant days before the sea retreated and left this once prosperous port high and dry. Then the wooded ramparts would have been bare and lashed by salt winds. Today, they guard a garden planted with exotics, including the national collection of arbutuses (strawberry trees).

▶ *E of Minehead on A396.*

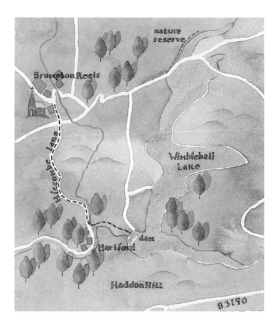

Pick of the paths *There are footpaths by Wimbleball Lake, but one of the best walks follows Hiccombe Lane, south along a wooded valley from Brompton Regis to Hartford. There, a path climbs to the top of the 50m (165ft) high dam.*

The secretive heart of an ancient land

In the watery world of the Somerset Levels, man has for centuries battled against flooding to tame the land

1 Burrow Mump ▶ *Off A361. NT.*

2 Peat Moors Centre ▶ *Westhay, 5 miles NW of Glastonbury. Sat-Sun and bank hols Apr-Oct; daily in school hols*

3 Lake Village Museum ▶ *Glastonbury. Daily all year.*

4 Muchelney Abbey ▶ *2 miles S of Langport, off A378 or A372. EH. Daily Apr-Oct.*

5 West Sedgemoor ▶ *Battlefield along drove road from Westonzoyland village (booklet from post office), on A372, SE of Bridgwater. RSPB reserve 1 mile E of Fivehead, off A378 Langport road; Tel 01458 252805 for details.*

It is easy to get lost in this empty place of silvery willows, glinting water and shivering reeds. Buildings are scarce, riverbanks can be more than 3m (10ft) higher than the road, and few sounds break the silence, save the birds and the wind in the rustling bulrushes along the drainage ditches called 'rhynes'. The Somerset Levels and Moors cover some 250sq miles inland from the mud flats of the Bristol Channel. Bounded by the Mendips to the north, the Dorset downs to the south and the Quantocks to the west, they are like a geological saucer, once full of sea water with scattered islands of eroded limestone like **Burrow Mump**. As the sea receded at the end of the last Ice Age, 10,000 years ago, peat formed on the wetter lands north of the narrow spine of the Polden Hills, blue clay to their south. The peat lands are called Avalon; to the south are the Sedgemoors, King's, Queen's and West.

A hard marshland life

People were living in the Levels more than 2000 years ago, building villages and trackways on oak piles or peat bogs. Excavations in the 1890s showed them to have been skilled craftsmen, well adapted to their watery home. You can see how they lived at the **Peat Moors Centre** at Westhay and the **Lake Village Museum** in Glastonbury. Why they should have chosen this place, rather than the kinder Polden Hills nearby, has never been explained.

The Romans put up some defences to control the world's second-highest tidal range at Bridgwater Bay, but after their departure few outsiders dared to enter these waterlogged lands. Then in AD 878 King Alfred hid from the invading Danes on the Levels island of Athelney. When he defeated the Danish army, Alfred baptised Guthorm, the Danish king, at Aller, near Langport, and celebrated the peace across the Polden Hills at Wedmore. For the next 700 years the Church wielded power over the Levels and began to reclaim the 'summer saeta' – lands usable only in summer. Tall church towers, such as that at **Muchelney Abbey**, punctuate the landscape.

Conflict again broke the peace of the Levels when the last battle on English soil was fought in 1685 on **West Sedgemoor** between the armies of the Duke of Monmouth, illegitimate son of Charles II, and James II. The young pretender's cavalry were defeated not only by James's troops, but also by the treacherous rhynes that the horses struggled to cross. Now tens of thousands of wildfowl winter on the flooded plain, where the RSPB has a reserve, including a large heronry.

Much of the Levels can be explored on foot, on the 50-mile River Parrett Trail. You can find out more at the Langport and River Parrett Visitor Centre (Tel 01458 250350) and the Willow and Wetlands Visitor Centre at Stoke St Gregory (Tel 01823 490249).

RIVER CARY

SOMERSET

4 Tyntesfield 5 Montacute House 6 Glastonbury 7 Wells Cathedral 8 Cheddar Gorge

Tyntesfield

Victorian Gothic preserved

The essence of Victorian England has been preserved in this exuberant example of Gothic Revival architecture. Until taken over by the National Trust in 2002, Tyntesfield was the family home of four generations of the Gibbs Family. Its principal attraction is the wealth of original decoration, furnishings and the trappings of life above and below stairs. Conscientious maintenance by the late Lord Wraxhall has preserved carpets, wallpapers and wood panelling along with a productive kitchen garden and an exquisite family chapel. Visitors are encouraged to follow the conservation programme that will continue to make more areas of the property accessible.
▶ *7 miles SW of Bristol. M5 (Junction 19) via A369 and B3129. NT. House / Garden Sat-Wed mid Mar-Oct. Tel 01275 461900.*

Montacute House

Reality, or is it all an illusion?

There is a surreal quality about this glorious Elizabethan house. You almost expect to see Alice playing flamingo croquet with the Red Queen on the lawns below its glowing stonework – chiselled to such elegance and pierced by so many glinting windows that the building seems to float above the ground. In the North Garden a yew hedge has been clipped into fluid shapes reminiscent of a Salvador Dali painting.

Inside, staircases made of the same honey-coloured limestone used for the exterior complement fine tapestries, while faces from the Elizabethan and Jacobean establishment stare down from the walls of the Long Gallery.
▶ *S of A3088, W of Yeovil. NT. Wed-Mon Mar-Oct; garden also Wed-Sun Nov-Feb; park open at all times.*

Glastonbury

A past steeped in faith and legend

To climb the green cone of Glastonbury Tor is to follow in legendary footsteps. It is here that Joseph of Arimathea arrived from the Holy Land in about AD 60, bringing with him Christianity and the Holy Grail, supposedly buried below Chalice Well, at the foot of the tor. And this is also said to be Avalon, the last resting place of King Arthur. By comparison, the 14th-century tower of the chapel of St Michael, crowning the tor, is a latecomer.

In the town, Joseph is believed to have built England's first Christian church, a little wood-and-wattle forerunner of the abbey that was by Saxon times one of the greatest centres of faith and learning in the land. Although in ruins, the abbey still conveys a sense of the power it held over the lives of all around.
▶ *S of Wells on A39.*

Wells Cathedral

Kings, bishops and apostles watch over life in an elegant city

Drop down from the Mendips and more than 300 intricately carved figures on the west front of Wells Cathedral rise before you. Christ sits in majesty at the top and the figures beneath descend through a hierarchy of apostles, saints, kings, bishops and knights.

St Andrew's cathedral and adjoining moated Bishop's Palace are surrounded by the city's bustle, with twice-weekly markets held under the arch called The Bishop's Eye. Through the arch all is serene – croquet is played on the palace lawns and the cathedral's interior is cool and tranquil. The nave is dominated by huge scissor-arches, built in 1338 when the newly heightened tower began to crack. Look out for the jousting knights of the cathedral clock (installed in 1390) and the octagonal chapter house – its vaulted ceiling supported by a single pillar. The nearby Vicar's Close, built in the 1360s, remains a perfect medieval street.
▶ *Wells is at junction of A39 and A371. Daily.*

Cheddar Gorge

A narrow canyon colonised by bats

Rocky crags tower almost 152m (500ft) over the twisting gorge road, dwarfing vehicles that travel along it. Formed 300 million years ago, Cheddar's limestone buckled and eroded until the first Ice Age, a million years ago. Its melting ice floes sculpted these caverns for thousands of years. The hollowed out spaces were colonised by horseshoe bats, which can be seen sleeping in Gough's Caves.

Climb Jacob's Ladder – a flight of 274 steps – to take the 4 mile walk around the gorge or to enjoy the views. The landscape is a mixture of rare limestone grassland, heath and woodland where you can see peregrine falcons and the flowers of the Cheddar pink, only found in the Mendips.
▶ *Take B3135 gorge road from A371 or B3151.*

GLASTONBURY TOR

SOMERSET

Clifton Suspension Bridge

Stone towers threaded with metal chains crown the dramatic beauty of Avon Gorge

Two huge towered piers, 26m (85ft) high, support the chains that span Avon Gorge's 214m (702ft) breadth. The structure looks delicate, stretched 75m (246ft) above high water, but is strong enough to carry 4 million cars a year. The chains that curve above it are anchored in solid rock to take the downward force of 162 suspension rods. Far below, the tidal river winds between bare limestone crags on the north side and steep woods on the south. The bridge was designed by Isambard Kingdom Brunel and completed in 1864, five years after his death. Sadly, it can be a lure for the desperate, and few are as lucky as Sarah Henley whose billowing skirts formed a parachute when she jumped off the bridge in 1885. She landed gently in the river and lived into her seventies.

▶ *From Bristol city centre, follow signs for Clifton and then Clifton Suspension Bridge.*

Clifton Observatory

A room with an unconventional view

Inside the round tower of an old mill, high on the Bristol Downs with magnificent views of the Avon Gorge, is a secret. In the top room is a large concave dish in which, as your eyes adjust to the dark, you will see an image of the world outside. The view is created by a camera obscura – a lens and mirror in a box at the top of the building project it into the dish. Use the wooden pole to turn the image 360 degrees. It was built by an artist, William West, in 1829, and its effect is still magical today.

From Bristol, follow signs for Clifton and Suspension Bridge, but do not cross. Park nearby and follow signed footpath to right. Or walk across Clifton Downs. Daily.

SS *Great Britain*

Step on board the first iron ship to cross the Atlantic

Prince Albert launched the SS *Great Britain* from Bristol in 1843, amid great celebration. It was the world's first iron steamship, and was built for transatlantic travel.

Brunel's design was revolutionary – it was also the first ship to be driven by a screw propeller. The vast hull is 98m (322ft) long and is topped by a wooden deck and masts that rise to 30m (100ft). Inside, passengers enjoyed the epitome of carpeted, gilded luxury. *Great Britain* spent nearly 100 years at sea, carried the English cricket team to its first ever Australian tour in 1861, and travelled more than a million miles. It was rescued from the Falkland Islands in 1970 and towed 7000 miles to its home port for restoration.

▶ *On S side of Bristol's floating harbour, signed from city centre. Daily.*

The American Museum

Centuries of American history come to life in an English manor house

The Star-Spangled Banner flying boldly above an elegant Georgian mansion is the only clue that the interior might be anything other than British. Each room is an authentic re-creation of American life – from the charm of a 17th-century New England 'keeping room' (a sitting-dining room), through the worlds of Red Indians and Scarlett O'Hara, to the simple elegance of the Shakers. Collections of folk art, maps and quilts are also displayed here.

The gardens incorporate an arboretum of North American trees and a replica of George Washington's rose garden at Mount Vernon. In 1785 he was sent seeds from friends who lived near Bath, and descendants of his plants in Virginia now grow here.

▶ *Signed from Bath city centre and A36 Warminster Road. For museum and garden opening details, Tel 01225 460503.*

CLIFTON SUSPENSION BRIDGE

On foot in a Georgian gem

Revel in the 18th-century glories of Bath, Britain's most elegant city, built for pleasure and fashion

6 Bath

ROYAL CRESCENT

Begin on the south slopes of **Bath** at the Palladian mansion of **Prior Park** (gardens only, Wed-Mon Mar-Oct, Sat-Sun Nov-Feb; NT). This was home to Ralph Allen whose business acumen provided the pale honey-coloured stone for the city's buildings. In 1726 he bought the nearby stone quarries when the architect John Wood the Elder was drawing up his city plan. Already Bath was attracting visitors, due in part to the energy of 'Beau' Nash, its master of ceremonies. These three men made Bath both fashionable and beautiful.

From Prior Park, head north for the river and take the riverside walk, continuing north. On the opposite bank are the Parades, among John Wood's first property developments, built high above ground on vaulted cellars. Upriver is **Pulteney Bridge**, built by Robert Adam, lined with shops on both sides: climb the riverside steps and look east down Pulteney Street to what in Georgian times was the Sydney Hotel, now the **Holburne Museum of Art** (closed Mon, except bank hols, and mid Dec-mid Jan).

Across Pulteney Bridge, New Bond Street curves round to the paved precinct of Old Bond Street. Look up at the formal simplicity of the Royal National Hospital for Rheumatic Diseases, originally the Bath Hospital built in 1738. Walk up Milsom Street, where Jane Austen was once among the shoppers. Higher still are the

Assembly Rooms (daily), where dances were held. Westward is **The Circus**, begun by John Wood in 1754 and completed by his son, John Wood the Younger. From here walk to **Royal Crescent**. It scoops up the sun as it looks south over green lawns to the city. Call at No.1 (Tues-Sun, and bank hol Mon, mid Feb-late Nov) for perfect Georgian interiors.

Take the Gravel Walk that curves behind The Circus, stopping at the **Georgian Garden** (open all year). Notice the shelters for sedan chairmen in Queen's Parade Place. Then Gay Street, the earliest of John Wood the Elder's projects, runs into **Queen Square**, his first masterpiece. From here walk down to the **Theatre Royal**, which opened in 1805 with a performance of Shakespeare's Richard III. Opposite is The Garrick's Head pub, once the house of 'Beau' Nash.

The new Thermae Bath Spa complements the 18th-century **Hot Baths** and **Cross Bath** with the Abbey Churchyard and the **Pump Room** beyond. This is the heart of fashionable Georgian Bath. Look down on the green steaming water of the **King's Bath** below, in which you would then have bathed in a yellow canvas gown. Refresh yourself with a glass of spa water – or a cup of tea and a Bath bun.

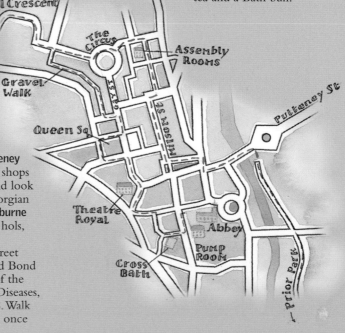

SOMERSET

The Roman Baths

The closest you are likely to get to Roman life in Britain

As you stand in the steamy dimness and watch the steady torrent of hot spring water, the iron salts staining the stone vermilion, it is easy to understand the awe that inspired the Romans to build their great baths and temple here in the 1st century AD.

These are the only hot springs in Britain. Every day, for thousands of years, 250,000 gallons of water at a constant temperature of 46°C have bubbled out of the ground. The early Celts dedicated the springs to their goddess Sulis, to whom the Romans added their own deity, Minerva. Her power is symbolised in the haunting and wild-haired face of the Gorgon that stares down from the re-created temple pediment.

The green expanse of the Great Bath, with its Roman columns, steps and paving, was revealed more than a century ago. The lead pipes and lining of the bath look little different from when they were laid 2000 years ago. Close your eyes for a moment and you might hear the echo of voices, smell the anointing oil and feel the hot steam. You can even throw a coin, a curse or a prayer into one of the baths, just as the Romans did before you.

▶ *Entrance in Abbey Churchyard, Bath. Daily.*

Stoney Littleton Long Barrow

Enter the ancient twilight world of Stone Age burials

The approach to the low, dark entrance, set in the curved stone wall of a whaleback hump in a high cornfield, evokes a sense of both curiosity and foreboding. Almost unwillingly you enter. There is a smell of cold damp earth. In places the huge lintel makes it impossible to stand upright.

But go on and you reach the musty darkness of seven stone chambers, built into a mound around 30m (100ft) long 5000 years ago to bury the dead of the Neolithic peoples who lived here. When you emerge again into the light, this dark place stays with you, a chill reminder of the unknown.

▶ *Take narrow lane to Wellow from A367 S of Bath (or from A36 across B3110 at Hinton Charterhouse). Pass Fox & Badger pub on left and take left turn beyond Wellow into narrow lane leading to Wellow Brook, where path leads to long barrow. EH. Daily.*

Farleigh Hungerford Castle

An idyll of English medieval life in a serene valley landscape

It may have warlike crenellated towers, but this little castle on its green promontory in a deep Somerset valley was never in combat. Sir Thomas Hungerford added the battlements to his manor house in the 1383; he was pardoned for not asking the king's permission first. His descendants enjoyed mixed fortunes: Sir Walter Hungerford was the first Speaker of the House of Commons; Sir Edward Hungerford had to sell the castle in 1711 to clear his debts, after which the place fell into decay.

Now the castle exhales an air of almost domestic tranquillity, with house martins nesting in the old gatehouse and flowers growing in the grassy moat. Two towers remain of the original four, together with parts of the walls, foundations and cobbled courtyards. The chapel, once the parish church until enclosed by the outer wall of the castle in the 15th century, contains one of the finest English medieval wall paintings – a huge figure of St George killing the Dragon.

▶ *8 miles S of Bath off A366. EH. Daily Apr-Oct, Sat-Sun Nov-Mar.*

WEST COUNTRY

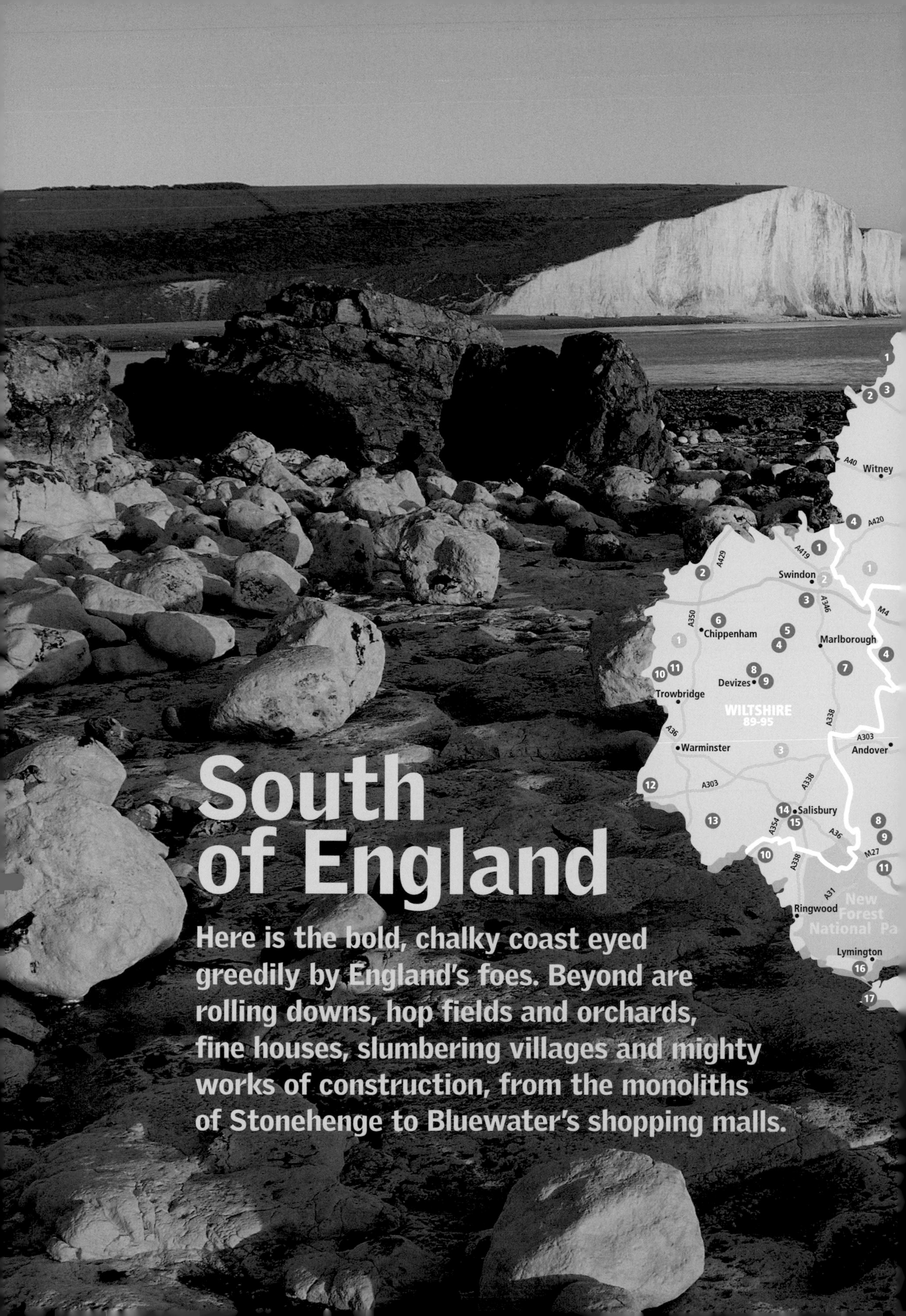

South
of England

Here is the bold, chalky coast eyed
greedily by England's foes. Beyond are
rolling downs, hop fields and orchards,
fine houses, slumbering villages and mighty
works of construction, from the monoliths
of Stonehenge to Bluewater's shopping malls.

Witney

Swindon

Chippenham

Marlborough

Devizes

Trowbridge

WILTSHIRE
89–95

Warminster

Andover

Salisbury

New
Forest
National Pa

Ringwood

Lymington

Key

1 Main entry
2 Feature entry
County boundary
Motorway
Principal A road

(See 'Finding your way', page 7)

Banbury

Milton Keynes

A428 1 2 A421 A1
Bedford
Biggleswade 3
6 5
BEDFORDSHIRE 42-45
A422 1
Buckingham
2
A4146
A421
4
10 M1 8
9
Leighton Buzzard
A505
5
12
A5
A1(M) A10
Stevenage
A602
A120
6 7 9
Hertford
8
A414
HERTFORDSHIRE 62-65
A10
3
Tring
A41
1
St Albans
2
M25
Watford

BUCKINGHAMSHIRE 50-53
3
Aylesbury
A4010
A413

A44 A34
5
Oxford
6 7-10
OXFORDSHIRE 72-76
11
A34
12 Didcot
13
14
15
M40
The Chilterns
High Wycombe
7
6
Beaconsfield
8
1
Maidenhead
10
Windsor
7-9
9

1
5 6
3
BERKSHIRE 46-49
Newbury
Reading
A322

1 A339
Basingstoke
3
M3
A33
HAMPSHIRE and Isle of Wight 54-61
A31
Winchester
7
5 6
4
A3
Haslemere
3
Woking
7
A3
12 4
11
16
Guildford 6
Farnham
5 1
4
2
13
Dorking
14
Reigate
15
M23
M25
6 5
SURREY 77-81
Crawley
A24
A22

Southampton
M27
A3(M)
13
1
Chichester
2
A27
7
Bognor Regis
8
Worthing
10
11
Petersfield
A272
4
5 6
A24
9
Haywards Heath
A23
The South Downs
SUSSEX 82-89
A26
A27
Lewes
14
Brighton
1
13
Eastbourne
12

14
Portsmouth
12
15
Newport
18

Gravesend 1
Rochester
A228
8
Chatham
7
A249
M26
2
M2
A2
11
12
The North Downs
Maidstone
4
6
9
A20
KENT 66-71
3
Royal Tunbridge Wells
A26
A228
10 A229
Crowborough
Ashford
A2070
A28
A2
A256
16
15 18
Dover
Folkestone
17
A259
3
2 1
5
17 Rye
A259
16
8
2 Hastings
Bexhill-on-Sea
15
A21

A299 14
Margate
A253
13
Canterbury

BEDFORDSHIRE

1 Bromham Mill **2** Bedford Butterfly Park

3 St John's, Cockayne Hatley **4** Houghton

House **5** Shuttleworth Collection

Bromham Mill

The clanks and splashes of a bygone industrial age on a sleepy riverbank

The rhythmic churning and thumping of the enormous iron mill wheel at Bromham, interspersed with whooshing cascades of water, soothes and mesmerises. Try tearing your eyes away from the intricate web of wheels and pulleys that drives the system.

There has been a mill on this spot since before the Domesday survey of 1086. Bromham Mill dates from the 17th century, the lone survivor of many such mills that once stood along the banks of the Great Ouse. For centuries, the wheel was turned only by the river water, then in the 1920s a steam engine was installed to provide extra power. The charming rosy-brick mill building is set in 3ha (7 acres) of water meadows, and its creaking, groaning machinery has been renovated to allow visitors to watch flour milling at close quarters. The mill also houses an art gallery and craft centre.
▶ *Bromham village, 2 miles W of Bedford, off A428. Wed-Sun and bank hol Mon Mar-Oct. For other times Tel 01234 824330.*

Bedford Butterfly Park

Keep your eyes peeled on a journey to the faraway tropics

Yes, this is Bedfordshire, but as you stand enveloped in a cloud of brightly coloured butterflies in the hot, steamy tropical house, you might think yourself in the Amazonian rain forest or the jungles of Malaysia. Among the hundreds of exotic butterfly species to be seen are the African citrus swallowtail, the giant purple emperor from Japan and Korea, and the zebra, postman and gulf fritillary from South America. The centrepiece of the house – heated to 28°C (84°F) and filled with lush flowering plants – is a cascading waterfall, which maintains the humidity the butterflies require and feeds a stream that flows between ponds of water lily and koi carp.

To follow the life cycle, you can study the caterpillar feeding station and an 'emerging cage', where rows of butterflies hang upside-down to dry their wings before release. A nature trail, leading through 4ha (10 acres) of wild-flower meadows, and a millennium garden, filled with butterfly-attracting plants, lets you observe native British species.
▶ *From A1 take A421 towards Bedford; turn right at Great Barford and follow signs for Wilden. Daily mid Feb-Oct, Thur-Sun Nov-early Feb.*

St John's, Cockayne Hatley

The antique-mad rector who went on a European spending-spree

Startlingly elaborate and intricate Flemish wood carvings adorn 16 stalls with tip-up seats and misericords that face each other across the aisle of St John's Church. The brilliance of their craftsmanship is echoed in the oak figures – Catholic saints and writers wreathed in foliage and fruits – lining the chancel.

The very un-Anglican woodwork, which dates from 1689, was looted from the Abbey of Oignies during the Napoleonic invasion of Flanders. It was brought to St John's by Henry Cockayne Cust, who became both squire and rector of the parish in 1806. A descendant of the Cockayne family, who had acquired the local manor in 1417, Cust embarked on a major restoration of the ancient church. Among the many other precious items he rescued is a vividly coloured 13th-century stained-glass window from Yorkshire depicting the Saxon kings Oswald of Northumbria and Edward of East Anglia, and the saints Dunstan and Theobaldus.
▶ *NE of Biggleswade, on minor road, off B1042 at Wrestlingworth. Church ½ mile outside village on signed lane. Key from 23 Village Road (towards top of village on left) or Well House (first house in village on right).*

Houghton House

The once great mansion that impressed a local hero

The gaunt three-storey remains of the early 17th-century Houghton House – a ruin for more than 200 years – command a superb position above Marston Vale. It is said that the Bedford preacher and writer John Bunyan used Houghton as a model for 'House Beautiful' in *The Pilgrim's Progress* (1678).

The bay windows, corner towers and shaped gables are typically Jacobean, but there are also still-magnificent elements of the radical Italian Renaissance style introduced to England by the architect Inigo Jones. He is thought to have designed the Tuscan arcade on the north front and the west front's elegant columned loggia.

Houghton was built for Mary, Dowager Countess of Pembroke, the sister of the poet and courtier Sir Philip Sidney. In 1738 it passed to the Russells, dukes of Bedford, and in 1794 was stripped of its fittings and partly dismantled.
▶ *1 mile NE of Ampthill, off B530 Ampthill-Bedford road on signed track; house is ¼ mile beyond car park. EH. Daily.*

Shuttleworth Collection

Those magnificent men take to the air over Biggleswade

You can hear the insistent drone of engines overhead, smell the oil and aircraft fuel – and share the fear and excitement of the aviation pioneers – at Old Warden aerodrome. Displayed in eight vast hangars are more than 40 lovingly restored aircraft dating from 1909 to 1947. These include a 1910 Bristol Boxkite, which featured in the film *Those Magnificent Men In Their Flying Machines*, a 1919 Sopwith Dove, a 1928 Gipsy Moth, a 1935 Gloster Gladiator and, both from 1941, a Hawker Sea Hurricane and a Supermarine Spitfire.

The man behind the collection – one of the largest in the world – was Richard Shuttleworth, a motor racing enthusiast and keen aviator. He inherited the Old Warden estate in 1932 but was killed in a flying accident eight years later, at the age of 31. Among the other fascinating vehicles he assembled are veteran, vintage and classic motor cars, motorcyles, cycles and horse-drawn carriages. Visitors can watch maintenance and restoration in progress in the workshop hangar, and there are regular flying displays.
▶ *Old Warden Park, signed from B658, off A1 roundabout NW of Biggleswade. Daily all year, except Christmas week. Flying displays first Sun of month May-Oct, and some Sats in summer.*

SOUTH OF ENGLAND

BEDFORDSHIRE

The Swiss Garden

An exquisite ornamental garden with a heady whiff of alpine air

This garden of velvety lawns, rose arbours and subtly landscaped ponds and streams, crossed by decorative ironwork bridges, transports you to a different age. Only the intermittent screech of peacocks and the occasional rumble of aircraft engines from the Shuttleworth Collection next door (see page 43) disturb the tranquillity.

Little has changed at the compact 4ha (10 acre) garden since it was laid out by the 3rd Lord Ongley in the 1820s. Its precision, neatness, delicate beauty, and even architecture, reflect the creator's fondness for all things Swiss, following a vogue at the time. Grass and gravel paths, some lined with classical urns and statues, interlace the garden and lead to exotic follies. In an exquisitely crafted glasshouse, ablaze with wisteria in early summer, are a grotto and fernery. To see an exhibition about the history of the garden, head for its central and most intriguing feature – the tiny thatched Swiss Cottage.
▶ *Old Warden Park, next to Shuttleworth Collection (see page 43). Daily.*

Wrest Park Gardens

An elaborate and extravagant setting for afternoon tea

A fabulous domed pavilion draws visitors to the head of the lake known as the Long Water. The architect Thomas Archer built it from 1709 to 1711 with red and yellow brick that forms a squat star shape. Six rooms, or 'closets', lead off a large central hall, and although it was intended only for taking tea, the interior is elaborately decorated with trompe l'oeil columns and figures.

Many ornate follies and statues are found in the woodland on either side of the lake. These include the Bowling Green House with its wedding-cake decoration, the rustic Bath House (a fake ruin), a pagan altar and a column to 'Capability' Brown, who made alterations to the gardens in 1758-60.
▶ *Follow signs from Silsoe village W of A6. EH. Sat, Sun and bank hols Apr-Jun and Sept-Oct; Thur-Mon Jul-Aug.*

De Grey Mausoleum

In loving memory of one family

Attached to the parish church of St John at Flitton is an unassuming white-painted building that houses one of Britain's largest collections of funerary monuments. This is the mausoleum of the de Grey family, lords of the manor of Wrest for 600 years. Inside are several cool but light-filled rooms crammed with magnificently sculpted tombs, many of them carved in marble with a likeness of the deceased. The monuments span three centuries – the earliest is a brass sculpture dated 1545. Among the more fanciful is a memorial dated 1740 to Henry de Grey, Duke of Kent and creator of the woodland garden at Wrest Park, who is depicted in Roman dress.
▶ *From A507, take minor road to Flitton. EH. Sat-Sun. Key kept at 3 Highfield Road, off Wardhedges Road, ½ mile from mausoleum.*

Sharpenhoe Clappers

An Iron Age fort besieged by natural colour

Hundreds of wild flowers, including clustered bellflowers and bee orchids, thrive on the chalk downland of Sharpenhoe Clappers. Brown argus, chalk-hill blue and green hairstreak butterflies flit along hedgerows and in the wooded glen. An Iron Age hill-fort once stood on this 160m (525ft) high promontory offering wide views, between trees, of the Bedfordshire plain. It is a high point on the Icknield Way, a pre-Roman track linking Wiltshire with Norfolk.
▶ *6 miles N of Luton off minor road between Harlington and Barton-le-Clay. Follow signs from Sharpenhoe village to NT car park. 1 mile walk to Clappers. NT.*

Canaletto Room

From the grandeur of Woburn Abbey to the splendour of Venice

The majestic curve of the Rialto Bridge, the vast expanse of Piazza San Marco, the Basilica and the Doge's Palace – many sights and colours of 18th-century Venice jostle for space on the walls of Woburn Abbey's dining room, home to one of the world's greatest collections of works by Antonio Canale (1697-1768), known as Canaletto. The scenes, commissioned by the 4th Duke of Bedford after a visit to Venice in 1731, transport the viewer to a regatta on the Grand

Canal, awash with gondolas, to the Scuola San Rocco, or to the entrance to the Arsenal. When the paintings arrived in the dining room, the Venetian west window was blocked in to hang three more Canalettos there. The boards were removed later and the paintings re-hung: one in the Blue Drawing Room and the two others between the Ante-Library and Long Gallery.

▶ *From M1 (Junction 12 or 13) follow signs to Woburn Abbey. Tel 01525 290333 for Abbey opening times – dining room sometimes shut.*

LEIGHTON BUZZARD RAILWAY

Leighton Buzzard Railway
Engines of a working steam railway retire to a life of passenger service

Take a leisurely trip on the steam railway at Leighton Buzzard and prepare for a large dose of nostalgia. It was once a vital commercial artery, built in 1919 to carry sand – the local gold dust, used to make bricks – from quarries to distribution sites. In its early years the 2ft gauge track transported up to 3000 tonnes of sand each week, but it has carried a steam passenger service since 1968, and is now devoted to a celebration of industrial heritage.

From Page's Park Station, trains trundle at approximately 5½ miles per hour, negotiating steep gradients and sharp curves, and halting the traffic on numerous minor roads. Their destination is Stonehenge Works, almost 3 miles away, the only survivor of the Leighton Buzzard sand industry. The former quarry and brickworks is now home to more than 50 steam locomotives from around the world, including examples from India, Africa and Spain, as well as numerous artefacts from the history of the line, a number of tiny diesel engines and sand skips among them.

▶ *Follow steam train signs from A4146 to Page's Park Station. Tel 01525 373888 for opening times and timetable details.*

Whipsnade Tree Cathedral
A place for peaceful contemplation

In a secluded corner of Whipsnade Downs, flanked by wild-flower meadows, is a unique glory: a grass-floored cathedral made entirely of mature trees and shrubs. Stately avenues of limes delineate the nave. The chancel is a semicircle of silver birch. Horse chestnuts line the north and south transepts, and each chapel is sculpted from a different tree species. A cloister walk of ash trees edges a dew pond enclosure that collects rainfall. Its four entrance points are marked by pairs of vast cypresses. Shrubs planted here include berberis, cotoneaster, hazel, holly, laurel, privet, may, rhododendron and wild rose.

A visit to Liverpool's Anglican cathedral, while it was under construction, inspired a local landowner, E.K. Blyth, to create a symbol of faith, hope and renewal after the First World War. It was planted in 1931-8 in memory of three friends, two of whom had died in 1918.

▶ *2 miles S of Dunstable, signed from B4540 outside Whipsnade village. NT. Daily.*

BERKSHIRE

1 St Mary's, Aldworth **2** The Living Rainforest **3** Watermill Theatre

4 Walbury and Inkpen hills **5** Basildon Park **6** Beale Park

St Mary's, Aldworth

Worshippers at a little Norman church have giants for company

Locals know them as the Aldworth Giants: nine breathtakingly lifelike stone effigies of members of the de la Beche family, Norman lords of the manor. They recline in decorated niches down the sides of the nave of the church, and under the central arcade – knights and their ladies from the early 1300s, made immortal by the skill of medieval stone carvers. The creak of leather and clank of steel can be sensed in the warriors' armour and weaponry; the softness of silk in the frozen folds of the women's garments.

One of the most impressive figures is that of Sir Philip de la Beche, said to have been more than 1.4m (7ft) tall and represented life-size, squeezed uncomfortably into his niche. His mantle marks him as valet to Edward II, and a dwarf at his feet emphasises his height.

▶ *9 miles NE of Newbury on B4009. Junction 13 off M4.*

The Living Rainforest

Tread a jungle footpath among exotic plants and wildlife

Tropical trees and giant climbing plants press close on either side of the path, their huge leaves intertwining overhead, creepers dangle, exotic blooms flaunt their gaudy colours and bright butterflies flit among the foliage. It is not what you expect in Berkshire, but at Hampstead Norreys two huge greenhouses maintain a convincing illusion that you've just stepped into Amazonia or the heart of Africa. Follow the path to the centre of the rain forest and you find a pool, covered with the 1.8m (6ft) leaves of the giant Amazon water lily. There are monkeys, marmosets and turtles, and an impressive plumed basilisk, a type of iguana, which looks like a plastic dragon – until it blinks.

▶ *Hampstead Norreys, 6 miles NE of Newbury on B4009. Junction 13 (A34) off M4. Daily.*

Watermill Theatre

Players tread the boards of an old mill as a stream murmurs applause

Aptly enough, the continual murmur of running water supplies an insistent motif at the Watermill Theatre in Bagnor. A millrace channelled from the River Lambourn, which fringes the lawns, flows under the theatre, and visitors walk past a 6m (20ft) cast-iron waterwheel on their way into the auditorium, which was converted from the 1820s mill building in the 1960s. Surrounding barns have been turned into a bar and restaurant, while the converted stable block houses directors, actors and designers.

The Domesday Book commissioners valued the original mill on this site at 20 shillings, which is rather less than the reasonable price of a ticket to a performance. Even so, you can enjoy the setting of this playhouse-in-a-garden without attending a performance.

▶ *Bagnor is W of A34, 2 miles N of Newbury. Tel 01635 46044.*

Walbury and Inkpen hills

Twin summits linked by a ridge walk

You will come for the stunning four-county view across Berkshire, Hampshire, Oxfordshire and Wiltshire, but down the centuries people have had many other motives for clambering up Walbury Hill – at 297m (974ft) the highest point in southern England's chalk downlands.
The Celts noted its commanding outlook and built a fort on the summit – the track to the top leads across its ramparts. British forces saw that it resembled German coastal batteries in Normandy, and rehearsed for D-Day here, as a tablet near the parking space records. For around 200 years, up to the mid 19th century, spectators trooped by to gawp at public hangings on neighbouring **Inkpen Hill**, where a replica of the original gibbet stands. Its unusual T-shape enabled two victims to be strung up together, which was what happened to a local villager and his mistress, convicted in 1676 of murdering the man's wife.

▶ *4 miles S of A4, Newbury-Hungerford road.*

TREAD A JUNGLE FOOTPATH AMONG

Basildon Park

The county's finest house, saved from demolition by a press baron

Gazing up at an elaborately moulded and gilded ceiling in one of Basildon Park's sumptuously decorated rooms, it is hard to imagine that just 50 years ago it all nearly fell victim to the wrecker's ball and chain. At the end of the war, Berkshire's finest mansion was feeling the full ravages of four decades of neglect, coupled with the effects of billeting troops and prisoners there during the two world wars. Then, in 1952, the press baron Lord Iliffe and his wife bought the faded Palladian house and set about restoring it to its 18th-century grandeur, complete with contemporary fittings and furnishings.

The long façade of the house – built in 1776 by John Carr of York for Sir Francis Sykes, an East India Company 'nabob' – is made up of a three-storey main block in Bath stone, its tall columns set in sharp relief against a recessed portico, with two flanking two-storey pavilions. All this and 400 acres of wooded parkland impressed the head of the papermaking firm Dickinson so much that he named his firm's high-quality letter paper after the house.
▶ *7 miles NW of Reading on A329. NT. Wed-Sun pm and bank hol Mon late Mar-Oct; Dec opening Tel 0118 984 3040.*

Beale Park

Meerkats, monkeys and model boats on meadows by the Thames

Every turning along the trails winding through Beale Park's 122ha (300 acres) of ancient water meadow at Lower Basildon brings the visitor face to face with a different member of the animal kingdom. Meerkats rear up to stare back at their audience, terrapins pose motionless on rocks in a lake, chipmunks scurry among boughs and parrots flash a kaleidoscope of colour from spacious aviaries. There are deer, llamas, emus, Highland cattle and Soay sheep.

The park, founded by Gilbert Beale in 1956, has patches of woodland containing extraordinary statues and lawn-fringed pools separating the wildlife enclosures. There are paddling pools and a steam train for children, and half-hour boat trips on the Thames. A classical-style pavilion houses a fine collection of model boats. Here, perfect in every detail, are more than 400 replicas of vessels, from Roman galleys to modern trawlers, from Viking longships to the battleship Bismarck.
▶ *6 miles NW of Reading off A329. Daily Mar-Oct.*

EXOTIC PLANTS AND WILDLIFE
THE LIVING RAINFOREST

The Cookham of Stanley Spencer

Simple village scenes that inspired one of Britain's most original artists to create stunning religious images

1 Cookham

In Stanley Spencer's vision, the events of Christ's life took place in the painter's home village of **Cookham**. The Nativity he set in a local garden; Christ makes his triumphant entry into Jerusalem down Cookham High Street; and its same gabled buildings flank him as he carries the Cross towards Calvary. A walk today round the compact village (3 miles N of Maidenhead on B4447) passes scenes clearly recognisable as the background to many of Spencer's best-known paintings.

Start at the Stanley Spencer Gallery (Tel 01628 471885 for opening times), a former Methodist chapel at the heart of the village. The huge unfinished *Christ Preaching at Cookham Regatta* fills most of the wall facing the door: Christ sits in a basket chair on an old ferry surrounded by villagers listening from punts near Cookham Bridge, where the landlord at the Ferry Hotel surveys the profitable scene.

From the gallery, cross the road to the Tarry Stone, an old mounting block, and turn left into the churchyard of Holy Trinity (above), where Spencer set one of his most important paintings, *The Resurrection, Cookham,* and where a stone and a Judas tree commemorate the artist. Go through a gate to the riverside, where there is a view of the bridge that appears in many of Spencer's paintings. Turn right and ascend steps to the bridge for a view of the hotel, then return to the towpath and follow it for 180m (200yd). Before reaching the sailing club, turn left up a path and continue along Berries Lane, past a magnolia tree, painted by Spencer, in the grounds of Westward House to Cookham Moor. Turn left into the High Street, where a blue plaque on a house called 'Fernlea' identifies it as the artist's birthplace in 1891.

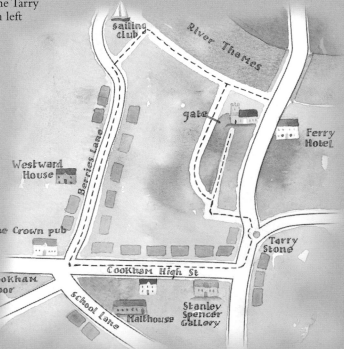

BERKSHIRE

7 Queen Mary's Dolls' House **8** St George's Hall and Chapel **9** Royal Mausoleum,

Frogmore House **10** Eton College

Queen Mary's Dolls' House
A little palace, perfect in every detail

In a single room of Windsor Castle, the world's largest inhabited castle, stands the smallest of all royal homes. Despite its name, Queen Mary's Dolls' House is no child's toy but a complete palace in miniature, designed by the architect Edwin Lutyens at one-twelfth normal size as a present for Queen Mary, and brought to Windsor in 1925. There are 40 rooms on four levels, including suites for a king and queen, just as there are in Windsor Castle.

There is electric light throughout, running water in all five bathrooms, and two working lifts that stop at every floor. More than 1500 leading craftsmen, artists and writers of the day gave their skills, writing finger-nail sized books for the bookshelves, painting royal portraits for the walls, and embroidering every item in the linen cupboard with a tiny royal monogram.
▶ *Windsor Castle. Daily.*

St George's Hall and Chapel
Chivalric knights in glorious gothic

When fire rampaged through one wing of Windsor Castle's state apartments in 1992, it caused such damage that over 7000 dustbins were used to collect the debris. The restoration of rooms to their former splendour by more than 4000 workers included the replacement of the lost ceiling of **St George's Hall** with the largest oak hammerbeam roof built in the 20th century. On the ceiling and walls of the hall are the numbered shields of every Knight of the Order of the Garter – note Winston Churchill's at No. 912.

The spiritual home of the Order is **St George's Chapel**, its soaring piers and graceful fan vaulting making it one of Britain's most beautiful ecclesiastical buildings. In its choir the brightly coloured banners of every living Knight of the Garter hang over stalls carved in the 15th century and bearing the plates of Knights from the inauguration of the Order in 1348 to the present day.
▶ *Windsor Castle. Hall daily. Chapel daily, except Sun (services only).*

Royal Mausoleum, Frogmore House
The final resting places for two of history's most constant couples

Queen Victoria loved the handsome white stucco Frogmore House, built originally in the 1680s and set in the tranquillity of Windsor Home Park. In its grounds is the huge Royal Mausoleum, completed in 1871, where Victoria and her husband Prince Albert are buried side by side in a sarcophagus of Aberdeen granite resting on a base of black marble. The interior of the mausoleum is painted and sculpted in the style of Raphael, Albert's favourite artist.

In stark contrast, outside the mausoleum are the simple tombs of the no less devoted Duke and Duchess of Windsor.
▶ *1 mile S of Windsor Castle, in Home Park. House, garden and mausoleum limited days May and late Aug. Tel 020 7766 7305.*

Eton College
Meet the 'boys in black'

A sartorial surprise awaits visitors to Eton. Top hats were doffed for the last time in 1940, but Eton College boys still wear black tailcoats dating from around 1850 and pin-striped trousers adopted about 1900. To this school garb the 70 King's Scholars of Henry VI's original foundation of 1440 add an academic gown, and there are blazers for boating, brown jackets for beagling, and fancy waistcoats.

Within Eton's walls, a collegiate calm prevails. In the chapel, raised 4m (13ft) above ground to escape floods, are 15th-century wall paintings found in 1847, three centuries after the college barber whitewashed over them.
▶ *N bank of Thames, opposite Windsor. College daily late Mar-Sept, except am termtime.*

SOUTH OF ENGLAND

49

BUCKINGHAMSHIRE

1 Stowe Landscape Garden **2** Claydon House **3** Waddesdon Manor **4** Coombe Hill

5 Ivinghoe Beacon

Stowe Landscape Garden

Where man improves on nature

Stepping into Stowe is like taking a trip back to the world of ancient Greece and Rome, but here temples are set in the sweeping grassy vistas of one of the greatest landscaped gardens in England, rather than among Mediterranean olive groves. The Grecian Valle, and the imposing Temple of Concord and Victory are two of the triumphs of the most famous of landscape gardeners, Lancelot 'Capability' Brown, who made his reputation during the ten years he worked here from 1741.

Brown did not start from scratch. Other great architects and landscape designers, including John Vanbrugh, William Kent and James Gibbs, had worked at Stowe before him.

▶ *3 miles NW of Buckingham off A422 Buckingham-Banbury road. NT. Wed-Sun, and bank hol Mon, Mar-Oct; Sat-Sun Nov-Feb.*

Claydon House

The ultimate rococo makeover

If you have a taste for ornate decoration, visit 16th-century Claydon House, refurbished in grand rococo style by the 2nd Earl Verney between 1757 and 1771. Festoons of foliage and drapery, fantastic snake-necked birds and monsters, clambering vines – all intricately carved in wood or moulded in plaster – cover the vast ceilings and frame doors, mirrors, windows and fireplaces in this showpiece.

Much of the decoration – including the inlaid mahogany staircase and the house's crowning glory, the Chinese Room, with its fretwork teahouse and frieze depicting a tea ceremony – is the work of the stonemason and woodcarver Luke Lightfoot.

▶ *6 miles S of Buckingham off A41 Aylesbury-Bicester road or A413 Aylesbury-Buckingham road. NT. Sat-Wed pm late Mar-Oct.*

WHERE MAN IMPROVES ON NATURE
STOWE LANDSCAPE GARDEN

Waddesdon Manor

Money no object when the baron went on his collecting sprees

Baron Ferdinand de Rothschild was a man who enjoyed spending his money. The results are to be seen at Waddesdon, the French chateau-style manor he built between 1874 and 1889. But this is more than a home of an exceptionally wealthy man: the baron was an avid collector, and he filled the house with the fruits of 35 years of buying the best that galleries and auction houses had to offer.

There is Sèvres and Meissen porcelain, portraits by Gainsborough and Reynolds, Beauvais tapestries, Aubusson and Savonnerie carpets, and countless pieces of exquisite French furniture. The gardens match the house, with a rococo-style aviary housing exotic birds such as kookaburras and Siamese fireback pheasants.
▶ *6 miles NW of Aylesbury on A41 Bicester road. NT. Wed-Sun and bank hol Mon late Mar-Oct, Nov-Dec opening Tel 01296 653266 (grounds all year, not daily).*

Coombe Hill

A break from Downing Street

Grand houses abound in Buckinghamshire, but the name of one that you can see from the top of Coombe Hill is world-renowned. Given to the nation by Lord Lee of Fareham in 1918 in the belief that regular exposure to 'the high and pure air of the Chiltern hills and woods' would lead politicians to saner government, this is Chequers, the prime minister's official country residence.

To see the imposing neo-Gothic façade, walk a short distance downhill past the summit monument and look sharp left. But before leaving the 260m (853ft) hilltop spare a moment for the monument itself. It is to the men of Buckinghamshire who fell in the South African War, 1899–1902.
▶ *3 miles NW of Great Missenden off A413 Amersham-Aylesbury road. NT car park 1 mile W of Dunsmore.*

Ivinghoe Beacon

Set your feet on an ancient route

Save the walk to the top of Ivinghoe Beacon for an early summer's day. The view gradually revealed in the clear air builds anticipation, culminating in a superb panorama that takes in a sweep of southern England. From the flat expanse of the Bedfordshire plain and the nearby chalk figure of the Whipsnade lion, the eye is drawn southwest to the Chilterns, following the line of the Ridgeway, Britain's oldest road, which starts on this 230m (770ft) hilltop and ends 85 miles away, at Avebury in Wiltshire. The nature reserve of the beacon is also best in early summer, carpeted with wild flowers and alive with butterflies.
▶ *Grassy car park 1½ miles on right hand side down minor road E of Ivinghoe (signed to Ivinghoe Beacon) off B489 Dunstable road.*

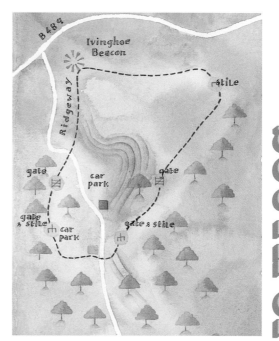

Breezy ramble *The circular walk from the car park over Ivinghoe Beacon takes about an hour. Cross road, take broad track downhill and go through a gate. At foot of hill, go through kissing gate on left, then turn right along grassy track. At line of trees on right, turn left and walk to top of ridge, then turn left again to reach beacon. At summit, turn left and walk down steep hill, joining the Ridgeway, marked by acorn symbols. Turn right, cross road and follow Ridgeway for ½ mile. Shortly after emerging from hawthorn copse, cross stile on left to return to car park.*

BUCKINGHAMSHIRE

6 Jordans **7** Bekonscot **8** Burnham Beeches **9** Cliveden

Jordans

Serene resting place of a Quaker leader

Some years after carrying the Pilgrim Fathers to North America in 1620, the three-masted, 180-tonne carrack, the *Mayflower*, was broken up. But some of her timbers lived on – ending up as part of the Mayflower Barn, one of the cluster of 17th-century farm buildings at the heart of Jordans, the original meeting place of William Penn and other early members of the Society of Friends.

Like the ship, Penn also made the return journey across the Atlantic, coming back to England in 1684, two years after founding Pennsylvania. From the barn (part of a hotel, but a simple request will get you inside) a path leads to the Friends Meeting House of 1688, currently being restored following fire damage. In the graveyard plain headstones mark the graves of 400 Quakers, including Penn, his two wives and ten of his 16 children.

▶ *2 miles NW of Chalfont St Peter off A413. Graveyard daily.*

Bekonscot

A model time and place where modern reality is put on hold

A working coal mine, a busy fishing port, a place where the trains always run on time, where windmills grind corn: all these elements of England between the wars – and hundreds more – are captured in miniature at Bekonscot. The world's oldest model village opened in 1929. It contains miniature lakes, streams, bridges, turreted castles, a zoo, an aerodrome and a caravan park, as well as rows of neat houses, shops and churches.

Farmworkers joyfully harvest the corn, villagers play cricket on the green and model children laugh with delight at the steam fair. The children's author Enid Blyton was a frequent visitor to Bekonscot, and it includes a replica of her house. More than 3000 shrubs and conifers, kept to scale using the Bonsai technique, complement the buildings.

▶ *Beaconsfield town centre. Junction 2 off M40, then A40 and A355. Daily mid Feb-Oct.*

Burnham Beeches

Mysterious ancient woodland preserved for city dwellers

The gnarled, twisted trees in this ancient wood – protected as a public open space 'for the enjoyment of Londoners' since 1880 – create a haunting atmosphere. Among the wood's 220ha (540 acres), which are crisscrossed by paths, are many mighty trees – beech and other kinds, such as the Druids Oak, thought to be nearly twice as old as the 400 years stated on the board beside it.

One of Britain's foremost 'wood pastures', Burnham Beeches is home to many wild creatures, including rare insects and fungi, as well as cattle, ponies, sheep and pigs. Walk if you can, but if you cannot, travel down Lord Mayor's Drive.

▶ *3 miles N of Slough off A355 Beaconsfield road. All times. Lord Mayor's Drive 8am-dusk.*

Cliveden

The sex scandal of the swinging 60s started here

The 19th-century American Ralph Waldo Story's erotic Fountain of Love stands at the head of the grand Lime Avenue, setting the scene for a visit to Cliveden. It carries echoes of the fateful meeting here in 1961 (when the estate was owned by Waldorf Astor) between John Profumo, secretary of state for war, and the call-girl Christine Keeler – the start of an affair that nearly toppled the government.

Cliveden has moved on since then. The house, the third on the site, was built in 1851 by Charles Barry, architect of the Houses of Parliament, and is now a hotel. Its true splendour is its magnificent position overlooking a lovely stretch of the Thames, which can be enjoyed from several points along paths through the gardens, including a broad flight of 170 steps leading down from the great parterre. Garden styles range from 17th-century formality to the more natural designs of the 20th century.

▶ *4 miles N of Maidenhead on A4094 Woodburn road (M4 Junction 7). NT. Gardens daily mid Mar-end Dec. House (3 rooms only) Thur and Sun pm Apr-Oct.*

Welcome to the Hell Fire Club

Rendezvous for the great and not so good in search of high jinks and underground antics

1 West Wycombe

West Wycombe Park ▶ *2 miles W of High Wycombe off A40 Stokenchurch road. NT. House and grounds Sun-Thur pm June-Aug; grounds only pm Sun-Thur and bank hols Apr-May.*

West Wycombe Caves ▶ *Daily Apr-Oct; Sat, Sun and bank hols Nov-Mar.*

Sir Francis Dashwood, politician, free thinker and second baronet, could have taught today's high-living club-goers a thing or two. The Brotherhood of St Francis, which he founded, had nothing to do with asceticism and religious devotion, and everything to do with a congregation of young bloods having a party. With members of the Establishment, including the Prince of Wales, Earl of Sandwich, Marquis of Granby and Archbishop of Canterbury's son rushing off to the Dashwood home at **West Wycombe**, it was no time before mid-18th-century London society was revelling in talk of wild goings on there. Wine, women and lascivious satanic rituals were rumoured to be on the menu. Soon the brotherhood had a more catchy nickname: the Hell Fire Club. At **West Wycombe Park** you can see the ultimate palace of pleasure where Sir Francis entertained high society friends. Originally a relatively modest, three-storied brick house, it was rebuilt by the eccentric aristocrat in around 1750 in Palladian style, with a colonnaded façade, frescoes and painted ceilings.

Inspiration from the classical world

The grounds, which owe their present form to remodelling by the landscape designer Humphrey Repton in the late 18th century, are overlooked by the **Mausoleum** on West Wycombe hill. Sir Francis took Constantine's Arch in Rome as inspiration when he built this vast hexagonal monument in 1763. It is open to the sky, and full of wild flowers as well as funerary urns and shrines to the Dashwood family and friends. Alongside the mausoleum stands **St Lawrence's Church**, the interior of which was redesigned with typical Dashwood brio to resemble the Sun temple at Palmyra near Damascus. Like the mausoleum, it can be visited at any time.

Deep under the hill on which mausoleum and church stand are **West Wycombe Caves**. Here, in a series of tunnels and galleries dug out to provide chalk for local roadstone, there are reconstructions lit by electricity, depicting Sir Francis and members of his notorious club, which used to meet in subterranean workings.

ST LAWRENCE'S CHURCH

A RUSH OF EXCITEMENT AS THE LOOMS BURST INTO LIFE

WHITCHURCH SILK MILL

HAMPSHIRE & ISLE OF WIGHT

1 Sandham Memorial Chapel **2** Whitchurch Silk Mill **3** Brickworks office, Basingstoke

4 Noar Hill, Selborne

Sandham Memorial Chapel

Evocative images of life behind the front lines in the First World War

Making jam sandwiches in the hospital ward, sorting the laundry, scrubbing the floor, kit inspection – there is something immeasurably moving about the murals by Stanley Spencer (1891-1959) in Sandham Memorial Chapel. Nineteen panels detail the minutiae of soldiers' lives without revealing any of the horror, while *The Resurrection of the Soldiers* covers the entire east wall.

Spencer served in the First World War with the Royal Army Medical Corps at Bristol and then in Macedonia with the infantry. He had already planned a series of paintings depicting the human companionship engendered by war when a Mr and Mrs Behrend decided to build a chapel in Burghclere to house them. Spencer painted the murals, considered by many to be his greatest work, between 1926 and 1932. The chapel was dedicated to Mrs Behrend's brother, Lieut. H.W. Sandham, who died from an illness contracted in Macedonia.

▶ *Burghclere, off A34, 4 miles S of Newbury. NT. Wed-Sun, and bank hol Mon, Apr-Oct; Sat-Sun Mar and Nov-Dec.*

Whitchurch Silk Mill

A rush of excitement as the looms burst into life

Shuttles fly from side to side, reeds frantically clunk and clack back and forth: when Whitchurch Silk Mill's power looms are in action (there are 16 in all) the sound is deafening and the building vibrates. Yet the lengths of silk fabric that are the end product of this frenzy of activity could hardly be more delicate. They include taffeta and organza in exclusive designs, mainly for theatrical costumes and other short runs of up to 50m (164ft).

The red-brick mill building, dating from 1800, is situated on an island in the River Test. Its waterwheel once powered all the machinery. Nowadays, electricity is used, but on some occasions the big wheel turns to drive the 19th-century winding gear on the top floor, which purrs gently as it coils hanks of Chinese silk onto wooden bobbins ready to feed the warping mill.

▶ *Winchester Street, near Whitchurch centre, off A34, 10 miles W of Basingstoke. Tues-Sun and bank hol Mon. Power looms operated Tues–Fri.*

Brickworks office, Basingstoke

A tiny Lutyens masterpiece revealed in a modern industrial estate

The best-kept secret in Basingstoke is this architectural gem designed in 1905 by Edwin Lutyens to house the offices of the Daneshill Brick & Tile Company. The single-storey building, dwarfed by the modern industrial units of the Kingsland Business Park, was designed to show off the newly formed company's products. The building is in effect a 3D catalogue of differently shaped bricks incorporated into window frames and mullions, door frames, parapet and – the *tour de force* – the central, twisting chimney.

Lutyens (1869-1944) had visited two splendid local houses, the Vyne and Basing House, while staying with his friend Walter Hoare and, having admired their brickwork, suggested Hoare set up a brickmaking company using local clay. This Hoare did, subsequently supplying the bricks for many of Lutyens's most famous buildings. Basingstoke Heritage Society has created a pretty garden from which to view the exterior brickwork.

▶ *Bilton Road. Leave Ringway (A339) at Reading Road roundabout, on Faraday Road for Daneshill. At next roundabout, take 1st left, Wade Road, then left into Bilton Road.*

Noar Hill, Selborne

Chalk grassland from the pages of an 18th-century naturalist

Selborne's most celebrated resident, the parson and naturalist Gilbert White (1720-93), spent much of his time riding round his parish on horseback noting the flora and fauna. His diaries are a delightful account of what he saw. Noar Hill, a nature reserve just south of the village, was one of his haunts. Here, medieval chalk quarries are now grassy hollows where Duke of Burgundy butterflies dance, birds sing and rabbits graze between musk orchids and other downland wild flowers. There is a real sense that time has stood still and that this piece of chalk grassland looks just as it did when White wrote his classic *The Natural History and Antiquities of Selborne* in 1789.

▶ *Off B3006 S of Selborne – 1st right (Newton Valence), then 1st left and track up to hill.*

SOUTH OF ENGLAND

HAMPSHIRE & ISLE OF WIGHT

5 The Church in the Wood **6** The Pub With No Name **7** Winchester Cathedral

8 Mottisfont Abbey gardens

The Church in the Wood
A Romany church in a beech wood glade

A wooden fence marks out a clearing in the woods of Bramdean Common. Here stands a tiny green, corrugated-tin church, founded 100 years ago to serve the local Romany population. Bramdean Common has long been popular with Romanies, and wedding and funeral ceremonies still take place in the church. It is little more than a hut, yet there is an intensely spiritual feel about a place of worship this close to nature. For a true sense of the unexpected, it is best to come across it almost by chance while walking in the woods.
▶ *W off A32 just N of West Meon Hut traffic lights, signed Alresford. Follow road for 2 miles. Park on left of road, beside drive to Wood Farm. Walk back along road to church notice board at end of path into woodland.*

The Pub With No Name
Ale house of old that captured a poet's imagination

'It hides from either road, a field's breadth back, and it's trees you see, not the house,' wrote the First World War poet Edward Thomas in *Up in the Wind*. He was describing the Pub With No Name, off a lane, up a track, in the middle of fields high on the downs (officially known as the White Horse Inn, but no name-board hangs from the pub sign frame).

Thomas (killed in action in 1917) loved the area. There is a memorial window engraved by Laurence Whistler in nearby Steep Church, and a plaque in the Edward Thomas Bar in the 17th-century pub, where open fires, wooden settles and candlelight evoke a bygone age.
▶ *Priors Dean, from A32, 5 miles S of Alton, turn left to Steep and Froxfield, then 3rd left at crossroads on brow of hill and 2nd right.*

Winchester Cathedral
The great church saved by a diver

From the peaceful Dean Garnier's Garden in The Close, you will see that the east end of the cathedral tips dramatically downwards. Today this is not a worry, but in 1905 there was a real danger of complete collapse. The Norman cathedral – Europe's longest medieval church at 169m (556ft) – had been built on a bog, and its foundations of beech logs, laid on a gravel bed, were rotting. The high water table meant that any attempt to remove the logs and underpin the walls with concrete would be thwarted by water rushing in.

The consulting engineer proposed the use of a diver, and William Walker was taken on in 1906. First, liquid cement was injected into cracks in the walls, then trenches, or 'drifts' – 235 in all – were dug under the base of the walls and allowed to fill with water. Walker, working alone, in the dark and in full diving gear, then began filling the drifts with bags of dry cement, which he slit open so they would absorb the water. It took him five years to complete the task, a feat commemorated at the east end of the cathedral with a statue. Be sure to seek out the crypt, under the east end, which regularly floods. When it does, the beautiful vaulting is perfectly reflected around Antony Gormley's contemplative figure, Sound II, standing up to his ankles, and sometimes knees, in water (right).
▶ *Winchester centre. Tours Mon-Sat.*

Mottisfont Abbey gardens
Sweet smell of old-fashioned roses

The heady fragrance of roses hits you even before you enter this quintessentially English summer garden. More than 300 varieties dating from the Middle Ages to 1900 are collected in two walled gardens in the grounds of a former Augustinian priory. Along with such ancient hybrids as Rosa gallica, Rosa damascena and Rosa moschata, there are China, Bourbon, Hybrid Perpetual and Tea roses. As most bloom only once a year, visit in June – though herbaceous plants and climbers keep the borders colourful all summer. Leave time to see Rex Whistler's amazingly deceptive trompe l'oeil plasterwork in the house and an excellent small collection of 20th-century art.
▶ *4½ miles NW of Romsey, 1 mile W of A3057. NT. Tel 01794 340757 for opening details.*

THE GREAT CHURCH
SAVED BY A DIVER

WINCHESTER CATHEDRAL

The ships that ruled the waves

Britain's key strategic harbour shows 400 years of naval life, from a Tudor warship to the first submarine

1 Portsmouth

Portsmouth Historic Dockyard ▶ *Daily; Warships by Water: boat tour of modern naval base, seasonal; Tel 023 9283 9766.*

Royal Navy Submarine Museum ▶ *Haslar Jetty Road, Gosport. Daily, Tel 023 9252 9217. Waterbus Harbour Tours: between Historic Dockyard and Submarine Museum, Tel 023 9261 2743.*

Explosion! ▶ *Priddy's Hard, Gosport. Sat and Sun Tel 023 9250 5600.*

The harbour at **Portsmouth**, a natural south coast haven, has always played an essential role in Britain's maritime trading and coastal defences. The Romans made a base at the north end in Portchester (see page 61). In the 1490s, when ships purpose-built for war became too large to repair on the beach, the world's first dry dock was created here, and in 1512 the town became an official centre for the construction of Henry VIII's warships. By the 17th century, Portsmouth had pride of place among the naval dockyards of southern England. The Georgian Royal Dockyard buildings are now a handsome backdrop for both the modern navy and the museums and historic ships of 'Flagship Portsmouth'.

Raised from the seabed

On October 11, 1982, the world held its breath as the hull of Henry VIII's favourite ship, *Mary Rose*, was lifted from the seabed where it had lain for 437 years. The vessel had sunk during enemy action in 1545 just outside Portsmouth Harbour, not far from where it had been built in 1509-11. Now in No. 3 Dry Dock, the surviving half of the hull of the first purpose-built battleship is back in an upright position. From this Tudor time capsule of life at sea, divers brought up 19,000 objects, astonishingly well preserved by the silt. On display in the **Mary Rose Museum**, they range from cast-bronze guns with Henry's coat of arms and the only surviving Tudor longbows to personal possessions such as silk embroidered purses and headlice combs. The star of the show is the barber-surgeon's threatening tool kit.

When Nelson sailed **HMS *Victory*** to fight in the Battle of Trafalgar 260 years later, warships had become larger and stronger. The admiral's quarters were grand and spacious, with furniture that could be folded away to make space for guns. Life for the 500 crew, by contrast, was severely cramped on the lower gun deck, even without the 90 tables that were fitted up at meal times, or the hammocks slung from the beams at night. Luckily, the average height of a sailor in those days was no more than 1.8m (5ft 8in). Nelson was a mere 1.7m (5ft 6in), which explains his tiny cot.

The launch of **HMS *Warrior*** in 1860 instantly rendered all other warships obsolete. Steam power had already been introduced into some wooden warships, but *Warrior's* trump card was its iron hull. In addition, it had a central, armour-plated box to protect its machinery. The ship's iron construction also meant it could be divided into watertight compartments, limiting the water taken on board if the ship was holed.

Warrior had four engines fuelled by ten boilers, but could not steam more than 2000 miles without reloading with coal. So it was fitted with masts and made long hauls under sail. Compared with *Victory*, the crew's quarters were spacious. They even had the luxury of washing machines; stokers and engineers had baths.

Also in Portsmouth dockyard are the **Royal Naval Museum** and **Action Stations**, an exciting hands-on, high-tech experience of life in today's navy, including warship command and helicopter flight simulators.

Underwater fire power

In Gosport, a short boat trip across the harbour, is the **Royal Navy Submarine Museum**, where two subs are on view. *Holland I*, named after its inventor, John Philip Holland, was Britain's first practical operational submarine. Launched in 1901, the sub was outdated by 1913 and sank on its way to the scrap yard. It was lifted and brought to Gosport in 1982 and then conserved. *Holland I* is now displayed to the public in its final stripped-down form, with torpedo tube, engine propeller and ballast tanks still in place, but otherwise empty.

HMS *Alliance*, by contrast, is preserved fully equipped, as it was when its service ended in 1973. Raised out of the water, the boat looks surprisingly large. Inside you can only wonder how 65 crew could possibly have survived for months at sea with pipes and wheels and levers covering every inch of wall and ceiling, bunks slung in every nook and a galley no bigger than a cupboard.

To complete the overview of naval history, take the bus link to **Explosion!** at Priddy's Hard (its buildings were a State secret for 200 years) to learn of the people who supplied ammunitions from Trafalgar to the Gulf War.

'...A BLACK SNAKE AMONG RABBITS.'

Napoleon III on HMS Warrior

HAMPSHIRE & ISLE OF WIGHT

Romsey Abbey
How to buy a Norman masterpiece

It was £100 paid to Henry VIII in 1544 that saved this church for posterity. The abbey, built between 1120 and 1240 to replace a nunnery church destroyed by invading Vikings, is second only to Durham Cathedral for its wonderful Norman architecture. The triforium arcading in the chancel, with a column over each pair of sub-arches, is unique to Romsey.

The north aisle and transept, screened from the nuns, were allocated to the townsfolk as their parish church. The fact that they had worshipped here for centuries probably persuaded Henry, when he dissolved the abbey, to allow them to keep the building. The Bill of Sale, with the king's great seal, is in the south choir aisle. Also notable are a Saxon rood, some vividly carved Norman capitals, and Lord Mountbatten of Burma's grave.
▶ *Romsey town centre.*

Martin Down
Butterfly and orchid heaven

In the northwest part of this nature reserve, between a Romano-British earthwork called Bokerley Dyke and a Bronze Age enclosure, there is a Second World War rifle range with a row of stop butts. Sitting atop the highest butt, at peace with the world as the skylarks twitter, you have a fine view of one of Britain's largest areas of chalk downland and scrub, parts of which have never been touched by a plough. With patches of heath and woodland too, Martin Down has a mixture of habitats that provides shelter and food for a wide range of wildlife. Orchid enthusiasts will be delighted: frog, pyramidal, fragrant, burnt-tip and early purple are common. And for butterfly fanciers, the list of possible sightings includes Duke of Burgundy, meadow browns, small blues, gatekeepers, dark green fritillaries, silver-spotted skippers. Don't forget your field guide.
▶ *For NW area, National Nature Reserve car park on S side of A354, 7 miles SW of Salisbury. For E end, NNR car park in Sillens Lane, Martin village, off A354. Daily.*

Eling Tide Mill
Harnessing the sea to make flour

Heath Robinson comes to mind, but it all works, and has done since about 1782, when Eling Tide Mill was built on the Test estuary. In fact, there has been a tide mill on Eling causeway since at least 1086, and possibly much longer. The causeway is in effect a dam. Twice a day the rising tide fills the estuary behind the dam and the water is held back by sluice gates. When the tide turns, water flows out through a millrace driving the waterwheel, which in turn operates the grinding machines. Each tide guarantees 4 hours' milling time. That's reliable, cheap power 8 hours a day. Reflect on this as you leave with your bag of stoneground wholemeal flour under your arm.
▶ *Eling Lane, Totton, off A35. Follow brown signs; park S end of causeway. Wed-Sun, bank hol Mon; Tel 023 8086 9575 for milling times.*

Spinnaker Tower
A futuristic icon sailing into the sky

Built on the seabed and designed to represent billowing sails, this striking 170m tall tower draws strongly on Portsmouth's maritime heritage. Look out from the viewing decks on a clear day and you might be lucky enough to see the Isle of Wight, in fact you could see magnificent views stretching as far as 23 miles. A high speed internal lift and an external lift offering panoramic views take visitors to the three viewing platforms, or you can always choose to walk up the 572 steps to the top. Feeling brave? Then stand on the glass floor in the centre of the concrete and steel structure, the largest glass floor in Europe, and look down to the ground underneath. Or step out onto the 'Crow's Nest' viewing platform at 110m high and feel the wind whistle around you. It really is quite an experience.
▶ *Portsmouth Historic Waterfront. Daily. Tel 023 9285 7520 for opening times.*

Portchester Castle

Norman stronghold and church behind the walls of a Roman fort

At high tide, the sea laps against the walls of the amazingly well preserved 3rd-century Roman fortress. The 3m (10ft) thick walls and most of the bastions survive, with courses of red tiles breaking the grey flint.

In the 12th century, Henry I added the square keep, from the top of which the whole fortress can be seen – and where the names of some of the 10,000 prisoners held at Portchester during the Napoleonic wars are carved. The Norman church inside the walls, also built by Henry I, is an architectural gem, with bold zigzag moulding and other motifs.
▶ *6 miles N of Portsmouth off A27 Fareham road. EH. Daily.*

Buckler's Hard

Home for shipwrights and sawyers, slipway for men-o'-war

Look down the grassy strip between cottages at Buckler's Hard to Beaulieu River at low tide, and the stumps of the cradles for three ships commanded by Nelson – *Agamemnon, Swiftsure* and *Euryalus* – are still visible, rising from the mud. The cottages lining the single car-free 'street' look much as they did when built in the late 1700s, with the interiors of some portraying daily life at the time.

The shipyard at Buckler's Hard was established in the 1750s and continued until 1880, when steel ships made it redundant. A model in the museum shows how the yard was in 1803, at the height of the wars with France, complete with sawmill and models of ships.
▶ *7 miles E of Lymington off B3054 Beaulieu road. Museum daily.*

The Durbar Room, Osborne House

Bringing home the jewel in the crown

It resembles a baroque wedding cake: an extraordinary encrustation of moulded plasterwork on the ceiling and a larger-than-lifesize plaster and papier-mâché peacock over the mantelpiece. In 1890 an ageing Queen Victoria, Empress of India, decided to bring a flavour of the subcontinent, which she never visited, into the Italianate villa designed by Prince Albert as a homely retreat. Lockwood Kipling, the writer's father, and master craftsman Ram Singh realised her desire.
▶ *1 mile SE of East Cowes off A3021. EH. Daily Apr-Oct; Nov-Mar Tel 01983 200022.*

Hurst Spit

Big guns and racing tides

The narrow finger of shingle seems to have the Isle of Wight as its destination, but at Hurst Castle it makes a sudden U-turn for the Hampshire shore, encircling mudflats and saltmarsh full of wildfowl and waders.

Henry VIII built the castle (open daily from April to October; EH) in the early 1540s to defend the Solent against possible French invasion. The tower where the king's men kept watch looks out on the boiling water between the spit and the isle as tides rampage through a gap just 3/4 mile wide. The two low-slung wings sweeping out from the castle are defence batteries added in the 1870s, this time with the French navy's new iron-clad warships in mind; two of their 38-ton guns are preserved in place.
▶ *3 miles S of Lymington off A337.*

Old Battery, The Needles

Stop firing the guns, the cliffs are shaking to bits!

An exposed walk leads to old coastal defences on the tip of the headland – and a spectacular view of The Needles. As long as there is not a wind of gale-force 8 or higher blowing, you can descend into a tunnel leading to the cliff edge and an armoured searchlight, installed in the 1890s to sweep the same turbulent stretch of water covered by the guns at Hurst Castle on the mainland (see above).

A small exhibition relates how First World War firing trials made the chalk cliffs unstable, forcing the battery's relocation further from the edge. The coloured sands of Alum Bay, reached by a chair lift from the clifftop, dominate the walk back.
▶ *4 miles SW of Yarmouth at end of B3322. Mar-Oct. Tel 01983 754772 to check if open. NT.*

Dinosaur Farm Museum

Dig in the graveyard of giants

Come to this simple dairy farm if you want to enrol in a hunt for dinosaur fossils or handle their gigantic bones instead of looking at them in glass cases. Ever since the skeleton of a brachiosaurus – the heaviest known dinosaur at around 50 tonnes – was discovered near the farmhouse in 1992, fossil hunters have been digging up remains of the great reptiles and cleaning them in the farm's barns. No wonder a TV series about the beasts was filmed here and called 'Live from Dinosaur Island'.
▶ *Lower Sutton Farm, 2 miles SE of Brighstone on A3055. For details of opening Tel 01983 740844.*

SOUTH OF ENGLAND

Romans at work, rest and play

Remains and artefacts at St Albans bring Verulamium,

a provincial town of the Roman Empire, vividly to life

1 St Albans

Roman theatre ▶ *Just W of A4147 (Bluehouse Hill). Daily.*

Verulamium Museum ▶ *E of A4147 in Verulamium Park. Mon-Sat, Sun pm.*

St Albans Cathedral ▶ *Town centre, off Holywell Hill.*

Looking down on the **Roman theatre** at **St Albans** from the path that surrounds its majestic remains, it is easy to imagine the excited roars of the crowd 1600 or more years ago as they thrilled to a gory bout of bear-baiting or bullfighting.

Along the north side of the theatre, reached through a vast triumphal arch, ran Watling Street, the road built by the Romans to link their garrison at Wroxeter (see page 178), near Shrewsbury, with London. This part of its route, still obvious today, highlights the great importance of Verulamium as a stronghold – important enough to attract the wrath of Boudicca and her East Anglian tribes, who laid waste to the town in AD 60. Despite this and two major fires Verulamium was rebuilt repeatedly, on an ever grander scale, reaching its zenith around 300, when up to ten aristocratic families had estates there.

Near where the Basilica and Forum once stood, at the heart of the Roman town, is the **Verulamium Museum**, which houses the results of the excavations begun in the 1930s by Mortimer and Tessa Wheeler. Its displays include vibrant mosaics, decorated with dolphins, lions, stags and flower patterns, and intricate ceiling paintings in rich brown and red pigments. A stroll across parkland from the museum takes you to the mosaic floor and hypocaust, or underground heating system, of an excavated villa.

Flint and bricks carried across the River Ver from the ruins of the Roman town provided building materials for the Norman **St Albans Cathedral**. It was on this spot around 210 that Alban, a citizen of Verulamium, was beheaded for professing Christianity, then a proscribed religion in the empire. Alban was Britain's first Christian martyr, and his shrine in the cathedral's chapel of St Alban has been a place of pilgrimage for centuries.

ROMAN THEATRE, ST ALBANS

HERTFORDSHIRE

1 Walter Rothschild Zoological Museum **2** De Havilland Aircraft Heritage Centre

3 Hatfield House **4** Shaw's Retreat

Walter Rothschild Zoological Museum

Nose-to-nose with all creatures great and small – safely stuffed

A startlingly realistic polar bear with a mysterious grin greets you – a disturbing encounter, until you notice that almost every exhibit in the Walter Rothschild collection, part of the Natural History Museum, is equally lifelike. From the shy okapi, a rare member of the giraffe family, to huge pythons and anacondas, giant turtles and flamboyantly colourful hummingbirds, cassowaries and butterflies, the place is full of eye-popping surprises, with the prize for the most bizarre going to a group of fleas dressed in painstakingly created 'clothes'.

Walter Rothschild was given the land and money for the museum in 1889 as a 21st birthday present from his father, the financier 1st Baron Rothschild. The young naturalist commissioned the most skilled Victorian taxidermists for his collection of more than 4000 species – some, such as the dodo and the zebra-like quagga, now extinct – and displayed them in the handsome floor-to-ceiling cases still used today.

▶ *Akeman Street, off High Street, Tring centre, signed off A41. Mon-Sat, and Sun pm, all year.*

De Havilland Aircraft Heritage Centre

Home of one of the most remarkable planes of the Second World War

Historic Salisbury Hall was chosen by the de Havilland Aircraft Company in 1939 as a site for the top-secret design and manufacture of the Mosquito bomber – arguably the most versatile and agile of all the Allied aircraft used in the Second World War.

The original prototype of this plywood, high-speed, unarmed bomber can now be seen at this lovingly maintained museum – the oldest aircraft museum in the country. A further 18 types of de Havilland aircraft ranging from DH Moths to modern military and civil jets are also on show. Visitors are encouraged to gain a hands-on experience of what it was like to pilot one of these impressive machines by inspecting, and even sitting in, the cockpits of the planes on display.

▶ *3 miles NW of South Mimms on B556. Tues, Thur, Sat pm, Sun and bank hol Mon Mar-Oct.*

Hatfield House

Getting close to the virgin queen

Four hundred years of power and influence emanate from the walls, floors and ceilings of Hatfield House. It is the place that brings you nearer than anywhere else to Elizabeth I. Two haunting representations of the Tudor queen – the Rainbow and Ermine portraits – dominate rooms on the lower floors, and upstairs, in the Long Gallery, are her yellow gloves, hat and silk stockings, believed to be the first worn in England.

The queen spent much of her childhood at the adjacent Royal Palace of 1497, and held her first council in its Great Hall. Robert Cecil, 1st Earl of Salisbury and chief minister to James I, built Hatfield House itself in 1611. It has been near the centre of national power ever since, scaling another pinnacle under the 3rd Marquess of Salisbury, three times Tory prime minister in the 1880s and 1890s.

▶ *Signed from A1(M) (Junction 4). House Wed-Sun and bank hols pm (tours Wed-Fri) Easter Sat-Sept. Park and West Garden daily (East Gardens Thur only) Easter Sat-Sept. Tel 01707 287010.*

Shaw's Retreat

The rotating shed where a Nobel laureate escaped his admirers

Almost hidden by trees at the end of a country garden is a writer's surprising hideaway: a revolving weatherboarded hut, 2m (7ft) square, that resembles a child's Wendy house. Raised on a base, the hut can be turned through 360 degrees to improve the light or to change the view. George Bernard Shaw, the Irish dramatist and Nobel prize-winner, used this shack as a study. His wife built it as a summerhouse in the grounds of his home at Ayot St Lawrence, but Shaw – desiring peace – avoided uninvited callers and wrote many of his plays there, including *Pygmalion* and *St Joan*. He called it 'The Retreat'.

▶ *2 miles W of Welwyn, signed from B653. NT. Wed-Sun and bank hols mid Mar-Oct.*

SOUTH OF ENGLAND

MONUMENTAL
ARTISTIC
MASTERPIECES
DISPLAYED IN AN
OPEN-AIR GALLERY
HENRY MOORE FOUNDATION

HERTFORDSHIRE

5 Welwyn Roman Baths **6** Knebworth Gardens **7** Scott's Grotto **8** Great Amwell

9 Henry Moore Foundation

Welwyn Roman Baths

Roman bathhouse preserved in a quiet vault beneath a motorway

Cut into an embankment near the A1(M) are doors reminiscent of a wartime bunker. They open to reveal a dank tunnel winding down to the substantial remains of a Roman bathhouse. Signs and wall displays identify the *frigidarium*, *tepidarium* and *caldarium* (cold, warm and hot rooms), as well as the hypocaust and the stoke hole, where a fire generated heat. As you walk around, it is easy to forget that the A1(M) is just 9m (30ft) above your head. The baths were part of Dicket Mead Villa, built in the 3rd century AD and unearthed in 1969. Soon after they were found, a new motorway route was announced that ran straight through the site. A protective steel vault was built over the baths, but the rest of the excavations were bulldozed.
▶ *Welwyn, signed from A1(M) Junction 6. Sat, Sun, bank hols pm Jan-Nov; daily in school hols.*

Knebworth Gardens

Subtle gardens versus Gothic excess

Exquisite Victorian and Edwardian gardens are being reclaimed in the grounds of Knebworth House. At the heart of the restoration, begun in 1980, is the sunken lawn, set in avenues of pleached limes by the architect Edwin Lutyens in 1910. He offset the flamboyant, mid-19th-century Gothic additions to the house with simple garden designs. Gertrude Jekyll used the same approach – her 1907 design for a herb garden, not laid out until 1982, produces a feast of aromas and textures. A new walled garden sets borders of ornamental vegetables around a spectacular central fountain.
▶ *Accessible only from A1(M) Junction 7. Tel 01438 812661 for opening times.*

Scott's Grotto

A glittering suburban gem

Thousands of shells, minerals and smooth flints glimmer and glisten so that the interior of Scott's Grotto appears to be jewel-encrusted. It is Britain's largest underground folly, extending 20m (67ft) into a hillside, and has six chambers linked by passageways and dotted with niches for seating. Beautifully restored, it is one of the surviving elements of the Amwell estate's grand gardens. A Quaker poet, John Scott, laid out the grotto in the mid 18th century and his friend

Dr Samuel Johnson described it as 'a fairy hall'. It was saved from destruction in the 1960s, when houses were built all around it.
▶ *Scotts Road, off A119, S of Ware. Sat and bank hol Mon pm Apr-Sept, or Tel 01920 464131 for appointment. Take a torch.*

Great Amwell

Quenching the thirst of Londoners

A delicately landscaped water-garden with elegantly swaying willows commemorates a feat of engineering. When London needed a fresh water supply in the 17th century, Hugh Myddleton, a Welsh engineer, cut the New River – which flows through the garden. Dug out in 1609-13, it carried water 25 miles from chalk springs in Great Amwell to Clerkenwell. A large urn-like monument in the garden marks Myddleton's achievement. Follow New River to Amwell Marsh Pumping Station, built in 1884, which pumps 16 million litres of water a day from a depth of 120m (394ft).
▶ *S of Ware off A1170. Park near St John the Baptist Church and walk through churchyard.*

Henry Moore Foundation

Monumental artistic masterpieces displayed in an open-air gallery

Vast, sinuous sculptures bring an otherworldly feel to a meticulously tended garden and sheep pasture in the English countryside. They are part of the largest collection of works by Henry Moore (1898-1986), whose organic, semi-abstract forms seem entirely natural in this context. Moore and his wife Irina moved to the quiet corner of Perry Green after their London studio was damaged in the Blitz. They converted two 15th-century cottages into a house where they spent the rest of their lives, and gradually acquired 28ha (70 acres) of land. The estate includes studios, workshops and barns containing hundreds of works by Moore. Among several restored studios, the light and airy Sheep Field Barn incorporates three galleries displaying sketches, carvings and sculpture. Sheep graze carelessly between the immense and primal pieces set in the surrounding fields. *Large Standing Figure: Knife Edge* (left, foreground) and *Three Piece Sculpture: Vertebrae* (left, background) are among more than 30 sculptures that rise out of the gentle landscape.
▶ *Perry Green, SW of Bishop's Stortford, off B1004. Tues-Sun Apr-mid Oct. Visitor numbers limited, Tel 01279 843333 in advance.*

SOUTH OF ENGLAND

KENT

Bluewater Shopping Centre
Through the checkout to art and architecture

A shopping centre seems an unlikely subject for artists, but on a fine day dozens of them are lured to Bluewater with their sketchpads and paints. Built in the dramatic amphitheatre of a disused chalk quarry half a mile across, it is surrounded by 20ha (50 acres) of parkland planted with trees and shrubs, and a ring of six lakes fringed with rushes, hostas and other water-loving plants.

Construction is mainly ultra-modern steel and glass, with a reminder of the Kentish setting in the shining metal ventilation cowls on the roof, imitating the wooden ones on oasthouses. Inside, shoppers can stroll along a triangle of three spacious gallery-arcades of shops and cafés, with a major department store at each corner. Decoration is used everywhere to great effect. The upper walkways contain abstract and figurative sculptures, one gallery is lined with reliefs showing medieval trades, while the floor of the longest gallery is inlaid with a sinuous mosaic depicting the River Thames, from its source in far-off Gloucestershire all the way to its estuary on the coasts of Kent and Essex.
▶ *N of A2, Junction 2 off M25. Daily.*

Lullingstone Roman Villa
Roman riches in a plain container

The destination – an anonymous modern hangar – seems to hold little appeal after the approach through the picture-postcard village of Eynsford and under a magnificent Victorian viaduct. But the plain packaging disguises a wonderful surprise: laid out under the protective roof are the remains of a spectacular Roman villa, probably built in the 1st century AD for a prosperous Romano–British farmer.

Portions of the fine mosaic floors and the elaborate heating system that ran under them have survived, but what sets the villa apart from others is its Christian chapel. This dates back to about 380, which means that the owner must have been a convert two centuries before Christianity became the official religion of Kent. But the chapel's life was short: the villa burnt down soon after 400 and was lost until workmen discovered it in 1939.
▶ *1 mile S of Eynsford off A225 Dartford-Sevenoaks road. EH. Daily Feb-Nov, Wed-Sun Dec-Jan.*

Penshurst Place
Under these spreading chestnut beams the barons banqueted

Towering 18m (60ft) to its massive chestnut roof timbers, the Barons' Hall in Penshurst Place is one of England's grandest medieval interiors and the centrepiece of this sprawling mansion of golden-brown stone. The hall was completed in 1341 and is still much as it was six centuries ago, with logs piled in its central fireplace, trestle tables stretching on either side, and a floor of well-worn medieval tiles.

In the grounds stands Sidney's Oak, already 500 years old when the house was built. It is named after the Elizabethan hero Sir Philip Sidney, the most famous member of the family that has lived here since 1552.
▶ *4 miles W of Tonbridge, in Penshurst village. Sat and Sun Mar, daily Apr-Oct.*

Ightham Mote
Reversing the march of time

There is an eternal quality about this moated medieval manor house; its stone, brick, half-timbering and water have a harmony that seems rooted in time. Yet Ightham is a masterpiece of recent restoration by the National Trust.

By the 1990s, acid rain had dissolved much of the masonry, deathwatch beetle had mined the timber and damp ruined the plaster. Then craftsmen in traditional building skills were called in to rescue the house from seemingly certain death. How they breathed new life into it can be seen in a permanent exhibition.
▶ *3 miles SE of Sevenoaks off A227. NT. Sun-Fri, except Tues, Mar-Oct.*

Garden Organic Yalding
Follow the plots and sift the wisdom of Adam and his heirs

Here, laid out on a wide expanse of the Medway valley, is a showcase for the virtues of manuring and mulching over reliance on artificial fertilisers and chemical pest controls. The plots, which radiate from central lawns, take visitors on a horticultural journey through time – from a medieval 'physick garden' where mandrake and henbane grow, past 1820s self-sufficiency and

HOP FARM COUNTRY PARK

1940s 'Digging for Victory' gardens, to a modern ecological ideal of interdependent plants and wildlife.
▶ *5 miles SW of Maidstone on B2010. Wed-Sun Apr-Oct, and bank hols.*

Hop Farm Country Park
A fine draught of the old days

Half a century ago thousands poured out of the capital's East End in late summer to work in Kent's hopfields, picking the pungent-smelling flowers, and sleeping in airless tin-roofed huts. Today the process is mechanised; but in September visitors to the hop-pickers' festivals at Beltring (left) can enjoy the smells and camaraderie of old.

Among the array of 31 oasthouses there is an exhibition relating the story of the twining hopbine (vine) and its flower. Outside, gentle giants haul families around the farm on brewers' drays – pensioned-off shire horses, their polished harness glittering with brass.
▶ *Beltring, 5 miles E of Tonbridge on A228 Pembury-Mereworth road. Daily. Tel 0870 0274166 for festival dates.*

The Historic Dockyard, Chatham
Sail back to the time when Britain ruled the waves

The days of British naval glory are brought to life in the Historic Dockyard. Ships fill the dry docks, rope is still twisted in the quarter-mile long Ropery and a submarine awaits the intrepid investigator. The dockyard began under Henry VIII in the 1540s, closed down in 1984, and is now being meticulously restored. The surviving buildings date mainly from the years around 1800. In the dry docks stand more recent naval vessels – HMS *Gannet*, a graceful Victorian sloop; HMS *Cavalier*, a Second World War destroyer; and the submarine *Ocelot*, the last warship to be built at Chatham for the Royal Navy, and launched here in 1962.

The dockyard's giant roofed slipways, where ships were built under cover, are marvels of Victorian cast-iron design. The late 18th-century Ropery was the longest brick building in Europe when it was constructed. Visitors can watch rope – still in demand for re-rigging tall ships – being made on 19th-century machines.
▶ *Off Dock Road, Chatham. Daily Feb-Oct, Sat-Sun Nov.*

KENT

Rochester bridges
See the Medway crossed six times

The Romans blazed the trail at the busy Medway port of Rochester with the town's first and longest surviving bridge. It was made of wood and served until the 1380s when the stone bridge that Charles Dickens knew as a child was constructed. This one was paid for by two Kentish knights, together with a small chapel, still standing, where travellers could give thanks for their safe crossing. The bridge was blown up in the 1850s in a road-widening scheme.

In its place, two road bridges and a Victorian railway bridge stand side by side. Upstream, a trio of concrete bridges soar above the mudflats: the four-lane M2 road bridge, erected in the 1960s, a second motorway crossing and the bridge carrying the Channel Tunnel rail link. Climb to the top of Rochester Castle's Norman 37m (120ft) high keep for a view of all six bridges.
▶ *Rochester Castle, town centre. EH. Daily.*

Leeds Castle
Accessories for the well-dressed dog at the most romantic of castles

The castle, serene on its island in the middle of a lake where black swans glide, was made for romance – the favourite retreat of medieval queens of England, including Eleanor of Castile, wife of Edward I. The picturesque setting is completed by an aviary crammed with brilliant parrakeets and cockatoos, and a maze with an underground grotto.

Within the castle walls, the state rooms are still furnished as they were in the days of medieval royalty. The gatehouse has a collection of dog collars from the past 400 years. They include fearsome 16th-century German collars of chains and spikes to protect against bears, an Italian collar of intricately pierced brass made about 1630, and an Austrian 18th-century leather collar covered in red velvet.
▶ *3 miles E of Maidstone off M20 (Junction 8). Daily.*

Bedgebury National Pinetum and Forest
Stroll among the world's finest collection of conifers

The Old Man of Kent – a giant double-crowned silver fir (*Abies grandis*) – stretches its lofty limbs 54m (176ft) above the national conifer collection. It is the tallest of some 6500 trees that make up the 120ha (300 acre) Bedgebury Pinetum, including examples of more than 60 per cent of all conifers that grow in the world's temperate zones. Notions of conifers being boringly similar are soon dispelled as you bask in a rich array of colours from deep blue-green to brilliant yellow.

Bedgebury was begun in 1924 as an offshoot of Kew Gardens, to protect conifers from the fatal effects of London's air pollution. A timber-built visitor centre has a cedar shingle roof and is heated by the Pinetum's wood chippings.
▶ *2 miles S of Goudhurst on B2079. Daily.*

Chart Gunpowder Mills
Explosives for Wellington and Nelson from a Kentish powder keg

The sweating powder-monkeys who scrambled along the decks of Nelson's warships were carrying gunpowder made at the Chart Mills in Faversham, Britain's only surviving gunpowder mill. It was established about 1560 and remained a centre of explosive manufacture for almost 400 years. It closed in the 1930s and was restored and reopened by local enthusiasts in the 1970s.

Inside the mill, enormous water-powered grindstones crushed saltpetre, sulphur and charcoal to make the gunpowder. Explosions were always a risk: in 1916 a TNT blast killed more than a hundred workers, and the shock-wave was felt as far away as Norwich.
▶ *Faversham, off Stonebridge Way. Sat, Sun, and bank hol Mon pm, Easter-Oct.*

Brogdale Horticultural Trust
The fruitiest place in England

Where can a Bloody Ploughman, a Chorister Boy, a Northern Spy and a Red Devil all be found together? The answer is, within sight of the thundering M2, at Brogdale, near Faversham. The names are those of apple trees whose fruit will never grace the supermarket shelves. Brogdale is home to the National Fruit Collection, dedicated to ensuring the survival of rare and threatened varieties. Its 60ha (150 acres) of orchards are planted with more than 2000 varieties of apple trees, 550 varieties of pear, 350 of plum and 220 of cherry.

Guided walks lead through avenues of blossom in spring. Fruit can be sampled in autumn, trees bought for planting, and pruning and grafting skills learned from the experts.
▶ *Brogdale Road, 1 mile S of A2 at Faversham. Garden centre daily, tours Apr-Nov.*

Canterbury Cathedral
Miracles in glass and lead give a graphic portrayal of Christian life

Glowing dark blue, crimson and vivid green, the 800-year-old stained-glass windows of Canterbury Cathedral are a visual revelation. High above the worn stone floor, Adam delves outside the Garden of Eden, the Magi bring their gifts, and the murderers of St Thomas Becket burst in on his devotions. These windows are the 'Poor Man's Bible'. In the centuries between the death of Becket in 1170 and the desecration of the cathedral by Henry VIII in the 1530s, they taught thousands of illiterate pilgrims about the Old Testament, the life of Christ, the martyrdom of Becket and the miracles performed at his tomb.

In spite of vandalism by Henry VIII's men, and a century later by Puritans, the cathedral has some of the world's best early medieval stained glass, much of it in the windows where it was first set. Eight of the 12 great windows of the Trinity Chapel, the site of Becket's shrine at the eastern end of the cathedral, survive. The miracles shown include a nun cured of epilepsy. Other scenes depict cures of afflictions ranging from toothache to leprosy.
▶ *Central Canterbury. Daily.*

Powell-Cotton Museum
Exotic animals, tribal art and an Eiffel Tower on the Isle of Thanet

Animals that once roamed the jungles and plains of the wilder parts of the world in the 19th century can be seen in a quiet corner of Kent. Before colour photography, the only means of showing exotic creatures in their natural habitat was to shoot them, stuff them and mount them in dioramas. This art is shown to the full at Quex Park, Birchington. In the 1890s Major Percy Powell-Cotton, a hunter and naturalist, set up a museum here to display animals, such as antelope and white rhinoceros, that he had shot on his travels. He was also a collector of tribal art and weaponry.

A short walk from the house, a striking spire soars above the trees in Quex's 100ha (250 acre) park. This graceful cast-iron structure looks from a distance like a small relation of the Eiffel Tower. It crowns the Waterloo Tower, around 18m (60ft) high, built by John Powell-Powell about 1820. An enthusiastic bellringer, he installed a ring of 12 bells in the tower, which are still in use.
▶ *Quex Park, Birchington, off Canterbury Road (A28). Sun-Thur and bank hols Apr-Oct; Sun only Nov-Mar. Tel 01843 842168.*

Bronze Age Boat, Dover Museum
The original cross-Channel ferry

The remains of a Bronze Age boat, estimated to be about 3500 years old, form the prize exhibit of Dover Museum. Centuries before Moses led the Children of Israel out of Egypt, sailors from Kent were crossing to France in stout seagoing vessels made from oak planks, stitched together with twisted yew withies and waterproofed with moss and wax. Powered by 18 paddlers, such a boat could have carried passengers, goods and even livestock across the Channel. On a calm day, it could have made the crossing in about 5 hours.

About half the boat has been recovered from the Dover mud. It measures 9.5 x 2.4m (31 x 8ft) and would have been at least 18m (60ft) long. Though blackened by age, it is still easy to make out the withies, wedges and other details of its construction. Also on display is a section of a modern replica boat, made with copies of Bronze Age tools.
▶ *Market Square, Dover. Mon-Sat, Sun Apr-Aug.*

Timeball Tower
Time-keeping on a grand scale

At 1pm every day the large ball at the top of Timeball Tower suddenly drops. On the dot. It is so accurate that you can set your watch by it. And that is exactly why it is there. In 1853, it was built to pass a direct electric signal from Greenwich to Deal, so that ships in the area could be sure of working out their longitude on outward journeys. This, the last working example in Britain, was crucial in this once very busy port on the English Channel.

The Timeball Tower followed a long line of signalling posts that have stood at the same spot – from bonfires in Tudor times to announce the arrival of mail to the Shutter Telegraph of 1796 which used 6 shutters in 63 different combinations to send messages to the Admiralty in London. Working models of many of the previous signalling mechanisms can be tried out at this unique museum.
▶ *Victoria Parade, Deal. Sat-Sun and bank hol mon Easter-end Sept. Other times by appointment, Tel 01304 360897.*

Explore a secret realm stolen from the sea

Between the Kentish downs and the coast there lies an other-worldly place of dykes and water meadows

1 Brookland   **2** Fairfield   **3** Royal Military Canal   **4** Martello Tower   **5** Dungeness

Romney Marsh is truly atmospheric – a wide, empty triangle stretching south of the M20 and Eurostar line to a stranded fringe of seaside bungalows. On clear days, the sky is an enormous vault above the billiard-table-flat landscape, but often fog seeps in from the Channel, shrouding every sight, carrying in its dense folds the forlorn hooting of the lighthouse at Dungeness and the bleating of invisible sheep.

It was on the backs of these sheep – the Romney breed with their long, lustrous fleeces – that the marsh built its wealth. Symbols of the old wool trade prosperity make frequent landmarks in the featureless sweep of fields: grand churches, such as those at New Romney and Lydd, which swagger over their humble towns.

There are smaller, intimate places of worship too, such as **Brookland** (7 miles north of Rye on the A259), where the separate triple-coned belfry looks like three giant candle-snuffers one inside the other, and the interior holds a rare lead font. Two miles west, isolated in water meadows, lies tiny, skilfully restored **Fairfield**, which until a century ago could be reached only by boat.

The retreat of the sea – accelerated by the cutting of numerous drainage channels, which mark the boundaries of fields and force roads into frequent 90 degree bends – gave life to the marsh. But the most impressive of these artificial waterways was excavated for strategic reasons.

The **Royal Military Canal**, which defines the marsh in its 28-mile-long sweep from Hythe round to Rye, was dug as a third line of defence against Napoleon: if his forces got past the Navy's ships and the Martello tower forts on the coast, cannon and troops would open fire when they tried to cross this watery barrier. On the coast at Dymchurch, you can see how the whole plan worked at an exhibition in the little town's **Martello Tower** (EH. Tel 01304 211067 to visit).

The beat of drums and dragonflies' wings

Napoleon never invaded, but nature did, and the canal, which has a footpath beside it, is a reedy haven for kingfishers, dragonflies and frogs. The soldiers had another duty: to help to stamp out smuggling, for which the area, with its lonely beaches, treacherous fogs and secret ways, was notorious. In the 20th century, the local novelist Russell Thorndike romanticised this war of wits

between excisemen and smugglers for later generations, and it is celebrated each summer in Dymchurch's Dr Syn festival, named after the books' pirate-turned-clergyman hero.

At the foot of this triangle lies **Dungeness**, where the waves heap high shingle ramparts along the flank of fortress-like **Dungeness Nuclear Power Station**, a structure visible for miles around. Its cuboid architecture, scale and striding pylons complement this elemental spot, the bleak majesty of which is best appreciated by climbing to the top of the old lighthouse, which is situated immediately east of the power station, right on the blunt tip of Dungeness point. From up here one of the miniature steam trains puffing to the southern terminus of the **Romney, Hythe and**

Dymchurch Railway appears even more Lilliputian. The railway operates daily from April until mid October with other dates in winter (Tel 01797 362353 for timetable details).

Back on the ground, you can crunch north over the pebbles, past shacks black-tarred against the salt spray, to **Derek Jarman's Garden**, which is not signposted, or turn inland and follow either of the two roads towards Lydd for a mile to reach the flooded gravel pits of the **RSPB Dungeness Nature Reserve**. Its visitor centre, one of the best places for birdwatching in England, is open daily all year, enabling the comings and goings of spring and autumn migrants to be observed.

THE LITTLE AND LARGE SHOW

DUNGENESS POWER STATION AND DYMCHURCH RAILWAY.

KENT

St Leonard's, Hythe
Bones by the thousand

High on the hill above the seafront boarding houses and cramped old streets of Hythe, the parish church of St Leonard's houses one of the strangest sights to be seen in any British ecclesiastical building. The crypt is filled with 2000 human skulls and 8000 thighbones from people of all ages. The skulls are displayed neatly on racks, and the thighbones are stacked end-on to the wall. They are thought to be at least 1000 years old, and were once believed to be the bones of battle casualties or plague victims. But it seems more likely that as new graves were dug earlier bones were removed and stored in the crypt. It is one of only two ossuaries – vaults for holding bones – left in England.

When St Leonard's was built looking out across the Channel from this one-time Cinque Port, it stood on a pilgrims' route. Its huge pillars still have crude crosses and the outlines of medieval ships scratched into their stone. Below the chancel runs a covered passage or ambulatory, built to allow processions to walk right round the church on holy ground. This was later turned into the crypt in which the bones are exhibited.
▶ *Church Road, Hythe. Crypt daily May-Sept.*

Dover Castle
Defender of fortress England

Dominating the skyline above Dover, this multi-layered castle has played many roles in the defence of the British Isles since 1198 when the first keep was built by Henry II on the site of an Anglo-Saxon fortress. This fortress formed a vital link in the chain of castles along the south east coast, commissioned by Henry VIII as a defence against the threat of invasion from Europe. Later, fears of another invasion from across the English Channel during the Napoleonic Wars prompted the excavation of the extensive network of tunnels deep into the cliffs below the castle. During the Second World War these same tunnels were used as the focal point for planning the evacuation of British troops from Dunkirk in northern France. The Command Centre has been preserved along with corridors used as a wartime hospital.
▶ *E of town centre. EH. Daily Feb-Oct; Thur-Mon Nov-Jan. Tel 01304 211067.*

SOUTH OF ENGLAND

OXFORDSHIRE

1 Swalcliffe Barn **2** Rollright Stones **3** Great Tew **4** Kelmscott Manor **5** Blenheim Palace

6 Oxford Botanic Garden **7** Christ Church **8** Pitt Rivers Museum **9** Tradescant Room

Swalcliffe Barn

Wonder at the mighty oak, and the men who worked it to such effect

The tithe barn, built between 1401 and 1407, in Swalcliffe village is one of England's finest: testimony to the skill of medieval carpenters and the durability of English oak. The defining feature of this breathtaking building is the roof, its huge span supported by nine mighty crucks. Each cruck consists of two massive blades of timber, obtained by a pair of sawyers, who cut the tree lengthways over a pit with a huge double-handled saw – one sawyer working on top, the other in the pit. The two lengths of green timber were then jointed and pegged to make a giant roof support.

▶ *5 miles W of Banbury on B4035. Sun and bank hols pm, Easter–end Oct.*

Rollright Stones

Is there treachery afoot in the ranks of the stone army?

When mist wreathes their ridgetop site, it is easy to understand why the 5000-year-old scattered henge known as the Rollright Stones are equally shrouded in folklore. Even their name bows to local superstition – the idea that the stones uproot themselves occasionally and roll downhill to drink from a stream. Such a thought fits in with the legend that they are really a king and his invading army, turned to stone on the spot. The arrangement of the stones in turn inspired storytellers to embellish the legend. There is the King Stone, once one of the uprights of the doorway to a burial chamber but now standing in regal isolation. Not too far away are the King's Men, a stone circle that seems to defy accurate counting. Then, to one side, is the huddle of burial chamber uprights and capstone known as the Whispering Knights. Was this an army riven by dissent?

▶ *1 mile S of Long Compton on A3400 (21 miles N of Oxford). EH.*

Great Tew

A vision of pre-industrial England preserved in amber stone and thatch

Great Tew is the place to see your image of a perfect English village realised. The terraces of honey-coloured cottages with their undulating thatched roofs were built for estate workers in the 1630s by Lucius Carey, Lord Falkland.

All the other vital ingredients of an unforgettably picturesque village are here too. There is a village green and traditional general stores, and a good old-fashioned pub, renowned for its English country wines and real cider. Last but not least, there are cottage gardens with foaming phlox and twining honeysuckles behind clipped box hedges.

▶ *On B4022, off A361 (Banbury–Chipping Norton road) and A44 (Woodstock–Chipping Norton road).*

Kelmscott Manor

Flower and leaf forms that inspired the Arts and Crafts leader

A stroll around the gardens of this charming Tudor house on the banks of the upper Thames soon reveals why they so inspired its most famous resident, William Morris. Every wall and border provides stunning images of foliage and flowers, immediately reminiscent of the vivid wallpaper and textile designs of the leader of the Arts and Crafts Movement.

There was something essentially English about the movement, with its nostalgia for a pre-industrial age, and Morris found its perfect evocation at Kelmscott. More than a century after his death, we can still see the pleasure he got from the work of 'simple countryfolks of the long-past times'.

▶ *2 miles E of Lechlade off A417. Wed Apr–Sept; 3rd Sat in Apr, May, June and Sept pm; 1st and 3rd Sat in July and Aug pm.*

Blenheim Palace

National monument, symbol of power, titanic piece of sculpture

In a country renowned for stately houses, Blenheim is in a class of its own. Even the term 'palace' is an inadequate description; none of the royal palaces compare in scale – for that you have to travel to Versailles, in many ways the model for Blenheim. Nikolaus Pevsner, the architectural historian, likened it to a titanic piece of sculpture – a good way to regard it, especially on a first visit. When John Churchill, 1st Duke of Marlborough, won the greatest victory since Agincourt at Blenheim, on the Danube, in 1704, queen and country built a mixture of home and stunning patriotic monument for the national hero. It was designed by Vanbrugh and Hawksmoor, and eventually cost around £300,000: by the standards of the day, a simply staggering sum.

▶ *8 miles N of Oxford on A44. Daily mid Feb-Oct, Wed-Sun Nov-mid Dec. Park daily.*

Oxford Botanic Garden

Famed resource of herbalists and botanists

Immediately west of Magdalen Bridge, across the road from the college that also bears that name, gates lead into one of the most famous gardens in the world. The University of Oxford Botanic garden was the first 'physick garden' in England – founded in 1621 for the study of the use of plants in medicine.

The enterprise got off to a flying start, thanks to its establishment on '4000 loads of mucke and dunge' – the contents of college cesspits – and an energetic first keeper. Jacob Bobart gathered a great number of plants and seeds, largely from continental Europe, and laid the foundation for today's collection of around 8000 different plants from all over the world. Beyond the garden walls, a bog garden and glasshouses lead down to the River Cherwell.

▶ *From Rose Lane and High Street in city centre. Daily.*

Christ Church

A cardinal's ambition produces the largest college in Oxford

Step into the vast 80m (262ft) square main quadrangle of Christ Church to sense the grand scale of the college. It was founded as Cardinal College by the ambitious Cardinal Wolsey in 1525 with the intention of making the most splendid in Oxford. Henry VIII renamed it in 1546. Christopher Wren added an octagonal tower in 1682, which rises above the main gateway and holds 'Great Tom', a 7 tonne bell. Beside Tom Quad is the 12th-century cathedral, the only church in the world to be both a college chapel and a cathedral. Part of its nave was demolished by Wolsey to build the main quad, and, as a result, it is one of the smallest cathedrals in Britain.

Christ Church is the only Oxbridge college to own a gallery filled with works by the Old Masters. There are more than 2000 drawings and 300 paintings by such artists as Carracci, Leonardo, Raphael, Michelangelo, Tintoretto and van Dyck.

▶ *Oxford city centre, off St Aldate's. Cathedral daily all year; gallery daily Mon-Sat, Sun pm.*

Pitt Rivers Museum

Weird and wonderful souvenirs gathered from faraway lands

More than 500,000 exhibits are displayed in the huge warehouse-like space of the Pitt Rivers Museum. Prepare yourself for many breathtaking discoveries here: from shrunken heads and severed fingers to a Tahitian mourner's costume collected during Captain Cook's second voyage in 1773-4 and Hawaiian feather cloaks. General Pitt Rivers, an English soldier and archaeologist, donated his collection to Oxford University in 1884. The handwritten labels and traditional cabinets used for exhibits add to its eccentric charm.

▶ *Oxford city centre. Entrance through University Museum on Parks Road. Daily.*

Tradescant Room

A royal gardener sowed the seeds of the Ashmolean Museum's collection

John Tradescant, gardener to Charles I, toured the world in search of new plants. The natural and man-made specimens he acquired on his travels became the basis for the collection at the Ashmolean, Britain's oldest public museum, which opened in 1683.

A shell-decorated cape of deer hides worn by Powhatan, father of Pocahontas, is displayed here, as is the lantern carried by Guy Fawkes when he was arrested in 1605 and Henry VIII's stirrups and hawking gear.

▶ *Oxford city centre, Beaumont Street. Daily Tues-Sat, Sun pm and bank hols.*

SOUTH OF ENGLAND

OXFORDSHIRE

10 Radcliffe Square **11** Dorchester Abbey **12** Didcot Railway Centre **13** Nuffield Place

14 Maharajah's Well **15** Mapledurham

Radcliffe Square

Architectural flair creates a grand stage for academic study

Nowhere in Britain is so much learning concentrated into such a compact area. The **Radcliffe Camera**, in the centre of the square, opened as a science and medical library in 1749 and is now a main reading room of the Bodleian Library. Nicholas Hawksmoor drew up an early plan for the domed building, but it was modified and completed by James Gibbs. In 1814, the Allied powers met here for a premature celebration of Napoleon's defeat.

Opposite the Camera is the **Divinity School**, built in 1483 as a lecture room for theology students. An elegant fan-vaulted ceiling rises over it, with the initials of its patrons carved into 455 roof bosses. Above the school is **Duke Humfrey's Library**, built five years later to house 300 manuscripts given to the university by the Duke, Henry V's brother. It is part of the Bodleian Library, the university's research library, which has almost 7 million books on more than 100 miles of shelving.

▶ *Oxford city centre, off Catte Street. Library tours Mon-Sat, Tel 01865 277224.*

Dorchester Abbey

Stone branches and stained-glass figures create a biblical family tree

Three ornate windows dominate the chancel of Dorchester's 12th-century abbey. The most magnificent depicts Christ's family in the Tree of Jesse. Five foliage-covered branches rise from Jesse's reclining form and carry statues of Old Testament prophets and kings. Sadly, carvings of Christ and Mary have been lost.

The abbey's Norman font is a rare survival – to preserve holy water from seeping through the stone, the font is made entirely of lead and decorated with figures of Christ and ten apostles (Judas and Thomas are missing). An effigy of a crusader knight lies in the aisle. The figure, created in the 13th century, is captured in urgent movement, reaching for his sword.

▶ *S of Oxford, signed from A4074. Daily.*

Didcot Railway Centre

God's wonderful railway is kept alive by schoolboy dreams

In 1961, as steam was giving way to diesel, four train-spotting schoolboys decided to try to preserve one of the Great Western Railway's engines. Their ambition led to the formation of the Great Western Society, which moved into an old engine shed at Didcot in 1967. Today it houses more than 20 of the railway's brunswick green steam locomotives, many of its chocolate-and-cream carriages, a re-creation of a small country station and restored signal boxes.

None of the centre's locomotives has travelled as far as *Pendennis Castle*. It was built in 1924 to haul express trains, but on withdrawal from service was shipped to work on an Australian railway. It was rescued in 1994 and returned to England – one of very few locos to have circumnavigated the world.

▶ *10 miles S of Oxford, signed from M40 (Junction 13). Access via Didcot station. Sat-Sun all year and in school hols. Tel 01235 817200 for times.*

Nuffield Place

The modest home of an extraordinary man

When its owner died in 1963, Nuffield Place was preserved exactly as he left it, with rooms decorated and furnished largely in the style of the 1930s. But this is no maudlin monument full of musty memories. It was the home of the unstuffy industrialist and philanthropist William Morris (Lord Nuffield), who founded the company, Morris Motors, which once made half of all cars sold in Britain. Morris gave millions of pounds to charity, established the Nuffield Foundation and endowed the Oxford University college that bears his name.

The house, set high in the Chilterns, reflects the man: it is confident but not ostentatious, more a cameo of upper middle class than aristocratic life, and so homely that it would be no surprise to see the owner himself come striding into one of its rooms. The contents include many fine examples of 20th-century craftsmanship, from clocks, rugs and tapestries to specially commissioned pieces of furniture.

▶ *2 miles W of Nettlebed on A4130 (Henley-Wallingford). 2nd and 4th Sun pm, May-Sept.*

Maharajah's Well

Never was there such a grand place from which to draw refreshment

It is the last thing you expect in a leafy Oxfordshire village like Stoke Row, but there it is: the Maharajah's Well, a little piece of exotic, faraway India in English arcadia. The Maharajah of Benares made a gift of the well after Edward Anderson Reade, of nearby Ipsden, completed a water scheme in the potentate's holy city on the River Ganges. Whatever engineering problems Mr Reade faced, they were probably matched here in miniature: the 1.2m (4ft) diameter shaft had to be dug to the daunting depth of 112m (368ft) – twice the height of Nelson's Column – before the workers eventually struck water.

The elaborate and exquisite structure which crowns the head of the well ensures the feat doesn't go unnoticed. A canopied dome, supported on eight cast-iron columns, covers winding-gear machinery embellished with an exuberant cast-iron elephant.

▶ *2½ miles S of A4130 (Henley-on-Thames to Wallingford road) at Nettlebed.*

Mapledurham

A Tudor mill and mansion preserved in a backwater of time

Give the modern world the slip and visit Mapledurham. Across the Thames, distant trains flash by and the roofs of Reading crowd along the horizon, but this small village is a lovely backwater: by-passed by the Industrial Revolution, never mind the high-tech one.

The 16th-century water mill is the last working one along the entire length of the river. Mapledurham House, one of the largest Elizabethan homes in England, has a moulded plaster ceiling dating from the early 1600s and an imposing staircase.

▶ *4 miles NW of Reading off A4074 Oxford road. Sat, Sun and bank hols pm, Easter-Sept.*

Myth and reality vie for territory

Fabulous creatures and Stone Age chieftains haunt the Ridge Way south of Uffington

1 Uffington

All features ▶ *9 miles E of Swindon off B4507 Wantage-Ashbury road. EH/NT. Daily.*

Legend and historical record are entangled around the hilltops and henges near **Uffington**. Legend says St George slew the dragon on **Dragon Hill**; the record shows that King Alfred defeated the invading Danes somewhere near here, at the Battle of Ashdown in AD 871.

Then there is the **Uffington White Horse**, perhaps the most extraordinary of all the figures carved on England's chalklands. Close up, the 115m (377ft) long and 33m (108ft) high 'horse' is an incomprehensible, seemingly random arrangement of bare strips of ground, made by ramming chalk into trenches cut into the turf. But from farther away these resolve themselves into the few deft brushstrokes of the famous landmark: a wonderfully bold, abstract steed galloping over the steep escarpment. The line of the horse's lower body has been left uncarved, suggested instead from the position of the off foreleg and hind leg. How the people who carved the figure were able to execute it with such élan when they could not stand back and view their efforts easily is a mystery – as is its exact age. It is known that the Uffington White Horse dates from at least the 1st century BC because coins from that time are marked with its image, but some experts believe it is older – possibly the most ancient chalk figure in Britain. The horse's representation on coins also offers one explanation of why it was created: as a huge sign advertising the territory of the Iron Age tribe that controlled the area.

Silent sentinels to the dead

The chalk-cutters had only a few uphill yards to walk before reaching the safety of their hill fort – **Uffington Castle** – the ramparts of which shoulder onto the Ridge Way, Britain's oldest trade route. From here, they would have had a good view of a Stone Age long barrow just a mile to the west, yet separated by a gulf of time almost as wide as that separating us from them. What they called the spot, we do not know. Nowadays, the stones of the 3600-year-old burial chamber, which stand in a prominent copse of beech trees, are known as **Wayland's Smithy** – a name derived from the Saxon, Welandes Smidthan. According to Norse legend, Welande, who eventually became the armourer of the gods, would shoe the horse of any traveller on the Ridge Way if it was left tethered here overnight, together with a coin.

UFFINGTON WHITE HORSE

SURREY

Watts Chapel and Gallery

Shrine and collection celebrate a colossus of Victorian art

Two buildings in the little village of Compton capture the life and times of one of the most revered figures of Victorian art – the painter and sculptor George Frederic Watts. The simple chapel exterior gives no hint of the interior, where the artist's wife and collaborator, Mary, together with local people taught in her pottery, created a symbolic Tree of Life. Every inch of the walls and ceiling is covered in vividly painted plaster decoration – a blend of Art Nouveau and Celtic forms.

The gallery, too, is a simple building holding unexpected treasures: more than 250 of the Watts' works, from heroic, morally weighty pieces on classical and allegorical themes to portraits of the famous of his day. Dwarfing all is the full-size model for his monumental bronze statue *Physical Energy*, which stands in Kensington Gardens and earned Watts the nickname of 'England's Michelangelo'.

▶ *3 miles SW of Guildford off A3 Hindhead road. Chapel daily. Gallery daily, except Thur.*

Waverley Abbey

Tantalising fragments of a great church among guarding woods

The seclusion that motivated Cistercian monks to site their first monastery in England here – and inspired Walter Scott to name the first of his historical novels after the place – still survives nearly 900 years on. The ruins of their church stand in a grassy expanse, fringed on one side by the order's fishpond and ringed by dense woods that shut out the everyday world.

Excavations and the few remaining fragments of the abbey, started in 1128, indicate that it was immense – about 85m (280ft) long and 36m (120ft) wide. A great oak grows out of one wall, arching over what would have been the church's central crossing, and from a corner of the ruin a yew rises from a hillock of gnarled roots. The most substantial remains are those of the chapter house, where supports for a fan-vaulted ceiling and parts of the upper floor survive, and where the gable is pierced by two tall lancet windows and a rose window. A mown path and a few information panels are the only concessions to the visitor.

▶ *2 miles SE of Farnham off B3001 Elstead road. EH. Daily Apr–Sept.*

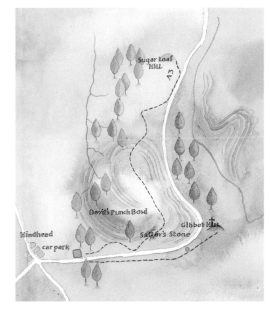

Devil's Punch Bowl

Villainous spot marked by murder and the sword of justice

Legend says the devil scooped out a handful of earth to throw at Thor, the god of thunder, so creating this bowl-shaped depression of heath, birch and pine from which mists sometimes rise over the rim like steam. Fact links the spot with the killing in 1786 of a sailor by his three companions.

To find the Sailor's Stone recalling this 'barbarous murder', cross the A3 from the car park and walk along the bridleway on the left for about ten minutes. Just beyond the stone a signposted path leads to Gibbet Hill, where the killers were hanged in chains; a granite cross stands near the exact spot. Back at the car park, the gap in the trees behind the café leads to the rim of the Punch Bowl and a view of what the 18th-century traveller William Cobbett called 'the most villainous spot God ever made'.

Across the wilderness the mound of Sugar Loaf Hill stands out; a path, reached by turning right and following the rim then going down a long flight of steps, leads to the hill.

▶ *NT car park ¾ mile E of Hindhead on A3 Guildford road.*

SOUTH OF ENGLAND

SURREY

Winkworth Arboretum

Dr Fox's exotic hillside hidden among the North Downs

Spring and autumn set Winkworth ablaze with colour, but the paths that crisscross its hillside and lead down to its two lakes make enjoyable woodland walking at any time of the year.

Dr Wilfrid Fox started planting these slopes with exotic trees and shrubs in the 1930s, aiming always to complement the English downland scenery on the opposite side of the valley. Overhead, native oaks and beeches jostle for space with giants of the North American forest and colourful maples from Japan. Beneath them nature is allowed free play: the plants that flank the paths are wild ones, and there are copses bright with wood anemones, primroses and bluebells.

▶ *2 miles SE of Godalming off B2130 Hascombe road. NT. Daily.*

Bramley

Walk a green lane that follows two lost routes to the sea

From the crossroads in the village of Bramley, a short stroll of a couple of hundred yards in the direction of Wonersh transports the walker back in time by a century. On the left is the platform of Bramley and Wonersh Station on the former Guildford to Shoreham Railway – completed in 1865 and axed in 1966, hence the tag 'the Hundred Years Railway'. The station sign still stands among the brambles and nettles, and a solitary pillar box is all that is left of the stationmaster's office.

Turn left on the path along the old line, and you soon meet the Wey and Arun Canal, cut to link London and the south coast, and so bypass French privateers in the Strait of Dover. Soon the path goes under a road bridge, itself built on top of an earlier foot bridge by which barge horses were led over the canal: the three ages of transport in microcosm.

▶ *3 miles S of Guildford on A281 to Horsham.*

Guildford Cathedral

From ancient hunting ground to 20th-century sanctuary

Light, airy and unmistakably modern, yet with a clear touch of the Gothic in its soaring, pointed arches, Guildford Cathedral is a subtle blend of 20th-century tastes and techniques with older traditions of church architecture. The redbrick building, its tower crowned by a golden angel, was designed by Sir Edward Maufe and begun in 1936. The Second World War halted construction and it was not until 1961 that the cathedral was consecrated.

With no screen or organ to interrupt its length, the spatial possibilities of the broad nave, lined by pillars of pale limestone, are exploited to the full. One long vista stretches to the altar, which is backed by a great gold curtain. A brass stag set in the marble floor marks the centre of the cathedral and the top of Stag Hill – the name of the old royal hunting ground on which the church stands.

▶ *½ mile NW of city centre. Daily.*

Brookwood Cemetery

Walk in a Victorian city of the dead, and remember those fallen in war

Under spreading yews and towering redwood trees stand stone and bronze angels, tall crosses and broken pillars, and giant tombs in the form of classical temples or Gothic chapels. Brookwood is an enduring memorial to Victorian attitudes to death. In 1852 the London Necropolis Company bought this expanse of heath to create a burial ground for London's dead, when the city's graveyards were full. Guided walks among the 240,000 graves include some at night for the stout-hearted.

In sharp contrast to the overgrown disorder of Victorian Brookwood are the neat lawns and uniform headstones in the neighbouring Brookwood Military Cemetery, for more than 5000 Commonwealth, American and Allied dead of two world wars. The two graveyards cover 200ha (500 acres) – the second largest cemetery in Europe after one in St Petersburg.

▶ *S of Brookwood village, 5 miles NW of Guildford off A322 Bagshot road; Military cemetery off A324 Pirbright road. Daily. Guided walks first Sun of month.*

Hatchlands Park

First hear an overture, the house is the main theme, the grounds a finale

Music is at the heart of Hatchlands. The mansion's ground-floor rooms contain the world's finest collection of composer-related keyboard instruments. There is the piano on which Chopin played his recitals in England, another autographed by Johann Christian Bach and a third on which Edward Elgar first tapped out the notes of 'Land of Hope and Glory'. Their sound is re-created on an audio guide, played by Alec Cobbe, who collected the instruments and lives in the house.

Hatchlands' uncluttered, bright red brick façade looks almost new. In fact, the house was built in 1758 for Admiral Boscawen. Much of the interior decoration, including moulded ceilings and elaborate fireplaces, is among the earliest known work of Robert Adam.

A third glory of Hatchlands is its 160ha (400 acre) park, landscaped by Humphry Repton. Partings between trees reveal carefully planned views of the mansion.
▶ *5 miles E of Guildford off A246. NT. Tel 01483 222482 for opening details.*

Leptis Magna ruins

From a Mediterranean shore of Africa to an ornamental lakeside

A 10-minute walk from the car park on the A30 along the side of Virginia Water is rewarded by the unlikely sight of Roman columns from a temple in sun-baked North Africa. Once they were part of the Temple of Serapis at imperial Rome's major port of Leptis Magna, near Tripoli. In 1816 they were brought to England to decorate the portico of the new British Museum. But they proved unsuitable for the purpose, so in 1826 the columns were erected at Virginia Water to form a picturesque ruin.
▶ *3 miles SW of Staines off A30 Sunningdale road. Daily.*

Brooklands Museum

Pistons and propellers, chequered flags and chocks away

The birthplace of motor racing and aviation captures the fascination with speed. Stand on the bridge below which the 1907 concrete circuit banks steeply upwards like a wall of death and it is easy to imagine the crowds cheer as drivers battled to break the lap record. Nearby is the world's first ticket office for plane passengers: a building the size of a bus shelter where enthusiasts paid two guineas for a flight round the aerodrome. Many of the cars and planes of the era can be seen in the restored garages, workshops and hangers. They range from the humble Austin Seven to the mighty Duesenberg, and from a replica of A.V. Roe's flimsy No. 1 Biplane to a Wellington bomber salvaged from Loch Ness and painstakingly reconstructed.
▶ *1½ miles S of Weybridge on B374 to Byfleet. Daily.*

BROOKLANDS MUSEUM

SURREY

Chatley Heath Semaphore Tower

Signalling all the way to the Navy

At the top of the 28m (90ft) high brick tower are two movable signal arms – and a 360-degree view extending from the North Downs to the London Eye. Chatley Heath Tower was one of 13 semaphore stations by which messages were passed between the Admiralty in London and the Naval Dockyard in Portsmouth from 1822 until 1847. Working models show how the system worked, and describe the duties of the naval lieutenant in charge. The tower, long derelict, was gutted by fire in 1984 – its spick-and-span condition today is a triumph of restoration.
▶ *2 miles SW of Cobham off A3 to Guildford. Tel 01372 458822 for opening details.*

Painshill Park

A magical blend of nature and art in a reawakened 'sleeping beauty' garden

Surprises lie around every turn of the path in Painshill's 80ha (200 acres): successive scenes in a theatrical landscape created by Charles Hamilton in the 18th century and lovingly restored over recent years. The marked 'historic route' first crests a gentle rise to reveal a lake stretching along the foot of a slope planted with vines – just as Hamilton made it. Across a lawn stands a little Gothic temple, an elegant wooden folly painted to resemble stone. The path descends to a ruined abbey wall – another folly – and crosses a willow-pattern Chinese bridge to Grotto Island (open weekends only), where amazingly convincing plaster stalactites hang from the roof of an artificial cavern.

There is a crescent-shaped cascade, a waterwheel 10.6m (35ft) across which raises water from the River Mole into the lake, a four-storey Gothic Tower and a resplendent Turkish Tent.
▶ *At Cobham on A245 Leatherhead-Woking road. Daily.*

Holmbury Hill

To Heaven's gate, by sandy paths

An on-top-of-the-world view is the reward for only 15 minutes not-too-steep walking from a car park on the slope of Holmbury Hill. The path leads through the pines of Hurtwood, known as Surrey's 'Little Switzerland', to the grassy 261m (857ft) summit, where a toposcope identifies the main landmarks – including, on clear days, a glint of the sea through Shoreham Gap, 25 miles away.

From the top, half an hour's walk down the signposted path leads to Holmbury St Mary, where the 1873 village church was the gift of G.E. Street, architect of the Law Courts in London, who retired here. His wife was so struck on first seeing the beauty of the setting that she exclaimed 'It is heaven's gate!'
▶ *Hurtwood Control car park 1, 1½ miles S of Peaslake off A25 Dorking-Guildford road.*

Mill Church, Reigate Heath

Beneath crosses of oak and sails

Within the redbrick base of the windmill on the heath, next to the golf club (which holds the key), a tiny church with room for only about 50 worshippers was created in 1880. Above their heads a cross of huge oak beams supports the central post round which the weatherboarded tower of the 240-year-old mill – now restored and with a new set of sails – was turned to catch the wind.
▶ *1 mile W of Reigate off A25 Dorking road.*

Chaldon Church

Rewards and punishments in a violent medieval picture show

It dominates the west wall: a macabre mural, 5.2m (17ft) across and 3.3m (11ft) high, discovered under layers of whitewash in 1869. Painted in around 1200, it vividly depicts the torments of the damned and the rewards of the saved at a terrible Last Judgement.

White figures, made all the more powerful and poignant by a red background, portray St Michael weighing good and bad deeds, and Christ transfixing the Devil with his Cross. The souls of the dead struggle to reach Heaven by a ladder of salvation, but evil spirits pluck many down to Hell, where grotesque demons with cloven hooves await to mete out blood-curdling punishments.

▶ *2 miles W of Caterham off A22 Purley road (Junction 6 off M25).*

Denbies Wine Estate

A taste of France on a sunny downland slope

England's largest vineyard turns 107ha (265 acres) of the North Downs into a scene reminiscent of the Champagne region of northern France. The estate is broken up by patches of woodland and crisscrossed by footpaths, including the North Downs Way. A short Vineyard Trail winds among the plantations on the lower slopes, while the 'vineyard train' carries passengers to the highest point of the estate, with its extensive views.

The train starts from the low, flint-built visitor centre – part of a complex of buildings that, with their central courtyard, are a Surrey version of the French chateau. There is a tour of the wine-producing process, too, ending with a tasting session in the cellars.

▶ *½ mile N of Dorking on A24 Leatherhead road. Daily. Train Apr-Oct.*

Fiery furnaces & deafening mills

Quiet woods and streams were once scenes of bustling industry

1 Friday Street 2 Chilworth 3 Shalford Mill
4 Cobham 5 Haxted 6 Outwood Common

Few places are more peaceful than **Friday Street**, yet three centuries ago this hamlet four miles southwest of Dorking, off the A25, was a centre of an iron industry that turned large tracts of south Surrey and north Sussex into a 'black country'.

Iron ore was dug from the hills. Trees were felled to fire the furnaces. 'Hammer ponds' like that at Friday Street were dug to provide water power for the bellows and tilt hammers – logs of ash bound with iron that were raised then dropped to shape hot metal on the anvil.

The local iron industry declined as coal replaced timber as fuel and the centres of industry moved to the coalfields, but reminders live on. In Abinger Hammer, for example, a village three miles northwest of Friday Street, there is a village clock commemorating the ironmasters, with the figure of Jack the Smith striking the bell with his hammer to mark the hour.

Explosives for musketshot and shell

The little Tillingbourne river which flows through Abinger supplied other industries; just three and a half miles downstream, on the A248, lies **Chilworth**, where gunpowder mills were built in 1625. Their 1885 concrete replacements, which closed after the end of the First World War, can be reached along the signposted Vera's Path near Chilworth Station. A mile down the same road is **Shalford Mill**, a fine timber-frame-and-brick corn mill, working until 1914 and now owned by the National Trust (open Wed and Sun Tel 01483 561389). Go north from Guildford, up the A3 for ten miles, to discover the corn mill at **Cobham** – restored to working order in 1993, and open on second Sundays of the month from April to October. On the county boundary with Kent, the 17th-century watermill at **Haxted**, four miles east of Lingfield off the B2028, contains an exhibition about the milling industry.

Domesday Book listed 5600 watermills in 1086. Windmills, by contrast, are not recorded until the 12th century. On **Outwood Common**, off the A23 five miles southeast of Reigate, stands the oldest working windmill in England – built in 1665 – with 18m (60ft) sails still driving huge millstones. It is a reminder of the days when wind power, alongside timber and water, played a major part in supplying the energy for industry.

SUSSEX

1 Weald and Downland Open Air Museum 2 Goodwood 3 Black Down

4 St Botolph's, Hardham 5 Bignor Roman Villa 6 Parham 7 Arundel Castle

8 Church of the English Martyrs, Goring-by-Sea 9 Leonardslee Gardens

Weald and Downland Open Air Museum

Every day is 'open house' in a village made up of homes from the past

More than 40 buildings from Sussex, Surrey, Kent and Hampshire have been re-erected to create the illusion of a real village in a fold of the South Downs. To walk through the rooms and up and down the stairs is to move through five centuries of domestic architecture.

Alongside a timber-framed market hall stand a medieval hall house and a pair of shops with projecting upper floors. The village smithy works under a chestnut tree, and a water mill produces stone-ground flour. There is a Victorian schoolroom and, on a slope above the village, a Tudor farmhouse with its own garden, orchard and livestock.

▶ *W of Singleton off A286. Daily mid Feb-mid Dec; Wed, Sat and Sun Jan-mid Feb; daily Dec 26-Jan 1.*

Goodwood

Look down on the loveliest of racecourses from a hilltop viewpoint

From the the 206m (676ft) high summit of The Trundle, 'Glorious Goodwood' can be seen at its most magnificent. You may not be able to pick out the jockeys' numbers as they streak towards the winning post, but the compensation is a splendid view of the entire racecourse, set against a vast panorama of downland and forest.

The road to Chichester passes the pavilioned grandstand, then descends towards Goodwood House, seat of the Dukes of Richmond and centre of a 4455ha (11,000 acre) estate, which includes the racecourse, a motor racing circuit, country park, airfield and golf course. Motor sport enthusiasts flock to the Festival of Speed in June or July, when cars race along a private road through Goodwood Park, and a Revival Meeting in September when spectators dress in period costume to watch great cars and drivers of the past compete on the preserved 1950s circuit.

▶ *To reach The Trundle, use The Triangle car park on Singleton road, 3½ miles N of Chichester, off A286. Cross road and take marked path to summit. Tel 01243 755022.*

Black Down

Share a poet's favourite view at Sussex's hilltop 'temple'

Climb to the highest point in Sussex and the reward is a breathtaking view described by the poet Lord Tennyson as 'Green Sussex fading into blue, with one grey glimpse of sea'. The ascent does not require exceptional stamina, as Black Down is only 280m (917ft) above sea level and is reached by an easy half-hour walk from a car park below.

The track passes through woodlands of beech, birch and Scots pine to emerge at a panoramic viewpoint known as the Temple of the Winds at the southern edge of the sandstone ridge. A curving stone seat looks out over a patchwork of Wealden woods and fields stretching towards the South Downs.

▶ *National Trust car park on Tennyson's Lane, a continuation of Haste Hill off B2131, ¼ mile SE of Haslemere.*

St Botolph's, Hardham

Adam and Eve star in a Norman wall painting masterpiece

Lift the latch, step into St Botolph's and blink in wonder at the paintings that cover every wall of Hardham's tiny Norman church. Along both sides of the nave, over the chancel arch, and on either side of the altar, in two horizontal tiers, a sequence of paintings tells Bible stories for villagers unable to read.

Painted by a group of travelling artists around 1100, the works were subsequently plastered over and unseen until their rediscovery in 1866. In strip cartoon form the life of Christ unfolds: annunciation, birth, baptism, Last Supper and betrayal. Images of Adam and Eve cover the west wall, including one of Adam watching Eve from a tree while she milks a huge cow. Among some 40 individual subjects there are visions of the torments of hell, images of the apostles, and a narrative of the legend of St George.

A soft red-ochre shade predominates, though there are blue backgrounds and green haloes. Subtle lighting can be switched on to allow the paintings to spell out their message.

▶ *1 mile S of Pulborough off A29. Daily.*

Bignor Roman Villa

Goddess of love and her heavenly gladiators uncovered

Under thatched huts in the shelter of the wooded north slope of the South Downs are some of the finest Roman mosaics in England. Glowing pictures, made up of tiny multi-coloured cubes of stone, cover the floors of room after room, including a 25m (82ft) blue-grey, red and white mosaic along one corridor. The most impressive shows the head of Venus, flanked by long-tailed birds and fern leaves, and accompanied by winged cupids bizarrely dressed as gladiators. In other rooms appear Ganymede borne aloft by an eagle, a gambolling dolphin and a Medusa's head.

The mosaics formed part of one of the largest Roman villas found in Britain. Begun in the 2nd century, it lay buried until 1811 when a farmer's plough revealed its splendours.
▶ *5 miles SW of Pulborough off A29. Daily May-Oct; Tues-Sun, and bank hol Mon, Mar-Apr and Oct.*

Parham

A Downland mansion warmed by four centuries of family life

Only three families have occupied Parham in its 400-year history, and the sumptuous Elizabethan house has the welcoming atmosphere of a family home. Not that Parham lacks grandeur. It has a Great Hall of light-oak panelling and tall leaded windows, a 49m (160ft) Gallery that runs the length of the house, and in the Green Room a painting of a kangaroo by George Stubbs, the first likeness of the animal seen in Europe. Stubbs painted it from a skin brought back in 1771 from Captain Cook's first voyage round the world.
▶ *3 miles S of Pulborough on A283. Wed, Thur, Sun and bank hol Mon, Easter-Sept; Tue-Fri and Sun Aug. Info line 01903 744888.*

Arundel Castle

Victorian palace behind the walls of a romantic fortress

Even the cascade of battlements, towers and turrets that spills down the hillside into the little town of Arundel hardly prepares you for the astonishing size and baronial splendour of Arundel Castle's interior.

The original Norman fortress was largely destroyed in the Civil War, and most of what stands today is the creation of successive dukes of Norfolk and earls of Arundel in the 18th and 19th centuries. A tour takes the visitor through chambers breathtaking in scale and magnificence of decoration, including the 40.5m (133ft) long Baronial Hall, which has an oak hammerbeam roof 15m (50ft) high, and a vast library containing 10,000 books.
▶ *8 miles E of Chichester off A27 Brighton road. Tues-Sun, Mons in Aug and bank hol Mon Apr-Oct.*

Church of the English Martyrs, Goring-by-Sea

Inspired to imitate Michelangelo

When Sussex artist Gary Bevans went to see the early 16th-century frescoes of the Sistine Chapel in 1987 he spotted that the building in Rome had the same sort of barrel-vault ceiling as his own church. There and then he offered to reproduce Michelangelo's ceiling frescoes in the Church of the English Martyrs. The labour of love, which is two-thirds the size of the original, took five years and presents a remarkable spectacle. A kaleidoscope of colour lifts the eye heavenward, to marvel at the Biblical scenes that stretch out on either side of the Creation of Adam.
▶ *1½ miles W of town centre on A259. Daily except Mon Easter-Dec.*

Leonardslee Gardens

Marsupials in the shrubbery, a model and a miniature lakeland

These 97ha (240 acre) gardens outside Lower Beeding village are full of surprises. A colony of wallabies live in a wooded enclosure, although bolder individuals have jumped over the fence and hop around the grounds. The gardens are at their brightest in May, when azaleas and rhododendrons splash the slopes of a valley with many colours. Seven ponds spread along the valley floor – at different levels, like the steps of a watery staircase.

Do not miss the marvel near the park entrance. Called 'Behind the Doll's House', it is a re-creation, at one-twelfth real size, of an Edwardian country estate. A lodge-keeper picks strawberries, a hedgehog flees from a bonfire, a gardener plants out lettuces, an elderly colonel slumbers in his Bath chair. As daylight dims, lamps come on in buildings.
▶ *4 miles SE of Horsham off A281 Henfield road. Daily Apr-Oct.*

SOUTH OF ENGLAND

BOLD ARCHITECTURAL STATEMENT
FROM THE EARLY DAYS OF AVIATION

SUSSEX

Lancing College Chapel
Reaching for heaven from deep roots

Accentuated by its narrowness, the nave of Lancing College Chapel seems to soar forever upwards. Clusters of graceful columns, reflecting the light from tall windows of clear glass, eventually meet 27m (90ft) overhead. The foundations below the visitor's feet are scarcely less impressive – driven 21m (70ft) into the sandstone of the Gothic-style building's downland site above the River Adur.

A splash of colour at each end of the nave relieves the simplicity of the bare stonework. Over the altar, there are tapestries in red and gold, while high above the organ pipes at the west end is a rose window 10m (32ft) across, consisting of 30,000 pieces of glass.
▶ *¾ mile NE of North Lancing off A27 Arundel-Lewes road. Daily Mon-Sat; pm Sun and bank hols.*

Shoreham Airport
Bold architectural statement from the early days of aviation

Few buildings in Britain present a more classic example of Art Deco architecture than the terminal building of Shoreham Airport - the interior of which is pictured oppposite. Its geometric lines, bold curves, contoured surfaces and bright colours are typical of the design style that was in fashion when the terminal was built in 1936. It is a welcoming place, with a cafe from which visitors can watch light planes on an airstrip that has been in continuous use since 1910.

Next door to the main terminal building, the Archive and Visitor Centre offers a wealth of information to the enthusiast capturing the feeling of an earlier, more leisurely era of air travel. The Archive contains photographs and records covering almost one hundred years of flight. From the Visitor Centre it is possible to tour the airport and visit the Municipal Hangar containing aircraft dating from the 1940s. Amongst projects to restore and recreate old aircraft has been the completion of a replica of the 'Flying Flea', a 1935 Pou de Ciel. This oddly shaped, midget machine can be seen as a forerunner of today's microlight aircraft.
▶ *1 mile NW of Shoreham-by-Sea between A259 coast road and A27. Archive and Visitor Centre daily Tel 01273 441061.*

Seven Sisters Country Park
Mighty white ramparts flanking the English Channel

The South Downs are surprised by the sea, brought up short in great chalk cliffs stretching from Cuckmere Haven to Beachy Head. Walkers on the South Downs Way follow a switchback course that dips and rises through the beds of old river valleys that once cut through the downs. For a taste of these breezy delights, follow the marked nature trail which sets off along this long-distance footpath from the Seven Sisters Country Park visitor centre before dropping to the beach at the foot of the first of the seven towering cliffs that give their name to the area. It then crosses the shingle at Cuckmere Haven before returning to the visitor centre along a backwater of the River Cuckmere.
▶ *6 miles W of Eastbourne off A259 Brighton road. Visitor centre daily Apr-Oct; Sat and Sun Nov-Mar.*

Charleston
Bloomsbury comes to a Sussex farm

Walls, doors, fireplaces, bookcases, chests, tables, even bedsteads and baths: every imaginable surface at Charleston is covered in paintings by Bloomsbury Group artists who made it their country meeting place for half a century. The painters Vanessa Bell and Duncan Grant, and their friend David Garnett, moved to Sussex in 1916, and there played host to many of the artists, writers and intellectuals of their time, including Clive Bell, Virginia Woolf and Maynard Keynes. The house has been preserved and partly re-created to appear as it was in the 1950s.
▶ *7 miles E of Lewes (A27). Wed-Sun, and bank hol Mon, Apr-Oct. Tel 01323 811626.*

SUSSEX

Michelham Priory
Where canons found island serenity

Doubly encircled by a loop of the River Cuckmere and by its own moat, Michelham Priory still preserves the tranquillity once enjoyed by the Augustinian canons who established a priory here in 1229. Henry VIII shattered their peace in 1537, destroying their church: its outlines marked on the lawns show what a vast edifice it must have been. The priory was then converted into a mansion.

The gatehouse survived and stands proudly 18m (60ft) high over the lily-covered moat. Bridges lead across the moat onto a tree-fringed walk, with views across the grounds of the 3ha (7 acre) island. You can buy flour from a restored mill powered by water channelled from the Cuckmere.

▶ *Upper Dicker, on minor road 2 miles W of Hailsham, signed from A22 and A27. Wed-Sun, and bank hol Mon, Mar-Oct; daily Aug.*

Brightling
'Mad Jack' and his half-dozen follies

Six bizarre 'follies' – an obelisk, an observatory, a cone, a temple, a round tower and a pyramid – created by an eccentric squire, John Fuller, in the early 1800s surround Brightling village.

The obelisk, Brightling Needle, is visible for miles around. It marks the 196m (646ft) summit of Brightling Down. Close by is the observatory – now a private house – built to satisfy Fuller's interest in astronomy. At Wood's Corner is the 10m (35ft) high Sugar Loaf, the result of an unwise wager: a friend challenged Fuller's claim that he could see the spire of Dallington church from his estate and proved him wrong, so Fuller put up this replica spire within sight of his house at Brightling Park. The rotunda temple is in the park, the round tower southeast of Brightling Church, and Fuller's own mausoleum – an 8m (25ft) high pyramid – in Brightling churchyard.

Fuller is thought to have planned his follies, which earned him the nickname 'Mad Jack', to keep local men employed as the Wealden iron industry declined.

▶ *3 miles S of Burwash off A265.*

Battle
Relive the day when quiet meadows rang to the cries of combat

The Battle of Hastings was literally an uphill task for the forces of William of Normandy as, on October 14, 1066, they launched their assault on King Harold's Anglo-Saxon army. Walking the ground today, you can imagine yourself a Norman knight, ordered to charge time after time towards the seemingly impenetrable wall of Saxon shields lining the top of the slope.

A one-mile Battlefield Walk circles the slopes of Senlac Hill, with an audio guide interpreting events through the eyes of Saxon thane and Norman knight. The savagery of the hand-to-hand fighting is chillingly realised.

On the hilltop, William founded an abbey to commemorate his victory. He set the high altar of the abbey church on the spot where Harold is supposed to have fallen. Although little of the original church remains, the tall walls of the monks' quarters still catch the eye as William intended, and the impressive Great Gatehouse of the 1330s is well preserved.

▶ *6 miles NW of Hastings on A2100. EH. Daily.*

Rye
Medieval port that the sea left behind

When the original guardians of the 13th-century **Ypres Tower** at Rye kept watch across the Channel for French invaders, waves lapped at the rocks below their feet. Two centuries later the sea receded, and the town once renowned for its boat-building was left stranded on a rocky outcrop 2 miles inland.

For the best vantage point over the town's higgledy-piggledy red-tiled roofs and cobbled streets, climb the winding steps to the top of the tower of **St Mary's Church**. From half way up you can look down into the nave, where the 5m (18ft) long pendulum of one of Britain's oldest church turret clocks, dating from 1562, can be seen swinging slowly to and fro. Ladders complete the ascent among the giant bells and sturdy ropes.

A walk around Rye reveals half-timbered houses jostling with their Georgian neighbours. The **Mermaid Inn** has close-set timbers, leaded windows and huge stone fireplaces; at its tables, 18th-century smugglers sat with loaded pistols in defiance of customs men. **Lamb House**, named after a former mayor, became the home of American novelist Henry James. In the **Heritage Centre** on Strand Quay, an exquisitely detailed Town Model depicts Rye as it was a century ago.

▶ *On A259. Ypres Tower, Thur-Mon Apr-Oct, Sat-Sun Nov-Mar. Mermaid Inn, Tel 01797 223065. Lamb House, Thur and Sat pm Mar-Oct; NT. Heritage Centre, daily.*

Bodiam Castle

A battlemented castle rises as if from the pages of a fairy tale

The setting could hardly be more spectacular. As the path from the car park crests a slight rise the moat suddenly comes into view, ringing a fortress that looks at first glance as though the centuries have left unsullied the work of the medieval castle architect in its most perfect form.

With its intact corner towers, battlemented gates and high ramparts pierced by arrow slits, Bodiam appears to be quite capable of giving a good account of itself if invaders approaching along the valley of the River Rother chose to attack it tomorrow. In fact, its 14th-century builder, Sir Edward Dalyngrigge, never had to face the feared French marauders, and lived secure in grand style behind his imposing walls.

Once across the moat, the apparent solidity of Bodiam Castle proves to be an illusion. The interior was reduced to a shell during the Civil War, although the layout of Dalyngrigge's great hall, chapel, kitchen and living quarters can still be traced. Spiral staircases climb to the battlements for a bird's-eye view of the castle, its moat and the surrounding green countryside.

Many of today's 'invaders' arrive by steam train on the Kent & East Sussex Railway from Tenterden 11 miles away.

▶ *3 miles NE of Robertsbridge off A21. Daily mid Feb-Oct; Sat-Sun only Nov-Feb. NT. Kent & East Sussex Railway, Tel 01580 762943 for timetable information.*

BODIAM CASTLE

Pavilioned in splendour

Oriental fantasy and Modernist marvel: seafront spectacles that span a century of South Coast architecture

1 Royal Pavilion ▶ *Brighton, daily.*
2 De La Warr Pavilion ▶ *Bexhill-on-Sea, daily.*

From the driving force of two powerful personalities sprang two of Britain's most sharply contrasting buildings, one eccentric and elaborate, the other understated and sleek.

More than a century apart in their creation, the **Royal Pavilion** in Brighton and **De La Warr Pavilion** (right) in Bexhill-on-Sea have become icons of two very different architecture styles. Both have had their critics. To Queen Victoria, the Royal Pavilion was 'a strange, odd, Chinese-looking place'. To a Bexhill commentator of the 1930s, the new De La Warr Pavilion was 'the most hideous thing I have ever seen, a good hoarding for advertisements'.

When in 1787 George, Prince of Wales, began to turn a simple farmhouse into a seaside palace, he directed his designers to decorate the interiors in the prevailing Chinese style. After becoming Prince Regent in 1811, George employed John Nash to enlarge the neo-classical building of Henry Holland into the present Pavilion, its flamboyant rooftop array of domes, minarets and turrets inspired by Indian Mogul architecture. Inside, two designers, Robert Jones and Frederick Crace, took charge of different rooms. The Pavilion took seven years to complete, by which time the prince had become George IV.

Oriental themes predominate. Dragons and serpents chase each other along curtain pelmets, support paintings and lamp standards, and writhe around sideboards and chair legs. One giant silvery dragon holds in its claws the huge 9m (30ft) high, 1 tonne chandelier, that hangs from the ceiling of the Banqueting Room. The equally spectacular Music Room has a domed ceiling covered in 26,000 gilded cockle shells. Once inside his Royal Pavilion, the king and his guests were sealed off from the outside world. A view of the seaside was no part

A FUTURISTIC ARTS SPACE
DE LA WARR PAVILION

of George's plan. Lamps burned day and night to heighten the atmosphere.

In sharp contrast, the architects who designed a pavilion for the promenade at Bexhill-on-Sea in the 1930s sought to merge their building into its seaside setting. Walls of glass occupy a large part of the seaward façade of the De La Warr Pavilion. People using the building look out on the seafront and the breaking waves beyond, while from outside the shifting shapes of those walking the pavilion's sun terraces and climbing its great spiral staircase appear an integral part of the architecture.

A futuristic arts space

The De La Warr Pavilion was designed by Erich Mendelsohn and Serge Chermayeff, winners of an architectural competition inspired by the Mayor of Bexhill, the 9th Earl de La Warr, to promote the town as a seaside resort. The brief for a combined entertainment hall, restaurant, conference room and lounge, specified a building in the Modernist style, of which Mendelsohn was an acknowledged master.

The winning design by Mendelsohn and Chermayeff, chosen from a total of 230 entries, embodied many of the key features of Modernism. These included the use of concrete and steel: the De La Warr Pavilion was the first major building in Britain constructed around a framework of welded steel. Interior design was based on cubic and other geometrical shapes, windows and doors were standardised in form, and there was little decoration. Instead of Brighton's exotic skyline, Bexhill in 1935 found itself with a sleek, flat-topped pavilion, every detail of its form designed to echo its function as the centre of the arts that it remains today.

WILTSHIRE

1 North Meadow **2** Malmesbury Abbey

North Meadow
Where ancient rights still flourish

By mid April, North Meadow is a purple haze as thousands of snake's head fritillaries flower. This rare plant, slow to establish but easy to eradicate, is proof that the land has been managed in the same way for centuries.

Under old laws, livestock can be grazed here from Lammas Day, August 1, hence the meadow's description as Lammas land, but the animals must be removed by February 12 to allow the grass to grow for hay. The pasture, untreated with modern fertilisers, is full of the bulbs and seeds of wild flowers. When the rare fritillaries have died back – most of those growing in Britain are found on the 40ha (100 acres) of this nature reserve – the meadow becomes a knee-high June kaleidoscope of marsh orchid, knapweed, meadow rue, great burnet, oxeye daisy and flowering grasses. By early July, the show is over and the hay crop is cut, revealing old stones marking the limits of the parcels of hay.

▶ *¾ mile N of Cricklade, off minor road to A419 Cirencester-Swindon road. Daily.*

Malmesbury Abbey
Scenes from the Bible set in stone

In medieval times the 12th-century church must have soared over the little town, inspiring awe among inhabitants and travellers. Today, people come to admire what remains, chiefly the extravagantly decorated south porch, which contains some of the finest figurative Norman carving in Britain.

Eight arches over the entrance to the porch are intricately carved, three with biblical scenes. Look, for example, for the Creation of Eve in the inner arch. Inside the porch are three superb panels – a Lord in Majesty above the door, and studies of the apostles on the side walls.

▶ *15 miles W of Swindon, Junction 17 off M4.*

SOUTH OF ENGLAND

Swindon arrives with a roar

When railway fever swept Britain, a backwater of Wiltshire found itself in the right place at the right time

1 **Box Tunnel**

2 **STEAM** ▶ *¾ mile SW of Swindon centre, M4 Junction 16. Daily.*

The toss of a sandwich, the story goes, determined the site of the locomotive works that transformed Swindon from a sleepy little market town of about 2000 people into a booming railway centre. In 1840 Isambard Kingdom Brunel, engineer of the Great Western Railway, and his superintendent of locomotives, Daniel Gooch, were picnicking beside the route of the new line when they decided to throw a sandwich and build workshops to service the railway wherever it landed.

The first trains on the new broad-gauge line between London and Bristol ran in 1841, and were drawn by locos such as the North Star (below), built in George Stephenson's Newcastle works. Swindon's own works opened in 1843. Initially, they were for the maintenance and repair of rolling stock, but soon locos such as Gooch's *Firefly*

and *Lightning* classes were being built in them – by workers with train-building skills, who moved south from Scotland and the north of England, and rapidly overtook the ability of the little town to accommodate them. In about 1850, work started on New Swindon, a planned estate of terraced houses, complete with church, school, theatre, library, a medical centre, and a park where GWR fêtes were held. The initial 300 dwellings were built with Bath stone excavated during construction of the **Box Tunnel**, which at nearly two miles was the world's longest railway tunnel at the time. But setting records was not enough for Brunel, who created in the tunnel's western portal a piece of architecture grandiose enough to complement his Bristol Temple Meads Station and Royal Albert Bridge over the River Tamar. The triumphal western archway to the tunnel is visible from the A4 – on the edge of Box village, half-way between Bath and Chippenham.

Re-creating the golden age of the train

The spirit of the railway era is brought vividly back to life in **STEAM**, the Museum of the Great Western Railway, which occupies some of the old workshops – they were closed in 1986. Apart from chronicling the history of the line – God's Wonderful Railway, as it was known – and the larger-than-life personalities associated with it, the museum presents a lively and noisy evocation of the lives of the navvies and shop-floor workers who built the line and kept the trains running. And if you have ever wanted to walk beneath a 120 tonne steam loco or take a (virtual) ride in a driver's cab, this is your chance. In workshops adjoining the museum, former GWR workers restore old engines (above). Nearby, you can visit No. 34 Farrindon Road, one of the original New Swindon houses, preserved by the museum.

WILTSHIRE

3 Science Museum, Wroughton

4 Silbury Hill **5** Avebury **6** Maud Heath's

Causeway **7** Crofton Pumping Station

Science Museum, Wroughton
Plenty of room, no matter how big

This former airfield is a store for the Science Museum's largest objects. The seven hangars hold some 18,000 items ranging from the first Hovercraft to the last Fleet Street printing press, from part of ZETA (an apparatus used to examine thermonuclear reactions) to the only Comet 4B airliner left in the world. Parts of the collection are open on Event Days, so phone for details.
▶ *4 miles S of Swindon off A4361 road to Avebury. Tel 01793 846200 for details of events.*

Silbury Hill
The mystery of the mighty mound

Around 4500 years ago, with antlers for pickaxes and animals' shoulder blades for shovels, Neolithic man quarried some 250,000m3 (327,000cu yd) of chalk and soil to build the largest manmade mound in Europe. At 40m (130ft) high, and covering 2.2ha (5½ acres), the hill is about the same size as a small Egyptian pyramid. Why it was made is an archaeological puzzle – none of the exploratory shafts sunk into it has provided a clue.

Climbing the hill is prohibited, but a footpath from the car park in Avebury enables people to approach quite close. There is also an exhibition in the village's Alexander Keiller Museum, which reveals the high degree of sophistication required to construct Silbury.
▶ *7 miles W of Marlborough beside A4. EH/NT. Museum daily.*

Avebury
Where every direction is a journey into the distant past

A long tide of history has swept over the village and its surroundings, leaving an extraordinarily fascinating heritage. In Avebury itself, part of which lies within a 5000-year-old stone circle and earthwork, there is a church (St James) going back to Saxon times and a grand Tudor house incorporating fragments of a medieval priory that previously stood on the spot.

Leading southeast from the circle is the **Stone Avenue** – dozens of pairs of standing stones stretching nearly two miles to **The Sanctuary**, a second ceremonial site. From here, ancient monuments crowd across all points of the compass. Northeast are the hundreds of standing stones on Fyfield Down. West lies the **West Kennett Long Barrow**, a huge Neolithic tomb, and just beyond the A4, a modern highway paved over a Roman road, is Silbury Hill. Cherhill Down with its 2500-year-old hillfort, **Oldbury Castle**, lies another three miles in the same direction, while northwestwards, beyond Avebury, lies the great livestock enclosure of **Windmill Hill**, constructed nearly 6000 years ago.
▶ *6 miles W of Marlborough off A4 Calne Road. Public footpaths to all sites. EH/NT.*

Maud Heath's Causeway
An enduring gift of dry feet for the folk who followed her

Chippenham market trader Maud Heath was generous as well as successful: when she died in 1487 she willed sufficient property to construct a road and causeway over the soggy Avon meadows so that her successors would not have to endure the discomforts that bedevilled her journey to and from the town. She also left £8 a year for the upkeep.

Two monuments commemorate the widow. At one end of the 64 arches that carry the causeway along the lowest stretch of its 4½ miles, there is a pillar and ball. A mile east, on Wick Hill, a bonneted statue sits on top of a tall column, looking out on the flood plain below.
▶ *3 miles NE of Chippenham off B4069, beside Langley Burrell-East Tytherton road.*

Crofton Pumping Station
Steam-powered leviathans to get water to the canal's high point

A 25m (82ft) high chimney, a big, riveted red boiler and two magnificent beam engines (a Boulton & Watt of 1812 and a Harvey & Co of Hayle, dated 1846): this is engineering history at its most thrilling, especially at weekends, when it is set in motion (phone for times). William Jessop designed the station to pump water to the highest point of the Kennet & Avon Canal, a sharp 123m (401ft) above the Kennet, from which water could be fed into the locks leading in both directions.
▶ *6 miles SE of Marlborough off A346 at Burbage. Daily Easter-Sept. Tel 01672 870300.*

SOUTH OF ENGLAND

WILTSHIRE

8 The White Horse, Devizes

9 Caen Hill Locks

The White Horse, Devizes
Chalk charger for the Millennium

The steed cut into the slope of Roundway Hill is the most recent of Wiltshire's eight white horses, all connected by a 90-mile long circular walk. It took about 200 people to construct it in 1999, cutting and removing turf, then infilling the shape with chalk to create a figure 46m (150ft) from prancing hoof to pricked ear, and virtually the same dimension from nose to flowing tail. As a last act, a time capsule was buried on December 31. There is a car park on the approach lane, and a footpath leading onto the horse, where you can sit on the big boulder that is its eye.
▶ *2 miles N of Devizes off A361 Avebury road.*

Caen Hill Locks
How Mr Rennie made water climb uphill

For the crew of a narrowboat, the flight of 16 locks on the edge of Devizes is a daunting prospect. It takes more than two hours to work a vessel through them, opening and closing successive gates to raise or lower the water in a lock and convey the craft to the next level. For a bystander, however, the giant watery staircase on the side of the hill is an awe-inspiring sight.

The challenge facing John Rennie, engineer of the Kennet & Avon Canal, which opened in 1810, was to raise the waterway 72m (237ft) in the short distance of two and a half miles between the valley of the Avon to the west and the town. His solution was to build 29 locks, 16 in close succession up the side of Caen Hill. Each one has a side pond or pound – reservoirs from which the canal is replenished. Photographs in the tearoom at the top of the flight illustrate the restoration of the locks during the 1980s, the last act before the reopening of the canal in 1990.
▶ *2 miles E of Devizes off A361 Trowbridge road.*

Pay homage to the lord of the rings

Dozens of prehistoric monuments surround Stonehenge, perfect spots from which to view the great circle

3 Stonehenge

In a tantalising game of now you see it, now you don't, the best-known ancient monument in Britain pops into sight then hides with each crest and dip as you travel east along the roller-coaster A303, until, 2 miles west of Amesbury, the road sweeps by, almost indecently close. **Stonehenge** (EH): the image is so familiar yet retains such a capacity to shock when the traveller finally comes face to face with its sheer scale, majesty and aura.

But the 4000-year-old stone circle is just the last phase of a building process going back at least another millennium, to around 3000 BC: a sequence of events that reveals growing ambition and technical expertise – a burning desire to build an ever bigger, more permanent structure. To start with there was no stone, just a simple 'henge' consisting of a circular ditch and earth rampart. Within a few centuries a ring of massive timber uprights had appeared inside the rampart, so that it resembled **Woodhenge** (EH), 2 miles northeast, whose long-eroded timbers are now marked by concrete posts. Then, around 2600 BC, the monument began to take on its present character with the replacement of the timbers by

about 60 bluestones from the Preseli Mountains in Wales, probably arranged in a double crescent at first, but much altered since. With each of the stones about 2m (6ft 6in) in length and weighing 4 tonnes, their transportation and erection show great engineering skill, but the henge is overshadowed by what happened next. During the following three centuries the giants arrived: dozens of sarsen, or sandstone, megaliths brought 20 miles from the Marlborough Downs. Thirty of these 25-tonne slabs were arranged in a circle and capped with lintels, and within this five even bigger trilithons – each composed of two uprights supporting a lintel – were erected.

Stonehenge is not a stupendous balancing act, however, but an elegant feat of architecture. The uprights have been shaped so that they taper, the lintels sculpted into curves, and the two components fitted together with rudimentary mortice-and-tenon joints – the shaped top of the uprights slotting into a hole cut on the underside of the lintel. No wonder Stonehenge still stands, instilling awe among the hoards who visit every year.

Explore the surroundings

After a close-up look at the stone circle (open daily; EH), a walk is recommended: one that escapes the crowds and rewards with unusual views of the monument from some of the other prehistoric sites in the surrounding National Trust land – all described in a leaflet available in the car park. Turn right on the track that exits the car park at its far end, then cross a stile on the left to reach **The Cursus**. This 1¾ mile long narrow enclosure, edged by a low bank and ditch, dates from the earliest of the building phases of Stonehenge and may have been used by Neolithic man for processions and to run races. Towards its western end, on land so close to the stone circle that it was probably reserved for the dead of powerful families, clusters of Bronze Age burial mounds dot the downland.

But it is another Bronze Age cemetery – the **Old King Barrows** – reached from the opposite, eastern, end of The Cursus, that affords one of the most potent views of the monument. From here, with visitors around the stones reduced to the size of ants and road traffic almost out of sight and earshot, Stonehenge takes centrestage in a haunting landscape embroidered with barrows, tumuli, fortifications and other ancient earthworks. South, and running in the direction of the car park, is **The Avenue**, a 12m (40ft) wide route along which the giant stones were probably transported. Although largely obliterated by intervening centuries of ploughing, its banks and ditches are visible close to the road.

WILTSHIRE

The Peto Garden at Iford Manor
An Italian twist to the hills of rural Wiltshire

Pencil-thin cypresses, terraced walks, fluted columns, marble lions, Byzantine roundels, a Romanesque-style cloister – but for the Friesian cows grazing in the fields across the River Frome, you could well be in Tuscany.

This intimate garden is the creation of the architect-turned-garden–designer Harold Peto, who lived here from 1899 to 1933. Attracted by the Italian style of gardening, where planting is secondary to architecture, he saw the hillside against which Iford Manor is built as the ideal setting for his pools and waterfalls, paths and vistas, colonnades and statuary.
▶ *6 miles S of Bath off A36. Tues-Thur, Sat-Sun, May-Sept; Sun and Easter Mon only Apr and Oct.*

St Laurence's, Bradford-on-Avon
A tiny, intact Saxon church, taller than it is long

St Laurence's is a rare Saxon survival. It is remarkably tall and narrow, with windows few and small, in Saxon style, and unusually rich exterior detail. Inside, the nave is higher than it is long and the extraordinary proportions are accentuated by plain walls, now decorated only with two stone angels. The church was built probably in the 11th century for the nuns at Shaftesbury, in Dorset, to whom King Ethelred had granted Bradford. It fell into disuse and was turned into cottages, but is now restored as a supremely peaceful place of worship.
▶ *S of Town Bridge, across footbridge from car park on A363.*

Stourhead and Stourton House gardens
A great classical garden and an informal floral gem side by side

Stourton House Flower Garden is, as the owners say, the sort of garden you need to poke about in – at one moment there is a vegetable patch or a tumble of roses, at the next a splendid clipped leylandii hedge.

From the endearingly shambolic Stourton, it is only a short step to Stourhead, perhaps the finest example of the 18th-century English landscape garden. It is the natural-looking but minutely planned work of Henry Hoare II, a banker, who, inspired by the idealised Italian landscapes painted by artists such as Claude Lorrain, Nicolas Poussin and Gaspard Dughet, began in 1741 to create similar scenes around the house built by his father 20 years before.

Whatever the season, Stourhead is a place of enchantment, where you can drink in the carefully composed views of classical temples and Gothic follies, the shifting reflections on the tranquil lake, and the changing light on the backdrop of magnificent specimen trees.
▶ *Stourton, off B3092, 3 miles NW of Mere on A303. Stourhead Garden daily; (house Fri-Tues mid Mar-Oct); NT. Stourton House Flower Garden, Wed, Thur, Sun and bank hol Mon Apr-Nov.*

Old Wardour Castle
A romantic ruin at the centre of an 18th-century pleasure park

Peace and tumult have both left their mark on Old Wardour Castle. Built as comfortable home more than fortress for Lord Lovel on his return from the Hundred Years' War in 1393, it was besieged and bombarded in the Civil War by both sides. In the 18th century the Arundell family turned the eerie remains into the centrepiece of their fashionably landscaped pleasure ground, designed by 'Capability' Brown. A lake, mock-Gothic Banqueting House and a grotto completed the idyll. Climb to the top of the 18m (60ft) walls for a distant view of New Wardour Castle, the classical home built for the family in the 1770s.
▶ *2 miles SW of Tisbury off A30. EH. Daily Apr-Oct, Sat-Sun Nov-Mar.*

SALISBURY CATHEDRAL

Wilton House

Ornate design is woven into the fabric of the house

The name Wilton is synonymous with quality carpet manufacture and there is no grander setting in which to view the products of the local industry as the home of the Earl of Pembroke. It was the earl's ancestor who founded the Royal Wilton carpet factory in 1655 and so keen were the family to encourage the industry that they once secretly smuggled in French weavers hidden in a wine barrel.

Standing on the site of an 8th century abbey, the house was extensively redesigned after a disastrous fire in 1647 by Inigo Jones and his son-in-law, John Webb. The jewels of their legacy are the magnificent Single and Double Cube State Rooms. Each highly ornate 'cube' is 30ft in each dimension and they were designed to display a series of family portraits by Van Dyck.

▶*3 miles W of Salisbury off A36. House Sun-Fri and Sat on bank hol weekends Apr-Aug. Grounds daily.*

Salisbury Cathedral

Medieval genius in stone and vellum

Salisbury Cathedral has much to marvel at: England's tallest spire at 123m (404ft), the large, elegant Close, the purity of the Early English architecture. For many the highlight is the splendid little octagonal Chapter House off the 13th-century cloisters. Light floods in through the delicate stained glass windows, illuminating intricate rib-vaulting that fans out from one slim column, and a carved stone frieze depicts 60 scenes from Genesis and Exodus. Here one of only four copies of the Magna Carta is displayed. It was drawn up to appease King John's rebellious barons and signed by the king at Runnymede in 1215. Written on vellum in Latin, the Magna Carta is a corner stone of civil rights in English law.

▶*Central Salisbury. New Street car park.*

London

The great metropolis is forever changing: glass and steel towers spring from Georgian docks; a ferris wheel casts its shadow on the mother of parliaments; a Hindu temple rises over suburban semis; and at the city's heart is the one constant – the rhythmic ebb and flow of the Thames.

A41
9
Regent's Park
22 A5205 A41
A400
A501
A40
Marylebone
A5
Paddington
10
Hyde Park
A4202
20
21
19
A4
A308
18 A3212
3 A302
A202
Victoria
A3213
4
St James's Park
Green Park
3
4
2
5 1
Waterloo
A201
A3204 A3
A2
King's Cross
St Pancras
Euston
A501
A1
A501
A10
15
7
A1202
9
8
12
10
11
Liverpool Street
8
6
A11
5
13
17
13
12
Blackfriars
16
Cannon Street
Fenchurch Street
7
17
6
14 16
14
11
London Bridge
Thames
A100

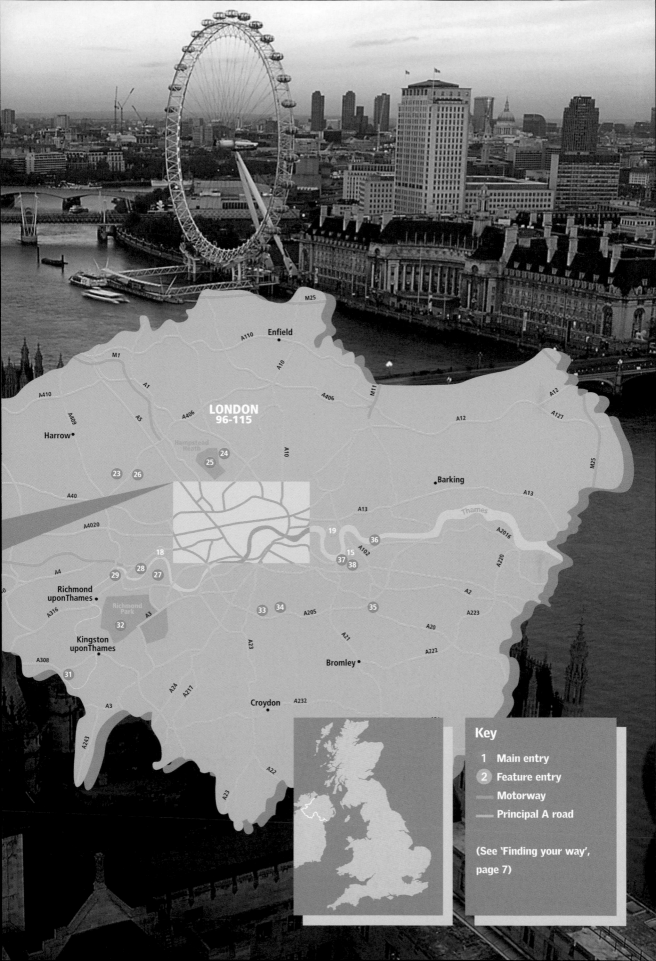

LONDON
96-115

Enfield

Harrow•

•Barking

Richmond
uponThames•

Kingston
uponThames

•Bromley

Croydon•

Thames

M25
A110
A10
A1
M1
A410
A409
A5
A406
A406
A10
A12
A127
A13
A2016
A220
A2
A223
A20
A222
A13
A13
A102
A205
A21
A23
A24
A217
A232
A22
A23
A243
A3
A308
A316
A3
A4
A4020
A40
M11

23 26 25 24 18 28 27 29 32 31 33 34 35 19 36 37 15 38

Key

1   Main entry

2   Feature entry

     Motorway

     Principal A road

(See 'Finding your way',
page 7)

LONDON

1 London Eye

2 Houses of Parliament

3 Westminster Abbey

4 Churchill Museum
and Cabinet War Rooms

5 The Banqueting House

6 Somerset House

Houses of Parliament
Government reality, Gothic fantasy

The Gothic Revival masterpiece that houses England's parliament is so familiar that it can almost appear commonplace. But approach it by passing through the sharply contrasting interior of Westminster Jubilee Line station and its glory shifts back into focus. From platform to street level, you move upward on an Escher-like stairway, through grey steel and concrete, past pipes and girders. It is like travelling through the innards of a machine, or cruising the set of Fritz Lang's *Metropolis*.

A medieval royal palace once occupied the site of Parliament, of which only Westminster Hall's stone walls and impressive hammerbeam oak roof remain. The rest, designed by Sir Charles Barry to blend with the nearby Abbey, was begun in 1837 and largely completed by 1860. Its style reflects sentimental longing for a mythical age of knights and chivalry. There are no maidens imprisoned in the towers here, however, only the 13.5 tonne Big Ben bell, that reassuringly continues to strike out the hours. And the battles fought now are with words not swords, on the floor of the Commons. Queue for a seat in the Strangers' Gallery – evening sessions are easier to get into – then sit back and enjoy the free show.
▶ *Westminster tube. Each MP has a limited number of tickets for Strangers' Gallery. For information, Tel 020 7219 4272.*

London Eye
Revolutionary London

Much more than a ride in the sky, the Eye is a major addition to the London skyline, a marriage of art and technology, with a flavour of the funfair. At 135m (450ft) above the ground, it is one of the capital's tallest structures and the world's highest observation wheel.

One circuit on the continuously moving wheel, aboard one of the 32 futuristic glass-enclosed pods, takes 30 minutes. With views of up to 25 miles all around you, it is like being circled by a giant map of the capital and its suburbs. By day, you can play spot the landmark, and on evening rides you will have the thrill of seeing London decked out in all its sparkling finery.
▶ *Waterloo/Westminster tube. Daily (closed 1 week Jan). To book, Tel 0870 5000 600.*

Westminster Abbey

The ghostly power of monarchy

Nowhere else can you stand in the presence of the mortal remains of so many major players in English history. Besides the graves of literary figures such as Chaucer and Ben Jonson – buried upright in the nave – burial space is heavily populated by kings and queens, from Edward the Confessor, who founded the abbey in 1065, to George II, the last monarch to be interred here in 1760. The body of the saintly Edward lies at the heart of the Abbey, in a magnificent tomb behind the High Altar. But continue past it into an even more glorious shrine to absolute power – Henry VII's Lady Chapel. Go through the fine bronze gates, displaying the Royal Tudor badges, and gasp at the intricacy of the vaulted roof soaring high above. Authority still radiates from the marble effigies, particularly from that of perhaps the greatest of England's rulers, Elizabeth I.

▶ *Westminster tube. Mon-Sat; Sun services only. For tours, Tel 020 7654 4900.*

Churchill Museum and Cabinet War Rooms

Relive the fight against Hitler

Picture the scene – 1940, and London is under attack, bombs cascade from the sky, and the streets are unsafe. Below ground in a heavily fortified Whitehall basement, Churchill, his Cabinet, the Chiefs of Staff and other high ranking officials live in a warren of cramped rooms and direct the Second World War.

Now you can get a taste of those years, descending to view the Cabinet Room, the typing pool, the telephone with a 'secure' line to the American president, and the hub of the action, the Map Room, where battles were plotted and won. The Churchill Museum shows the Churchills' restored private living areas. It is the first national museum dedicated to the life and times of the wartime leader.

▶ *King Charles Street off Whitehall. Westminster or St James's Park tube. Daily.*

The Banqueting House

Height of the English Renaissance

If Charles I had glanced upward just before his execution at the Banqueting House in 1649, he may have thought he had already entered heaven. Adorning the ceiling were the nine baroque canvases that he had commissioned Rubens to paint to celebrate the life and rule of his father, James I. And they are still there, the crowning glory of the only surviving building from the royal palace of Whitehall.

Today, Inigo Jones' Palladian masterpiece is open to all, although few seem to notice it among the other grand edifices on Whitehall. Yet as well as Rubens' paintings, there is the lavish grandeur of a building that was a revelation at a time when Tudor red brick and timbering still prevailed, and a wonderfully atmospheric vaulted basement, the Undercroft, once used as a drinking den by James I and his cronies, and by Charles II to hold lotteries.

▶ *Corner of Whitehall and Horse Guards Avenue. Embankment or Westminster tube. Mon-Sat, except bank hols.*

Somerset House

Skate over the ice to view an eccentric yet dazzling bequest

The old custodian of Births, Marriages and Deaths has thrown open its doors. And the first impression is perhaps the best. Pass through the gateway on the Strand and you are in a vast courtyard that rivals the Place des Vosges in Paris for scale and beauty. For years, employees of the Inland Revenue used this centrepiece of William Chambers' 18th-century neoclassical design as a car park. Now it is a public space, dominated by a show of dancing water jets. Since 1999, an ice rink has sat at the centre for nine weeks each winter. When lit by flaming torches in the evenings it makes a truly uplifting sight.

Within the complex are the Courtauld Gallery of mainly Impressionist works and one of London's latest and most generous bequests. The Gilbert Collection of decorative arts, the gift of the British-born entrepreneur Sir Arthur Gilbert, includes priceless gold and jewel-encrusted snuff boxes, miniature portraits and Italian micro-mosaics. Among its exhibits is a bizarre replica of Gilbert's Beverly Hills office, with a waxwork of him on the phone at his desk, dressed in tennis gear.

▶ *Temple tube. Daily.*

Everything new under the sun

From modest 19th-century roots London's department stores have become the grand palaces of retailing

EAST MEETS WEST END
AT LIBERTY

No other European city can match London's department stores for their sheer scale, surprising diversity of goods – 'from a pin to an elephant' was the boast of Whiteley's, one of the first of the breed in the 1870s – or the striking differences between them.

The greatest concentration of stores is on Oxford Street, the capital's main shopping artery. But this familiar streetscape is relatively recent. Oxford Street had been just a highway to the west, linking the City with Oxford from Roman days until the late 17th century. At this time, although there were a few shops at the Tottenham Court Road end, on the northern fringe of Soho, there was no sign of the development that was to follow, turning the 'West End' into the axis of commerce and Oxford Street into the main avenue of a new 'central' London.

Then, in the 18th century, the growth of estates to the west of the City, such as Grosvenor and Portman, allowed Oxford Street traders to take advantage of an influx of well-to-do inhabitants. In 1790 a small shop called Dickins and Smith (later Dickins & Jones) opened at 54 Oxford Street, then in 1833 Peter Robinson began a drapery business at number 103. Thirty years later his silk buyer, John Lewis, set up on his own close by at 132.

At the turn of the 20th century, the increasing spending power of the middle class pushed retail on to a grander scale. The Gillows had been furniture makers on Oxford Street since 1765. In 1906, now in partnership with S.J. Waring, they opened a giant department store, Waring & Gillow. This was eclipsed three years later by the opening of a shopping colossus, **Selfridges**, at number 400. Today it is the old matriarch of the tribe, a huge carcass of consumption instantly recognisable from its façade of Greek columns. The store attracts 17 million shoppers a year, including around 3 million tourists, fulfilling the promise of its founder – Chicago millionaire Gordon Selfridge – that 'Selfridges is for everyone'.

Such was the success of Oxford Street that stores spread south along the elegant terraces of Regent Street, designed by John Nash in the early 19th century. These included Messrs Farmer and Rogers, where Arthur Lasenby Liberty became manager of the store's Oriental warehouse at the age of 20. Impatient at not being made a partner, he set up on his own, convinced that he could change the look of homewares and fashion. In 1874 he took a lease on a small store opposite his old employer, selling ornaments, fabrics, carpets and *objets d'art* from the Far East. Within 18 months Liberty had expanded the store into neighbouring properties and his sources into Java, India, Indochina and Persia, turning later to English manufacturers to dye and print Eastern designs. The store became London's most fashionable place to shop. Today **Liberty** (210-220 Regent Street) is a magical grotto filled, behind its mock Tudor exterior, with exotic goods – intense colours, rich textures and fabulous printed fabrics – in a setting as intimate as a private club.

Moving west and upmarket

As London expanded west, spurred on by the new Metropolitan underground line in the 1860s, shops began to meet the demands of well-healed residents in streets linking Knightsbridge with the north bank of the Thames. They also developed a new style of retailing, with restaurants and retiring rooms for customers – particularly women, barred from their husbands' clubs – in the hope of their spending longer on the premises.

In 1813 Benjamin Harvey opened a small linen shop in a terraced house on the corner of Knightsbridge and Sloane Square. The business passed seven years later to his daughter and her partner Colonel Nichols, extending their wares into oriental carpets, silks and luxury goods. The present premises were acquired in 1880 and by the end of the next century **Harvey Nichols** (109-125 Knightsbridge) had become a byword for sophistication, famous for its bold window displays, the chic Fifth Floor food market and restaurant and particularly the wide range of designer clothing, beloved of the society crowds. To launch into a sea of fashionable labels, go to the first floor, pausing in the ground-floor cosmetics section – probably the most fragrant space in London.

And yet, ask the world to name one London store and it is likely to be **Harrods**, which opened in 1849 close to Harvey Nichols and now sells more than a million different goods. The Egyptian Hall, a £20 million homage to ancient Egypt with gold-leaf ceilings, was designed with the help of experts from the British Museum. The grandest department is the Food Hall, where surrounded by spectacular Edwardian tiled walls and ceilings you can buy anything from a potato to a £5000 bottle of Chateau Cheval Blanc '47. At night, the exterior, illuminated by more than 11,000 bulbs, is one of London's most impressive light-shows.

LONDON

LONDON

Royal Opera House

A spellbinding new version now playing to bigger audiences

The colonnaded mid 19th-century Royal Opera House was never one of Europe's grandest. But its ambitious restoration and renovation has transformed it into one of the most exciting public spaces in the capital, open not just to audiences but visitors as well.

In addition to the undercover 'Link' walkway between the Piazza and Bow Street, visitors can step inside the cavernous Floral Hall, part of the original flower market, which is now the main bar and congregating area. There are restaurant tables on the mezzanine gallery (only open to ticket holders in the evening) and a further eating and drinking area on the upper floor with an open terrace overlooking the Piazza.

▶ *Bow Street. Covent Garden tube. Daily Mon-Sat. For backstage tours, Tel 020 7304 4000.*

James Smith's umbrella shop

Brolly amazing!

It looks as though it has not changed a jot since its doors opened in 1830, this enchanting emporium dedicated to every sort of umbrella and walking stick you could imagine – and then a few thousand more. Everywhere, there are shiny mahogany racks, stands and glazed cases, full of handles, from everyday to exotic, craning from furled fabrics from plain to sumptuous.

▶ *New Oxford Street. Tottenham Court Road tube. Daily except Sun.*

The British Museum

Secrets made transparent, and bars on public access removed

Known the world over for its collections, the British Museum is becoming equally famous for a part that few people, until recently, ever saw. A £100 million development by the architect Norman Foster has transformed the **Great Court**, with its pale Georgian stone walls and imposing side porticos, into Europe's largest covered square: a space that could swallow 17 Olympic-size swimming pools. Having remained hidden for 150 years, the courtyard is now enclosed by a soaring glass and steel roof. On display are several of the museum's treasures including a lion statue from the ancient city of Knidos in Turkey.

But the museum's top architectural treasure is the historic **Reading Room**, restored to its original 19th-century splendour and for the first time open to the public. Some of the masterminds of revolution, including Trotsky, Lenin and Marx, studied in the huge circular room; any complaints about communism, the Russian leader Gorbachev once remarked, should be addressed to the British Museum.

▶ *Great Russell Street. Tottenham Court Road/ Holborn tube. Museum, Great Court and Reading Room daily (museum closed Good Fri). For guided tours, Tel 020 7323 8181.*

BROLLY AMAZING!
JAMES SMITH'S UMBRELLA SHOP

Sir John Soane's Museum

The most eclectic collection of objects you will ever see

The home of Sir John Soane, the architect of the Bank of England, opened as a museum during his lifetime ('except in wet and dirty weather') to show his rather eccentric collection of objects. Mainly assembled after the death of his wife in 1815 – some say as a therapeutic means of dealing with his grief – the Aladdin's cave of treasures contains paintings (including works by Canaletto, Reynolds and Turner), architectural models, original Hogarth satirical masterpieces (*The Rake's Progress* and *The Election* among them), a shrine to Shakespeare, Apulian vases and the sarcophagus of Egyptian pharaoh Seti I.

There are also timepieces, Napoleonic medals, 325 items of furniture, many designed by Soane, a model of his wife's tomb and the grave of Fanny, her lapdog. The museum of this remarkable man, the son of a country bricklayer, is unique, highly eclectic and short on breathing space but it delivers what Soane wanted – an emotional punch.

▶ *13 Lincoln's Inn Fields off Kingsway. Holborn tube. Tues-Sat.*

Smithfield Market

The best joint for the meat trade

Smithfield Market is a remarkable survivor. Other wholesale food markets have been shunted out of the city centre, but the daily – early morning – business of buying and selling meat still takes place in a triumph of Victorian architecture. The 4ha (10 acre), cast iron, much embellished and now fully restored structure is fancy enough to hang works of art in, let alone sides of beef.

Meat – the livestock was once slaughtered on the spot – has been traded on the site for more than 800 years, with the space also used for jousting, horse sales, executions and St Bartholomew's Fair, named after the nearby church, London's oldest and one of the few survivors of medieval times. But more than a market, Smithfield today stands at the hub of a fashionable part of town, especially on the northern side, where a number of restaurants have sprouted up, and not just serving meat dishes. This is also the place for pubs that are open in the small hours of the morning, and cafés that serve cholesterol-laden breakfasts.

▶ *Charterhouse Street off Farringdon Road. Farringdon/Barbican tube. Mon-Fri 4am-noon.*

St Paul's Cathedral

Whisper a prayer of thanks for Sir Christopher Wren's masterpiece

Even as late as the 1950s St Paul's reigned magnificently over the capital's skyline, a constant presence with the rest of the city sprawling around its feet. These days Wren's immense 17th-century church tends to announce itself with more of a flourish: appearing suddenly among city high-rises, or in that much-photographed view from Fleet Street and Ludgate, the dome appearing behind two tiers of Corinthian columns, framed by the twin towers of the west front.

The dome is its most impressive feature. A pewter tureen from without, ornately painted within, it is one of the largest in the world, comparable to that of St Peter's in Rome. The ceiling is a false one, a matter of architectural aesthetics best appreciated from the perspective of the Whispering Gallery. Such are the bizarre acoustics here that a sotto voce murmur on one side can, when the church is empty, be heard by someone putting an ear to the wall 30m (100ft) away on the far side of the dome.

▶ *St Paul's Churchyard off Cheapside. St Paul's tube. Mon-Sat.*

LONDON

30 St Mary Axe
Green thinking among grey streets

Ask a Londoner what they think of 30 St Mary Axe, and they may not have an answer. Ask them what they think of The Gherkin and you can be sure of an opinion. The distinctive shape of the 179.8m tall office building on St Mary Axe, opened in 2004, has made as much impact on the public as it has on the skyline.

But the shape is not a whim. The radical design of Norman Foster used green principles to make London's first ecological building. The external aerodynamic form of the building lets wind pressure differentials form natural ventilation within the building, reducing energy consumption. The use of glass for much of the outside of the building ensures maximum daylight penetration, reducing the need for artificial lighting. Even the building's bulging middle and the tapering top and bottom have a benefit – on street level the huge size of the building is not as obvious. It really is a building of the future.

▶ *Liverpool Street/Fenchurch/Bank tube.*

Tate Modern
An architectural art powerhouse

A gentle slope leads you into the depths of a former power station on the banks of the River Thames. The Bankside station, built by Sir Giles Gilbert Scott between 1947 and 1963, has been transformed into the Tate Modern, a £134 million showcase for the gallery's collection dating from 1900 to the present day. It quickly became Britain's leading visitor attraction when it opened in 2000, with more than 5 million visitors in its first year.

As you enter the immense space of the Turbine Room (pictured), its interior engulfs you like a whale swallowing plankton. Tall, cathedral-like windows illuminate the bolted pillars and industrial lifts inside and the hum of the transformer station – still operating on the building's south side – creates a quiet background chant. The effect of the space is every bit as thrilling as that of the collection by Picasso, Matisse, Rothko, Dali, Warhol, Pollock, Giacometti and other masters.

▶ *Bankside. Southwark tube. Daily.*

Geffrye Museum
A history of changing rooms

In 1715 a terrace of almshouses was founded in Shoreditch by a wealthy Cornish merchant. Nearly 200 years later the poor were moved to more comfortable surroundings and the buildings became a museum of furniture, Shoreditch then being the centre of the East End's furniture trade. Today you can observe 400 years of domestic history here, by walking through a series of rooms furnished in various period styles. They span the heavy dark oaks of the 17th century, through Victorian chintz and clutter to the pale woods and shocking colours of a contemporary loft apartment. If the sun is shining, explore a series of exterior rooms in the gardens outside, including an aromatic display in the walled herb garden.

▶ *Kingsland Road. Old Street tube. Daily except Mon. Sun and bank hol Mon pm only.*

Shakespeare's Globe
Tragedy, comedy and romance – as our greatest playwright saw it

Take yourself back to 16th-century London at the Globe, a faithful reconstruction of the riverside theatre for which Shakespeare wrote many of his plays. Twenty wooden bays make up the circular, open-air theatre three storeys high. Like the original, it is the work of master craftsmen, using traditional techniques and materials such as 6000 bundles of Norfolk water reed on the roof, some 36,000 hand made bricks and heavy oak beams.

Plays, of course, are the thing, staged from May to September in authentic style. But you can visit the theatre all year as well as enjoy the 'Shakespeare's Globe' exhibition, which brings Shakespeare's London to life. Enter the recording booths to add your voice to prerecorded scenes of his plays and to hear actors read familiar lines – you may be surprised by the many different deliveries of 'To be or not to be'.

▶ *New Globe Walk, Bankside. Southwark tube. Exhibition and theatre tours daily. Box office, Tel 020 7401 9919.*

AN ARCHITECTURAL
ART POWERHOUSE
TATE MODERN

COLUMBIA ROAD FLOWER MARKET

Streets ahead for the best bargins

The goods might not all be new, but a visit to one of London's street markets is always a fresh experience

5 Petticoat Lane **6** Brick Lane **7** Columbia Road Flower Market **8** Spitalfields Market
9 Camden Lock **10** Portobello Road

They are the best free shows in town: colourful, noisy multi-cultural events with a strong dose of the theatrical; centuries old but stunningly contemporary, as much about people as content. 'They' are London's street markets – wonderful places for characters, food (all the myriad flavours of the 21st-century metropolis) and the bonhomie of crowds bent on having a good time. They are also the best places to go on a Sunday, since that is usually, though not exclusively, market day for the city's thronged bazaars.

For the ultimate London market experience head for Liverpool Street (tube and station) on a Sunday morning. Within walking distance, there are no fewer than four distinctly different East End markets.

Fed by waves of immigrants

Just across Bishopsgate from the station lies Middlesex Street, better known by its previous name of **Petticoat Lane**. It is here that you will find racks of leather jackets, cut-price fashions, fake designer-label wear, bolts of fabric and, yes, silky underwear – all a legacy of the rag trade established by Jewish and Huguenot refugees in the 17th century, and reflected in the names of streets such as Clothier and Fashion, as well as the Petticoat which so offended Victorian morality that it was renamed.

Follow the throng into Wentworth Street – heart of the market's Monday to Friday persona – and in the blink of an eye the production changes: different lane, different set, different players. This is **Brick Lane**, main thoroughfare of 'Bangla Town' and centre of another sprawling street market, where old tools, used furniture, bric-a-brac and yet more clothes are sold to the accompaniment of the latest hit from Dhaka.

There are fruit and vegetable stalls, and at least one selling jellied eels, and several beigel bakeries. But it is as the hottest place for curries – served in a score of restaurants – that Brick Lane really earns a place on the capital's gastronomic map. The variety of food is just one reflection of the area's changing cultural identity. The building at the corner of Fournier Street that now houses a mosque serving the thriving Bangladeshi community is another: in its time it has also been a place of worship for protestant Huguenot silk workers and a synagogue.

Follow your nose up Brick Lane, across Bethnal Green Road, and before long you will catch the scent of **Columbia Road Flower Market**, where a million blooms have burst by 9am and been picked by 2pm. There are flowerpots of all shapes and size, rooted trees and shrubs, houseplants and cuttings – in fact, every green thing that Londoners need for their flats, balconies, backyards and gardens. Back towards Liverpool Street, and there is time to walk along Commercial Street and into **Spitalfields Market**, which closes around three hours later than its neighbours at 5pm. Light spills through the roof glazing and ironwork of this old covered market, formerly for fruit and vegetables, onto stalls stuffed with organic food, craftworks, collectables and secondhand books.

Another day, another part of town, another market. **Camden Lock** (Camden Town tube), bustles every day. This most youthful of street markets is something of an alternative fashion parade, and has stalls selling music, arts and crafts, and books. Antiques are also sold at Camden Lock, but the main place for these is **Portobello Road** (Notting Hill Gate or Ladbroke Grove tube) on a Saturday. Head north, beyond the Westway flyover, to find a bargain, or turn right into Goldborne Road, home of the capital's Moroccan community, where the stalls sell some of the best bric-a-brac in town.

LONDON

17 Lloyd's of London

18 Chelsea Physic Garden

Lloyd's of London

Space-age look for established name

Lloyd's is associated not only with insurance, but also with a fantastic edifice designed by Richard Rogers in 1978-86. Its inside-out look is a radical statement for a conservative city institution. Its functional workings, such as air conditioning ducts, are worn on its sleeve for practical as well as aesthetic reasons, making the interior a vast uncluttered space and adding a sculptural edge to the building. For the merchants and underwriters who met in Edward Lloyd's coffee house in the 1680s, it would have been inconceivable that such a superstructure would rise here 300 years later.
▶ *1 Lime Street. Bank or Monument tube.*

Chelsea Physic Garden

An abundance of natural remedies in London's secret garden

Step through a gate in a high brick wall that runs down busy Royal Hospital Road and you find yourself in one of the city's most unusual gardens. Established in 1673 by the Society of Apothecaries on the banks of the Thames – then the only means of access – the Chelsea Physic Garden is the second oldest botanic garden in England after Oxford's (see page 73).

The 1.5ha (3½ acre) green oasis was intended to show early medics how to recognise and use plants to cure all manner of ailments. It remains a place of research and education as well as pleasure. Aside from medicinal plants, the garden includes Britain's tallest outdoor olive tree, over 9m (30ft) high, and one of Europe's oldest rock gardens, made from volcanic lava imported from Iceland. A small crop of cannabis grew here until 1982 when a dedicated home botanist jumped over the wall during the night and harvested it.
▶ *Royal Hospital Road. Sloane Square tube. Wed-Fri pm and Sun pm Apr-Oct.*

LONDON

Natural History Museum
London's Jurassic Park

Step inside the cathedral-like entrance hall of the Natural History Museum, a triumph of Victorian design, and you come face to knee with the huge 26m (85ft) long Diplodocus. The dinosaur skeleton is a plaster cast but the effect is just as riveting, and there are plenty of real bones to see. Dinosaur fans should turn left out of the cavernous gallery, with its grand staircase, painted ceiling and terracotta monkeys, birds and reptiles, into room 21. It has helped to transform a slightly stuffy world of 68 million specimens into an inspiring place to learn. Take the 61m (200ft) long catwalk to the animatronic show, where a roaring T-Rex with bloodstained jaws guards its kill.
▶ *Cromwell Road and Exhibition Road. South Kensington tube. Daily.*

Kensington Roof Gardens
Lofty horticultural delights

Europe's largest roof garden flourishes 30m (100ft) above Kensington High Street. It was created in 1938 as the ultimate adornment to one of London's finest department stores, Derry and Tom's (no longer in business). Its 0.6ha (1½ acres) are themed. An area of English woodland has a hundred trees, including oak, birch, willow, apple and lime, growing in soil less than 1m (3ft) deep. Secret corners, archways and lots of trailing wisteria add charm to a walled Tudor garden, while a Mediterranean feel is created by the vine-covered walkway, fig trees, manicured lawns and fountains in the Spanish garden.
▶ *99 Kensington High Street. High Street Kensington tube. Daily. Tel 020 7937 7994.*

Leighton House Museum
Inspired by *The Arabian Nights*

The residence of Frederic, Lord Leighton, a Victorian painter and president of the Royal Academy, is a lavish fantasy home. At its centre is the Arab Hall, inspired by a Moorish palace in Sicily. The room is decorated with lattice work and tiles from the Middle East, and a gilt mosaic frieze depicting mythological scenes. A gentle fountain spouts in the middle.

The house also contains Leighton's 18m (60ft) long studio with its gilt dome, a collection of Victorian paintings, including works by Burne-Jones and Millais, and many souvenirs collected on the baron's travels.
▶ *12 Holland Park Road. High Street Kensington tube. Daily except Tues.*

Lord's
Bowled over by cricket's HQ

As you walk into Lord's through the Grace Gates – a memorial to England's first sporting hero, W.G. Grace – you gain a sense of the site's heritage. Resident here since 1814, it is the spiritual home of cricket. Go to a match, or take a tour that includes a museum with exhibits ranging from Sir Donald Bradman's boots to a sparrow (now stuffed) bowled out by Jehangir Khan in 1936 and the diminutive urn that holds the Ashes. You will also walk through the Long Room in the Victorian Pavilion, where MCC members keep an eye on the game under the gaze of a gallery of past heroes. The tour ends in the futuristic media centre – an alien form that seems to have landed on the two columns that support it. The gleaming structure is made of glass and aluminium and accommodates more than 200 journalists on match days.
▶ *St John's Wood Road. St John's Wood tube. Tel 020 7616 8595 for tour and museum information.*

Wembley Stadium
The sports venue of the future

When what is arguably the best-known football stadium in the world needed a facelift, no-one was sure what to expect. But £757 million later, the world's most expensive and largest sports stadium opened in 2007. Designed by Norman Foster, it is an enormous futuristic arena that seats 90,000 people and comes complete with a sliding roof. The famous Twin Towers of the old stadium have been replaced by a triumphant arch, visible across London. Its state-of-the-art facilities and design make this an unrivalled sporting arena.
▶ *Empire Way. Wembley Park tube, Wembley Central tube & rail and Wembley Stadium station (from Marylebone). Tel 020 8795 9000 for opening times.*

Highgate Cemetery

Eerie decay of a monumental necropolis

Extravagant statues and ornate Victorian symbols of death – stone urns, lilies, fancy spires and spectral angels – rise proudly from the ground and lurk ominously in the undergrowth of Highgate Cemetery. More than 167,000 people are buried in the 52,000 graves here, the final resting places of Michael Faraday and George Eliot among them. The 15ha (36 acre) site, a 19th-century graveyard for prosperous classes, has two distinct halves. The east side is better known because it is open to visitors and contains Karl Marx's tomb. The west (only open for guided tours) is overrun by wild flowers, ivy, weeds and brambles. Its impressive Egyptian Avenue, built into a hillside, leads to 36 vaults, with vast iron doors and Egyptian pediments, in the Circle of Lebanon.
▶ *Swain's Lane. Archway tube. East side daily, except during a burial. For times of West Cemetery guided tours, Tel 020 8340 1834.*

Hampstead Heath

Enclave of pastoral and porticoed splendour in the metropolis

Drop strangers into the heart of these 800 leafy acres and they will swear that they have been abandoned in some remote English shire. Only when their ears ignore the birdsong and tune into the distant hum of traffic will they accept the heath's urban coordinates. If in need of a refreshing dip, the Lido to the south and the bathing ponds offer a chance to swim in the open air.

As befits the setting, there is a classic 18th-century mansion in this rural idyll. The very large and very white Kenwood House is the work of Robert Adam, called in by Lord Mansfield in the 1760s to enlarge and embellish his red-brick residence. The property contains paintings by, among others, Turner, Gainsborough, Reynolds, Rembrandt and Vermeer.
▶ *Hampstead tube. Heath daily. Kenwood House (EH) daily. Tel 020 8348 1286.*

Shree Swaminarayan Mandir

Oriental vision in suburbia

The building popularly known as the Neasden Hindu temple is a labour worthy of the gods – it is also one of love. More than 2000 tonnes of limestone from Bulgaria, and a similar weight of marble from the quarries of Carrara, in Tuscany, were shipped to India. There, more than 1500 volunteer craftsmen chiselled the stone into 26,000 pieces of intricate carving and sculpture. These were then shipped to England, where they were assembled like a giant jigsaw. The whole business took three years. Leave your shoes at the door, step inside and admire gods in their elaborate finery, and visit the exhibition on Hinduism.
▶ *Brentfield Road, off A406 North Circular. Neasden tube. Daily.*

The Wetland Centre

Webbed feet and waders galore

Europe's largest wetland-creation project is built on the site of four redundant reservoirs. Five years in the making, the mosaic of lagoons, lakes, ponds and pools, which opened in May 2000, covers just over 40ha (100 acres). Fourteen habitats – from Australian billabong to Siberian tundra – have been created in the outdoor exhibition areas and some 140 species of birds recorded – as many as 70 in one day, including the kingfisher, and, in 2002, a bittern. The observatory in the Peter Scott visitor centre lets you birdwatch in comfort.
▶ *Queen Elizabeth's Walk, Barnes, off A306. Hammersmith tube (then 'Duck Bus'). Daily.*

Chiswick House

Superb imitation of the Italian master

Lord Hervey, a rival of Richard Boyle, 3rd Earl of Burlington, described Chiswick House, the earl's Palladian villa, as 'too small for a house, too big to hang on a watch chain'. His lordship was no judge of buildings. The young Burlington had returned from the Grand Tour inspired by the work of the 16th-century Italian architect Palladio. Working to his own designs, and with his protégé William Kent in charge of the interior decoration, Burlington completed this homage to Palladio's Villa Capra (near Vicenza) in 1729. The simple ground floor contrasts with the ornate upper floors, which contain three velvet-lined rooms.
▶ *Burlington Lane, off Hogarth Lane (A4). Chiswick station (from Waterloo). EH. Wed-Sun and bank hols Apr-Oct. Tel 020 8995 0508.*

LONDON

Kew Gardens
Collecting passions flourish behind glass and cast iron

Seven miles southwest of the capital's centre lies one of Britain's great legacies of empire. The 120ha (300 acres) of flowerbeds, glasshouses and hothouses of the Royal Botanic Gardens, Kew, are largely the creation of Joseph Banks. This eminent botanist, who accompanied James Cook on one of his round-the-world voyages, was president of the Royal Society for over four decades and started the plant collection at Kew. It is now the biggest in the world, with more than 30,000 species. Despite the larger Temperate House, a new alpine house and the Princess of Wales Conservatory, where ten climatic zones share the same roof, the most thrilling structure in the gardens is still Decimus Burton's Palm House, completed in 1848. In this 110m (363ft) long masterpiece in cast iron and glass, staircases and walkways lead visitors on a steamy walk among tropical plants.
▶ *Kew Gardens tube and station (from Waterloo). Daily.*

Heathrow Airport
Climbing to statistical heights

When Heathrow started life in 1946 there were 9000 flights a year. There are now more than that number every week. Sixty-four million people pass through its gates each year, arriving or departing on one of around 90 airlines flying to some 180 destinations: it all adds up to the busiest airport in the world – and a place that there are plenty of reasons to visit, apart from catching a plane.

With half the airport's revenue coming now from retailing, the range of shops in the terminals is more impressive than that of most high streets. And when the shops lose their attraction, you can visit the Heathrow Academy, off Perimeter Road, which houses an exhibition with highlights of Heathrow's history. The new aircraft viewing platform offers great views of the jumbo jets thundering down the runways. The first phase of Terminal 5 is due to open in 2008 with completion scheduled for 2011.
▶ *Heathrow tube and Heathrow Express (from Paddington). M4 (Junction 4). Heathrow Academy weekends and school hols, Tel 020 8745 6655.*

ONCE A HAUNT OF RIVER THIEVES AND SMUGGLERS, THE PROSPECT OF WHITBY WAS KNOWN FORMERLY AS THE DEVIL'S TAVERN

Finest taverns in the town

A rich seam of history runs through London's pubs, from city centre gin palace to riverside rendezvous

11 George Inn **12** Princess Louise **13** Prospect of Whitby **14** Anchor **15** Cutty Sark
16 Black Friar **17** Lamb and Flag **18** Dove

Conduct a straw poll of jolly patrons in any of London's 6000 or so pubs and you are bound to record overwhelming support for the proposition that their particular watering hole is one of the best. And the more the evening wears on, the greater that support is likely to get. As Dr Johnson – a pub regular – once declared, 'There is no other place where the more noise you make the more you are welcome'.

In the Middle Ages, the better-off chose the comfort of taverns. Here food and accommodation were offered to weary travellers, including pilgrims such as those in Chaucer's *Canterbury Tales* who begin their journey from the Tabard Inn in Southwark. The lower classes favoured the more functional alehouses, many the private homes of individual brewers: more than 40 were recorded in Domesday Book. This brewing free-for-all ended only when 'tippling houses' had to be licensed, in 1552.

With the arrival of regular stagecoach services in the mid 17th century, the coaching inn appeared in London. Many inns had galleries on three sides around a central courtyard, where visiting players would perform, watched by the customers. The **George Inn** (77 Borough High Street, SE1; NT) is the last of these London coaching stops. It dates from the 1540s, and one of the two-storeyed galleries, built in the 17th century, remains.

The industrial age, railways in particular, killed off the coaching trade but brought in a new working population with a keen thirst. This was slaked by the elaborate 'gin palaces' of the Victorian and Edwardian ages. Gin shops had first opened in the late 17th century when William III made the potent drink tax and licence free, to the delight of the poor, but with devastatingly drunken results. With technical advances in plate glass and gas lighting in the early 19th century, 'gin palaces' appeared in often grim surroundings like heavenly escapes from the misery of London poverty. The **Princess Louise** (208 High Holborn, WC1), with its flamboyant décor of etched glass, yards of brass and elaborate tiling stretching even into the toilets, is a fine example.

All human life is there

Pubs with the longest pedigree can be found along the banks of the Thames, the city's original commercial artery. The **Prospect of Whitby** (57 Wapping Wall, E1) was built in 1520. Samuel Pepys and J.M.W. Turner were regulars, as was Dr Johnson, although he preferred the warren of small, dark, intimate rooms of the **Anchor** across the river (34 Park Street, Bankside, SE1) as the place to work on his dictionary. Farther east, in Greenwich, is the **Cutty Sark** (Ballast Quay, off Lassell Street, SE10), built in 1804 but with its origins in the 16th century. It has changed little since Charles Dickens stood on its flagstoned floors in front of roaring fires.

You may not be able to see the river from the bars in the **Black Friar** (174 Queen Victoria Street, EC4), at the north end of Blackfriars Bridge, but you can enjoy a triumph of the Arts and Crafts movement. The pub, built in 1875 on the site of the medieval Blackfriars monastery, was decorated around 1905 in marble, alabaster, copper and bronze, with friezes devoted to cavorting friars.

Moving west, and in Covent Garden is a pub that has remained largely untouched since 1623. The **Lamb and Flag** (33 Rose Street, WC2) is a rarity: a wood-framed building that has survived in central London. Its snug interiors heave of an evening, the patrons spilling onto an alleyway where the poet John Dryden was beaten up for writing unflattering verses about a mistress of Charles II.

Back to the river but way upstream from the ancient pubs that served the wharves, docks and markets where most of their regulars spent their working days is the equally historic **Dove** (19 Upper Mall, near Hammersmith Bridge, W6). The building dates from the 17th century, when it is said Charles II and Nell Gwynne were customers. James Thomson wrote 'Rule Britannia' there around 1740, perhaps in Britain's smallest bar – 1.3m (4ft 3in) wide, 2.4m (7ft 10in) long. Today, you can watch rowing clubs practice their strokes from the pub's open terrace while you down a glass of Fullers brewed just up the river in Chiswick.

LONDON

31 Hampton Court Palace 32 Isabella Plantation 33 Dulwich Picture Gallery

34 Horniman Museum

Hampton Court Palace

A marriage of royal architectural passions beside the Thames

The sheer magnificence and location of this riverside palace – built by Cardinal Wolsey, then coveted and eventually possessed by his master, Henry VIII – are special enough, but what makes it unique is the way it combines the best of 16th and late 17th-century English architecture. Behind the new façades and state apartments that Christopher Wren built for William and Mary in the 1690s, much of the rambling medieval Tudor palace built by Wolsey and Henry VIII remains. This includes the Chapel Royal, Great Hall and the Tudor kitchens, where time appears to have stopped on midsummer's day 1542 when Henry entertained his court to the banquet to end all banquets. Parts of the exterior, including Wolsey's gatehouse, also date from the palace's Tudor era.

Henry VIII was Hampton Court's most flamboyant royal resident, William III the one who loved it best, but in length of tenure they are all upstaged by a horticultural occupant. The great vine, planted by 'Capability' Brown in 1768, is not only the oldest but – subject to dispute from a cutting planted in Windsor – the biggest in the world, with a 1.8m (6ft) girth, 30m (100ft) limbs and an annual yield of around 230kg (500lb) of grapes. An even more venerable feature of the gardens, the maze, was planted in 1702.
▶ *Hampton Court station (from Waterloo). Boats from Richmond and Kingston. Daily.*

Isabella Plantation

Glades full of birdsong and blooms

At the heart of Richmond Park's rolling expanses lie 16ha (40 acres) of shaded walks, lawns, streams and ponds. Here, fenced off from the deer that roam the royal hunting ground created by Charles I, lies a leafy wonderland of beech, oak, sweet chestnut and other trees. Beneath this canopy, spring orchestrates a concerto of colour as the woodland garden, started in 1949 and planted over following decades, comes into bloom, with rhododendrons, azaleas and magnolias succeeding each other. The plantation, like the rest of the park, is a National Nature Reserve and excels in birds. This is the place to see greater and lesser spotted woodpeckers and nuthatches, and to hear summer songsters such as the chiffchaff and willow warbler.
▶ *Richmond Park. Richmond tube and station (from Waterloo). Daily.*

Dulwich Picture Gallery

How a sovereign's lost dream enriches all

The story behind England's first purpose-built public art gallery is remarkable. It begins in the late 18th century when King Stanislaus Augustus of Poland commissioned two London art dealers (Noël Desenfans and Sir Francis Bourgeois) to acquire a collection worthy of a monarch. Five years later, in 1795, the king was exiled, Poland disappeared from the map, and the dealers were left holding the fruits of the enterprise – an assembly of works by the likes of Canaletto, Gainsborough, Murillo, Poussin, Rembrandt, Rubens, Van Dyck and Watteau.

They bequeathed the collection to Dulwich College in 1811 on condition that the paintings should be available for the 'inspection of the public' and that the architect for the new gallery should be the good chum of Bourgeois, Sir John Soane. After extensive refurbishment, the building lives up to its contents – Soane included pioneering roof lanterns in the design, which bathe the works in a subtle wash of light.
▶ *North Dulwich (from London Bridge) or West Dulwich (from Victoria) stations. Gallery Road off Thurlow Park Road (A205 South Circular). Daily except Mon (open bank hol Mon).*

Horniman Museum

Mr Tea's wonderful collection kept in an Art Nouveau pot

There is a whole world in the striking Art Nouveau building designed by the architect C.H. Townsend to house the eclectic collection started by the Quaker tea merchant F.J. Horniman. A quarter of a million specimens – everything from fossils to stuffed animals and aquaria brimming with sea life – are kept in the natural history collection. In the ethnography displays, myriad tribal masks stare out from among the textiles, jewellery, art, puppets and other items in the 60,000-strong collection. But it is the musical instruments collection, one of the finest in the world, that is the museum's particular glory, with 6500 music-related objects on display.
▶ *100 London Road (A205 South Circular). Forest Hill station (from London Bridge). Daily.*

DULWICH PICTURE GALLERY

Things are looking up in Docklands

Where cargo ships and liners tied up, skyscrapers now soar above a cavernous shopping mall and tube station

19 Docklands

Their glittering shapes can be seen right across London – from as far off as the Chiswick flyover, where the M4 disgorges traffic on the western fringe of the metropolis, and the watershed of the North Downs. The cluster of tall buildings at Canary Wharf rises above the city roofscape like steep cliffs from a barely ruffled sea. Forty times a minute, the beacon on top of One Canada Square, the architect Cesar Pelli's 244m (800ft) high, stainless-steel-and-glass skyscraper and centre of **Docklands**, flashes a warning to aircraft.

The most dramatic way to reach this vision of an urban future is on one of the computer-driven trains of the **Docklands Light Railway** (DLR), a combination of mass rapid transit system and fairground ride that transports many of the wharf's 50,000 commuters to and from work. Trains go from deep underground at Bank tube station, emerging among East End flats before sweeping on a viaduct into Canary Wharf, where the glass-canopied station has a vast underground shopping mall spreading out below it.

Transforming Mr Milligan's grand vision

Impressive though it is, the DLR stop is dwarfed by the nearby **Jubilee Line tube station** (right). Here, a curved steel and glass canopy pours light down a wide bank of five escalators onto a ticket hall 223m (732ft) long – just 21m (68ft) less than the height of One Canada Square. The sense of exhilaration conveyed by this immense space, created in the expanse left by a drained dock, is only rivalled in London by the turbine hall in Tate Modern (see page 105).

From Docklands in its new guise to a reminder of the area's heritage: a stroll across Cabot Square leads to **West India Dock**, on the opposite side of which stand numbers 1 and 2 warehouses. This long, four-storey brick range contains apartments, restaurants, bars, shops and a Docklands museum (daily) behind the loading bays and ornately grilled, arched windows of the original exterior. At one end stands a life-size statue of a man in Georgian dress. The inscription on the plinth records that Robert Milligan was a London merchant to whose genius the creation of the huge dock, opened in 1802, and the flanking warehouses owed their creation. Two centuries on, he would probably approve of the area's latest transformation.

LONDON

Eltham Palace

A brilliant bound from the medieval to the modernist

Like a streamlined 1930s liner tied up to ancient harbour walls, the ultra-chic Art Deco residence created by Stephen Courtauld, son of the rayon entrepreneur, and his wife Ginnie nudges against the medieval palace, former abode of Plantagenet and Tudor monarchs. An 18th-century Chinese screen is all that separates the 15th-century great hall from the Courtaulds' apartments. It is an extraordinary transition – from the bravura carpentry and carving of a soaring hammerbeam roof to the Hollywood-style mansion, with the ceiling of its entrance hall decorated in a chic aluminium leaf design. Elsewhere in the house lie Ginnie's onyx and gold bathroom, and the purpose-made quarters of the couple's pet lemur, decorated with tropical forest scenes.
▶ *Court Road off A20 London-Folkestone road. EH. Mottingham station (from Charing Cross). Tel 020 8294 2548 for opening times.*

The Thames Barrier

Where the tide waits on mighty gates

The shiny structures straddle the Thames between Woolwich and Silvertown like a row of up-ended boats. Inside are the hydraulics to raise the 5-storey, 3700-tonne gates of the barrier, the capital's defence since 1982 against a surge tide – when a high wind gets behind a rising spring tide – and the devastating flood such conditions can bring.

The best way to see the 520m (567yd) wide barrier, the largest moveable flood barrier in the world, is from the river. It can also be viewed from the Thames Barrier Park on the north bank, London's first major new park for over 50 years. For a close encounter, travel to the barrier visitor centre, which lies on the south bank, preferably on a monthly test day, when the gates are raised.
▶ *Unity Way, Woolwich. Charlton station. Daily. Tel 020 8305 4188 for test dates.*

Royal Observatory

The official home of stargazers

Charles II commissioned the Greenwich observatory in 1674 to discover 'the so-much desired longitude of places for perfecting the art of navigation'. Christopher Wren designed the original building – an octagonal room for making astronomical observations, with apartments below for John Flamsteed, first Astronomer Royal. The north windows of what has long been known as Flamsteed House still look down Greenwich Park, inviting visitors to climb the hill and explore the interior. The Time and Space project is an ambitious redevelopment of the historic site and includes an education centre, new galleries and a state-of-the-art planetarium.

Exhibits in the observatory include John Harrison's sea-going chronometers, which finally enabled mariners to calculate exactly how far east or west of Greenwich a ship was. At 1pm precisely the red time ball plummets down its mast on Flamsteed House – a signal by which sailors on the Thames have been setting clocks since 1833.
▶ *Greenwich Park. Greenwich (from Charing Cross) and Cutty Sark (DLR) stations. Daily.*

National Maritime Museum

Embark on voyages of discovery

This refurbished museum lies at the heart of maritime Britain. Here the nation's nautical heritage is spread through 16 galleries and across a colossal courtyard enclosed by a soaring 2500m2 (26,900sq ft) glass roof. In the Ship of War gallery, glass cases contain minutely detailed shipwrights' models of the mighty wooden vessels on which the country's naval strength was built. The original 17th-century shop front to Lloyd's Coffee House, the meeting place for shipping brokers that grew into the large insurance business of that name, leads into the Maritime London gallery. In the **Queen's House**, designed in 1616 by Inigo Jones, portraits of admirals and Jack Tars of all ranks line the walls.
▶ *Trafalgar Road, Greenwich. Greenwich (from Charing Cross) and Cutty Sark (DLR) stations. Daily.*

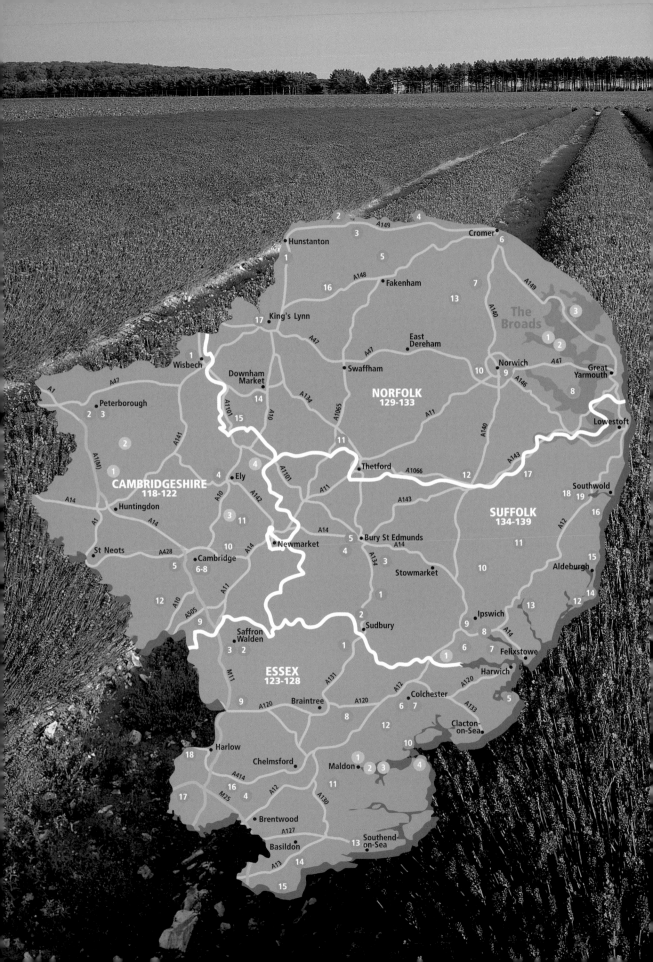

Hunstanton

Cromer
6

NORFOLK
129-133

King's Lynn
17

Wisbech

Downham
Market

East
Dereham

Swaffham

Norwich
9

Great
Yarmouth

The
Broads
3

1
2

8

Lowestoft

CAMBRIDGESHIRE
118-122

Peterborough
2 3

2

1

Ely
4

Huntingdon

Thetford

Southwold
18 19

16

Newmarket
5

Bury St Edmunds
4

SUFFOLK
134-139

11

St Neots

Cambridge
6-8

10

Stowmarket
10

Aldeburgh
15

12

5

9

1

Ipswich
9

13

12 14

8

6
7

Felixstowe

Sudbury

1

Harwich

Saffron
Walden
3 2

ESSEX
123-128

Colchester
6 7

5

9

Braintree

8

12

Clacton-
on-Sea

Harlow
18

Chelmsford

Maldon
1
2 3

4

10

17

4

11

Brentwood

13

Southend-
on-Sea

Basildon

14

15

East Anglia

Under immense skies, an ocean of woods, fields and fens flattens and stretches to low horizons. It sweeps around ageless towns, beautiful churches, haunting waterways and engineering feats before fading on lonely shingle beach, shifting sand and tide flat.

Key

1 Main entry

2 Feature entry

━━━ County boundary

━━━ Motorway

━━━ Principal A road

(See 'Finding your way', page 7)

CAMBRIDGESHIRE

1 Rose fields of Wisbech 2 Flag Fen Bronze Age Centre 3 Ceiling of the nave,

Peterborough Cathedral 4 Octagon Tower and Lantern, Ely Cathedral

5 Cambridge American Cemetery and Memorial

Rose fields of Wisbech

A floral feast for the senses

As you approach the old fenland town of
Wisbech on a summer's day, eyes and nose work
overtime to take in the brilliant colours and
overwhelming scent of the rose fields. The slight
rise on which Wisbech stands, together with the
peaty soil, make this an ideal place for the most
popular and romantic of flowers. Growers
cultivate different fields each year to give the soil
a chance to rest and rid itself of disease, but you
will soon spot the big, bright splashes of colour –
or you could simply follow your nose.
▶*Around Wisbech, especially on NE of town.*

Flag Fen Bronze Age Centre

Give gifts to the gods, or go under

Why did Bronze Age people cut down tens of
thousands of trees to construct a long causeway
and a huge building at the end of it? And why
did they throw animals and deliberately broken
swords, spears, tools and jewellery into the
adjoining mere?

An exhibition at Flag Fen visitor centre, in
Peterborough, explores these mysteries, and offers
the solution that this was an island with a great
religious centre. Here, in return for the recession
of the waters in spring, ancient gods were
placated with gifts and animal sacrifices during
winter floods. Many of the finds dredged from
the peat date from the centuries immediately
before and after 1100 BC, when climate changes
brought more severe weather. They include the
oldest known wheel in Britain – dating back to
around 1300 BC.
▶*3 miles E of city centre off A1139. Tues-Sun.*

Ceiling of the nave, Peterborough Cathedral

What the hereafter holds – in wide screen and technicolor

That common subject of medieval church
decoration, the depiction of good and evil in the
shape of angels, saints, devils and beasts, is given
uncommon vigour and colour here. Built in
1220 of oak from north Germany, this earliest
and largest expanse of painted ceiling in Britain
is a tour de force of medieval art. Use binoculars
to get close up to the saints and prelates, and
grotesque characters like the ape riding a goat –
and to get closer to the medieval mind.
▶*Peterborough city centre.*

Octagon Tower and Lantern, Ely Cathedral

Crowning glory of the fenlands

Sailing the flat fenland barley fields like a stately
ship in a black and green sea, the great Octagon
Tower of Ely Cathedral, topped by a huge
wooden lantern, is an unforgettable sight.
Nothing in Britain compares with this wonder
of medieval engineering.

The Octagon – 22m (72ft) in diameter and
weighing 400 tonnes – was created in 1322-8
by a monk, Alan of Walsingham, to replace a
collapsed Norman tower. It then took William
Hurley, Edward III's master carpenter, 14 years to
build the 200 tonne lantern.
▶*Central Ely. Off A10/A142. Daily.*

Cambridge American Cemetery and Memorial

Haunting and dignified shrine to America's war dead

In front of a tall flagpole carrying the Stars and
Stripes are drawn up rank upon curving rank of
white stone crosses – the graves of 3812 American
service personnel who died during the Second
World War while based in Britain. Stretching away
on one side of the flagpole, the 144m (472ft) long
Wall of the Missing is inscribed with the names
of 5125 others – those whose remains were never
recovered or positively identified.

The men and women who are buried and
remembered in this foreign field – a gift from
Cambridge University to the American Battle
Monuments Commission – represent every service
from the US Coastguard to the Marine Corps,
and every theatre of the war in Europe, from
North Africa to Normandy. They represent every
state too: the youth of Maine and Mississippi,
New York and Nebraska, who laid down their
lives to defeat fascism, and now rest in the shade
of tulip trees, liquidambars and American oaks.
▶*2 miles W of Cambridge off A1303, Junction 13
off M11. Daily.*

Where rivers and sea battle for land

Murder and mayhem preceded an ambitious scheme to transform the watery Fens into prime farmland

1 **Wood Walton Fen** ▶ *6 miles N of Huntingdon off B1090.*

2 **Holme Fen** ▶ *Whittlesey Mere, 6 miles S of Peterborough.*

3 **Stretham Old Engine** ▶ *4 miles S of Ely off A10. Second Sun each month, and bank hols, Apr-Sept. Tel 01353 648578*

4 **Prickwillow Drainage Engine Museum** ▶ *Main Street, Prickwillow, on B1382, 4 miles E of Ely. Fri-Tues May-Sept; Sat-Sun and bank hols Apr and Oct.*

Fenlanders tell you with pride: 'We live in a man-made landscape; there's nothing natural about it.' And the thing about Fenlanders, say their neighbours, from Lincoln south to Huntingdon, and from Peterborough east to Wisbech, is that they are *different*.

The Fens in the 17th century were a vast, swampy wetland covering 200,000ha (500,000 acres) and bedded on a mattress of thick black peat, much of it lying below sea level, prone to flooding by rivers and by sea-surges. Settlements on islets of silt held a scanty population of wildfowlers, reedcutters and fishermen. Those on the fringes of Fenland saw them as webbed-footed watermen, slow to react but dangerous once roused. Part of their enduring reputation for bloody-mindedness comes from the ferocity with which they opposed the great 17th-century drainage schemes in their homeland.

The plans hatched in the 1630s by the 4th Earl of Bedford and the Dutch engineer Cornelius Vermuyden were extraordinarily ambitious: nothing less than the drainage of the Fens for agriculture by cutting giant artificial rivers across the land. The feat was accomplished, too, in the face of local resisters, known as the 'Fen Tigers', who blew up river banks and murdered the Scots prisoners of war drafted in to work. But they could not hold back progress. Today, original Fenland still exists in a few places, such as **Wicken Fen** (see page 122) and **Wood Walton Fen** southwest of Ramsey.

Digging and draining the land

The most remarkable feature of the project is the parallel waterway of the Old and New Bedford Rivers, running 20 miles northeast from Earith in Cambridgeshire to Denver Sluice in Norfolk. The Old Bedford River was cut from 1630 to hurry the water of swollen rivers towards the sea in a flood-proof channel; the New Bedford River was dug 20 years later to funnel sudden sea surges coming the other way into the reservoir of low ground between the two artificial rivers. Stand on the bridges at Sutton Gault, Mepal or Welney to see the rivers arrowing away in gleaming geometrical directness.

Drainage of the Fens caused the sodden peat to dry and shrink, a process most vividly demonstrated at **Holme Fen**. As the level of the land started to fall below the newly constructed rivers, the water could no longer be channelled straight from the fields into the rivers, but had to be lifted into them. Windpumps did the job at first, but soon the fields lay so far below the rivers that more potent pumps had to be used. One of these, a 19th-century steam-powered pump, is preserved at **Stretham** near Ely. At **Prickwillow** to the northeast there is an impressive collection of diesel engines.

Almost all the land in the Fens is high-quality arable farmland these days. Some dismiss it as flat and boring, but it is easy to fall under the spell of a landscape where rows of black plough furrows, green vegetable shoots, gold cereals or brilliantly coloured flowers converge on the horizon like an object lesson in perspective, under vast cloud-splashed skies.

CAMBRIDGESHIRE

6 King's College Chapel 7 Scott Polar Research Institute 8 Fitzwilliam Museum

9 Imperial War Museum, Duxford 10 Anglesey Abbey

King's College Chapel

Surging and arching heavenwards – a firework display in masonry

The glory of King's College Chapel is its delicate fan-vaulted ceiling, which runs the 88m (289ft) length of the chapel. Supported by slender, soaring piers and ribs, it conveys a sense of weightlessness. There is also a Baroque organ decorated with trumpet-tooting angels. It accompanies the chapel's famous choir, which can be heard every day at evensong, Mondays excepted, much as the chapel's founder, Henry VI intended. The vivid purple, reds and blue Tudor stained glass, and a Rubens altarpiece of the Adoration of the Magi, are among the chapel's other treasures.

▶ *King's Parade, Cambridge. Tel 01223 331212 for opening times.*

Scott Polar Research Institute

Meet the heroes of polar exploration

Dramatic photographs at the Institute, founded in 1920, capture the loneliness and desperation of early polar expeditions. None tells more of heroism than the sail-rigged ship of Ernest Shackleton locked in a prison of ice off the Antarctic coast in 1915 – from here the explorer sailed and trekked more than 1000 miles to raise help for his crew.

The Institute is the world's most important polar research body, but it is the human details here that fascinate – the displays of letters, diaries and photographs from Captain Scott's doomed 1911-12 expedition, for instance, as he raced the Norwegian, Roald Amundsen, to the South Pole; and the flag that the victorious Amundsen planted at the Pole in 1911.

▶ *Lensfield Road, Cambridge. Tues-Sat pm.*

Fitzwilliam Museum

Cambridge's temple for lovers of art

A wandering policy is best at the Fitzwilliam, letting its huge number of treasures surprise and delight. Exquisite Ming vases, Egyptian mummies and paintings such as Flemish village celebrations by Pieter Bruegel the Younger all add to one of Europe's finest small museums.

The Fitzwilliam grew out of the £100,000 and the books and paintings bequeathed in 1816 by the 7th Viscount Fitzwilliam of Merrion.

Today, free lectures and concerts are regular attractions, and the museum café is a favourite Cambridge meeting place.

▶ *Trumpington Street, Cambridge. Tues-Sun and bank hol Mon.*

Imperial War Museum, Duxford

Europe's largest collection of military and civilian aircraft

All the classic aeroplanes of an enthusiast's dreams are here in the 180-aircraft collection of the Imperial War Museum, Duxford. Wander at your will from Spitfire to Lancaster, from First World War stringbags such as the Bristol Fighter to big delta-winged Vulcan bombers of the Cold War era, from Mustang fighters of the Second World War to a sinister B-52 bomber that pounded the jungles of Vietnam.

The cream of the American collection is displayed in one of Britain's boldest modern buildings, a glass-walled hangar 18m (60ft) tall, designed by Norman Foster. It has been dedicated as a memorial to the 30,000 American airmen who died while flying wartime missions from Britain – many from Duxford airfield.

▶ *Duxford, 8 miles S of Cambridge on A505, 1 mile W of M11 (Junction 10). Daily.*

Anglesey Abbey

One man's fascinating fancies

The spirit of a single man permeates Anglesey Abbey, a mellow-stoned Tudor mansion that incorporates the chapter house and monks' parlour of a 12th-century priory. It was bought by Huttleston Broughton, later Lord Fairhaven, in 1926 to house his spectacular collection of furniture, porcelain, clocks and paintings, including landscapes and studies by Thomas Gainsborough, John Constable and Claude Lorrain.

The abbey's 45ha (100 acre) Georgian-style gardens were laid out by Lord Fairhaven on reclaimed fenland in the 1930s. There are snowdrops along the winter walks, thousands of hyacinths to herald the spring, herbaceous borders bright with dahlias in summer, and a wonderful autumnal display in the arboretum.

▶ *Lode, on B1102, 6 miles NE of Cambridge. NT. House, Wed-Sun mid Mar-Oct. Garden, Wed-Sun all year.*

EUROPE'S LARGEST COLLECTION OF MILITARY AND CIVILIAN AIRCRAFT
IMPERIAL WAR MUSEUM, DUXFORD

CAMBRIDGESHIRE

11 Wicken Fen 12 Wimpole Home Farm

Wicken Fen

A vanished fen landscape

Where can you find more than 200 bird species, 1400 kinds of beetle, 1000 categories of moth, and 1700 types of fly? Wicken Fen is the place. It was the National Trust's first nature reserve, set up in 1899 when it looked as if drainage for agriculture would abolish East Anglia's primal wetland.

As you approach Wicken Fen, the 245ha (605 acre) reserve appears as a dark-coloured island of undisciplined tree foliage in a neat sea of chemical-green grain prairie. Strolling the fen's grassy walkways, you soon see that the island is an oasis. Willows and birches are full of bunting song, lagoons and streams ring with coot and waterhen cries. Ponds wrinkle with ripples from water spiders and beetles. There are rare birds such as marsh harrier and water rail, and wigeon in winter by the skyful. Water plants and orchids, wet woods and reedswamps are nurtured and protected within a patchwork of meadows, ditches, riverbanks and woods. To witness the hum and buzz of insect and bird activity at Wicken Fen, perhaps from Britain's oldest hide, is to experience something long vanished from the surrounding landscape.

▶ *Signposted in Wicken village on A1123. NT. Reserve daily. Visitor Centre daily Apr-Oct; Tues-Sun Nov-Mar.*

Wimpole Home Farm

Byres and barns in keeping with the elegance of their grand house

Farm buildings are not normally works of grand design, but when Philip Yorke, 3rd Earl of Hardwicke, engaged his friend Sir John Soane to improve Wimpole Hall, the family mansion, he also commissioned the eminent architect to draw up a model home farm for the estate. The result, completed in 1794, is a harmonious collection of soberly stylish buildings, with the vast Great Barn as its high point. The imposing stable block with its campanile-style clock over a grand entrance arch was built in mid-Victorian times. Today the rare livestock breeds, including some sturdy Suffolk Punch draught horses, and the collection of farm machinery housed in these buildings give a fascinating glimpse of farming over the past 200 years.

A visit to Wimpole Hall – the biggest 18th-century house in the county – is a must, too, if only to see Soane's bath house and the Yellow Drawing Room that he created out of several existing rooms on two floors. Niches and recesses frame a huge floor area under a vaulted ceiling, and the whole space is suffused with the muted light falling through an arcaded, glazed dome.

▶ *10 miles SW of Cambridge off A603. NT. Farm Sat-Wed mid Mar-Oct (also Thur Jul-Aug); Sat-Sun Nov-Mar. Hall times vary from farm. Tel 01223 206000.*

BESPOKE BRICKS IN A FANTASY SETTING STRAIGHT OUT OF TOLKIEN
BULMER BRICKWORKS

ESSEX

1 Bulmer Brickworks **2** Sun Inn and Turf

Maze, Saffron Walden

Bulmer Brickworks

Bespoke bricks in a fantasy setting straight out of Tolkien

You would not be surprised to see hobbits at work around the cylindrical kiln at Bulmer Brickworks, with its mossy cone-shaped roof puffing out smoke among the trees like a house in an enchanted forest. The brickworks is a curious survival from an era before mass-production. It produces small numbers of specialised items for particular jobs, especially bricks and tiles of odd shape needed for the restoration and repair of historic buildings such as Hampton Court Palace and Windsor Castle. The seams of clay from which the Bulmer bricks are made have been in almost constant use since Tudor times.

▶ *Signed off minor road, 1 mile SW of Bulmer Tye, between Castle Hedingham and Sudbury. Visits by appointment, Tel 01787 269232.*

Sun Inn and Turf Maze, Saffron Walden

Artistry in plaster and a pathway to forgiveness

What sets the 14th-century Sun Inn, a former coaching inn, apart from all other medieval buildings at Saffron Walden are the outstanding craftsmanship and inventiveness of its late 17th-century pargetting – the East Anglian art of moulding relief motifs and figures in plaster. Among the flowers, fruit and foliage, you will spot a dancing crane and a single stockinged leg. The liveliest scene portrays local hero Tom Hickathrift, armed with a wheel for a shield, vigorously battering the Wisbech Giant.

Nearby on the common is the 800-year-old Turf Maze, an intricate whorl of narrow brick-paved pathways winding for well over a mile towards a central grassy mound. Some say that the monks of Walden Abbey constructed it as a penitential labyrinth along whose tangled ways they would shuffle on their knees for hours, enduring bruises, cuts and cramps for the good of their souls.

▶ *Sun Inn, Church Street. Maze, The Common, off East Street (B184), E of town centre.*

EAST ANGLIA

ESSEX

Audley End House
Green men and gyrfalcons

Among the delights of this splendid Jacobean house, completed in 1614 for James I's Treasurer, are two fascinating eccentricities – Green Men and stuffed birds.

Down the centuries, the members of the Howard, Griffin and Neville families who embellished Audley End were all admirers of the Green Man, an ancient pagan presence often found in church architecture with foliage sprouting from his mouth or wrapped around his face. He is everywhere at Audley End – carved in human and lion form on the porch, on the Jacobean wooden screen and 1820s panelling in the Great Hall, and as a sinister, leering face in the ornate pillar capitals and plaster friezes added to the Saloon, the Drawing Room and the Library by the 3rd Lord Braybrooke in the early 19th century.

The dozens of cases of stuffed birds and animals in the Lower Gallery were collected by the 4th and 5th Lord Braybrookes in Victorian times. Bird of paradise, golden eagle and gyrfalcon, Tengmalm's owl and osprey jostle with fox, otter, badger and wild cat – and, in a case on his own, a little pet terrier confronting a rat.
▶ *Signed off B1383, 2 miles SE of Saffron Walden (M11 Junction 9). EH. Wed-Sun, and bank hols, Apr-Sept; 'Behind the Scenes' tours Sat-Sun Mar and Oct.*

Kelvedon Hatch Secret Nuclear Bunker

Cold War paranoia

Step into this unassuming bungalow and you will soon be 80ft underground, deep inside a Cold War nuclear bunker, built in 1952. Behind blast-proof doors, 600 people could hope to live through a nuclear war, with supplies lasting for three months. Explore the warren of rooms that would ensure man's survival in a new world.
▶ *Signed off A128 from Chipping Ongar to Brentwood. Mar-Oct daily, Nov-Feb Thur-Sun.*

Walton Backwaters
Secret water where the Swallows and Amazons sailed

October sees tens of thousands of wildfowl converge to overwinter on the wonderfully lonely Walton Backwaters. Walking the sea wall you may spot golden plover, lapwing, curlew, brent geese, tern, godwit and short-eared owl.

The Backwaters – sometimes known as Hamford Water – are a tidal inland sea dotted with dozens of marshy islets, which lie tucked in behind the protective arm of The Naze on the north Essex coast. The children's writer Arthur Ransome loved to sail the Backwaters. He set *Secret Water*, one of his 'Swallows and Amazons' novels, on and around the biggest island, Horsey Island.
▶ *Behind The Naze foreland, NW of Walton-on-the-Naze.*

Colchester Castle
Slaughter in the Roman vaults

Colchester is the oldest recorded town in Britain – a Roman colony was established there in AD 44. The castle museum draws on Roman artefacts unearthed locally, including glassware, toys, jewellery, religious objects, statues and household tools. Try weighing up the replica of a Roman centurion's armour complete with chain mail to get a sense of how heavy and cumbersome it must have been to march and fight in.

The museum is in the castle's Norman keep, Europe's largest. It was built early in the Norman occupation, over the 2000-year-old vaults of the Temple of Claudius. The vaults still carry scorch marks from AD 61, when Queen Boudicca and the Iceni sacked Colchester, massacring its Roman inhabitants.
▶ *Castle Park, Colchester. Daily.*

Jumbo Water Tower

Colchester's elephantine folly

You can't miss it. This grand and grotesque Victorian water tower folly at the crest of a ridge looms 40m (131ft) above Colchester in florid red brick. When construction of the tower began in 1882, newspapers were full of the controversial sale of Jumbo the London Zoo elephant to Barnum & Bailey's circus in New York. A local rector, whose house stood a matter of feet from the tower, was moved to declare, 'Never mind, now I have a Jumbo in my own back garden.'
▶ *Balkerne Passage, off North Hill, Colchester.*

Barley, Wheat and Grange Barns

Mighty cathedrals of the harvest, once piled high with monastic grain

Three of the oldest barns in Europe are neighbours in west Essex – the twin **Barley** and **Wheat Barns** built in the 13th century by the Knights Templar at Cressing Temple, and the nearby **Grange Barn** built by Cistercian monks 100 years before at Coggeshall. Today, they stand bowed under immense tiled roofs, their forests of iron-hard oak timbers still raised high, the vast, cool interiors echoing with the solemn and peaceful air of cathedrals.

All three barns are more than 30m (100ft) long, 12m (40ft) wide and 11m (36ft) high. From a raised platform at the centre of the Wheat Barn you can marvel at the skills of the medieval carpenters.
▶ *Barley and Wheat Barns, Cressing Temple, 3 miles SE of Braintree, on B1018; Sun-Fri Mar-Oct; grounds & gardens Mon-Fri Nov-Feb. Grange Barn, Coggeshall, off A120, Colchester-Braintree road; NT; Tues, Thur, Sun and bank hol Mon, Apr-Sept.*

Stansted Airport

Uplifting architecture of the skies

Norman Foster succeeded in raising the spirits of even the most nervous of fliers with his bold, low-level design for Stansted Airport's terminal, opened in 1991. With all services banished below ground, passengers have only one level to negotiate. Light is a defining feature – it floods into the concourse from skylights and through glazed walls, while at night interior illumination bounces off the domed roof shells.
▶ *Passenger terminal, Stansted Airport, M11 (Junctions 8 and 8A).*

Old Hall Marshes

A haven for birdlovers in a remote and marshy coastal peninsula

Smugglers used to take advantage of the isolation and watery byways of this part of the Essex coast. Now you can combine the pleasures of walking in lonely country with high-quality birdwatching. In summer 10 per cent of the tiny UK breeding population of pochard come here to nest. You can spot bearded tits in the reed beds, and in winter nearly 5000 dark-bellied brent geese overwinter from their Siberian homelands.
▶ *Walk from Tollesbury on B1023 (off A12 Colchester-Chelmsford road), or drive onto reserve (permit in advance from Warden at 1 Old Hall Lane, Tolleshunt D'Arcy, Maldon, Essex CM9 8TP). RSPB.*

Thrift Wood

Explore woodland kept and cared for in its ancient state

Little remains of the wildwood that once covered medieval Essex. Thrift Wood is a rare survivor, its trees still coppiced, the trunks cut low to promote the growth of pole-like branches. Walking the peaceful pathways – at their best in May – you get an idea of the harmonious yet intense mix of butterflies, birds, flowers and trees that characterised such woods in the Middle Ages. In fact the whole landscape hereabouts is a medieval one, with a network of ancient green lanes between thick hedges dating from Norman times.
▶ *Bicknacre, on B1418 between Danbury and South Woodham Ferrers.*

Layer Marney Tower

Renaissance glories of the world's tallest Tudor gatehouse

Henry, 1st Lord Marney, built himself this extraordinary red-brick house early in the reign of Henry VIII, and he did not do it by halves. The twin-towered central gatehouse, rising 24m (79ft) from the east Essex flatlands, draws the eye with its eight storeys of windows. Renaissance-inspired decoration in pale terracotta – angels in the window-frames, heraldic dolphins on the parapet – contrasts with the tower's fortress-like aspect. The Reformation, in full flood less than 20 years after the tower was built, bred abhorrence of anything that smacked of Rome, and the new-fangled Italianate style fell completely out of use. Climb the spiral stair of the gatehouse to its roof for a fine view.
▶ *Signed off B1022 in Tiptree. Sun-Thur pm Apr-Sept.*

ESSEX

Southend Pier

Roll up, roll up, ladies and gentlemen, for the longest pleasure pier in the entire world

The Pier is a breathtaking spectacle at first sight, running well over a mile out into the Thames estuary on its thousands of spindly centipede legs. It was completed in 1889 at the height of the Victorian seaside boom, and stands today as a survivor of several disastrous fires and collisions with ships.

In spite of enormous changes in holiday habits, Southend Pier remains a magnet. Little red-and-white trains rattle the holidaymakers out to the pierhead where, beyond the café, the lifeboat station can be visited. The procession of giant ships near at hand, negotiating the estuary, tells you why the lifeboat is there.

▶ *Southend seafront. Visitor Centre Tel 01702 215620.*

Motorboat Museum

A collection of fine motor vessels

Some of the fastest and most revolutionary motorboats seen in the 20th century were designed and built in Britain, and this museum tells you all about them. Over 31 exhibits, dating from 1823 to the present day, include record-breakers and rare boats as well as full-size replica models. The fascinating stories of the boats and their designers, racers and owners bring the exhibits to life.

▶ *1 mile S of Basildon off A13. Thur-Mon.*

SOUTHEND PIER

Tilbury Fort

Protecting London with the ultimate in defence design

It comes as a shock to find this perfect late 17th-century fort with its arrowhead bastions marooned on the Essex shore of the River Thames between dockland cranes, a giant power station and sprawling oil refineries. Henry VIII had the first fort built here to guard the Thames approaches to London from possible attacks by the French; it was adapted during the reign of Charles II to deal with the threat of raids up the Thames by daring Dutch warships. Heavy guns were mounted on the river bank, with the low-lying ramparts designed to soak up artillery bombardment and angled to offer covering fire to all sides of the fort in a landward attack.

Standing out from the austere fortifications is the 17th-century Water Gate with its fine martial array of Ionic and Corinthian columns, and a frieze of chariots, spears, classical armour and mighty wheeled cannon. Some well-aimed cannon balls from the river would probably have brought the whole elaborate assembly tumbling. Luckily the fort never saw a shot fired in anger.
▶ *Signed off A1089 to Tilbury (A13). EH. Daily Apr-Oct; Thur-Mon Nov-Mar.*

Greensted log church

The world's oldest wooden church

The squat nave of St Andrew's Church at Greensted is made of great oak logs split in half, dark with age and weathering. They probably date back to very early Norman times, making St Andrew's the oldest wooden church in the world.

It is said that the body of St Edmund (martyred in AD 870 by the Danes) rested here in an earlier church on the journey to its final burial place at Bury St Edmunds in Suffolk in 1013. On the church wall hangs a 15th-century painting of the martyrdom, with the smiling saint stuck full of arrows while scowling Danish archers prepare to finish him off.
▶ *1 mile W of Chipping Ongar off A414 (M11 Junction 7).*

Epping Forest

A threatened forest, saved for posterity

As a 'green lung' for northeast London, Epping Forest does an incredibly efficient job. Among its 2430ha (6000 acres) of twisted and distorted old beeches and hornbeams, it absorbs and hides thousands of visitors. Complete solitude is never more than a step or two off the main paths.

In the 17th century the forest – then a royal hunting ground – was ten times its present size. Travellers hurried through, fearing the footpads who lurked among the trees; the most notorious was highwayman Dick Turpin, the Whitechapel butcher's apprentice turned mugger, who had a hideout in the 1730s in Loughton Camp, an Iron Age fort deep in the forest.

By mid-Victorian times smallholders, squatters, poachers, timber merchants and commoners had all encroached on the forest, but the Epping Forest Act of 1878 allowed the City of London Corporation to take control and weed out all the exploiters. That explains the weird distortion of so many of the trees – after centuries of being pollarded into stubs by commoners who wanted open, grassy ground for grazing, the trees have been allowed to shoot their gnarled old boughs in all directions, like prisoners stretching their limbs after the manacles have been removed.
▶ *M25 (Junction 26) or M11 (Junction 5), between Epping and Chingford.*

Hunsdon Mead

The way hay meadows used to be

A fabulous carpet of wild flowers colours the grass of Hunsdon Mead in spring and summer. Traditional management of these hay meadows yields primroses, marsh marigold, yellow rattle, green-winged orchid, quaking grass and other species that have long since vanished from most meadows. Winter floods bring silt to enrich the soil, and attract crowds of wading birds. Clouds of butterflies appear in summer.

The Abbey family have farmed the meadows between the River Stort and the Stort canal since the 1920s. They continue to do as they have always done – allowing the grass to grow and wild flowers to set seed between March and July, cutting hay until mid August, and then putting stock on to graze until the end of the following February. No chemicals; everything is done nature's way.
▶ *Path from Roydon rail station; Roydon on B181, signed from A414, 3 miles W of Harlow.*

EAST ANGLIA

Echoes of the past on a lonely estuary

Birds, boats and the ghosts of ancient struggles glide across the water where the River Blackwater reaches the sea

1 **Maldon** ▶ *E of Chelmsford, on A414.*

2 **Northey Island** ▶ *S of Maldon, off minor road towards Mundon, or walk along sea wall from The Hythe, Maldon. Access to island by permit from Warden, Northey Cottage, Northey Island, Maldon CM9 6PP, Tel 01621 853142. NT.*

3 **Osea Island** ▶ *Privately owned. Island best viewed from coastal path 2 miles E of Maldon, off B1026.*

4 **St Peter-on-the-Wall** ▶ *Signed from Bradwell-on-Sea, off B1021, 8 miles N of Burnham-on-Crouch.*

Of all the muddy estuaries that cut the Essex coast into tatters, the Blackwater Estuary with its tiny causeway islands and bird-crowded creeks is the most haunting. There is something moodily compelling about the Blackwater, whether it is in the shimmering blue heat-haze of summer when the marshes smell as rich as fruit cake, or on a freezing winter's afternoon with brent geese crowding the sky in their thousands and gabbling madly. In the late 19th century Squire Thomas Kemble of Runwell Hall near Basildon, a great sportsman, recorded: 'The sky darkened with wild-geese covering a space of half-a-mile by a quarter-of-a-mile as thick as manure spread upon the ground, and making a noise I could only compare with fifty packs of hounds in full cry.' These days around 50,000 brents overwinter here, a staggering sight and sound at dawn and dusk flighting times.

The little old port of **Maldon** sits 12 miles upriver of the estuary mouth. Red-sailed barges of ancient design, rescued from dereliction and lovingly restored, moor at The Hythe, a curving river quay. Here 'Knot Man', a local character, will demonstrate clove hitches, running nooses, reef knots and other rope-related skills to the summer crowds that gather. East of the town, straggling sea-wall footpaths on both north and south banks accompany the Blackwater to the sea.

Battling the Vikings and the bottle

A couple of miles downstream of Maldon lies the fragmented **Northey Island**, half flood and half firm land. It is a peaceful place, reached from the south bank by a short tidal causeway – the catalyst for fearful bloodshed in AD 991, when local Saxon leader Earl Bryhtnoth allowed a party of marauding Danes to cross to the mainland after he had had them penned up safely on the island. The Sea Wolves slaughtered the Saxons.

Just downriver is **Osea Island** with its long causeway zigzagging over the mud. The island is private, but you can view it from the coast path. It was once owned by the brewery heir Frederick Charrington, who in the early 20th century experienced a Pauline conversion from his family business when he saw a woman knocked into the gutter by her drunken husband outside a Charrington pub. He bought Osea and turned it into a drying-out place for well-heeled drunks and drug addicts. Local stories tell of high jinks as the inmates sought to outwit their attendants and retrieve bottles of booze hidden in rabbit burrows and tied to buoys in the Blackwater. Osea was also a motor torpedo boat base during the First World War. Up to 2000 men were billeted on the island, necessitating the construction of enormous underground sewage tanks, which still exist.

Sources of power and peace

The south shore of the Blackwater forms the upper edge of the blunt-nosed Dengie peninsula, one of the remotest places in southern Britain. Here, the hulking block of Bradwell nuclear power station, built in the 1960s, and the isolated 1350-year-old Saxon chapel of **St Peter-on-the-Wall** stand just a couple of miles apart, adding to the strange, other-worldly feeling of the Blackwater.

NORFOLK

1 Norfolk Lavender **2** Scolt Head Island **3** Nelson's birthplace **4** Blakeney Point

Norfolk Lavender

A brilliant blaze of purple and a heady blast of perfume

For an exhilarating assault on your eyes and nose, go to Norfolk Lavender on a hot day in July before the hundred acres of flowers are harvested. With an immense carpet of purplish blue stretched out under a clear sky and the air laden with scent, you can imagine yourself in the plant's Mediterranean homeland. Lavender thrives at Heacham thanks to it being one of the driest spots in Britain and having ideal soil conditions. You can see lavender oil being distilled, and buy deliciously smelly soaps and perfumes.

▶ *Caley Mill, Heacham, 2 miles S of Hunstanton on A149. Daily.*

Scolt Head Island

Leave humankind behind and take a boat ride to bird land

The short boat ride from Burnham Overy Staithe to Scolt Head Island, which operates from April to September, transports you to a different world. Leaving creeks and mud flats behind, the boat eventually arrives at a bleak hook of dune, shingle and salt marsh 3½ miles long. The silence is overwhelming, until thousands of gulls, waders and terns break into raucous protest.

The island has sand dunes higher than houses, and is home to one of Britain's largest tern colonies. All three species of this pretty sea bird, with a distinctive forked tail, breed here: the common tern, with scarlet legs and matching, black-tipped beak; the black-crested sandwich tern, with a yellow-tipped black dagger of a beak; and the rarer little tern, which has a bill and legs of all-over yellow.

▶ *A149 Hunstanton to Wells-next-the-Sea road. NT. Access restricted at nesting time in spring and early summer.*

Nelson's birthplace

Try a grog ration with a difference and toast the hero of Trafalgar

If you fancy a glass of Nelson's Blood, pop into the Lord Nelson pub in Burnham Thorpe. Here you can sit in the old-fashioned snug bar among pictures of the Little Admiral, drinking this cockle-warming concoction based on high-octane navy rum. Horatio Nelson, England's greatest naval hero, was born in 1758 in the village rectory (since demolished), where his father was the minister, and spent his boyhood here before entering the Royal Navy as an undersized 12-year-old.

All Saints' Church, across the road from the pub, contains a lectern and rood cross made of timbers taken from HMS *Victory*, and there is an exhibition about the great man.

▶ *1 mile SE of Burnham Market (B1355, off A149 between Hunstanton and Wells-next-the-Sea).*

Blakeney Point

Crunch over shingle to a lonely landfall for migrating birds

The 3 mile shingle spit of Blakeney Point has been steadily growing westwards for the past thousand years – the result of offshore currents dragging and dumping millions of tonnes of pebbles, like some huge underwater conveyor belt. Already its long finger has cut off the harbours of Cley next the Sea, Blakeney and Morston; Stiffkey will be next, around 200 years from now if the spit keeps growing at its current rate.

Ferries run out from Morston and Blakeney, but the hour's walk from Cley beach is the most dramatic way to reach the point. As you crunch along the narrow pebble bar, watch the scene become ever wilder and more remote. The point broadens at its tip (on the map, it looks like a clawed foot at the end of a thin leg – the 'claws' being pebble bars stretching landward). This is nature's territory, a favourite hauling-out place for common seals, alive with geese and ducks in winter, and a home to breeding terns and ringed plovers in spring and summer. Most importantly, though, Blakeney Point is the first and the last place in Britain where tens of thousands of migrating birds rest after and before their flight over the North Sea in spring and autumn.

▶ *Off A149 between Wells-next-the-Sea and Sheringham. NT. Daily all year.*

EAST ANGLIA

NORFOLK

Little Walsingham

An exotic vision in an ancient place of pilgrimage

A religious vision first put Little Walsingham on the map as a place of pilgrimage nearly a thousand years ago. These days, it is the sight of the old railway station that gives visitors a jolt. There, on its roof, is a small onion dome, put up soon after Father David, a monk in the Russian Orthodox Church, arrived in 1967 and converted the building into a chapel to his faith – and a holy place open to everyone.

In Houghton St Giles, a mile to the south, you will find the 14th-century Slipper Chapel where, tradition says, pilgrims left their shoes before walking barefoot to the shrine of Our Lady of Walsingham.
▶ *Off B1105 4 miles S of Wells-next-the-Sea and A149.*

Cromer Pier

Roll up, roll up, come and see the summer show that never closes

Fancy taking in a traditional 'Seaside Special' end-of-the-pier show, complete with high-kicking chorus girls and an old-fashioned singalong? Keen to see whether those faded 60s crooners and bands a little past their sell-by date can still cut the mustard? Then the summertime shows in the old theatre at the end of Cromer Pier will be just up your street. The town itself, set behind a beautiful beach on the north Norfolk coast, is the very model of the safe and sandy British seaside resort. The pier opened in 1901 and is one of very few maintaining the 'Good Old Days' tradition of bright and cheerful live entertainment.
▶ *The Promenade, Cromer. Tel 01263 512495 for details of shows.*

Blickling Hall

Anne Boleyn's ghost searches for happier times at her former home

If you visit Blickling Hall on May 19, the anniversary of Anne Boleyn's execution in 1536, you might glimpse the unlucky second wife of Henry VIII. With her severed head in her lap, she is said to ride up the drive in a coach driven by a headless coachman and pulled by headless horses.

The Hall was built in 1616-28 on the site of Anne Boleyn's childhood home. Huge yew hedges frame the view of the symmetrical, red brick Jacobean mansion from the drive. It is homely looking in spite of its size, and surrounded by vivid flower gardens. A dense and intricate pattern of plasterwork covers the ceiling of the 39m (127ft) Long Gallery. Allegorical figures showing human attributes from wisdom to courage can be discerned there, as can symbols of the five senses. Original 18th-century wallpaper still hangs in the Chinese bedroom.
▶ *2 miles NW of Aylsham on B1354. NT. Wed-Sun mid Mar-Oct; Mon Aug.*

Berney Arms

Climb a towering mill and enjoy the peaceful countryside at its local inn

The black, imposing form of the windmill at Berney Arms stands 21m (70ft) high above the flat marshland of the River Yare. It was built as a cement mill in the 19th century, but mostly worked as a wind pump draining the marshes. The working mechanism can be explored through the mill's seven storeys, before you walk to the nearby Berney Arms pub for refreshment. Perched on the riverbank in a secluded spot, the marsh inn is a favourite haunt of boaters, birdwatchers and ramblers. The mill and pub can be reached by footpath from Reedham.
▶ *3½ miles NE of Reedham. Windmill (EH) Tel 01493 857900.*

Despenser Reredos

Miraculous survival of Norwich Cathedral's medieval altarpiece

Desperate measures were required during the Puritan purges of the 17th century. To preserve the wonderful reredos, or altarpiece, given to the cathedral by Bishop Despenser in 1387, it was turned painted side down and used as a table. It was not discovered until 1847, and was returned to St Luke's Chapel at the east end of the cathedral in 1957.

Painted in the 1380s, it is one of the finest examples of medieval church art in Britain. Red and gold blaze dramatically from the five panels depicting Christ's crucifixion and resurrection. Its skilful art conveys the pain and humiliation of Christ on the way to Golgotha, and his triumph as brute-faced guards cower when he emerges from the tomb.
▶ *Norwich city centre. Daily.*

Sainsbury Centre for Visual Arts

Architect's artful design to house a modern collection

Set in a green location beside the River Yare, this gallery-cum-museum was a revolutionary achievement when built in 1978, and still impresses today. Norman Foster designed it for the art collection of Sir Robert and Lady Sainsbury. As the mood of the collection is modern rather than classical, he incorporated the metallic ribs of its skeleton as part of the visual effect – a bold design that presents the building as a work of art.

The eclectic collection within lives up to the promise of its showcase exterior. Exhibits by sculptors as celebrated as Henry Moore and as obscure as African tribal artists stand beside Egyptian artefacts, carvings from South American civilisations, and paintings by Picasso and Modigliani.

▶ *At University of East Anglia, 2 miles W of Norwich, signed off B1108 in Earlham. Tues-Sun all year.*

Grime's Graves

Climb down the time ladder to a Stone Age mine worked for flint 4000 years ago

Thirty feet below the surface, your feet meet solid ground, and a rough-hewn arch leading to a gloomy gallery resolves in the half-light. This is the bottom of one of more than 300 shafts sunk deep into the heathland of Thetford Forest at Grime's Graves.

Our Dark Age forefathers gave the place its name, taking it for a vast and frightening burial ground dug by Grim, a giant pagan god. Today's exhibition centre strips away superstition, revealing the yawning holes for what they really are: entrances to a maze of flint mines, excavated in the chalk ground around 3500-4000 years ago.

Once underground, however, cold archaeological fact gives way to a sense of awe – and a feeling of kinship with those distant miners who worked the seams of grey nodules: source of axeheads, arrowheads, and other weapons and cutting tools in the days before iron. Down here, you can feel the knap marks created when they chipped out the flints, as fresh as if they were made yesterday.

▶ *7 miles NW of Thetford off A134. EH. Daily Apr-Sept; Thur-Mon Mar and Oct.*

Bressingham Steam Museum and Gardens

Sit back and enjoy the ride through gardens of dramatic colour

A vintage miniature steam locomotive carries visitors around the vibrantly coloured gardens of Bressingham Hall. The horticulturalist Alan Bloom combined his two passions at the hall in the 1950s and used steam power to show the garden flowerbeds, planted in superb mixes of colour and texture, to their best advantage. A few minutes' away is Foggy Bottom, the Blooms' peaceful private garden, glowing with the softer shades of conifers and heathers.

The museum has an extensive collection of restored locomotives, coaches and working stretches of track. You can fulfil your fantasies here by learning to drive a steam locomotive.

▶ *Bressingham, 2 miles W of Diss on A1066. Museum and gardens daily Apr-Oct including bank hols. Tel 01379 686900.*

NORFOLK

St Peter and St Paul, Salle
A structure borne on the wings of angels

Salle has a heavenly church, fit to grace a grand cathedral city. Instead it watches over a handful of cottages in rural Norfolk. Here you can see early 15th-century stonework at its best – towering, imposing and flooded with light. Wonderful carvings are all around: from the feathered angels swinging censers and fierce club-wielding figures (known as woodwoses) that guard the doorways, to the Seven Sacraments circling the font. The chancel roof, supported by hosts of wooden angels, is adorned by gloriously carved bosses – take your binoculars.
▶ *Signed from B1145 between Reepham and Cawston.*

Denver Sluice
Control centre in a balancing act between land and water

Stand at Denver Sluice and look out over the maze of converging waterways: the Relief Channel and the Cut-Off Channel, the Great Ouse and Popham's Eau, the River Delph and the River Wissey, the Old Bedford River and the Hundred Foot Drain. Most are man made; all are eternally busy. Some hurry floodwater from the Fens to the sea; others divert incoming seawater into safe channels, or hive off drinking water. It is all water, water hereabouts, but water under control – a process begun by the Dutchman Cornelius Vermuyden, who built the first sluice in 1651.
▶ *2 miles SW of Denver, signed off A10 1 mile S of Downham Market.*

Welney Wildfowl Reserve
Winged visitors turn the sky dark before a mass-splashdown

Some places are best in winter – the Wildfowl and Wetlands Trust's reserve at Welney is one. With the wetter months, water spills into the long strip of the Washes between the Old and New Bedford rivers, creating a vast overflow reservoir – and a paradise for water birds. From the observatory you can watch thousands of ducks, including pintail, pochard, shoveler, teal and wigeon, squabbling in the shallows, spot great crested grebes and see formations of pink-footed geese. But the grand feathery finale comes at dusk; then, the sky darkens as flocks of Bewick's swans, winter migrants from the Arctic, arrive at feeding time. Honking and swooping, they land in curtains of spray on a floodlit pool.
▶ *1 mile NE of Welney suspension bridge on A1101 (5 miles NW of Littleport on A10). Daily.*

Houghton Hall
A space of measured grandeur

The first-floor State Rooms in the Palladian mansion of Houghton Hall (1731) may be its most opulent spaces, but for sheer drama the Stone Hall wins every time. This fantastic cube measures 12m (40ft) across and 12m (40ft) high. An elaborate chimneypiece by the sculptor John Rysbrack leads the eye up to a ceiling painted with cherubs.

Heavy horses, kept in a grand stable block, complement the architectural grandeur, while Shetland ponies and a 20,000-strong army of model soldiers are bound to please children.
▶ *1 mile N of Harpley on A148 King's Lynn-Fakenham road. Wed-Thur, Sun and bank hol Mon Easter-Sept.*

King's Lynn
Of whalers and merchantmen

The best way to approach this ancient port, once a lynchpin of the wool trade, later of whaling, is by water. Seen from the little foot ferry that crosses the Great Ouse from West Lynn, church towers, domes and warehouses make a photogenic huddle on the far bank in a view little changed since the days of sail.

Once ashore, too, it is on the quaysides and along cobbled streets near the river that the town's historic character really shines. Here, warehouses, once depots of the Hanseatic League – the commercial powerhouse of medieval Europe – stand close to the cupola-crowned Custom House of 1683 and the great Guildhall of the Holy Trinity (1421) in chequered flint.
▶ *A17 from W, A10 from S (Ely), A47 from E (Norwich).*

Where rivers twist beneath wide skies

Birds, butterflies and swaying reeds melt into the solitude and calm of the Norfolk Broads' haunting beauty

1 **St Helen's Church, Ranworth** ▶ *1½ miles N of South Walsham, on B1140. Daily all year.*

2 **Broads Wildlife Centre** ▶ *Ranworth Broad. Follow signs in Ranworth (directions as above). Daily Apr-Oct.*

3 **Hickling Broad National Nature Reserve** ▶ *Managed by Norfolk Wildlife Trust. Off A149, between Potter Heigham and Stalham, towards Hickling. Daily all year.*

A pale sun sucks up the morning mist, leaving a heavy haze in the air. Marsh harriers flap ponderously over the reed beds, and dark hobbies hunt for dragonflies. A boat, moving on an unseen river, appears to sail lazily across the meadows. Trees grow in lagoons and church towers take root on the vast East Anglian skyline – there is subtle magic in the Norfolk Broads.

Climb the tower of **St Helen's Church, Ranworth**, for panoramic views across 15 miles of typical Broads' country. For many years, the Broads were thought to be shallow lakes fed by undiscovered springs, or remnants of an ancient sea trapped inland. In the 1960s, local historians correctly identified them as 41 flooded pits made between the 11th and 14th centuries by medieval peat diggers. Connecting channels were dug by marshmen who settled among the lagoons. They eked out a tough living in this reedy, watery enclave in the flatlands between Norwich and the east Norfolk coast.

A delicate balancing act

When leisure yachting opened up the Broads' insular area to holidaymakers at the end of the 19th century, the environment suffered. Riverbanks were eroded by the wash from boats and diesel polluted the waterways. By the mid 20th century, intensive chemical farming and housing development in the surrounding country threatened the area's complex ecology. Fertiliser nitrates and phosphates from sewage treatment plants leached into the water. Both nourished algae, which spread to block out light and oxygen. Reed and sedge grew unchecked, and, as a result, woodland began to replace the diverse patchwork of open water, reed swamp, reed bed, fen, meadow and wet woodland.

By the 1970s the Broads were fast disappearing, and all but sterile. Since that low point, efforts have been made to clean up the mess. The Broads Authority was set up in 1989 to oversee the area. National, local and RSPB nature reserves have been created and are managed to keep the mosaic of different habitats in balance. Boat speeds are monitored, polluted mud has been pumped out and rare water plants encouraged to grow. The **Broads Wildlife Centre**, a thatched structure moored in Ranworth Broad, educates visitors about conservation without preaching. Follow trails on walkways through the Broad from here, or take a ranger-led expedition.

Hickling Broad National Nature Reserve is the largest of the Broads, covering about 570ha (1400 acres) with large areas of marsh, reed bed and open water, and it is another victory for the conservationists. The slow wing beat of adult swallowtail butterflies can be seen here during their flying season (from late May until mid July). The caterpillars feed on the tall white-flowered umbellifer milk parsley, which thrives at Hickling.

The result of all the hard planning and conservation work is seen in the expanding list of wildlife that seeks refuge in the Broads. Birdwatchers in particular will find an earthbound slice of heaven here with sightings of avocets, barn owls and kingfishers. Among the reed beds you can spot reed buntings and marsh tits, and hear the fishing-reel click of the grasshopper warbler, as well as the loud, staccato whistle of Cetti's warbler – a bird seldom seen or heard in Britain until only a few years ago. If luck is on your side, you might even catch the hollow, gobbling boom of the bittern, a rare and shy cousin of the grey heron, which has become a symbol for conservation success.

SUFFOLK

1 Lavenham 2 Holy Trinity, Long Melford 3 Bradfield Woods 4 Ickworth House

5 The Nutshell, Bury St Edmunds 6 Tattingstone Wonder 7 Pin Mill 8 Orwell Bridge

Lavenham

When bad times came to Lavenham a medieval town was left behind

Park the car and walk. Lavenham is so steeped in history that anything mechanical seems out of key. Its crooked streets are lined with the finest collection of timber-framed houses in England. Their painted beams, wonky plaster walls and lattice windows recall a time when everything was handmade from local materials.

For 150 years, from the 14th to the 16th century, this was a boom-town, the prosperous centre of Suffolk's wool trade. As trade grew, artisans acquired cottages of wood and plaster, while wealthy cloth merchants built on a grander scale. When Lavenham lost its hold on the trade in the 16th century, the town slowly crumbled until restoration began in the 19th century. Some 300 buildings are now listed.
▶ *5 miles NE of Sudbury on A1141.*

Holy Trinity, Long Melford

A mini cathedral built on the big business of wool

Holy Trinity is an impressive parish church, flooded with light through great clerestory windows, rich in flushwork (knapped flints and pale stone), fragments of wall painting and handsome tombs. Almost entirely rebuilt by a family of wool merchants – the Cloptons – in the 1480s, the enormous church is a telling statement about the wealth created by the medieval wool trade.

The glory of the church is its superb 15th-century stained glass. The many donors depicted in the windows include Elizabeth Talbot, the spitting image of the Duchess in John Tenniel's drawings in *Alice's Adventures in Wonderland*. Other windows portray a rare Lily Crucifix (Christ among lily leaves, found in the Clopton Chantry) and three rabbits, whose three shared ears symbolise the Holy Trinity.
▶ *2 miles N of Sudbury on B1064.*

Bradfield Woods

Traditional methods preserve a rich diversity of woodland life

For 800 years Bradfield Woods have been coppiced: tall trees, such as oaks, are left to provide shelter, while shorter species, such as hazels, grow from stumps into long poles, cut every ten years or so for fencing, tool handles, firewood, furniture and other uses. This management has encouraged a mixture of light and shade, rich and poor soils, and wet and dry areas to develop over the years.

The woods have one of the most abundant mixes of wildlife and plants species in Britain. Tread carefully through orchids, oxlips, wood anemone and dog's mercury as you walk through Bradfield Woods. The observant rambler may also see fallow, roe and muntjac deer, tawny owl, great spotted woodpecker, grass snake and stag beetle.
▶ *4 miles SE of Sicklesmere on A134.*

Ickworth House

The bishop's grandest folly

Two curving wings flow from the vast central rotunda of Ickworth House, based on the Pantheon in Rome. It was built in the 1790s for Frederick Hervey (1730-1803), 4th Earl of Bristol and Bishop of Londonderry, an eccentric and keeper of more than one mistress. He intended to use the two wings to house his art collections and build living quarters below the 30m (100ft) dome of the oval rotunda. Sadly, the Earl died before his impractical dream house was completed.
▶ *2 miles SW of Bury St Edmunds, signed from A143. NT. Fri-Tues pm late Mar-early Nov. Tel 01284 735270.*

The Nutshell, Bury St Edmunds

The smallest pub in Britain

It is claimed that more than 100 drinkers once squeezed into this tiny pub. The story takes some believing as the 16th-century building measures less than 5m by 2m (16ft by 7ft) – and there is certainly no room for more than half a dozen customers at the bar. But it is a friendly watering hole, even if you do find yourself nose to nose with the mummified pub cat or have to work out how to drink your pint with someone else's elbow in it.
▶ *The Traverse, Abbeygate Street. Daily.*

BRADFIELD WOODS

Tattingstone Wonder

The church that isn't...

From the back, it is a pair of ordinary red brick cottages. Walk round to the front and – hey presto! – it looks just like a medieval parish church, complete with sham tower. Edward White of Tattingstone Place built the Tattingstone Wonder in 1790 to provide him and his guests with something dignified to look at from the house windows.

▶ *On S shore of Alton Water reservoir, S of Tattingstone village, off A137 between Ipswich and Brantham.*

Pin Mill

A sailor's peaceful and untouched mecca on the mud

Anyone who loved Arthur Ransome's *We Didn't Mean To Go To Sea* (1937) will adore Pin Mill, the eccentric little sailing port on the Orwell estuary where part of the children's adventure story is set. Little has changed at Pin Mill – amateur sailors crowd the old Butt & Oyster smugglers' pub before striding over the mud to their dinghies. A fleet of ancient barges, some still mobile and others in retirement as houseboats, lies in the mud or is rocked by the river as it rises with each tide to lap the pub wall.

▶ *Signed in Chelmondiston on B1456 Ipswich-Shotley Gate road. NT.*

Orwell Bridge

Grace and strength combine in one of the world's longest concrete structures

Marching like soldiers across the River Orwell, 19 pairs of straight-backed concrete piers hold aloft a curving ribbon of roadway, rising and falling as it carries traffic over the tranquil estuary. A thousand vehicles an hour thunder over it, dwarfed by the project's scale: a span of 1287m (4222ft), rising to 39m (128ft) above the tide and set on 1138 piles driven 40m (131ft) into the valley bed. Completed in 1982, the Orwell Bridge was a critical element in the Ipswich by-pass leading to the expanding container port of Felixstowe. To appreciate the true scale of this feat of engineering, view it from the B1456, which runs along the south side of the estuary.

▶ *2 miles S of Ipswich, on A14.*

EAST ANGLIA

SUFFOLK

Willis Corroon building

Ground-breaking modern design brings drama to a town centre

When the Willis, Faber and Dumas (now Willis Corroon) building was created in 1973-5 it heralded a revolution in workplace design. Faced with an awkwardly shaped piece of land, the architect, Norman Foster, followed the sinuous medieval street pattern, filling the site right to its edges – like, as he said, 'a pancake in a pan'.

By day, the sweeping curves and huge planes of black glass strikingly reflect the sky, scudding clouds and surrounding townscape – particularly the modest, domestic character of the Unitarian Meeting House of 1699-1700, which is partnered but not dwarfed by its exuberant neighbour. At night, when the internal lights blaze, the building seems to become mistily transparent and to float like some futuristic airship at its moorings.
▶ *Friars Street, Ipswich.*

Helmingham Hall Gardens

Wander through gorgeous gardens around a moated Tudor hall

Few houses are as romantically sited as Helmingham, home of the Tollemache family since Tudor times. It rises from its own red brick reflection in a moat, the many mullioned windows faced with pale limestone, the crow-stepped gables topped off with fairytale pinnacles. To add to the romance, the moat drawbridge is still raised each night.

The house is a private residence, but you can amble around its beautiful gardens, past dozens of rose species, some extremely old and rare, and splashes of spectacular colour and fragrance from herbaceous borders. Then stoop through arched tunnels of sweet peas, runner beans and gourds, crossing bridges to an apple walk and wild-flower garden.
▶ *Off B1077, 2 miles S of A1120, 10 miles E of Stowmarket. Wed and Sun pm May-Sept.*

Howard Monuments

Fathers and sons, and Henry VIII

Three remarkable tomb monuments of the Howard family, dukes of Norfolk, grace the Church of St Michael in Framlingham. In 1547 Thomas, the 3rd Duke, and his son Henry, Earl of Surrey, were both condemned to death for treason by Henry VIII. Thomas had a stroke of good fortune – the king died the day before the sentence was due to be carried out, and he was reprieved. But the Earl, a soldier-poet, was not so lucky – he had been beheaded the day before. Both tombs are sumptuous, the Earl's richly painted, his father's wonderfully carved with exquisitely detailed figures of the 12 Apostles in shell-hooded niches.

Alongside stands the tomb of the 3rd Duke's son-in-law, Henry Fitzroy, Duke of Richmond and illegitimate son of Henry VIII. This is another superbly carved work of art. Adam and Eve being banished from the Garden of Eden, Cain murdering his brother Abel, Abraham about to sacrifice Isaac: these themes of family abandonment, regret and concealment are worked into the stone, perhaps with deliberate symbolism.
▶ *6 miles W of Saxmundham, on B1119.*

Havergate Island

Home of the avocet – a triumph for conservation

Join one of the summer boat trips to the low-lying marsh island of Havergate, just downriver of Orford Ness, and you are in for a rare treat. A series of lagoons in the heart of the island with carefully maintained water levels are the summer home to the avocet, symbol of the RSPB, a striking black-and-white wading bird with blue-grey legs and a long, upturned bill. Avocets were hunted to extinction in 19th-century Britain; it was Havergate Island to which they returned in 1947, establishing a stronghold where they continue to thrive and breed.
▶ *By boat from Orford Quay. Book in advance Tel 01728 648281. Thur, and first and third Sat and Sun, Apr-Aug; first Sat Sept-Mar. RSPB.*

A living gallery along the river

The scenes that inspired the artist John Constable's greatest paintings are still to be seen in these few miles

1 Constable Country

This stroll beside the River Stour, which marks the boundary between Suffolk and Essex, crosses from bank to bank on its way through countryside made so familiar by Britain's favourite landscape painter that it is known simply as **Constable Country**.

From its start – on the bridge over the river in Dedham – this 'living gallery' walk takes you past scenes immortalised in famous paintings and a million reproductions, and surprisingly unchanged in the two centuries since Constable depicted them. The bridge looks down on the millpond, sluice and lock depicted in *Dedham Lock and Mill* (1820), which hangs in the V&A, and several of the artist's oil sketches. From the village (for detailed directions see map and caption) the path joins the river and follows it to **Flatford**.

Golding Constable, the artist's father, was a successful businessman and, among other interests, owned the dry dock and flour mill here, both of which feature in paintings by his son. *Boat Building near Flatford Mill* (1814), also to be seen in the V&A, is an account of a barge being constructed. Men are working on various phases

of shaping the timbers, there are adzes and other tools lying about, and a cauldron of pitch (used to caulk the planks) is heating on a fire. In *Flatford Mill (Scene on a Navigable River)*, painted in 1816–17, the family mill is the background for a study, to be seen in Tate Britain, of a little boy astride a heavy horse on the towpath, while bargees pole a vessel around in a wide pool of the Stour.

Reflection in the millpond

The dry dock has gone, but the mill still exists with, behind it, a scene etched into the national consciousness. Here are the millpond and, reflected on its surface, a gabled and red-roofed **Willy Lott's cottage** – just as Constable painted them for his most famous picture, *The Hay Wain* (1821). At the time, a buyer could not be found for this huge study of a horse-drawn cart pulled up in the water, but now it is one of the prides of the National Gallery. From here, the walk follows a path off the lane towards East Bergholt, back to Dedham. On the way it passes the spot that inspired *The Stour Valley and Dedham Church* (1815), a painting now in the Boston Museum of Fine Arts, in America.

Walk in the footsteps of the artist *To follow this easy circular walk of about 2½ miles, take the drive to Dedham Hall from the centre of the village, then turn right on a footpath. This crosses fields before reaching the River Stour, where you should turn right and follow the bank downstream as far as the footbridge across to Flatford. After looking at the mill, and possibly visiting the thatched Bridge Cottage (for opening details, Tel 01206 298260; NT) with its permanent exhibition about Constable, take the lane towards East Bergholt, the artist's birthplace. Where the path leads left, just beyond the drive to Clapper Farm, you can either follow it back along the Suffolk side of the valley to Dedham or continue to East Bergholt first.*

SUFFOLK

Sutton Hoo

Resting place fit for a Saxon king

When a grassy mound in a Suffolk field was dug up in 1939 it revealed a 7th-century burial ship 28m (90ft) long. This was the grave of King Raedwald of East Anglia and inside was Britain's finest hoard of Anglo-Saxon treasure, including fabulous weapons and jewels. The site, open to visitors, offers a dramatic re-creation of the burial and displays of original objects loaned from the British Museum.
▶ *On B1083 2 miles E of Woodbridge. NT. For opening details, Tel 01394 389700.*

Orford Ness

Military secrets of the shingle spit

Europe has other vegetation-supporting shingle spits, but none is bigger than Orford Ness. It is a moody and mysterious place thronged with nesting seabirds, reachable only by ferry and visited by few. Stand in the dips of the spit, with shingle rising on all sides, and you can feel truly cut off. Succeeding storms have thrown up lines of pebbles to form the shingle, which lies in row upon row of furrows, with colourful flora including pink sea thrift and the rare sea pea.

From 1913 until the 1980s the Ness was used for secret weapons testing. The strange, lonely atmosphere of the spit is somehow enhanced by its scatter of gaunt observation towers, barracks and 'pagoda' buildings where atomic bomb casings were tested. The gaps between the slender pillars were filled with perspex, which, in the event of an accidental explosion, would have been blown out, forcing the blast upwards into the dense concrete roof.
▶ *By ferry from Orford Quay, on B1084 N of Woodbridge (A12), Tel 01394 450900. NT. Tues-Sat July-Sept; Sat Apr-June and Oct.*

The House in the Clouds

When is a cottage not a cottage? When it's a tank

A weatherboarded 'cottage' under a steeply pitched roof perches 26m (85ft) on top of a five-storey house in the model resort of Thorpeness. The house is genuine enough, but the cottage on its roof is a disguised water tank, supplied by a pump housed in a windmill alongside, built to supply water to the resort.

Stuart Ogilvie, a local landowner as much eccentric as inventive, began work on Thorpeness in 1910 by digging The Meare, an ornamental lake. The village, rich in mock Tudor half-timbered houses, took shape over the next 20 years and today it functions exactly as Ogilvie intended – as a quiet coastal hideaway.
▶ *2 miles N of Aldeburgh, at end B1353.*

Dunwich

The city that the sea swallowed

Impossibly romantic, but true, is the story of Dunwich, a tiny coastal hamlet with lumps and bumps of medieval masonry scattered around its cliffs and fields. In early medieval times it was the ancient capital of East Anglia, with nine churches, two monasteries, a leper hospital and a busy market place, all surrounded by a city wall. But the sea took the lot, as if in some parable of pride brought low.

Nowadays all that is left of the past glory of Dunwich is a couple of monastic gateways in knapped flint, a fragment of the leper hospital with a row of Romanesque arches, and a small museum with a model of the fabulous city. But if you listen carefully on a stormy night, some say, you can hear the bells of the nine churches tolling under the surging North Sea waves.
▶ *Signed off B1125, 2 miles S of Blythburgh.*

South Elmham Minster

Secluded remains of one of the greatest Saxon churches

Hidden in a dark thicket of trees lie the brooding, lonely ruins of South Elmham Minster. The shape of the church – an impressive structure more than 30m (100ft) long – is unique in Britain, with a wide apse or rounded section forming the eastern end and a square porch shape where the west wall would normally be.

No one knows the exact age of the Minster, although it has been dated as far back as the 7th century AD. It is more likely to be 10th or early 11th-century work, built by Saxon craftsmen as part of a Christian revival along the Suffolk/Norfolk border after the marauding Danes had wiped out all the churches and religious settlements in the area.
▶ *By footpath from South Elmham Hall, 3 miles S of A143 Bungay-Harleston road.*

THE HOUSE IN THE CLOUDS

Wenhaston Doom

A shock for the sexton who came face to face with heaven and hell

During a violent rainstorm in 1892 the sexton of St Peter's Church in Wenhaston had the biggest suprise of his life. The old whitewashed boarding that had blocked the chancel arch had been thrown out into the churchyard, and as he walked by he saw a hellish picture taking shape on the wooden surface: demonic faces, contorted naked bodies and devilish beasts. The rain was rinsing off the whitewash, to reveal what had lain hidden for 350 years, a spectacular Doom or Day of Judgment scene, painted by a crude but vigorous hand in the 1520s. It must have been whited out a few decades later, when the Reformation began to bite and such popish idolatry was outlawed.

Now the Doom stands proudly in the church. Christ sits in glory on a rainbow. St Peter welcomes kings and saints into the citadel of Heaven, while the wretched sinners, tormented by yelling, horn-blowing demons, are sent into the cavernous mouth of Hell, depicted as a monstrous beast. Souls are weighed in a balance centre-stage; the saved file off heavenwards, while for the damned waits the grinning Devil himself, complete with cloven hooves and huge carbuncled nose.

▶ *1 mile S of B1123, E of Halesworth.*

Cathedral of the Marshes

Seven sins, eleven angels bathed in marshland light

The first sight of Holy Trinity Church at Blythburgh is memorable. Like a ship, it sails on its green promontory above rippling waves of reedbeds along the River Blyth. Inside, the 15th-century bench-ends are carved with the Seven Deadly Sins – Gluttony bursts out of his shirt, Avarice sits on a heap of money, Slander pokes out his poisoned tongue. High above, washed in pale light from the big windows, eleven wooden angels fly on outstretched wings along the painted wooden roof, soaring as it was first built, slotted together ingeniously by medieval carpenters without the help of metal nails or bolts. Musket balls have been found lodged in the angels faces, possibly fired by Puritan soldiers in 1644 or by locals getting rid of jackdaws.

▶ *Blythburgh, 4 miles E of Southwold, on A12.*

EAST ANGLIA

Central England

Between the valleys, hills and castles that border Wales and the dunes and marshes of The Wash is England's very heart. Here lush country, deep caves, romantic manor houses and age-old forest rub shoulders with cities and towns where the industrial age was born.

msby• 1

A16

The Wolds

2

A1028

3 5 Skegness •

7

4

A52 6

Boston •

5

A16 A17

8 • Spalding

Key

1 Main entry
2 Feature entry
— County boundary
    Motorway
— Principal A road

(See 'Finding your way', page 7)

DERBYSHIRE

1 Mam Tor 2 Millennium Walkway 3 The Round Building 4 Riley Graves

Mam Tor

The mountain that 'shivers'

Locals call it the shivering mountain because great crumbly slices of shale rock periodically peel off its east face, adding to the slipping, sliding expanse of scree below. After yet another big landslip in 1974, engineers gave up repairing the road over the head of the Hope Valley and left it to become a curiosity: a fissured cul-de-sac of paving beyond the car park at the road end above Castleton.

The shortest route to the summit lies from Mam Nick on the Edale road, which winds up the opposite, west side, of the mountain. From the car park there, stone steps lead to the hill-fort ramparts that ring the mountain's top, and magnificent views across the Peak District.
▶ *2 miles NW of Castleton off A6187 Hope Valley road. NT.*

Millennium Walkway

Clinging to the side of the gorge

On one side you can touch the high, sheer stone embankments and rock faces of the gorge, on the other just a handrail separates you from a fall to the swirling rushing River Goyt, 6m (20ft) below. It is not something for the faint-hearted, a walk along the elegant walkway opened in 2000. But for those with a head for heights, the stainless-steel structure's 160m (175yd) length presents a thrilling, fly-on-a-wall experience, where the river's roar blocks out every other sound and its dappled reflections play among the overhanging trees of The Torrs Gorge Country Park. A heritage centre in New Mills, the town above the gorge, has descriptions of the valley's water mills and spinning industry.
▶ *10 miles N of Buxton off A6 Stockport road at New Mills.*

The Round Building

The factory a cut above the rest

The foundation of a disused gasometer in the village of Hathersage sounds like an unlikely choice for the site of an ultra-modern factory, but that is just what the architect Michael Hopkins chose for his innovative, award-winning 1990 building for the cutlery designer and maker David Mellor. From the outside it looks like a huge inverted top – the soaring 28m (92ft) diameter, lead-covered roof resting on the single-storey stone perimeter, which is breached by glass doors but no windows. Inside, the factory – which visitors may walk around on weekdays – is a huge airy space, with natural light flooding through a glazed area at the top of the roof. The circular shape lends inspiration to the arrangement of the production process, which progresses in circular fashion around the floor. There is a shop alongside the works.
▶ *Hathersage town centre. Shop daily.*

Riley Graves

Wife, mother, gravedigger

When the Great Plague came knocking in the village of Eyam in 1666, the inhabitants imposed a quarantine on themselves – sealing their doors against visitors, and for at least one-third their fates as well. There are many touching memorials to their selflessness in the churchyard, a parish register of the deaths in the church itself and plaques on several of the village houses. But the most poignant reminder of the terrible event often goes unnoticed by the visitor. A small circular enclosure in a field just outside what has become known as 'plague village' marks the spot where, in 1666, Mrs Hancocke, a farmer's wife, had the heart-rending task of burying her husband and six of their children in the space of a single week. Nothing else brings home quite as vividly the tragedy that struck Eyam as the Riley Graves, which are named after the location.
▶ *10 miles SE of Chapel-en-le-Frith off A623 Baslow Road. Graves on minor road to Top Riley Farm ½ mile E of Eyam. NT. Daily.*

THE FACTORY A
CUT ABOVE THE REST
THE ROUND BUILDING

DERBYSHIRE

Peter's Stone

Bound in chains and hoisted high

From the Three Stags Head pub in the hamlet of Wardlow Mires on the main road, a footpath leads to this domed 15m (50ft) high pillar of limestone, said to be named after its resemblance to St Peter's in Rome. It must have been over the same fields that the body of Anthony Lingard was carted in 1815. Lingard, a 21-year-old from nearby Tideswell, had been executed in Derby for the murder of the hamlet's toll keeper, but justice was not done with him yet. His body was hoisted on the stone in chains and left to rot, an example to passers by, and the last gibbeting to occur in the county. Back at the hamlet, you can contemplate this tale of crime and punishment over a glass of real ale in the traditional pub.
▶ ¾ mile SW of Wardlow Mires on A623 Baslow-Chapel-en-le-Frith road.

Buxton Opera House

Mr Matcham's masterpiece makes a matchless comeback

Artistes love to perform against its rococo elegance and gilded marble, recently restored to the original splendour. From foyer to cherub-embellished proscenium arch, the interior of the opera house is an Edwardian extravaganza of painted panel, gold leaf and moulded plasterwork. Frank Matcham (1854–1920), architect par excellence of places of public entertainment, designed the building, which opened in 1905. Among his other works are the London Coliseum, Hackney Empire and Blackpool's Grand Theatre.

Nearby is the former **Devonshire Royal Hospital** (now part of the University of Derby) which started life as stables for occupants of The Crescent; there was room for 120 horses. The dome – in its day the biggest unsupported one in Europe, with a span of 47m (154ft) – was added in the 1880s.
▶ Buxton town centre. Tel 0845 127 2190.

Chesterfield church

Blaming the Devil for poor work

Looking up at the 69m (228ft) twisted spire of St Mary and All Saints is a disorientating experience. Legend says it corkscrews out of true because the Devil got his tail tangled round it. The real reason is that the carpenters who constructed the eight-sided structure 700 years ago used unseasoned timber, which is prone to warp. In addition, no restraining cross-braces were installed, so the green wood could twist to the maximum degree.
▶ Town centre. Daily (Sun services only).

Chatsworth Park

Watery displays on tap in gardens brimming with fine fountains

The grounds of the dukes of Devonshire's home contain many memorable man-made features, starting with the Emperor Fountain. Built in 1844 by Joseph Paxton, this is the world's highest gravity-fed fountain, shooting water 80m (260ft) into the air. Paxton also developed elaborate glasshouses at Chatsworth, including one for exotics that incorporates a Conservative Wall – so called because it has a system of flues and hot-water pipes which conserve heat for the plants.

After Paxton's powerful water feature, the Willow Tree Fountain is a gentle affair, raining a shower of water from its copper branches. The stainless steel, lily-shaped 'Revelation', added in 2000 to the Jack Pond, has water-powered petals that open and close around a golden sphere. More naturalistic is the stretch of the River Derwent that flows past the house – diverted to this course in the 1750s by 'Capability' Brown.
▶ 8 miles N of Matlock off A6 Bakewell road. Daily mid Mar-late Dec.

Lathkill Dale

Where history turns full circle

The Lathkill is a 'disappearing' river, swallowed mysteriously by the limestone only to bubble up farther down the dale. Historically, too, the river has performed vanishing tricks. Izaak Walton described it as 'the purest and most transparent stream I ever yet saw' in his *Compleat Angler*, first published in 1653, but in the 18th and 19th centuries the area was polluted by lead mining. Nowadays, river and dale again resemble Walton's idyll, with just the ruins of an aqueduct and a pump house, and the disused 'soughs' (drainage tunnels for the mines) as reminders of the industrial past.
▶ *1½ miles S of Bakewell, reached by a short walk from village of Over Haddon.*

Arbor Low

Let the stones and the setting grip your imagination

Arbor Low is the Stonehenge of the North: an isolated, embanked Neolithic stone circle, over 4000 years old. In this isolated spot, nothing intrudes between the imagination of the visitor and an almost tangible sense of mystery clinging to the stones – 50 huge toppled slabs.

The magnificence of the location adds to the sense of awe. Lying at a height of 375m (1230ft), Arbor Low has all-round views across the surrounding Peak District National Park – a country of far horizons, beneath wide skies echoing to trilling skylarks and the lonely call of curlews. A couple of fields away, and constructed at around the same time, lies the burial mound or barrow of Gib Hill.
▶ *5 miles SW of Bakewell off Youlgreave-Parsley Hay minor road. EH. Daily.*

Robin Hood's Stride

Towering rocks and a hermit's cave

Climbers call the twin gritstone outcrops the Weasel and the Inaccessible Pinnacles, but they are better known as Robin Hood's Stride, after a folk tale which says that the outlaw bridged the 20m (22yd) between the two with a single step. Across The Portway, the ancient, paved track leading past this rocky spot, lies Cratcliffe Tor. Here, railed-off and hidden behind an ancient yew tree, there is the cave where a hermit lived in the Middle Ages, and carved a crucifix on the wall.
▶ *4 miles NW of Matlock off B5056 Grangemill-Bakewell road.*

Hardwick Hall

The house that Bess built

The first things to strike a visitor to Hardwick Hall are its six rectangular, four-storeyed towers with their regimented window arrangement. The towers' crowning balustrades frame repetitions of the owner's initials 'ES' (Elizabeth Shrewsbury), better known as Bess of Hardwick. But the whole house bears the uncompromising stamp of the woman who did not start building it until 1590, when already about 70 years old.
▶ *15 miles N of Nottingham, Junction 28 off M1. NT. Wed, Thur, Sat and Sun, late Mar-Oct.*

Cromford Mill, Cromford

Riverside launchpad for Britain's Industrial Revolution

A grey fortress-like building on the Derwent is one of industrial history's most important sites. It was here in 1771 that Richard Arkwright, attracted by the potential of the river for supplying power, established the world's first successful water-powered cotton-spinning mill. A large workforce working with powered machinery in a factory environment set the pattern for industrial development all over the world and earned Arkwright the title of 'Father of the factory system'. Alongside the factory an entire village was built. Only Cromford's remoteness and poor communications stopped it becoming another Manchester.

Cromford is one of the The Derwent Valley Mills, which were granted World Heritage Site status in 2001.
▶ *2 miles S of Matlock on A6; daily.*

Masson Mill, Cromford

Working machinery recalls early factory life

Get a glimpse of how life must have been for workers in an 18th century textile mill with a visit to the Working Textile Museum housed in Masson Mill. The noise and smells of well-oiled machinery will evoke the lives of those present at the birth of the factory system. Standing at the northern entrance to the Derwent Valley Mills World Heritage Site, the magnificent five-storey Masson Mill was the third mill built by Richard Arkwright. Established in 1783, the power available from the river Derwent at this point was ten times greater than that at the earlier Cromford Mill.
▶ *Matlock Bath, off A6; daily.*

A hollow country

The secret underground world of Derbyshire's limestone caves

1 Creswell Crags ▶ *On B6042, between A60 Worksop-Mansfield road and A616. Cave tours Sat and Sun Feb-Oct, Sun Nov-Jan, all week in school holidays; Tel 01909 720378. Visitor centre daily Feb-Oct, Sun only Nov-Jan.*

2 Poole's Cavern ▶ *Buxton, off Green Lane, between A53 and A515. Daily mid Feb-Dec.*

3 Peak Cavern ▶ *Castleton, off A6187. Daily Apr-Oct; Sat and Sun Nov-Mar; daily in school hols.*

4 Treak Cliff Cavern ▶ *1 mile W of Castleton. Daily.*

5 Blue John Cavern ▶ *1 mile W of Castleton. Daily.*

6 Speedwell Cavern ▶ *½ mile W of Castleton. Daily.*

More than 50,000 years before Sir Arthur Conan Doyle made the limestone country around Castleton in the Peak District the sinister backdrop for his short story The Terror of Blue John Gap, prehistoric man was using rock shelters and caves in the sides of Derbyshire dales as temporary homes, and bases for hunting expeditions. Some of the earliest evidence of human habitation in Britain has been found near the border with Nottinghamshire in the caves and crevices of **Creswell Crags** – a narrow gorge, its floor now filled by a lake. Axes, flint scrapers and other tools left by early Stone Age people 40,000-60,000 years ago, during the last Ice Age, have been excavated in the caverns lining the valley. You can take a tour around the largest cavern, Robin Hood's Cave, where later Stone Age hunters, stalking animals such as arctic hare and reindeer when glaciers still covered the land, left behind one of the first examples of British art – a tiny fragment of bone engraved around 12,500 years ago with a horse's head.

Across the county, at Buxton, Stone Age, Bronze Age and Roman artefacts have been excavated at **Poole's Cavern**. The spectacular cave, named after a 15th-century outlaw who used it as his secret lair, includes Derbyshire's longest stalactite, the 2m (6½ft) Flitch of Bacon, so-called because it looks like a cured bacon hanging in a butcher's shop. Another huge stalactite, the 1.8m (6ft) long Mary, Queen of Scots Pillar, is named after the Queen who visited the cavern in 1582. The most bizarre sight is The Poached Egg Chamber, where stalagmites are tipped in egg-yolk orange, stained by iron oxide dripping from the rock above.

The four great caverns of Castleton

The most extensive network of Derbyshire caves lies at the head of the Hope Valley, where the limestone of the White Peak meets the shales and gritstone of the Dark Peak. People lived for some 400 years in the great, gaping maw of **Peak Cavern**, the largest cave entrance in Britain, big enough to hold several cottages. The last of its community of rope-makers left in the early 20th century, although rope making has been revived at the cave, along with its earthy old local name, 'The Devil's Arse'. The river that issues from under the 76m (250ft) wide entrance crag was known as the River Styx, and when the cavern flooded, as it still does every winter, locals said it was the Devil relieving himself.

Inside, you stoop through the low-roofed Lumbago Walk to reach Roger Rain's House (right), named for its constant cascade of water, and the Orchestra Chamber, where concerts are still held by the village choir. Beyond, where no visitors venture, is Britain's deepest cave, the 152m (500ft) deep Titan.

For the most spectacular stalactite and stalagmite formations, venture into **Treak Cliff Cavern**, which like many Derbyshire caves was found by lead miners in the 18th century. It is the world's biggest supplier of Blue John, a purple-and-white banded semi-precious mineral, which you may see being crafted in the Treak Cliff workshops. At the top of the old Mam Tor road west of Castleton is **Blue John Cavern**, another former lead mine and a source of 8 varieties of Blue John mineral.

The strangest underground journey of all is at **Speedwell Cavern**, at the foot of the spectacular gorge of Winnats Pass. Here you can take a boat trip along an underground canal constructed by lead miners 200 years ago to the Bottomless Pit, a vast subterranean lake.

ALL THIS
COUNTRY IS
HOLLOW
COULD YOU
STRIKE IT
WITH SOME
GIGANTIC
HAMMER IT
WOULD
BOOM LIKE
A DRUM,
OR POSSIBLY
CAVE IN
ALTOGETHER...

SIR ARTHUR CONAN DOYLE
THE TERROR OF BLUE JOHN GAP

ROGER RAIN'S HOUSE, PEAK CAVERN

DERBYSHIRE

Silk Mill, Derby

Jet engines and the beginning of the factory age

The huge, stainless-steel prototype RB211 dominates Britain's biggest collection of Rolls–Royce aero engines, made in Derby since 1915. Alongside stands one of Frank Whittle's tiny pioneering jet engines from the 1950s. Through fascinating displays and galleries, the Silk Mill tells the story of Derby's rise from a minor silk town to become known as 'the city of the transport age'.

The coming of the railway in 1840 made the town a hub of the fast-growing new system, and when Frederick Henry Royce joined forces with C.S. Rolls to open their car factory in 1906 at Osmaston, Derby's position as a transport centre was sealed.

The museum is appropriately on the site of the first factory in England, a silk mill built by John and Thomas Lombe between 1717 and 1721. The large-scale production methods used there were to become the hallmark of the Industrial Revolution 50 years later.
▶ *Derby, off Full Street. Daily, pm Sun and bank hols.*

Swarkestone Bridge

A bridge too far for Bonnie Prince Charlie and his rebels

The medieval Swarkestone Bridge, which still carries the busy A514 road between Derby and Swadlincote, is the longest stone bridge in England. Its 17 ribbed arches wind 3/4 mile over the flood plain of the River Trent, with the remains of a chapel at the bridge's northern end.

Just over 250 years ago the bridge was the scene of one of the most momentous events in British history. It was here in 1745 that Bonnie Prince Charlie decided to turn back his army of Jacobean rebels, thus halting his headlong and largely unopposed advance on London and the British throne.
▶ *3 miles S of Derby on A514.*

St Michael with St Mary, Melbourne

The misogynist church

Tucked away in a quiet bywater of a small south Derbyshire market town is one of the finest Norman churches in Britain, with some surprises for the modern visitor.

The interior of the 12th-century St Michael with St Mary at Melbourne is like a cathedral in miniature. Great pillars dominate the nave. The tower crossing is made up of four Romanesque Norman arches resting on deeply carved, contrasting capitals. These include the 'Melbourne cat', a primitive female fertility monster with her legs spread to form the lobes of the capital. Vine leaves sprout from her mouth. Then there is a vivid wall painting of the Devil stamping on the heads of two women. Attitudes were different 900 years ago.
▶ *Melbourne, 5 miles S of Derby off A514.*

Calke Abbey

Travel back in time to family life in a late-Victorian 'big house'

A dark, long and winding brick-lined tunnel in the bowels of Calke Abbey leads to a crumbling brewhouse where the reclusive Harper Crewe family concocted homemade beer. This, like the rest of the intriguing mansion, has been frozen in time.

The Harper Crewes lived at Calke Abbey from 1701 to 1985, when it was bought by the National Trust. They were hoarders and the Trust found itself custodian of a house largely untouched for 100 years. The collections of stuffed birds and animals, fossils and minerals accumulated by Sir Vauncey Harper Crewe between 1886 and his death in 1924 recall Miss Haversham's house in *Great Expectations*. A magnificent silk-hung Chinese State Bed, found in its original packing, is now assembled and glows like new. In the Caricature Room, the walls, used like a child's scrapbook, are covered with 18th-century cartoons.
▶ *Ticknall, 10 miles S of Derby on A514. NT. House Sat-Wed late Mar-end Oct. Park daily.*

GLOUCESTERSHIRE

Cotswold Farm Park 2 Sudeley Castle

Cotswold Farm Park

Meet blue-fleeced Herdwick sheep and pigs with Iron Age ancestors

High on the stony Cotswold hills graze Longhorn cattle, sheep with six horns, and goats whose ancestors were brought back from the Crusades – as well as pigs, horses, poultry and waterfowl. Some are in danger of extinction, such as the White Park cattle with black ears and noses. Farmer Joe Henson founded The Rare Breeds Survival Trust at the Cotswold Farm Park in 1973 to combine a living museum with scientific research.
▶ *Guiting Power, S of B4077, 5 miles W of Stow. Daily Mar-mid Sept; Sat-Sun mid Sept-Oct.*

Sudeley Castle

Home to an English queen and restored by a glove-making dynasty

Set in one of the finest unspoiled swathes of Cotswold landscape, the honey-coloured castle of Sudeley has a queenly air about it. So it might, for the Anglo-Saxon King Ethelred gave the manor to his daughter as a wedding present. In 1547 it became the home of Catherine Parr, the last of Henry VIII's six wives. Before she married the king she was much admired by Sir Thomas Seymour of Sudeley. After Henry's death, she swiftly married Thomas, only to die in childbirth at the castle a year later.

Sudeley was left in ruins after the Civil War until bought by the Dent family, glove-makers of Worcester. In the late 1880s, Emma Brocklehurst, wife of John Dent, set about extending Sudeley and enriching its Tudor legacy. Today it is flowering under its most recent mistress, Lady Ashcombe: the gardens are one of its glories. Displays at the castle have included Civil War battles re-enacted by the Sealed Knot (above).
▶ *Winchcombe, 7 miles NE of Cheltenham on B4632. House and gardens daily Mar-Oct.*

A royal forest with a fiery past

The ancient oak woods of the Royal Forest of Dean conceal an even older industrial age when iron was king

1 Puzzle Wood ▶ *Coleford off B4228. Tues-Sun, and bank hol Mon, Easter-Oct. Tel 01594 833187.*

2 Clearwell Caves ▶ *1½ miles S of Coleford off B4228. Daily mid Feb-early Nov; 'Christmas Fantasy' Dec. Tel 01594 832535.*

3 Hopewell Colliery ▶ *On B4226 near Cannop. Daily Mar-Oct. Tel 01594 810706 to check that mine is open.*

4 Dean Heritage Centre ▶ *Soudley, on B4227, 2 miles S of Cinderford. Daily.*

5 Symonds Yat Rock ▶ *3½ miles NW of Coleford on B4432. Daily.*

A strange high saucer of limestone and sandstone lies between the rivers Wye and Severn, where iron and coal touch the surface of the earth under the mantle of Britain's greatest oak forest. Roads twist beneath steep woods, where the unwary walker may stumble on a rusty tramway, or crunch on cinders from some long abandoned furnace.

Iron ore has been mined in the Forest of Dean since before the Romans, but it was they who left behind open cast workings at **Puzzle Wood** (right), which have been turned into a fantastical moss-covered landscape and maze. The Normans hunted in the forest and bestowed on it the title 'Royal'. To this day ancient traditions are upheld: the four forest officials, or 'Verderers', still hold their court every 40 days, and there are 150 'free miners' – those born in the vicinity of St Briavels, who are over 21 and have worked in a mine for a year and a day – who have the right to dig for minerals anywhere in the forest. One of the domains of the Free Miners was **Clearwell Caves**, where iron ore has been mined for 4000 years creating caverns that descend 152m (500ft).

The forest takes hold

By the 16th century the Forest was Britain's biggest iron-producing area, but the charcoal furnaces used to smelt the iron ate up the woodlands. In 1688 an Act of Parliament enclosed land to grow trees for the Navy; the ironworks were demolished. Coal mining, however, flourished. Although the last major pit closed in 1940, Free Miners continue to work their own seams. At the **Hopewell Colliery** you can descend into miles of deep subterranean workings.

For the best introduction to the forest visit the **Dean Heritage Centre**. It is on the site of an old iron foundry and mill, part of an industrial landscape reclaimed by oak trees. For the best forest views, stand at the 144m (473ft) high **Symonds Yat Rock** and watch peregrines circle high above the River Wye as it tumbles over rapids below. While there, imagine the industry that once filled this limestone gorge with the drifting smoke of its ironworks.

PUZZLE WOOD

GLOUCESTERSHIRE

3 Tewkesbury Abbey 4 St Mary's, Kempley

Tewkesbury Abbey

Where Norman power and beauty overrode Saxon glory

The 12th-century tower of Tewkesbury Abbey, on the confluence of the rivers Severn and Avon, is the largest in England at 45m (148ft) tall. Fourteen great Norman columns dominate the nave, each more than 9m (30ft) high and 2m (7ft) in diameter. At Tewkesbury, as at so many places in England, the Normans destroyed an earlier Saxon abbey to build their own.

At the hamlet of **Deerhurst** downstream on the Severn, two Saxon survivals give an indication of just how much was lost to the conflict between Saxon and Norman. Odda's Chapel is a tiny church dedicated in 1056, and the priory church of St Mary, once a monastery, has fine examples of Saxon art and architecture, including the Deerhurst Angel, carved on the wall of the ruined apse.

▶ *Tewkesbury, 2 miles W of M5 (Junction 9). Deerhurst, 4 miles SW off A38.*

St Mary's, Kempley

Glorious frescoes illuminate an abandoned Norman church

The interior of St Mary's is full of joyous colour. In the early 12th century, when the church was built, hardly an inch of stone or timber was left unpainted. The chancel, beyond the finely carved Norman arch, is covered in frescoes glowing with pinks and terracotta. Christ sits on a rainbow on the vaulted ceiling surrounded by angels, the Virgin Mary, apostles and bishops. They were painted in about 1120, probably for Hugh de Lacy, who fought at the Battle of Hastings, and are the most complete set of wall paintings of their kind in England.

Yet the church sits alone and officially redundant – a small, stubby-towered grey stone building with only ancient yew trees for company. Centuries ago the villagers of Kempley left for higher ground.

▶ *1 mile N of Kempley off A449. EH. Daily Mar-Oct. Tel 01531 660214 to visit in winter.*

CENTRAL ENGLAND

GLOUCESTERSHIRE

5 National Birds of Prey Centre 6 Severn Bore 7 Westbury Court Garden 8 Berkeley

Castle 9 The Jenner Museum 10 Slimbridge Wildfowl and Wetlands Centre

11 Source of the Thames

National Birds of Prey Centre

On the wing over Gloucestershire

The most striking feature of the largest and most powerful owl in Europe is its orange eyes. This is no sweet little bird as it can kill a hare if necessary. It represents just one of the 25 species of owl that are to be found at the National Birds of Prey Centre, one of the most significant collections of birds of prey in the world. One of their aims is conservation through a captive breeding programme but the centre also rescues and rehabilitates many birds. Daily flying demonstrations allow visitors to appreciate the exquisite beauty and power of these birds.
▶ *S of Newent on B4216. Daily.*

Severn Bore

An awesome natural phenomenon

There is a stillness, then a low roar. A huge wave, up to 2m (7ft) high, crashes upstream at about 10mph, clouting the banks with spray. Surfers ride its crest. It is as if the muscular brown River Severn has suddenly decided to flow the other way. Then it is gone, leaving the swollen river flowing upstream towards Gloucester. The Severn has the second highest tidal range anywhere in the world, and the configuration of the river bed causes the extraordinary phenomenon of the Severn Bore. Although it occurs on 260 days of the year it reaches its maximum on only about 25, always near an equinox in spring or autumn.

The best places to see the Bore are at Minsterworth, Stonebench or Over Bridge. Severn Bore predictions are published annually and are given a star rating according to size.
▶ *Minsterworth, 4 miles W of Gloucester off A40/A48. Stonebench, 3 miles SW of Gloucester off A430/B4008. Over village, 1 mile W of Gloucester on A40. For details of Bore, Tel 08708 506506 (Environment Agency).*

Westbury Court Garden

A rare survivor of 17th-century Dutch garden design

Not a leaf or twig is out of place at Westbury Court; everything is in perfect order. Globes of holly and pyramids of yews are reflected in a long clear canal. A quincunx pattern (as in the five on a dice) of clipped evergreens and trees surrounds a Dutch pavilion with views across the River Severn. In 1696, when the garden was created, such formal Dutch designs were the height of fashion – their high cost, and the later fashion for 'Capability' Brown's 'natural landscaping', meant that few were to survive. This is the earliest example left in England, and none in Holland are as perfect.
▶ *10 miles SW of Gloucester on A48. NT. Wed-Sun and bank hols Mar-June and Sept-Oct; daily July and Aug.*

Berkeley Castle

Dark deeds behind high castle walls

Although it is set in the gentle surroundings of the Severn plain's watermeadows, Berkeley Castle is not a romantic castle, but one that has seen savagery and betrayal. Elizabethan terraced gardens do not soften the swagger of its rose-grey buttressed walls that look as if they were hewn out of solid rock.

The Castle is owned by the Berkeley family, descendants of Robert Fitzhardinge, who began to build the feudal stronghold in 1117. In 1215, a group of rebellious barons met on the site of the Great Hall before going on to Runnymede to force King John to seal the Magna Carta. The Hall itself has changed little since it was built in 1340 and its beamed roof rises to more than 9m (30ft).

Climb the stone steps to the King's Gallery where portraits of past kings and queens will briefly divert your eye from the dungeon in the corner – rotting animal carcasses were hurled into it to poison prisoners in the room above. Edward II, kept captive here, survived the stench but was savagely murdered by his jailers in 1327.
▶ *E of Berkeley village on B4066. For opening times Tel 01453 810332.*

The Jenner Museum
Scene of a life-saving discovery

A country doctor's modest white Georgian house in the shadow of Berkeley Castle was the scene of a vital medical advance. This is the home of Dr Edward Jenner. It was here that a milkmaid came to see him in 1796. She had cowpox, a mild skin rash. Jenner knew country people believed that if you had cowpox you would not catch smallpox, which at that time killed one in five people. He infected his gardener's son with cowpox taken from the milkmaid and then tried, unsuccessfully, to infect him with smallpox. Jenner called this vaccination, from the Latin – 'vacca' – for cow.

Jenner's study remains as he left it in 1823, and other rooms reveal his many interests – he discovered the cuckoo's nesting habits, studied heart disease and hunted for fossils. A computerised exhibition above the garden 'surgery' – where the poor were treated free of charge – traces immunology back to Jenner.
▶ *As for Berkeley Castle. Tues-Sun and bank hol pm Apr-Sept, Sun pm Oct.*

Slimbridge Wildfowl and Wetlands Centre
Flurries of feathers and the call of the wild

The sight of a black swan followed by her cygnets or the feel of a Hawaiian goose nibbling your hand are memorable encounters. As you walk across the shimmering islands in this watery landscape, most birds hardly notice you. Fluorescent pink flamingos quarrel by the café and ducklings huddle in the car park.

Slimbridge is the headquarters of the Wildfowl & Wetlands Trust, founded in 1946 by the naturalist and artist Peter Scott. Its mission is to conserve the world's wetlands. Watch from hides in the Centre some of the 20,000 birds that fly in every year and do not miss a tour of the 'Duckery'. Duck eggs are so vulnerable to predators that some are replaced by wooden replicas and taken to be hatched in incubators. To stand in the darkness as a torch illuminates an egg and see, inside it, a duckling tapping at the shell, is incredibly moving.
▶ *Signed from Slimbridge village, off A38, W of M5. Daily.*

Source of the Thames
See the birth of a great river

In winter, water bubbles out of the ground, spreading in a sequence of shallow pools as it meanders south through the meadows. In summer the spring is usually dry. A granite boulder marks the source of the River Thames in a pebbly hollow beneath an ash tree. Green depressions in hay fields reveal its course until it becomes a proper river 2 miles south at Kemble. It is hard to believe, in this supremely peaceful place, that from such a modest beginning Britain's second-longest river flows for 210 miles to the east, through the nation's capital to the North Sea.
▶ *Near Cirencester (see map).*

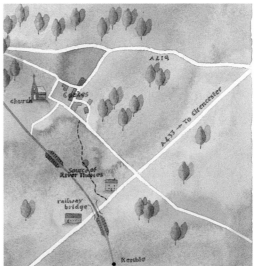

Finding the source *The path to the source of the Thames runs northwest from the A433 about 3 miles southwest of Cirencester. In a dip in the road, just before a railway bridge, look out for a wooden footpath sign to the right. Alternatively, find the Thames and Severn Canal tunnel on a footpath from the nearby village of Coates and follow the old towpath south for about a mile.*

GLOUCESTERSHIRE

Owlpen Manor

The sleeping beauty of manor houses

'A dream … among dark, secret rooms of yew, hiding in the slope of the valley.' So the writer Vita Sackville-West described Owlpen Manor. The romantic, mid-15th-century manor house is set in gardens of topiary yews and box parterres and the manorial estate includes outbuildings, a mill and 19th-century church. Below it, miniature hanging gardens drop into the secluded valley on the western edge of the Cotswolds. In 1850, the house fell into neglect and lay undisturbed until 1926 when Norman Jewson, a follower of the Arts and Crafts Movement, began its restoration. The interiors reveal Owlpen's mixed history – 17th-century painted wallcloths in the Great Chamber are a backdrop for Arts and Crafts objects.

▶ *Signed from Uley village, S of Stroud on B4066. Tues, Thur and Sun pm May-Sept.*

Severn bridges

Where elegant engineering complements natural beauty

When the huge foundations carrying viaducts at each end of the new Severn bridge are submerged at high tide, the supporting cables of the central span look like pale cobwebs floating above the Severn (below). The first bridge across the Severn estuary, with its lofty 136m (445ft) white towers, opened in 1966. As traffic increased, a new tollbridge was commissioned, downstream, to link Wales and England. Completed in 1996, it spans nearly three miles. A walk along the Severn Way between the two takes about an hour. Use the civil engineering exhibition on the English side at Severn Beach or the windy viewpoint on the old bridge at Aust as a starting point.

▶ *A403 links Severn Beach with Aust. Viewpoint at Aust reached from M48 service area. Visitor centre and exhibition signed from A403 – turn W on B4055 along winding lane to shore. Sat-Sun and bank hols Easter-Sept. Closes in bad weather, Tel 01454 633511 to check.*

WHERE ELEGANT ENGINEERING COMPLEMENTS NATURAL BEAUTY

SEVERN BRIDGES

Westonbirt Arboretum

Space and perfect calm beneath an ever-changing canopy of trees

Enter Westonbirt and escape into a more tranquil world. The arboretum covers 243ha (600 acres) of landscaped grounds, where 17 miles of rides pass through a magnificent collection of more than 18,000 trees begun in 1829 by Robert Holford, who made a fortune piping clean drinking water into London.

In spring seek out the rhododendrons and camellias, azaleas, magnolias and flowering cherry trees, and the wild flowers of the Silk Wood. In summer, explore leafy, sunlit glades, which become a riot of red and gold in autumn. Viburnum scents the January air.
▶ *5 miles SW of Tetbury on A433. Daily.*

Chedworth Roman Villa

All mod cons and an enviable position for a 2nd-century des res

For a Roman army officer planning to build a smart new villa in about AD 120 the wooded combe at Chedworth, overlooking the lovely valley of the River Coln, would have been the perfect site. It was just off the Fosseway and not too far from Glevum (Gloucester) or Corinium (Cirencester). Most important, it had a good supply of spring water – essential for the baths.

Over the next 300 years the villa evolved into an elegant mansion, complete with underfloor central heating, bathhouses and large reception rooms. Many of the fine mosaic floors survive, the best a particularly charming example in the dining room depicting the seasons. First excavated in 1864, Chedworth provides fascinating evidence of how a Roman family set up home in England.
▶ *7 miles N of Cirencester off A429. NT. Tues-Sun, and bank hol Mon, Mar-mid Nov.*

HEREFORDSHIRE

1 Croft Castle and Croft Ambrey

2 Hampton Court

Croft Castle and Croft Ambrey

Fortified homes that span 2500 years

Fine avenues of oaks, beeches and 350-year-old Spanish chestnuts lead to Croft Castle, set four-square on a high sweep of border country with all the confidence of a fortress home first mentioned in Domesday Book. In the 18th century the house was given one of the earliest 'Gothick' makeovers.

On the 305m (1000ft) high ridge behind Croft is an even older home, the Ambrey, where Celts farmed for over 400 years before the Roman conquest. You can see 14 counties from their fortified camp – here, in AD 50, the chieftain Caratacus faced the legions of Rome.
▶ *5 miles NW of Leominster off B4362. NT. Tel 01568 780246 for details. House and gardens Wed-Sun Apr-Oct, Sat and Sun Mar. Park and Ambrey daily.*

Hampton Court

An American dream comes true in a very English setting

Don't be confused. This is not *the* Hampton Court, but a square-towered and battlemented, early 15th-century castle set in sweeping parkland below a wooded hill, framed in the archway of a turreted gatehouse.

In 1994 the Van Kampens, an American family from Michigan, fell in love with the history and romance of the castle and swiftly bought it. Then, two years later, they began to create one of the largest and most ambitious gardens in Britain. In the Kitchen Garden rosy lettuces, peas and marigolds, cabbages and cornflowers, are laid out with the care and skill of a great painting. Pavilions, canals and cascades link huge massed borders in the Flower Garden and a dark tunnel leads to a Sunken Garden and waterfall. There is a Maze, a Dutch Water Garden, a Gothic tower. This is gardening in the grand tradition, extravagant and unabashed.
▶ *Hope under Dinmore, 5 miles S of Leominster, on A417, near junction with A49 Hereford-Leominster road. Tel 01568 797777.*

CENTRAL ENGLAND

HEREFORDSHIRE

3 Bromyard Downs 4 Lower Brockhampton 5 Eastnor Castle 6 Mappa Mundi

7 Kilpeck church 8 Hellens 9 Goodrich Castle

Bromyard Downs
A magical resting place

The market town of Bromyard is laid out like an ancient map below the Downs, where larks hover, bluebells fill the crowning beechwoods in spring and orchids appear like mauve candles by the dew ponds. Most of the 106ha (262 acres) of shimmering herb-rich grassland has never been cultivated, grazed only by a few sheep and cut for hay.

Welsh cattle drovers once rested here, paying a halfpenny a cow. In about 1815 a racecourse was laid out to provide work for soldiers returning from the Napoleonic wars; thousands came from as far as Birmingham to the annual races until the turn of the 20th century. The Downs are now left to local people who still have grazing rights here, and to wild plants, butterflies and birds.
▶ *E of Bromyard between A44 and B4203.*

Lower Brockhampton
A medieval house bound by an unbroken spell

Hidden deep in one of the secret valley bowls of Bringsty Common, down a long and winding lane, is an enchanting, perfectly preserved half-timbered manor house. It was built for John Domulton in 1380. When one of his descendants decided to replace it with a new mansion in the 18th century, Lower Brockhampton, with its moat, splendid timbered interior and exquisite detached gatehouse, was left like Sleeping Beauty to slumber undisturbed.
▶ *2 miles E of Bromyard, signed from A44 Worcester Road. NT. House Sat and Sun Mar; Wed-Sun and bank hols Apr-Oct.*

Eastnor Castle
The ultimate fairytale castle

If you were to dream of a castle, this is probably how it would look. Eastnor is huge and symmetrical, with cloverleaf towers at each corner and a battlemented tower in the middle. Castellated terraces descend to a broad lake and red deer graze in 122ha (300 acres) of parkland below the Malvern Hills. Buzzards circle over rare and magnificent trees in an arboretum. Even Eastnor village, with its school, cricket field and church, follows the idyllic English pattern.

Yet the castle was built in the early 19th century, not in the 12th. It is essentially a pastiche, a copy of a medieval fortress, built by Robert Smirke, architect of the British Museum,

for the 1st Earl Somers between 1810 and 1824. Somers wanted to impress his contemporaries and assure his family's place among the higher ranks of the ruling classes. Succeeding generations added to the interiors – the Gothic drawing room was designed by A.W.N. Pugin and J.G. Crace, collaborators on the Houses of Parliament – and today Eastnor is an elegant and richly welcoming family home as well as a magical castle.
▶ *2½ miles from Ledbury, on A438, off A449 between Ledbury and Malvern. Daily, except Sat, mid July-Aug; Sun and bank hol Mon Apr-Sept.*

Mappa Mundi
Lose yourself in the medieval world

Dimly lit in a cabinet of Derbyshire slate in Hereford Cathedral, the Mappa Mundi – a 13th-century world map – offers a glimpse of medieval learning. Drawn on a single sheet of vellum (calfskin) in about 1290, it is a theological diagram that presents the world in spiritual and geographical terms. Jerusalem is at the centre, with seas and rivers cutting across Asia, Europe and Africa. Dragons are illustrated here, as are 420 cities and towns, and images of people, plants, angels and devils, headed by Christ sitting in judgment. In one corner is a horseman on what was a white horse, until a medieval boy decorated it with very neat spots.
▶ *In New Library, Hereford Cathedral. Daily May-Sept; Mon-Sat Feb-Apr and Oct-Dec. Closed Jan.*

Kilpeck church
A morality tale carved in stone

Real and imaginary beasts like the Basilisk, hatched from a cock's egg by a toad, and the Mantichore, a lion's body with a man's head, leap from the exterior arches of Kilpeck church. The 12th-century church has survived from a time when few people could read, but everyone understood carved images. Sculptors drew on Celtic, Saxon and Viking imagery, and contemporary themes, to create sexually explicit figures such as the sheela-na-gig (a woman exposing her genitalia, thought to be a fertility symbol) as well as huntsmen, dogs and dragons: a panorama of life and fears. Only inside the church was there peace, personified by serene saints carved on the chancel arch.
▶ *9 miles SW of Hereford, signed from A465 between Hereford and Pontrilas.*

Hellens

Revealing scandals of a family's past

Step into the cobbled courtyard of Hellens, see the russet brick and diamond-paned windows with sweeping views across the Malverns and be transported back in time. A tour of the 13th-century manor acquaints you with family members who lived and loved here: James, a friend of the Black Prince, Hetty Walwyn, who ran off with a farmer and was confined to her room for 30 years, and adulterers who hung portraits of their mistresses by Hogarth and Reynolds on the panelled walls.

▶ *Much Marcle, off A449, 4 miles SW of Ledbury. Tel 01531 660504 for opening times.*

Goodrich Castle

A rocky baronial stronghold looming above the River Wye

Standing high on a rocky cliff, Goodrich Castle appears to have been carved from one enormous chunk of red sandstone – its foundations can be seen rising out of the deep dry moat. Godric Mappestone built the first fortress here in about 1086, but parts of two later constructions are incorporated within its great walls. The fourth and final additions to the building were made in the late 13th century with an architectural flair that created not just a castle but a splendid home. William de Valence, Henry III's half brother, owned it for nearly 50 years. A record of his widow's expenses from 1296 provides fascinating details of castle life, including the cost of a new pair of stockings (five pence) and boots (18 pence), and how a 'pipe' of wine – more than 700 bottles – was transported from Bristol for less than £4.

▶ *5 miles S of Ross-on-Wye, signed from A40. EH. Daily Mar-Oct; Wed-Sun Nov-Feb.*

Apples picked and pressed

Herefordshire's orchards fuel a potent cider industry

1 Cider Museum ▶ *Ryelands St, Hereford; daily.*

2 Westons ▶ *Much Marcle, 4 miles S of Ledbury off A449; Daily; Tel 01531 660233 for daily tours.*

3 Dunkertons ▶ *1 mile S of Pembridge on A44 Kington-Leominster road; Mon-Sat.*

4 Broome Farm ▶ *N of A49 at Peterstow, W of Ross-on-Wye, Tel 01989 567232. For other cider mills, Tel 01432 260621 (Visit Herefordshire).*

There are more than 3850ha (9500 acres) of cider apple orchards in Herefordshire. Pink and white apple blossom in spring is followed by jewelled apples in autumn, with names like Foxwhelp and Sheep's Nose. From them are produced more than half of Britain's cider.

An apple called Redstreak, raised from a pip in the 17th century, made Herefordshire cider the most prized in England. Cider became a fashionable drink, but in the next century its appeal waned with the custom of giving farm workers the dry, cloudy brew as part of their wages. This practice continued into the 1920s, but now cider making thrives again.

A good place to begin a quest for the finest cider among some 500 makers in Herefordshire is the **Cider Museum**. It tells the story of cider, and makes cider brandy in its own King Offa Distillery. **Westons** of Much Marcle, founded in 1880, is one of the largest makers but still relies on traditional methods. **Dunkertons** of Pembridge specialises in organically grown varieties. Visit between September and Christmas when the apples are pressed. To get right among the orchards, in full blossom in May, make for **Broome Farm**, where cider is produced on a small but passionate scale.

Standing on the edge of England

Wander away from the beaten track to savour the magnificent scenery that stands between two countries

5 Golden Valley ▶ *Valley of River Dore, between Dorstone and Pontrilas. B4347 runs through it.*

6 Abbey Dore ▶ *NE of Pontrilas off B4347. Daily, except services.*

7 Black Hill ▶ *E of Craswall on Monnow valley road.*

Four rivers – the Dore, Escley, Monnow and Olchon – flow through the southwest corner of Herefordshire and enclose an area of unparalleled beauty known as the **Golden Valley**. This is border country, a secret and wild chunk of landscape with the Black Mountains silhouetted in the distance.

The River Dore runs for 12 tranquil miles through the Golden Valley to the village of Ewyas Harold, which means 'the sheep land of Harold'. It is said that a one-eyed hermit lived in the Golden Valley in the 11th century and local legend alleges that it was King Harold, miraculously rescued after the Battle of Hastings and brought here by his mistress, Edith Swansneck.

French Cistercian monks founded **Abbey Dore** at Ewyas Harold in the 12th century. The name comes from the French for gold, 'or', to describe the river and its fertile valley, or perhaps the Welsh for water, 'dwr'. Local rose-grey stone was used to create the austere exterior, which brings a Gallic air to the rolling English countryside. Only the transepts and chancel remain, but they form an awesome, lofty space. The abbey was rescued from dereliction in the 17th century and became the local parish church. Its oak chancel screen was intricately carved with coats of arms by John Abel of Hereford in 1632.

The abandoned railway route through the Golden Valley is good walking terrain, but take the road west over the hills to Longtown and the land changes. The Black Mountains rise abruptly from the River Olchon's valley, forming a high and almost impregnable wall.

Between the valleys of the Monnow and Olchon rivers climbs the sharply defined **Black Hill**, an outrider of the Black Mountains. At 644m (2112ft) it is England's highest summit south of Yorkshire. It narrows from the peak to a rocky ridge that arches like a feline spine and is known locally as the Cat's Back (below). Views from it reach into the valleys below and extend as far as the Brecon Beacons, The Wrekin in Shropshire and the Cotswolds.

LEICESTERSHIRE & RUTLAND

1 Belvoir Castle **2** Donington Grand Prix Collection **3** Breedon on the Hill

4 Bosworth Battlefield

Belvoir Castle

Battles, sieges and high living at one of Britain's finest castles

Commanding wide vistas across the Vale of Belvoir, the lofty, turretted, castellated ancestral home of the dukes of Rutland dominates the skyline. Belvoir Castle is the fourth building on the site since Robert de Todeni, standard bearer to William the Conqueror at the Battle of Hastings in 1066, erected a castle here.

The romantic medievalism of the building dates only from 1830, when Belvoir (meaning 'beautiful view' and pronounced 'beever') was remodelled after a fire. Battles and sieges in the Wars of the Roses and Civil War had caused the destruction of the previous castles.

The interior features a dazzling array of oriental, Louis XIV-style and Georgian rooms. The 40m (131ft) long Regent's Gallery is hung with Gobelin tapestries depicting *The Adventures of Don Quixote*. Glorious gardens are laid out below the castle, and on the terraced hillside a statue collection includes work by Caius Cibber, Charles II's sculptor.
▶ *6 miles SW of Grantham off A1. For opening details, Tel 01476 871002.*

Donington Grand Prix Collection

Motor sport's hall of fame

For the motor racing enthusiast, there is nothing in the world like the Donington Grand Prix Collection. In five huge halls on the edge of Donington Park's race-track, motor sport is commemorated from its earliest beginnings in the 1900s to the present day. Exhibits include a three-wheeler Morgan raced at Donington Park when it first opened in the 1930s, the 1963 World Championship-winning Lotus 25 of Jim Clark, and the 1993 McLaren of Ayrton Senna in which he won the European Grand Prix on the neighbouring circuit.
▶ *Donington Park, Castle Donington, 2 miles from M1 (Junction 23a/24). Daily.*

Breedon on the Hill

A 9th-century carved angel keeps watch over a hill-top church

Above the village of Breedon a startling knoll of red-and-ochre dolomite and fossil-filled limestone thrusts out over the Vale of Trent. Its crowning glory is the isolated church of St Mary and St Hardulph, standing on the site of an Iron Age fort and a former Augustinian priory. The church contains one of England's largest collections of Saxon carvings, dating from the 8th to 10th centuries.

Foremost among the items of stonework is the Breedon Angel, considered to be the earliest carved angel in England. The figure is set in an arched panel in the tower's bell-ringing chamber. One hand holds a cross, while the other is raised to make a blessing. Elsewhere in the church, interlaced vine-scrolls stretch round the walls in a 19m (63ft) long frieze. Other friezes are studded with birds, fighting beasts, and huntsmen with spears.
▶ *4 miles S of Castle Donington off A453.*

Bosworth Battlefield

Ghosts of a bloody conflict

A single white rose, lying on a memorial stone, marks the spot where Richard III died in 1485. In August 1485, Henry Tudor – just arrived from France via Wales – confronted Richard's much larger army here. When he perceived that the day was going against him, Richard rode straight towards Henry's standard, declaring that he would 'make an end to war or life'. In the event, he lost both. Richard, last of the Plantagenets, also became the last English monarch to die in battle, and Henry VII, first of the Tudors, was proclaimed king on nearby Crown Hill.

The site has remained largely unchanged for the past 500 years. There is a visitor centre on Ambion Hill, where Richard's army had been encamped before Henry attacked, and a battlefield trail with viewpoints. A modern statue in Leicester recalls Richard's bravery, portraying him not as the crook-backed figure of Shakespearean drama, but as a kingly and athletic figure, 'a good lawmaker for the ease and solace of the common people'.
▶ *11 miles E of Leicester, signed from all routes. Visitor centre daily; Apr-Oct, Sat-Sun Mar, Sun Nov-Dec. Park and trail daily.*

CENTRAL ENGLAND

LEICESTERSHIRE & RUTLAND

St Luke's, Gaddesby

Vivid re-enaction of a scene from the Battle of Waterloo

A graceful broach-spired 13th-century church of golden ironstone dominates the village of Gaddesby. Most dramatic of its memorial monuments is a chancel sculpture by Joseph Gott, dedicated to the cavalry officer Colonel Edward Cheney, who lived at Gaddesby Hall and died in 1848.

The nearly life-size sculpture is the only equine statue in marble to be found in an English church. It depicts Cheney's heroism at the Battle of Waterloo. No fewer than four horses were killed beneath the officer, but he fought on, leading the Scots Greys through the final stages of the battle. As his agonised horse collapses with a bullet wound in its chest, the dauntless Cheney, hat dislodged, wields his sabre in swashbuckling fashion.

Notice that the horse has green teeth – an apple is customarily placed in its mouth each harvest festival.
▶ *Church Lane, Gaddesby, 3 miles E from A607 Leicester-Melton Mowbray road.*

Taylor's Bellfoundry and Museum

See bells made that toll out around the world

From a ladle nearly as big as a man, molten metal heated in a furnace to 1200°C (2200°F) is poured into a mould set in a sandpit to cast a new bell. When Great Paul, the 16 tonner that hangs in St Paul's Cathedral, was cast at Taylor's (right) in 1888 it took two weeks to cool.

Taylor's is a family firm founded in 1838 when the bells of All Saints Church in Loughborough needed recasting. It is the world's largest working bellfoundry. Church bells, hand bells, ships' bells and carillons are made or restored here. A tour reveals the intricate process of bell-making, from preparing the core of the bell mould using sand, hay and horse manure, to the delicate art of inscribing, the thrill of casting and the skill of tuning.
▶ *Freehold Street, Loughborough. Museum Tues-Fri, and Sat in summer. For tours, Tel 01509 233414.*

Abbey Pumping Station

The story of sewage in a grand Victorian setting

How did people manage before the WC was invented? And what was bathtime like without soap? These aspects of universal needs are considered at the Abbey Pumping Station, now the Leicester Museum of Science and Technology. The building opened in 1891 and still houses four beam engines that played a vital role in the city's public health by pumping 945,000 litres (208,000 gallons) of sewage every hour to the Beaumont Leys treatment works. Today it is home to the 'Flushed with Pride' exhibition, which follows the history of plumbing from Roman times. Washday blues at a Victorian laundry are re-created along with displays of prototype washing machines and shower-baths.
▶ *1 mile N of city centre, next to National Space Centre. Sat-Wed Feb-Nov.*

National Space Centre

Take one small step towards cosmic exploration

A transparent Rocket Tower of super-light plastic material hooped with curved steel tubes erupts 42m (138ft) above the car park like an alien chrysalis – the sleek form of the 18.5m (61ft) high *Blue Streak* rocket visible inside.
Next to the Tower, the Space Theatre's futuristic geodesic dome occupies an old storm water tank. At Britain's largest exhibition centre devoted to space exploration you can take a virtual trip across the known universe and glimpse our investigations of it.

Six themed galleries give you the chance to experience various aspects of space travel – you can launch a rocket, build a satellite and join the crew of the futuristic lunar base. The Centre's £11 million collection of authentic space gear and technology might make you ponder the big questions. Where do we come from? Is anybody else out there? How will it all end?
▶ *1 mile N of city centre. Tues-Sun and bank hol Mon; also Mon pm in school hols.*

SEE BELLS MADE THAT
T LL OUT AROUND
THE WORLD

TAYLOR'S BELLFOUNDRY AND MUSEUM

Clipsham Yew Tree Avenue

A forester's flight of fancy

A regiment of exotically clipped yew trees lines the carriage drive to Clipsham Hall. Many of the 150 ancient trees are crowned with perfectly sculpted whimsical topknots or animals, including an elephant and a deer, while varied shapes, initials and geometric patterns are carved on their sides.

Some designs represent historic events, such as a Battle of Britain Spitfire and Neil Armstrong's Moon landing in 1969. New ideas are continually added to the collection.

As many of these venerable trees are more than double the height of the forestry workers who look after them, trimming them into shape each September is a great challenge. At least modern topiarists enjoy the benefit of powered hedgecutters and mechanical hoists – advantages denied to Amos Alexander, the head forester of Clipsham estate, who started this unusual project as a hobby in 1870.

▶ *1 mile E of A1, 8 miles N of Stamford, just outside Clipsham, near Ram Jam Inn. Daily.*

Ye Olde Pork Pie Shoppe

The art of raised pie-making lives on in Melton Mowbray

The real pork pie, hand-made on the premises of Dickinson & Morris to a time-honoured recipe, is a revelation to the taste buds. This English delicacy originated in the market town of Melton Mowbray 160 years ago as a by-product of the Vale of Belvoir's dairy industry. Whey produced during the making of Stilton cheese was fed to pigs, enhancing the flavour of their meat.

Founded in 1851, Dickinson & Morris is the oldest and last-remaining of Melton's pork pie bakeries. With a little notice, you can see a pie-making demonstration or don an apron and create your own hand-raised, hot-water-crust pies. They are baked overnight for collection the next day.

▶ *8-10 Nottingham Street, Melton Mowbray. Mon-Sat. Book ahead for demonstrations and evening tuition sessions. Tel 01664 482068.*

SUBMERGED VALLEYS BRING SURPRISING BENEFITS
RUTLAND WATER

Rutland Water

Submerged valleys bring surprising benefits

When Rutland Water was created in the 1970s, it was western Europe's largest man-made lake, covering some 1255ha (3100 acres), or 4 per cent of Rutland, England's smallest county. The drowned valleys of the Gwash form an impressive stretch of water, slowly earning forgiveness for the disruption and hardship its construction caused to local people. Besides huge quantities of water for the expanding East Midlands, it provides a spacious outdoor leisure playground and a haven for wildlife, including an osprey colony.

On the lake's southeastern shores, Normanton church is preserved as a poignant reminder of the impact the rising waters had on the surrounding community. Just the tower and clerestory remain visible above the waterline. Inside, a small museum traces the history and geology of the reservoir. Walks and cycle tracks follow the lake's 25 mile perimeter, but its scope and scale is best appreciated from a boat.

▶ *Central Rutland. Normanton Church, daily Apr-Sept. Boat trips, Tel 01572 787630.*

Harborough Museum

The secrets of foundation garments laid bare for all to see

The name of Symington looms large in the annals of Market Harborough. James, son of a prosperous grocer, married a corset staymaker in 1830, and founded the underpinnings of the local economy.

Modest sales of handmade corsetry in his drapery and tailoring business soon blossomed into an empire employing hundreds of people. One of the factories now houses Market Harborough's museum, where the Symington Collection of Corsetry reveals the agony of the quest for the fashionable female form, achieved with steel, whalebone and high-tensile elastic. Displays show the development of corsets from the breathtaking narrow-waisted stays of the Victorian age to the comparative comfort of the Liberty Bodice. After cutting, garments were steam-heated, starched and preformed over hollow copper moulds known as Swedish Maidens.

In the Second World War, the Symington factories turned their skills to manufacturing parachutes for the armed forces.

▶ *Fox Yard, at rear of Council Offices, Adam and Eve Street, Market Harborough. Daily.*

Stanford Hall

A pioneering aviator who came so close to achieving his dream

The stable block museum of this fine William and Mary house contains a strange, fragile aircraft of bamboo struts and canvas lashed together by a cat's cradle of taut wire. It is a replica of *The Hawk*, the flying machine in which Lieutenant Percy Pilcher RN ended his aviation experiments in the grounds of Stanford Hall in 1899.

Pilcher flew numerous machines constructed on the principles of hang gliders, but he also experimented with aero engines, and was on the way to attaining the prize for the first powered flight. Tragically, *The Hawk* disintegrated in mid-air, and he crashed with fatal injuries on the banks of the Avon. His research ended up instead on the far side of the Atlantic, helping the Wright Brothers towards their successful maiden flight in 1903.

Pilcher was a friend of the 6th Lord Braye whose ancestors have lived on the estate since 1430. The present house dates from 1690 and contains antique furnishings and costumes, and a notable collection of Stuart portraits.

▶ *5 miles S of Lutterworth, N of Stanford-on-Avon, E of M1 (Junction 19). Sun and bank hol Mon (except Aug) Easter-Sept.*

Foxton Locks

Victorian boaters could climb the stairs or take the lift

Foxton is one of the prettiest spots on the British canal network. A sequence of ten locks raises water levels 23m (75ft) between the Grand Union Canal and the Leicestershire and Northamptonshire Canal. Opened in 1814, they were in their day an impressively engineered solution to the hilly terrain around these bustling Midland waterways.

In 1900 the Grand Junction Canal Company employed another solution to solve canal bottlenecks – it built a steam-powered Inclined Plane Lift next to the locks. Two counterbalanced tanks, each capable of loading two narrow boats at a time, plied up and down the slope on rails, taking just 12 minutes to travel between the two canals instead of 45 minutes through the locks. As railways replaced canals, the system became redundant, and the lift was abandoned. A museum tells the story of locks and lift.

▶ *3 miles NW of Market Harborough off A6. Museum daily, except Thur and Fri Nov-Easter.*

CENTRAL ENGLAND

A dynamic mix of Stilton and spice

Settlers from around the globe have created a rich and vibrant cultural life in the city of Leicester

1 Leicester

Over the centuries, **Leicester** has become one of Europe's most cosmopolitan cities. Romans, Danes and Normans once stamped their identity in walls, baths, mosaics, place names and institutions. Jewish, Irish and Italian communities have become established here and the city was a haven for Belgian, German and East European refugees during the Second World War. Since 1945, newcomers from Africa and the Caribbean, and especially from the Indian sub-continent, have made it thoroughly multi-cultural. There is a higher percentage of non-white residents here than in any other British city. They make a crucial contribution to the local economy – for example, some 10 per cent of the city's jobs are in Asian businesses.

Castle Park, on Leicester's west side, is the oldest part of the city, with architecture that reflects the cultures of its inhabitants. Several of its most ancient churches stand here, including the Anglo-Saxon St Nicholas Church and the 12th-century cathedral. A stark contrast is found in Oxford Street where a white marble façade encases the **Jain temple** (Tel 0116 254 3091). Originally a Victorian Congregational chapel, it was converted during the 1980s for followers of Jainism, an Indian religion founded over 2500 years ago. More than a million fragments of

mirror glass sparkle on the mosaic wall inside, and marble statues of prophets stand under the central dome, surrounded by 54 columns. In 1989 an old hosiery factory was converted into a Sikh temple, the **Guru Nanak Gurdwara** (9 Holy Bones, Tel 0116 262 8606). Its museum houses sacred paintings, handwritten manuscripts and elaborate models, including the Golden Temple of Amritsar. A prayer hall, library, school and a 'langar' (a communal free kitchen), where people eat together regardless of race or social status, are also part of the complex. Both temples are open daily for worship, but arrange sightseeing visits in advance and be prepared to remove your shoes and cover your head.

Go shopping to discover another facet of Leicester's cultural diversity. The city market, with around 400 stalls, displays enough ingredients to prepare any exotic dish, as well as the county's more traditional pork pies and Stilton cheese. Then head north of the city to the **Golden Mile** (along Belgrave and Melton Road, on A607), named after the jewellers who trade here. It is at the heart of the Gujarati-speaking community, and has a colourful range of restaurants and specialist shops selling spices, saris, silks, sweets and crafts from countries all over the world.

DIWALI FESTIVAL ON BELGRAVE ROAD, LEICESTER

LINCOLNSHIRE

1 National Fishing Heritage Centre 2 St James's, Louth 3 Gainsborough Old Hall

4 Lincoln Cathedral 5 Boston Stump

National Fishing Heritage Centre

Experience the fear and exhilaration of a life on the waves

A tour of the trawler *Ross Tiger* with a former trawlerman evokes the treacherous conditions on its fishing expeditions: the exhausting shifts, freezing decks, whiplash cables and the deafening roar of the engine room.

It is one of the highlights of a visit to the National Fishing Heritage Centre in Grimsby, the world's largest fishing port in the 1950s. The Centre captures the essence of this hazardous trade in recordings, tableaux and story boards with bracing icy blasts. For more fishy experiences join a tour to Grimsby's early morning fish auction, with a visit to a traditional dockside smoke-house.

▶ *Alexandra Dock, Grimsby. Daily.*

St James's, Louth

Canny perspective of a soaring spire

The pencil-slim spire of Louth's church dominates the wide skies of the Lincolnshire Wolds. Rising to 90m (295ft) above the market town, St James's has the highest steeple of any English parish church. It appears taller due to its elegant Perpendicular style, and a clever understanding of optical illusion by its medieval masons. The bobbles, or crockets, on the spire are unevenly spaced and subtly enlarged as they ascend the spire to counteract the effects of perspective.

The tower was strengthened in 1499 to support the ambitious spire. It grew for the next 15 years and was braced with flying buttresses and 15m (50ft) pinnacles.

▶ *In centre of Louth. Mon-Sat Apr-Dec; Mon, Wed, Fri and Sat am Jan-Mar.*

Gainsborough Old Hall

A medieval hall graced by kings and preachers

Richard III, Henry VIII and John Wesley all visited this rambling brick-and-timbered manor built in 1465-80. Perfectly preserved, and a surprising find in the centre of a modest market town, it has altered little since their visits. In the barn-like Great Hall, curved oak roof trusses soar above walls brightly decked with banners and hangings, and tables set for a medieval banquet. Passages from it lead to the original medieval kitchen with two fireplaces, each large enough to roast an ox fit for a king.

▶ *In centre of Gainsborough. EH. Mon-Sat; also Sun pm Apr-Oct.*

Lincoln Cathedral

Calamitous setbacks that helped to create awe-inspiring architecture

Walk around Lincoln Cathedral's ten-sided, flying-buttressed chapterhouse to sense the vast scale of an ambitious structure, completed against all odds. The cathedral's golden limestone was shaped by natural disaster: fire destroyed the 11th-century original in 1141, an earthquake in 1185 led to a Gothic-style rebuild, and when the spire blew down in 1548 it ceased to be the world's tallest building. A piece of the original Norman cathedral survives in the west front's round-arched bays and the Romanesque frieze of biblical scenes above. Inside, you'll find the demonic Lincoln Imp, perching cross-legged in the 13th-century Angel Choir.

▶ *Clearly signed in city centre. Daily.*

Boston Stump

Highest church tower in the realm

The good folk of Boston wanted the world – or at least every sailor for miles out to sea, and every landlubber on the fens – to know their town was the greatest port after London, so they built the highest church tower in England. It was started in the early 1300s and eventually, some 200 years later, a halt was called and plans to put up a crowning spire, or simply continue the tower, abandoned. In a masterpiece of understatement some wag gave it the sobriquet, the Stump. Some 'stump': by then, the pinnacled lantern tower had reached a giddying 83m (272ft).

The interior is just as remarkable. The nave pillars tilt on silty foundations. The misericords on the choirstalls depict medieval domestic scenes: a housewife chasing a fox carrying off her fowls; a teacher birching a pupil who has a book stuffed in his breeches.

▶ *Boston centre. Tower Mon-Sat. Church daily.*

CENTRAL ENGLAND

LINCOLNSHIRE

6 The Wash 7 Tattershall Castle 8 Pinchbeck Pumping Engine 9 Grimsthorpe Castle

10 Stamford 11 Burghley House

The Wash

Wildlife finds a peaceful haven in an isolated land of dunes and marshes

Thousands of seals, wading birds and wildfowl inhabit the remote, marshy flatlands and shingle beaches of The Wash. Rare plants, amphibians and insects colonise the shore – marsh orchids, natterjack toads and 12 species of dragonfly among them. Their movement, calls and song may be the only signs of life in these vast expanses of land. Nature reserves at Gedney Drove End, Frampton Marsh, Freiston Shore and Gibraltar Point provide access points, trails and information about the fragile ecosystem.

The North Sea took a broad, square bite from the low-lying coastline between Skegness and the bulge of East Anglia to form The Wash. Rivers draining into this shallow basin added peat and alluvium to tidal scourings deposited by the sea and the region slowly silted up – Boston, once England's second largest seaport, now lies four miles inland. Vast areas of saline marshland have been reclaimed since the Romans built sea banks and drains along the fertile silt ridges near Holbeach. Today, a system of banks, dykes and pumps protects the area. But visitors should take care not to stray from sea banks as tidal flows are swift and dangerous.

▶ *From Skegness to Hunstanton. Weekday bombing ranges at Holbeach St Matthew and Wainfleet Sand – obey signs.*

Tattershall Castle

Medieval high-rise that expresses its creator's vaunting ambition

More than a million bricks were used in the construction of Tattershall's formidable six-storey Great Tower (right), built in 1434-46. Its turreted battlements loom 34m (110ft) above the flatlands around Coningsby, and are visible as far as Boston Stump and Lincoln Cathedral. The tower is a fitting monument to its creator, Ralph Cromwell (1393-1456). He fought with Henry V at Agincourt, and became Treasurer of England. Among the sparsely furnished state rooms, his defiant motto 'Nay je droit?' (have I not the right?) can be seen carved on the parlour's chimneypiece.

Cromwell also commissioned the collegiate church next to the castle, built in Perpendicular style. Look out for the Treasurer's emblem – the purse – inside.

▶ *W of Coningsby, on A153 in Tattershall. NT. Sat-Wed Apr-Oct; Sat-Sun pm Nov-Dec and Mar.*

Pinchbeck Pumping Engine

A marvel of steam power that tirelessly drained the waterland

They'll start it up for you, this prodigious piece of 19th-century engineering: the hissing, pounding Pinchbeck Pumping Engine. Its gigantic 5 tonne flywheel dwarfs the interior of the modest brick housing. The precisely engineered pistons slide smoothly in their chambers – as good as when new.

The arrival of steam power and the pumping engine transformed the economy of the fens, removing the threat of flooding. From 1833 until an electrically powered replacement superseded it nearly 120 years later, this leviathan pumped up to 34,100 litres (7500 gallons) of water an hour from the surrounding marshes of South Holland into the embanked River Welland. Fenland life is explored in the small Land Drainage Museum.

▶ *1 mile N of Spalding off A16. Daily Apr-Sept.*

Grimsthorpe Castle

Vanbrugh's most impressive makeover for the new duke

It could be said that Grimsthorpe Castle is all front – but what a front. Part of a larger design by the playwright, soldier and architect John Vanbrugh, the great north front (completed about 1726) is a superb Baroque version of a medieval fortress – and symbolic of the 16th Baron Willoughby's ambition to see his new status as a duke reflected in the ancestral home. Here is a façade calculated to inspire awe. Soaring above the roof line, colossal statues on ancient classical themes crown great Tuscan pillars and frame a huge family coat of arms. The flanking towers project into the courtyard, their chimney-stacks disguised as Roman altars. Beyond the main entrance, the heroic theme continues in a spectacular arcaded hall before you enter the human huddle of the rest of the house.

▶ *5 miles NW of Bourne on A151. Sun, Thur and bank hols pm Apr–Sept; Sun-Thur pm Aug.*

Stamford

Preserved but not precious, an architectural gem of a town

The A1 takes a swing around it, but you should turn off and visit this lovely town – in 1967 it was the first in England to declare itself a conservation area. Stamford has more than 500 listed buildings of architectural or historic merit. No wonder it is a favourite backdrop for period costume dramas.

Many houses have the beautifully proportioned, trademark windows of the Georgian era. But some of Stamford's buildings, such as the almshouses, Browne's Hospital (1483), in Broad Street, belong to the years when the town was a prosperous cloth port on the River Welland. In a maze of medieval streets, the roofs are a particular delight: some have graded tiles that become smaller and thinner as they climb to the ridge; others are clad in frost-fractured Collyweston limestone, subtly shading from blue to brown.

▶ *1 mile E of A1 on Lincs/Cambs border.*

Burghley House

Home of Elizabeth's spymaster

Elizabeth I never visited the home of her trusted statesman and spymaster – perhaps wisely. Had she done so, she would have found that William Cecil had designed a residence fit for a king, with a roofscape of turrets and chimneys even more flamboyant than that at her own palace of Hampton Court.

Cecil founded a dynasty. The 5th Earl, a shopaholic, collected works of art from all over Europe and commissioned artists such as the *trompe l'oeil* specialist Antonio Verrio (1639-1707). Here, in Verrio's *Hell Staircase*, the visitor ascends into the gaping mouth of a gigantic cat, where the Grim Reaper scythes down lost souls. Oil and gas lighting blackened the work over the years, but, in 1993, it was cleaned – except for the lower legs of a female figure (on the edge of the picture), left to show its pre-restoration state.

▶ *1 mile SE of Stamford. Sat-Thur Apr-Oct.*

TATTERSHALL CASTLE

A county cleared for takeoff

Fly back in time to the 1940s, when Lincolnshire played a central role in the air campaign to win the war

1 **RAF Digby** ▶ *2 miles E of A15 (Lincoln-Sleaford road) on B1191. Sun May-Sept. Other times by appointment.* Tel 01526 327619.

2 **Metheringham Airfield** ▶ *5 miles E of A15 (Lincoln-Sleaford road) on B1202. Wed, Sat and Sun and bank hols Apr-Oct.* Tel 01526 378270.

3 **Thorpe Camp (RAF Woodhall Spa)** ▶ *2 miles N of A153 at Coningsby on B1192. Sun and bank hols pm Easter-Sept; also Wed July-Aug.* Tel 01526 342249.

4 **RAF Coningsby** ▶ *10 miles NE of Sleaford on A153. Mon-Fri.* Tel 01526 344041.

5 **Lincolnshire Aviation Heritage Centre** *(RAF East Kirkby)* ▶ *3 miles W of A16 (Boston-Louth road) on A155. Mon-Sat all year.* Tel 01790 763207.

6 **RAF Cranwell** ▶ *½ mile N of A17 (Sleaford-Newark road) on B1429. Daily Apr-Sept.* Tel 01529 488490.

In the days when Germany's industries and cities were being attacked from the air, Lincolnshire was known as 'Bomber County'. With 28 aerodromes of Bomber Command, and a score of fighter fields; with 30,000 flat acres taken over for military aviation; with skies that reverberated to the drone of planes taking off for or returning from raids, it seemed, for those who were there, as though the entire shire, from the North Sea to the Trent, was one great runway.

Fortunately those dramatic days are not just the stuff of memory, peopled by the ghosts of disused airfields and derelict hangars. Instead Lincolnshire's aviation heritage is preserved at more than a dozen places, where you can see everything from blockbusting displays of legendary wartime aircraft to an ops room and control tower. At former bases such as **Digby**, **Metheringham** and **Woodhall Spa** the atmosphere of what it was like to belong to one of these 'small towns', with its aircrews, ground staff, Naafi and debriefing rooms, is brought vividly back to life in exhibitions and displays.

Home of the Dambusters

There are, too, touching collections of personal memorabilia – blurred photographs of smiling aircrews, crumpled flying jackets and fragments of fuselage – and official telegrams informing a parent or wife that her son or husband was missing in action, presumed dead. One death is easier to comprehend than the overall toll: 25,611 personnel of Bomber Command were killed in action flying from airfields in Lincolnshire. They came from every part of Britain, and from Australia, Canada, New Zealand, Poland and Southern Rhodesia. Many of them are remembered in dozens of village memorials, such as the one in Bardney, where a Lancaster propeller on the village green commemorates the members of 9 Squadron, responsible for sinking the battleship Tirpitz off Norway.

Also taking part in that attack were the Lancasters of 617 Squadron, based at RAF Scampton, the one that became known simply as the Dambusters after Guy Gibson led the daring raid aimed at depriving Germany's industrial Ruhr of water and hydro-electric power. Although more than half of the 7366 Lancasters built flew out of Lincolnshire, many in massed 'thousand bomber raids', it was this single mission by a small force of 16 aircraft, of which eight never returned, that cemented the plane as a symbol of the county's role in the bomber offensive.

Taking to the skies

In spite of this, Lancasters are almost extinct: only two in the world are still airworthy, one of them at **RAF Coningsby**. There, Lancaster PA474 'City of Lincoln', together with the Spitfires (pictured left flying over Boston) and Hurricanes of the Battle of Britain Memorial Flight, can be seen in the flight's dedicated hangar. The planes are regularly wheeled out and take to the sky in air displays here and elsewhere around Britain.

A short distance away, at the **Lincolnshire Aviation Heritage Centre**, East Kirkby, another Lancaster is the star attraction. Visitors can thrill to the sound and sight of the plane's four mighty Rolls-Royce Merlin engines roaring into life and sending it taxiing along the runway, but NX611, 'Just Jane' is grounded. Among the other displays, there is a museum devoted to the imaginative ways in which stranded or captured aircrew sought to make it back home, and a full-size 'bouncing bomb' used in rehearsals for the Dambusters raid. A few miles to the west, an exhibition at **RAF Cranwell** charts the history of this working base since its Royal Flying Corps days in the First World War. Cranwell is the home of the Royal Flying School, where Battle of Britain pilot Douglas Bader and jet engine inventor Frank Whittle trained, and from which today's graduates may go on to fly the planes that streak across the skies of Lincolnshire – the Red Arrows, based at Scampton, or Coningsby's Tornados.

NORTHAMPTONSHIRE

1 Harringworth Viaduct **2** Deene Park **3** Rockingham Castle **4** Saxon churches

Harringworth Viaduct

Victorian engineering on a monumental scale

A startling landmark strides across the wide floodplain of the Welland between Harringworth (in Northamptonshire) and Seaton (in Rutland). The Harringworth railway viaduct's 82 arches, visible for miles around, rise 18m (60ft) above the valley floor, extend for ¾ mile and contain some 15 million bricks.

Two thousand men worked on the viaduct between 1876 and 1878 to carry the Midland Railway's branch line between Kettering and Manton. The skilful brickwork (battleship grey on the lower arches, terracotta on the upper sections) is apparent only at close quarters, but the full impact of this colossal structure is best experienced from a distance. Occasional trains are diverted across the viaduct, but it no longer carries regular passenger services.

▶ *12 miles W of Stamford off A47/B672.*

Deene Park

Home of horse and rider from the Charge of the Light Brigade

The country seat of the Brudenell family contains one of the most unusual exhibits to be found in a stately home: the preserved head of Ronald, an equine hero from the Crimean War. Deene Park was the home of the 7th Earl of Cardigan, who in 1854 led the heroic but disastrously mismanaged Charge of the Light Brigade. His beloved horse not only survived the war, but lived another 18 years, and led his master's funeral procession in 1868. Sedated with laudanum, Ronald was so drowsy that the bugler had to sound a battle charge to rouse him. Apparently Lord Cardigan arrived at his final resting-place ahead of schedule.

The manor of Deene predates Domesday Book. The Tudor part is built around a courtyard, off which is the Elizabethan Great Hall with a fine hammerbeam roof of sweet chestnut. Spectacular plaster ceilings and linenfold panelling decorate several rooms. Other parts of the house are Victorian in character, as the 7th Earl would have known it.

▶ *5 miles NE of Corby off A43. Sun pm June-Aug; Sun-Mon pm bank hols Easter-Aug.*

VICTORIAN ENGINEERING ON A MONUMENTAL SCALE
HARRINGWORTH VIADUCT

Rockingham Castle

Nine hundred years of home make-overs under one roof

Stout drum towers flanking the entrance confront visitors with the perfect image of a stalwart medieval fortress. Step through the gate, however, and you progress three centuries to find a cluster of gabled, honey-coloured buildings resembling a Tudor estate. For Rockingham Castle has assumed many guises, and combines with architectural flair a mix of styles chronicling the needs of its successive occupants – from the remains of the original fortified walls (now a terrace giving glorious views over five counties), to the 17th-century laundry adorned with clock and bell-tower.

Inside, magnificent rooms groan with choice antiques and paintings, while curios of fine pedigree recall distinguished guests. An iron chest in the Hall is said to have belonged to King John, and mementos of Dickens commemorate his visits to the castle, which he used as the model for Chesney Wold – home of the Dedlocks in the novel *Bleak House*.

▶ *1 mile N of Corby off A6003. Sun and bank hol Mon Easter-May; Tues, Sun and bank hol Mon June-Sept.*

Saxon churches

Rare survivals of England's earliest places of Christian worship

Northamptonshire has one of the richest collections of Saxon churches in England. Christianity spread across the region in the 7th century with the reign of King Paeda, the first Christian ruler of the kingdom of Mercia. A monastery was established at Peterborough, in Cambridgeshire, and between 750 and 850 the monks built **All Saints' Church, Brixworth**, a large and handsome church of golden stone with recycled Roman bricks embedded in its arches. It has an unusual rounded external stair turret attached to its tower, as does **St Andrew's Church, Brigstock**, which dates from around 900 to 1000, built after Vikings burnt down the original church.

All Saints' Church, Earls Barton, is noted for its superb tower, built around 970, decorated with distinctive ragstone strips in grey-gold patterns added by some exuberant Saxon masons. Later Norman work can be seen in its portal decked with chevrons and strange beasts, and the blind arcading of the chancel.

▶ *Brixworth, 6 miles N of Northampton on A508. Brigstock, 8 miles NE of Kettering on A43/A6116. Earls Barton, off A45, 6 miles NE of Northampton.*

NORTHAMPTONSHIRE

Tresham Trail

The Catholic enigmas of an Elizabethan courtier and builder

Sir Thomas Tresham is remembered for a bizarre series of 16th-century buildings, which are riddled with numerical puzzles and religious allusions. Tresham inherited the family estate at Rushton and was knighted by Elizabeth I for his loyal service at court. He had been brought up a Protestant, as required by the State, but publicly turned to Catholicism in 1580 and was imprisoned as a result. In the 1570s he built his first work, the **Market House, Rothwell**, which like his later buildings is lavishly adorned with coats of arms and Latin inscriptions. While in prison he planned **Triangular Lodge, Rushton**, a three-sided building signifying the Trinity.

Lyveden New Bield, begun about 1595, was intended as a garden lodge, but construction ceased on Tresham's death in 1605. The substantial building stands eerily roofless, two storeys high, with moated gardens nearby. It is embellished with religious scriptures.
▶ *Market House, Rothwell; Tel 01536 713252. Triangular Lodge, 3 miles E of Desborough off A6; EH; Thur-Mon Apr-Oct. Lyveden New Bield, off A427, 4 miles SW of Oundle; NT; Wed-Sun and bank hol Mon late Mar-Oct; daily Aug; Sat-Sun Nov-Mar.*

Eleanor Cross, Geddington

A king's heartfelt memorial to his devoted queen

In Geddington village stands a tall stone monument encrusted with time-worn carving. Three statues decorate its angled niches, each representing Eleanor of Castile, wife of Edward I. This is the best-preserved and least altered of the three surviving crosses erected in 1294 by the grief-stricken king to mark the places where Eleanor's funeral cortège rested overnight on its journey south to London.

The other two crosses are at Hardingstone (now a suburb of Northampton) and Waltham Cross in Essex. A Victorian copy outside Charing Cross station in London marks the final resting site.

Eleanor and Edward wed in 1254. During their 36-year marriage the couple were rarely apart, even on Edward's protracted military campaigns. In 1290, Edward set off to fight the Scots. Eleanor followed, but, already gravely ill, died at Harby, Nottinghamshire. She is buried in Westminster Abbey.
▶ *Geddington, 3 miles N of Kettering, on A43. Hardingstone on A508, S of Northampton.*

Cottesbrooke Hall

Sporting art in a fine setting

The greatest collection of sporting and equestrian art outside America can be seen at Cottesbrooke Hall. Sculptures and paintings by artists such as George Stubbs, John Ferneley, Ben Marshall and Alfred Munnings immortalise the horses and hounds of former owners, including Lord Woolavington, who formed the collection at the end of the 19th century.

The house, completed in 1713, is said to have been the model for Jane Austen's *Mansfield Park*. Its rooms, filled with exquisite tapestries, furniture and porcelain, include the Staircase Hall, its sea-green walls decorated in rare rococo papier-mâché work from 1750.

The gardens are adorned with parterres, water features and herbaceous borders bursting with unusual plants.
▶ *9 miles N of Northampton off A5199. For opening details, Tel 01604 505808.*

Northampton Museum

A shoe-lover's paradise in a county town

Kitten heels, absurd creations of the 1970s and even an elephant boot used in an expedition of 1859 to re-create Hannibal's crossing of the Alps are among the 12,000 outlandish items of footwear held at Northampton Museum. The shoe-making town has possibly the world's largest collection of historic footwear – so big that only a selection can be shown at any one time.

Dazzlingly impractical court shoes with 15cm (6in) heels play footsie with military attire (glistening jackboots, electrically heated flying boots, parachute boots with built-in shock absorbers) and Queen Victoria's silk wedding shoes. The desiccated remnants of Roman shoes unearthed in archaeological digs are on view, and the story is told of how in the 11th century the Chinese emperor ordered women to wear crippling foot bindings after his daughter was born with misshapen feet.

▶ *Guildhall Road, Northampton. Mon-Sat, and Sun pm.*

Holy Sepulchre, Northampton

A crusader's round church

Of Britain's four surviving medieval round churches, the best-preserved is the Holy Sepulchre. It was founded in 1100 by Simon de Senlis, 1st Earl of Northampton, to celebrate his safe return from the Crusades. Step inside and you could almost be in the 11th-century Holy Sepulchre in Jerusalem, said to have been built over the tomb of Christ. It was the prototype for Senlis's church.

The most striking architectural feature is 'the Round', which lies immediately inside the entrance door. The sunken crypt-like space, supported by 16 weighty vaulted pillars, formed the nave (it is now a baptistry). The long chancel (the present nave) was added in the 13th century, the tower and spire in 1375, and the apse by Sir George Gilbert Scott in 1860. Quaint stone corbels, some depicting musicians, decorate parts of the nave, along with Victorian glasswork and 17th-century memorial brasses. Holy Sepulchre is popularly known as the 'Soldiers' Church', and regimental colours commemorating many historic battles hang in its chapels.

▶ *Northampton town centre. Wed and Sat pm May-Sept.*

Express Lifts tower

Going nowhere fast in the 'Northampton Lighthouse'

A bizarre landmark projects 127m (418ft) above the industrial outskirts to the west of Northampton. The slender concrete obelisk, nicknamed the 'Northampton lighthouse', is the taller of Europe's two solitary lift-testing towers. Its summit is the highest point due east between Northampton and the Ural Mountains of Russia.

Built by the former Express Lifts company, the tower contains three separate shafts designed to test lifts of differing speeds. In 2001, a Grade II listing by English Heritage reprieved the structure from demolition. There is no public access to the site, but the tower is clearly visible from parts of the town.

▶ *On industrial estate on A4500 due W of centre of Northampton. Good views from southern orbital road, Daventry exit route.*

Stoke Bruerne National Waterways Museum

The hazardous life of bargees

A few moments up the towpath from the colourful canal village of Stoke Bruerne yawns the sunless mouth of the Blisworth Tunnel, the second-longest continuous bore still navigable on British waterways. Built in 1805, the tunnel is 1¾ miles long and reaches a depth of 36m (120ft) below ground. Although wide enough for two boats to pass, it presented a serious hazard to early traffic on the Grand Union Canal. Heavily laden barges were propelled through by the dangerous method of 'legging'. The bargees lay on the boat's wingboards, pushing against the tunnel roof with their feet. A steam tug introduced in 1871 made legging unnecessary, but accidents continued to occur when boats collided in the smoky darkness.

The museum near Stoke Bruerne's locks, housed on three floors of an old cornmill, tells the story of the tunnel and vividly portrays life on the waterways with working models and canal memorabilia. Hire a narrowboat for the day and you can tackle the tunnel yourself.

▶ *Off A508, 3 miles S of M1 (Junction 15) and A5. Daily.*

CENTRAL ENGLAND

NOTTINGHAMSHIRE

1 Hodsock snowdrops **2** Mr Straw's House **3** Clumber Park **4** The Major Oak

Hodsock snowdrops

Drifts of white below the trees

In the dark days of February, long before the garden-visiting season begins in most places, Hodsock Priory is besieged by visitors. For a few fleeting weeks, winter woodland in the 324ha (800 acre) grounds lies under drifts of snowdrops, intermingled with the yellow of winter aconites, green-tinged hellebores or Christmas roses, and the mauves and hot yellows of early crocuses.

▶ *SW of Blyth, ¾ mile W of B6045 (Blyth-Worksop road). Daily for 4-5 weeks from early Feb. Tel 01909 591204.*

Mr Straw's House

The clocks tick but time stands still

You will feel a sense of disbelief when you stand outside No. 7 Blyth Grove, Worksop. Is this unexceptional, early 20th-century semi, no different from its neighbours, really owned by the National Trust? Only once beyond the bay window and panelled front door does all become clear: No. 7 is a time capsule, exactly as it was when well-to-do grocer William Straw moved there in 1923, having first had the house refurbished in the style of the day.

After William senior and then his wife died, their sons, William and Walter, kept everything exactly as Dad and Mum had left it, down to the Sanderson wallpapers, grained woodwork and superior Axminster staircarpet with its fashionable Tutankhamun motifs (the tomb of the pharaoh had been discovered in 1922). Nothing was thrown out either – as larder shelves lined with ancient tins of treacle and bottles of salad cream, and neatly tied bundles of the parents' old letters testify.

▶ *Worksop, signed from Blyth Road (B6045). NT. Tues-Sat mid Mar-Oct; pre-booked ticket only, Tel 01909 482380.*

Clumber Park

The house that died and vanished

You cannot miss Clumber Park: 1538ha (3800 acres) of stately grounds, entered, for best impressions, down a 2 mile avenue of luminous lime trees. There is a 35ha (87 acre) lake, miles of footpaths and cycle trails, a Victorian kitchen garden complete with glasshouse, and a host of picnic places. But the house that once lay at the heart of all this – one of Europe's biggest estates – has vanished.

Clumber House is dead and gone, killed in the 1930s by death duties, then sold off bit by bit. Now, forlorn lines of paving slabs and yew bushes mark its vast groundplan, like the foundations of an ancient temple. Apart from the stable block, which somehow escaped the fate of the rest of the dukes of Newcastle's grand seat, nothing remains: the furniture was sold; the panelling was stripped from the walls; finally, even the masonry was carted off.

▶ *Bounded by A614 and B6034 SE of Worksop. NT. Daily.*

The Major Oak

Ancient survivor of a mighty forest

Once the royal forest of Sherwood rolled away as far as the eye could see: 40,500ha (100,000 acres) of huntin' and shootin' for kings and queens, and an infinity of hiding places for Robin Hood and his merry men. Little remains of the vast greenwood – long since felled for hearths, furnaces and ships – but, in the Sherwood Forest Country Park, near Edwinstowe, you can find a lingering essence.

Here, among 182ha (450 acres) of slender young birch trees are giant oaks, hollow and stag-headed in the last stage of their long lives. Grandest of all is the Major Oak, with a trunk measuring 10m (33ft) in circumference and branches spreading across 30m (100ft). It has taken about 800 years for this leviathan to reach these staggering dimensions: a lifetime encompassing the reign of King John, and, possibly, a certain Robin of Locksley and Maid Marian meeting under its sapling boughs.

▶ *W of B6034, ¾ mile N of Edwinstowe. Daily.*

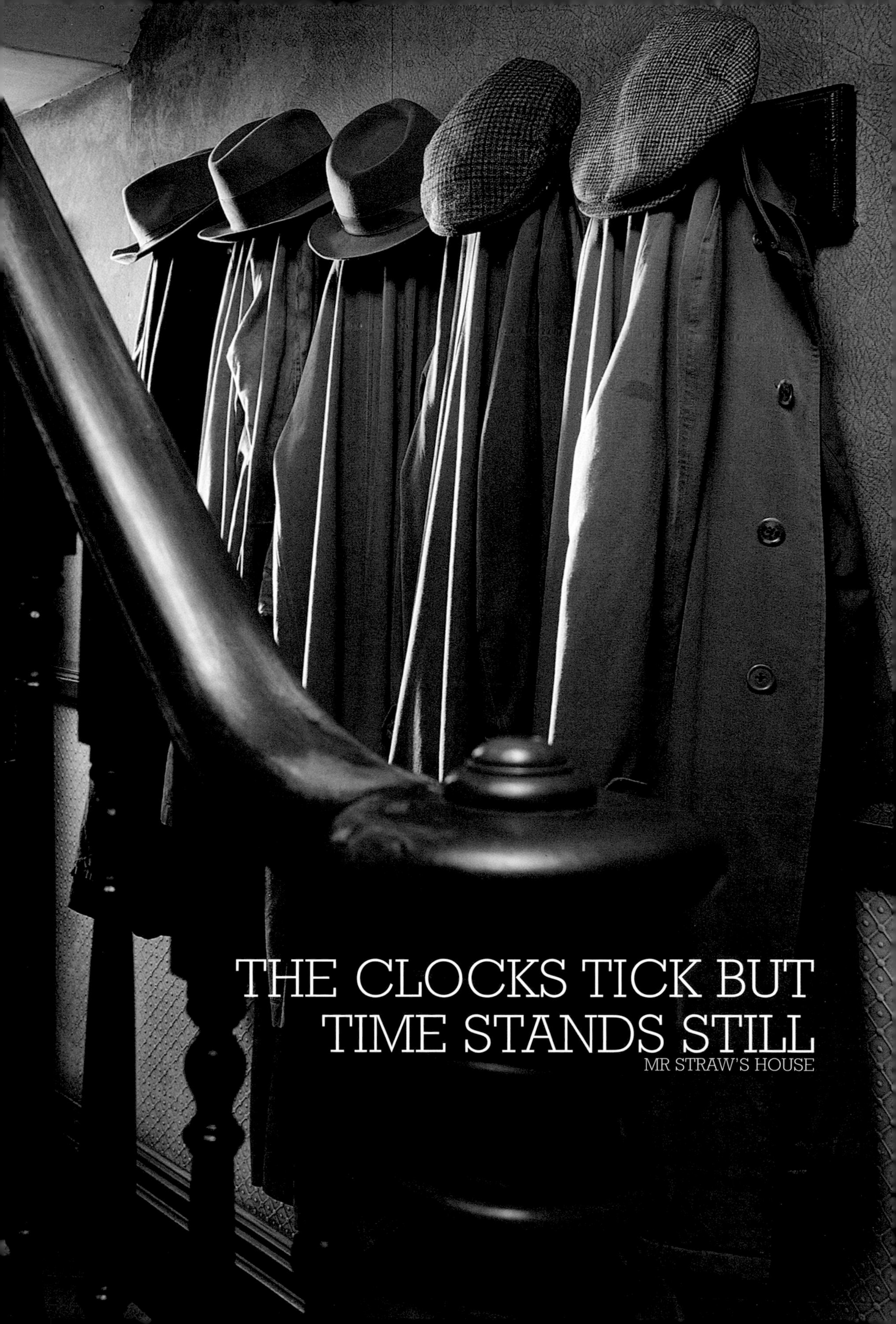

THE CLOCKS TICK BUT
TIME STANDS STILL
MR STRAW'S HOUSE

NOTTINGHAMSHIRE

Laxton

A unique chance to walk the fields of feudal England

Dry and dusty history lessons! Remember the teacher talking about the medieval open field system? What did it look like, this England without its patchwork of small fields and hedges? At Laxton, you can find out, for this is the only place in Britain where it is still possible to see and walk the rolling acres of a feudal past.

Three great open fields, first recorded in around 1200, surround the village. Here, on 810ha (2000 acres), the serfs, villeins and freemen of 'Laxintune', as Domesday Book called it, ploughed long, thin strips of land in ways still copied by Laxton farmers today. In another reminder of the village past, an ancient manorial court meets to check the field boundaries and adjudicate in disputes. There is a visitor centre at the Dovecote Inn with further information.
▶ *3 miles SW of Tuxford on A1.*

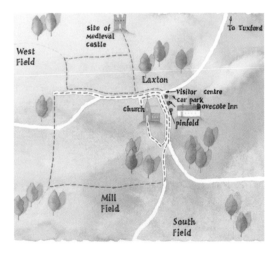

In the footsteps of peasants *Three walks across Laxton's medieval fields start and finish at the Dovecote Inn visitor centre. The shortest (green) one goes past the pinfold, where stray animals were penned, and the Church of St Michael and the Archangel. In the church, the tombs of the de Everingham family, lords of the manor, include a very unusual one carved out of oak. The red route goes around Mill Field – oldest and biggest of the open fields. A third path (blue) takes in the best-preserved motte-and-bailey castle in the county.*

Newstead Abbey

Home of the original Byronic hero

Like the scandalous great uncle from whom he inherited the ancestral home, a hard-up Lord Byron dug up the floor of the north cloister, searching for the monastic gold said to be buried there. No gold came to light, but the poet did disinter a human cranium, which he had made into a macabre but capacious wine goblet. It would have been a favourite topic of conversation when he entertained guests in his apartments – small islands of opulence in what one visitor described as 'an extensive ruin'.

The Great Hall resounded to the crack of pistol practice and the Great Dining Room to the clash of rapiers in fencing matches, while Byron's tame bear, wolf and numerous dogs had the run of the place. Can you sense the romantic ghosts at Newstead Abbey?
▶ *12 miles N of Nottingham on A60 (Junction 27 off M1). Daily Apr–Sept, pm only.*

Southwell Minster

Flourishes in stone, wood and metal embellish a vast Norman church

Intricate craftsmanship spanning many centuries enriches the interior of Southwell Minster. In the nave, Peter Ball's *Christus Rex* (1987) greets worshippers with open arms in gilded wood and beaten copper. The choir screen and stalls bristle with detailed carvings of leaves and figures. Look out for the mouse on the altar rails, signature of the workshop where they were made in 1950, and spot the elaborate 14th-century misericords.

In the impressive Chapter House, stone capitals and columns are encrusted with an array of 13th-century foliage carving – vines, buttercup, maple, hawthorn and oak. Small creatures peep between the delicate leaves, and here and there you can even discern the pagan figure of a Green Man.
▶ *In centre of Southwell. Daily, except during church services.*

The Workhouse
Where Oliver asked for more

Tiny top-floor windows, rows of lavatories, distempered walls and circular scars on the kitchen floors where huge coppers boiled cabbage, potatoes and tea – many stark details reveal the bleak history of Southwell's former workhouse. Built in 1824, it housed the local poor for over 150 years, and was the prototype for more than 600 workhouses built after the punitive Poor Law Amendment Act of 1834.

Its plain red-brick façade and regimented interior embodied the severe philosophy that shaped treatment of the poor. Inmates were segregated into classes and assigned quarters according to their status. Families were split up and men, women and children kept apart. In the hierarchy of poverty, each class had its own exercise yard, day room, separate entrances, exits and staircases – life was controlled and monotonous. It was the very system that drove Charles Dickens to write *Oliver Twist*.
▶ *On outskirts of Southwell, off A612. NT. Tel 01636 817250 for opening times.*

Upton Hall Time Museum
A brief history of time-keeping

Step inside this elegant Georgian mansion and you enter a world of unsynchronised ticking, clanking and chiming, as dozens of timepieces mark the passing hours. Upton Hall is home to the British Horological Institute. The largest collection of clocks and watches in Britain is displayed in its reception rooms. Prize exhibits include 'Tim', the original speaking clock, and the atomic 'BBC pips' machine. Be enchanted by the constantly rolling bagatelle ball of the Congreve Clock and sniff out a Chinese incense clock. Just don't set your watch by the exhibits – many are more than 300 years old and their accuracy cannot be guaranteed.
▶ *3 miles N of Southwell, on A612. Groups by arrangement, Tel 01636 813795.*

Galleries of Justice
You have the right to remain silent

Condemned to death, transported to Australia in chains, or cautioned by a modern custody sergeant. These and other alarming fates can be experienced in a museum set in Nottingham's former County Court. In the Crime and Punishment galleries, visitors are ushered into a Victorian court to take part in a reconstructed trial scene. The 'guilty' are taken down to a grim 18th-century cell, watched by a jailer who will oversee their hard labour.

Return to the right side of the law in the modern Police Galleries, where you can view a crime scene, collect forensic evidence and choose your witnesses to solve a case.
▶ *In Nottingham's old Lace Market district. Tues-Sun, bank hol Mon and Mon in school holidays.*

Nottingham Caves
A thousand years of history beneath a modern shopping centre

Underneath the city of Nottingham lies a honeycomb of caves – more than 400 in the centre alone. All were scraped by human hands from the soft sandstone mound on which the city stands. An escalator leading into a basement shopping precinct provides an improbable access point.

Visitors are directed through 14 different caverns, variously used throughout the centuries as storage areas and dwelling places, ale cellars, prisons, wells, privies, air-raid shelters and secret meeting rooms. One cave was used as a tannery, its pits filled with noxious substances for curing leather. Another section re-creates the appalling slum conditions endured by Nottingham's Victorian poor. Other caves are accessible from Nottingham Castle.

Ye Olde Trip to Jerusalem, a pub at the foot of the Castle rock and on the site of the castle's old brewhouse, has cave bars and cellars gouged into the creamy sandstone.
▶ *Under Broad Marsh Shopping Centre; daily all year. Ye Olde Trip to Jerusalem, 1 Brewhouse Yard, Nottingham NG1 6AD; daily all year.*

Ruddington Framework Knitters' Museum
Experience the drudgery of lives spent making socks and stockings

Flick a switch in the museum and prepare for the deafening din of 20 handframe knitting machines at full tilt. Workers in 19th-century Ruddington toiled at these repetitive, backbreaking, treadle-operated machines for more than 12 hours a day, six days a week.

This unique survival of a knitters' yard operated from 1829 to 1929, when over 90 per cent of Britain's hosiery output came from workshops in the East Midlands, before factory production made them obsolete. Cramped workers' cottages huddle in the yard, with tiny gardens, the communal pump, washhouse, privy and pigsty. To either side are frameshops, closely packed with restored handframes and ingenious circular machines on which visitors can try out their sock-making skills.
▶ *Signed in Ruddington, S of Nottingham. Wed-Sat, and bank hol Mon, Easter-Dec; Sun pm Easter-Sept.*

CENTRAL ENGLAND

SHROPSHIRE

1 Hawkstone Park and Follies 2 Shrewsbury Castle 3 Wroxeter Roman City 4 The Wrekin
5 Snailbeach Mine 6 Stiperstones 7 The Long Mynd 8 Clun 9 Stokesay Castle

Hawkstone Park and Follies

Grottoes, glades and fantasy at the world's first theme park

So striking and otherworldly is Hawkstone Park that it served as the backdrop for a television adaptation of C.S. Lewis's *Narnia Chronicles*. Set among rugged sandstone hills, the 40ha (100 acre) park with its caves, dizzying clifftops, glades and eerie rock formations offers a surprise at every turn. Adding to the visual feast is an array of follies, including the thatched Gingerbread Hall and the 34m (112ft) high Monument that affords expansive views of the area.

Hawkstone Park is the creation of the Hill family, who owned it up until 1906. They added fantastic constructions and walks to the park's natural features. In the late 18th century they published a guide to Hawkstone that encouraged visitors from across England and Wales, so staking a claim to be the creators of the world's first leisure theme park.

▶ *Weston-under-Redcastle village, near Hodnet, off A53 or A49, 11 miles N of Shrewsbury. For opening details of park, Tel 01939 200611.*

Shrewsbury Castle

A Norman fortress remodelled by an engineering genius

Shrewsbury's magnificent red sandstone castle perches atop the town, its lofty location clearly demonstrating why it was chosen as a defensive site. Built in the 11th century, the stronghold was refortified by Edward I around 1300. Its most recent 'improver' was the great civil engineer Thomas Telford. In 1790 he altered the castle to create a residence for his wealthy patron, Lord Pulteney, Shrewsbury's Member of Parliament. Today it houses the Shropshire Regimental Museum.

▶ *Castle Gates, Shrewsbury. Daily Jun-Aug; Tues-Sat mid Feb-May and Sept-Dec.*

Wroxeter Roman City

A once-flourishing Roman metropolis on the River Severn

One of the largest examples of Roman masonry still standing in Britain can be seen at Wroxeter. Known as The Old Work, the 8m (26ft) high wall formed part of a basilica, or gymnasium, in Viroconium, the fourth-largest Roman settlement in the province.

The city had developed from a simple fortress established around AD 58 to become an impressive urban area of 5000 inhabitants in the 2nd century. Laid out in a grid pattern on the banks of the River Severn, the site contains extensive remains, including the underfloor heating system of a bathhouse, and parts of a market hall and tavern.

▶ *5 miles E of Shrewsbury off A5. EH. Daily Mar-Oct; Wed-Sun Nov-Feb.*

The Wrekin

Grand views and a giant-sized legend

The Wrekin looms like a stranded sea monster above the Shropshire Plain, rising abruptly to 407m (1335ft). From the top, reached by a relatively easy climb, there are matchless views across the surrounding country – on a clear day you can see 17 English and Welsh counties. Legend has it that many of its most prominent features are the work of two giants who still live beneath its surface.

The Wrekin's name is derived from the Celtic terms *wre* and *ken*, meaning 'most conspicuous hill'. The ancient British *Cornovii* tribe recognised the hill's strategic value, making it their capital.

▶ *10 miles E of Shrewsbury off A5.*

Snailbeach Mine

Industrial relics from Shropshire's heyday as a lead producer

In a county mostly noted for its rural beauty, Snailbeach Mine is something of an oddity. It was Europe's largest lead producer during the 19th century, with an annual output of between 2000 and 3000 tonnes. After years of neglect, the site has been renovated and a waymarked walk takes in many points of interest, including reconstructed pit winding gear and the compressor engine house. The latter accommodated engines that powered compressed air drills, a testament to the position of Snailbeach at the forefront of mining technology. Twenty of the mine's original buildings are still standing.
▶ *10 miles SW of Shrewsbury off A488.*

Stiperstones

The Devil's own kingdom among boulders of ice-age scree

With its stark and jagged contours, the 3-mile long outcrop known as the Stiperstones stands in sharp contrast to the smooth, rolling outlines of other Shropshire hills. The ruggedly angular appearance is the work of the last Ice Age, when prolonged frost shattered the peak into a combination of boulder-strewn scree and jutting protrusions.

The strange landscape has given rise to many superstitions and associations with the supernatural. The Devil himself is said to hold court at one of the most striking rocky formations – the Devil's Chair.
▶ *13 miles SW of Shrewsbury off A488.*

The Long Mynd

Hills, heath and revitalising spring water for the keen walker

More than 30 miles of footpaths criss-cross The Long Mynd, an area of undulating heathland offering spectacular views to the Brecon Beacons in Wales and sightings of moorland birds such as stonechat and red grouse. The ridge-top track known as the Portway has been in use for thousands of years, and Bronze Age burial mounds dot the hillsides. Lovers' Walk, so called because of the many 'kissing gates' placed along its length, culminates at a natural spring – the 'pop works'. The bubbling waters were once believed to treat sluggish livers, gout and obesity.
▶ *The Long Mynd rises W of Church Stretton off A49, 12 miles S of Shrewsbury. NT.*

Clun

Ancient town that trades on trust

The Shropshire poet A.E. Housman described the riverside town of Clun as one of 'the quietest places under the sun'. Today it still seems untouched by the hurly-burly of modern life. But in the 12th and 13th centuries Clun and its castle (now ruined) came under frequent attack from the Welsh.

The town has a distinctly medieval layout, with narrow grid-patterned streets. Its timeless feel is exemplified by the habit traders have of leaving unattended goods for sale on the roadside, and trusting shoppers to leave the correct amounts of money for their purchases.
▶ *28 miles SW of Shrewsbury on A488.*

Stokesay Castle

The loveliest and best-preserved manor house in England

An exquisite Jacobean timber-framed custard-coloured gatehouse marks the entrance to Stokesay Castle, a fortified manor house built in the Onny Valley by a wealthy wool merchant 700 years ago. Lawrence of Ludlow was keen on home comforts by 13th-century standards. He built a 16m (52ft) long Great Hall with a central fireplace and unusually large windows for the time. After meals the family would retire upstairs to a wood-panelled solar, or drawing room, with peep holes onto the hall below.

Stokesay is astoundingly well preserved. Decorative tiles, mullioned windows and delicate carvings abound, such as a Flemish 17th-century overmantel. Climb to the top of the South Tower for sweeping views across rolling countryside.
▶ *7 miles NW of Ludlow off A49. EH. Daily May-Aug; Wed-Sun Mar-Apr and Sept-Oct; Thur-Sun Nov-Feb. Tel 01588 672544.*

CENTRAL ENGLAND

Three miles of furnace and forge

The industrial age was born in the Ironbridge Gorge, where Britain made the leap from field to factory

1 Ironbridge Gorge

With its steep sides shrouded in woodland, the **Ironbridge Gorge** is the epitome of rural Shropshire, yet in the 18th century this became the smoky, sulphurous, white-hot birthplace of Britain's Industrial Revolution.

It was up a little dingle on the northern slope of the gorge, at Coalbrookdale, that, in 1709, Abraham Darby discovered how to smelt iron using coke, obtained from local coal, instead of charcoal. The discovery sparked a chain of events that transformed this stretch of the Severn valley, and changed Britain and the world forever. That momentous transformation is recognised in the town's World Heritage Site status, and

remembered in its museums – of which Ironbridge has more than anywhere else of its size in Europe (although one 'passport' ticket will gain you admission to all of them).

Start by visiting the place where it all began. At the **Coalbrookdale Museum of Iron** (open daily) the Darby furnace is now protected by a glass pyramid. An old red-brick warehouse topped by a wrought-iron clock contains artefacts and interactive exhibits about the gorge's ironmasters.

Downhill from the old ironworks is the feature that gave the gorge and town its name. The world's first iron bridge (above) opened on New Year's Day 1781: a single graceful span

THE WORLD'S FIRST IRON BRIDGE, DESIGNED BY F.F. PRITCHARD, MAKES AN ELEGANT ARC OVER THE SEVERN.

across the Severn that required 400 tonnes of metal from the foundry, by now in the hands of Abraham Darby III. The bridge tollhouse contains an exhibition about the structure (daily), relating how it improved the supply of iron ore to local foundries and benefited other industries springing up in the vicinity. The **Museum of the Gorge** (daily), which is housed in an old warehouse near the bridge, contains a 12m (40ft) long model of industry's most vital 3 miles in the late 1700s – shortly after the bridge was built and at just the time when cottage industries based on the local clay were taking off.

Fine tiles and crockery

It was in 1796 that the Coalport China Works opened at the eastern end of the gorge, about 2 miles downriver from the bridge. The factory, one of the largest producers of porcelain in Victorian times, closed in 1926 and now houses the **Coalport China Museum** (daily), which has demonstrations of the production process, exquisite collections of china and galleries about the factory workers' lives. Nearby, on the opposite bank of the river, the **Jackfield Tile Museum** (daily) occupies part of another factory that was a household name a century or so ago: the grandly titled Craven Dunnill's Encaustic & Decorative Tile Works clad thousands of miles of Victorian walls with its ceramics. And in the village of Broseley, across the river from Ironbridge, the **Broseley Pipeworks** (daily mid May–Sept) is a reminder of the time when smokers puffed tobacco in clay pipes.

But if there is time for one reminder only of Ironbridge's heritage, visit the **Blists Hill Victorian Town** (daily), which lies on the eastern edge of the town. Here every aspect of life and work during its industrial heyday is recaptured – down to the inhabitants' clothes.

SHROPSHIRE

10 Ludlow **11** Hampton Loade

Ludlow

A walk through a thousand years

With a medieval street plan and nearly 500 listed buildings, Ludlow can rightfully claim, as a local guide book says, to be 'one of Europe's most beautiful towns'. Nowhere is this more apparent than on Broad Street, where you can stroll through nearly 1000 years of history. Beginning at the elegant Georgian town houses close to the River Teme, you pass timbered buildings from the 14th to 16th centuries, still in active use, as you climb to the castle, completed in 1086.

Ludlow Castle is large and dominating with robust defences. Edward IV's sons, later the 'Princes in the Tower', were raised here, and it was the venue for the premiere of John Milton's masque *Comus* in 1634.
▶ *24 miles N of Hereford off A49. Castle daily Feb-Dec; Sat-Sun only Jan.*

Hampton Loade

Where ferry and steam train are still the best ways to travel

The minute village of Hampton Loade is home to two fascinating examples of bygone transport, dating from the 19th century. The village stands astride the River Severn and the only direct means of access from one side to the other is a ferry powered ingeniously by nothing more than the river's current. Meanwhile, steam is used to power the trains on the restored Severn Valley Railway, which passes through Hampton Loade station on its 16 mile journey between Bridgnorth and Kidderminster.
▶ *9 miles NW of Kidderminster off A442.*

CENTRAL ENGLAND

STAFFORDSHIRE

1 Thor's Cave 2 Biddulph Grange Garden

3 Lud's Church 4 St Giles, Cheadle

5 St Chad's Gospels

Thor's Cave

Perfect lookout for cavemen

Film makers needing a location for prehistoric man have often looked no farther than Thor's Cave. It is the archetypal caveman's dwelling, a gaping void high on a limestone crag above the River Manifold. Early Victorian archaeologists were the first to discover that this many-chambered, many-fissured cavern, named after the Norse god of war, provided just such a home for our Stone Age ancestors. As you stand at the entrance and admire the Manifold Valley below, you can imagine how they must have scanned the same magnificent landscape, perhaps in search of game.

Thor's Cave can be reached by a stairway from the Manifold Track. This path follows the course of one of the Peak District's 'disappearing' rivers, which sink into deep cracks in the limestone.
▶ *Near Wetton, off A523, 10 miles SE of Leek.*

Biddulph Grange Garden

Around the globe in the time it takes to explore a garden

The remarkable themed gardens at Biddulph Grange take you on a world tour all within a compact area of 6ha (15 acres). From the neat beds of the Chinese garden, across a red-painted bridge reflected in tranquil waters to a temple decorated with gilded dragons and seahorses, you are then transported to the classical, formal world of the Italian garden or the grandeur of stone sphinxes and clipped yew pyramids and obelisks of the Egyptian Court. Closer to home are a Scottish glen and the Cheshire Cottage.

The gardens were designed by the horticulturalist James Bateman. He owned Biddulph Grange (now private apartments) from the mid 1840s, and set about creating 'mixed' gardens to display the plant specimens he had collected from all over the world.
▶ *3 miles S of Congleton off A527. NT. For opening times, Tel 01782 517999.*

Lud's Church

Legendary home of the Green Knight

A feeling of impending doom fills the air as you enter the dank confines of Lud's Church, a spectactular chasm hidden among the trees of Back Forest. Ferns and mosses drip from precipitous, 18m (60ft) high walls of gritstone as you pass through the 61m (200ft) 'nave'.

The 'church' was probably the model for the Green Chapel in the medieval poem *Sir Gawain and the Green Knight*, and the scene of the ritual beheading of the Green Knight. It was named after Walter de Ludank, a follower of John Wycliff, the 14th-century religious reformer. Ludank's beautiful daughter Alice was killed here when one of his illicit services was raided by soldiers.
▶ *Approach Back Forest from youth hostel at Gradbach Mill, near Leek on A523/A53.*

St Giles, Cheadle

Sensational evocation of a pious age

Even the ornate spire and red west doors with their magnificent gold lions – family emblem of the Earl of Shrewsbury, patron of St Giles – do not prepare the visitor for what lies within. What was lost when churches were stripped of their decoration in the Reformation? What sights greeted the 13th-century peasant on the Sabbath? At St Giles, in what has been called the outstanding English church of the 19th century, the architect A.W.N. Pugin, still only 29 years old, gave genius and imagination full rein to re-create the age of Decorated Gothic. It is a sight that leaves the modern-day onlooker speechless. Every inch of the interior is sumptuously decorated with gleaming metalwork, gorgeously painted walls and glowing floor tiles.
▶ *Cheadle town centre, 10 miles E of Stoke-on-Trent off A52 Ashbourne road. Daily.*

St Chad's Gospels

A light shone on to the Dark Ages

The gloriously illuminated manuscript belonging to Lichfield Cathedral gives the lie to the term Dark Ages. The work of a single unknown scribe, it is nearly as old as the cathedral itself, and may even have been commissioned for the foundation of the original, Saxon, church in 700. Originally one of a pair – hence 'gospels' – the manuscript's outstanding feature is a series of eight beautifully decorated pages, including the 'carpet' page, on which the scribe's skill reaches its highest point with an intricate design around the form of the cross.
▶ *Cathedral chapter house. Lichfield city centre. Daily.*

The city of English ceramic genius

For more than 250 years potters have thrown clay and fired their wares in the Potteries towns of Stoke-on-Trent

1 The Wedgwood Visitor Centre ▶ *Barlaston, off A34, 4 miles S of city centre (Hanley). Daily.*

2 Etruria Industrial Museum ▶ *Lower Bedford Street, Etruria, SW of Hanley. Wed-Sun Apr-Dec. Group visits Jan-Mar Tel 01782 233145.*

3 Potteries Museum and Art Gallery ▶ *Bethseda Street, Hanley. Daily (pm only Sun).*

4 Gladstone Pottery Museum ▶ *Uttoxeter Road (off A50), Longton. Daily.*

5 Spode Museum and Visitor Centre ▶ *Church Street, Stoke, off A500. Daily.*

6 Royal Doulton Visitor Centre ▶ *Nile Street, Burslem, off A50. Daily.*

At one time the whole world seemed to eat off and drink out of pottery and ceramics made in Stoke, Burslem, Tunstall, Hanley, Longton and Fenton, the six towns (Arnold Bennett forgot Fenton in his 'Five Towns') that now form the city of Stoke-on-Trent. Plentiful deposits of clay for pottery making, lead and salt for glazing and coal for firing made this the centre of the British ceramics industry by the early 18th century. Today, through museums and factory tours, you can relive the days when Stoke's skyline was pierced by hundreds of brick bottle-shaped kilns belching out thick smoke.

The man who did most to further the craft of English pottery was Josiah Wedgwood – scientist, artist, engineer and social reformer, as well as master potter – who opened his first factory, at Burslem, in 1759. **The Wedgwood Visitor Centre**, at Barlaston, examines his life and legacy, and allows you to see the entire ceramics production process, from raw clay to decoration – you can even try your hand at the potter's wheel.

The story of Etruria, the factory and workers' village that Wedgwood built in 1769, is told in the **Etruria Industrial Museum**, housed in a canalside bone and flint mill of 1857, and in the **Potteries Museum and Art Gallery**, Hanley, which has one of the world's finest collections of Staffordshire ceramics. The **Gladstone Pottery Museum**, Longton, is a working Victorian pottery factory complete with bottle kilns (right). The **Spode Museum and Visitor Centre**, Stoke, and the **Royal Doulton Visitor Centre**, Burslem, recount the stories of Spode and Royal Doulton ware with factory tours and demonstrations.

> You cannot drink tea out of a tea cup without the aid of the Five Towns, you cannot eat a meal in decency without the aid of the Five Towns.
>
> Arnold Bennett
> *The Old Wives' Tale* (1908)

STAFFORDSHIRE

Alton Towers

Get strapped in at the white-knuckle wonderland

As long ago as 1890, the former home of the earls of Shrewsbury was attracting the crowds – in that year alone, 30,000 came to see acrobats, lion-tamers, elephants and fireworks. But those figures and attractions pale beside today's visitor numbers and the white-knuckle rides that pull them in. In the score or so years since 'The Corkscrew' carried its first passengers, more than 40 million fun-seekers have passed through the turnstiles of Britain's biggest and best-known theme park. The building of each new ride is shrouded in secrecy. The newest big ride 'Rita', which opened in 2005, is said to take off faster than a shuttle launch while 'Air' gives you the chance to fly, face-down and inches from the ground, at more than 40mph.
▶ *12 miles E of Stoke-on-Trent off A52 Stoke-Ashbourne road. Theme park daily mid Mar-early Nov.*

Shugborough

A feast of neoclassical follies

There are three good reasons for visiting the seat of the earls of Lichfield. The 18th-century mansion contains collections of ceramics, French furniture, silver and paintings, along with restored domestic quarters giving a glimpse of life below stairs. In the park there is a replica Georgian farm with a collection of historic rare breeds and the newly opened original Walled Garden. But it is the estate's ornamental architecture that leaves the most lasting impression. Here James 'Athenian' Stuart, architect and painter, created several Greek-style monuments. The most striking is the Arch of Hadrian, built to commemorate Admiral George Anson (the Lichfield family name), who is largely credited with reviving the Royal Navy in the mid 18th century. Other follies include the Tower of the Winds and the Doric Temple, said to be the earliest building of the Greek Revival in England.
▶ *6 miles E of Stafford off A513. NT. Daily, including bank hol Mon, mid Mar-Oct.*

Fields of remembrance

Shared territories of war's victims

The statue of a blindfolded soldier stands in the **National Memorial Arboretum** at Alrewas (inset right). Private Herbert Burden lied about his age to join up and was only 17 when he was shot for desertion in the First World War. Nearby are memorials to the 1941-5 campaign in the Far East. A replica length of track and a plinth commemorate those who died on the Sumatra Railway. An original section of line, with sleepers and spikes, honours the 16,000 Allied servicemen who died during construction of the infamous Burma Railway.

Twelve miles away, near Broadhurst Green on Cannock Chase, there are more reminders of those who fell in the last century's conflicts. The lawns of the **Commonwealth War Cemetery** contain 97 white headstones for First World War servicemen, mostly New Zealanders. In the larger **German Military Cemetery** (right), ranks of granite headstones mark the 5000 combatants of that nation who died on British soil. They include the bodies of airship crews from the 1914-18 conflict, those of aircrews shot down in the Second World War and dead German seamen washed up on British beaches.
▶ *National Memorial Arboretum, Alrewas, 4 miles NE of Lichfield signed off A38 or A513; daily. Commonwealth and German cemeteries, 2 miles N of Cannock off A34 Stafford road; daily.*

Kinver Edge rock houses

Dwellings hewn from the cliff

People lived in caves at Kinver Edge as recently as the 1960s: cosy homes – some with several rooms, windows and doors – carved out of the soft red sandstone of the outcrop. The best of the rock houses, some of which have been restored, were in Holy Austin Rock at the northern end of the Edge, where six dwellings were noted in 1831, and where a café survived until 1967. The community seems to have reached a peak in the 1860s, when there were 11 families living here.
▶ *5 miles NW of Kidderminster off A449/A458. NT. Tel 01384 872553 for rock house details.*

SHARED TERRITORIES OF WAR'S VICTIMS

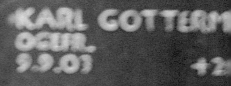

WERNER BOY
I.T.
11.7.21 +29.4.42

HUGO SAUER
UFFZ.
29.4.19 +10.10.39

ANS WYNANDS
GEFR.
.3.22   +31.5.45

RUDOLF MÜLLER
SCHTZ.
4.11.05   +17.5.45

KARL GOTTERM
OGFR.
9.9.03   +2

PA

WARWICKSHIRE & WEST MIDLANDS

1 The New Art Gallery, Walsall 2 Black Country Living Museum 3 Soho House

4 The Jewellery Quarter

The New Art Gallery, Walsall

Inspiring display case to match a generous gift of artworks

The building rises beside the canal, just off the shopping centre: a 30m (100ft) high austere tower pierced by windows of differing sizes that capture the sky, and clad with pale terracotta tiles that reflect the changing light.

Inside the £21 million gallery, which opened in 2000, surfaces covered in glowing Douglas fir contrast with others where the shuttered concrete-work has been left exposed. It is home to the Garman Ryan collection, created by Kathleen Garman, widow of the sculptor Jacob Epstein, and her friend the American sculptor Sally Ryan, and given to the people of Walsall in 1973.

There are more than 350 items in the collection, including works by Monet, Van Gogh and Braque, as well as 43 pieces by Epstein. Temporary exhibitions and events are held in other spaces in the building, while visitors entering the Discovery Gallery are encouraged to interact with the exhibits.
▶ *Walsall town centre. Junction 7, 9 or 10 off M6. Tues-Sat, and Sun pm; also bank hol Mons.*

Black Country Living Museum

Now that the smoke has cleared

The Black Country does not appear on any map. It spread as far as the smoke from the foundries and furnaces that inspired the name: an area about 10 miles by 12 miles, with Dudley at its centre. It is appropriate, then, that the town is home to this open-air museum, with its re-creation of the sort of village that sprang up hereabouts in the late 18th century.

Coal, iron ore, limestone for furnace flux and canals to bring the raw materials in and ship the finished goods out all came together here. Visitors can take a narrowboat trip along one of the canals into the mine workings, or stay above ground and explore the 10½ ha (26 acre) site. There are around 40,000 items on show – from early photographs to faithful reproductions of the workshops where the nails, bolts, anchors and chains for which the area was renowned were made.
▶ *½ mile NE of Dudley centre, off A4037 (M5 Junction 2). Daily Mar-Oct; Wed-Sun Nov-Feb.*

Soho House

Where the great minds of the day warmed to conversation

Once it was surrounded by parkland: today its neoclassical façade tries not to appear embarrassed by being tucked into crowded Handsworth. Soho House is clad in painted slate, the very latest thing when the silversmith and great entrepreneur Matthew Boulton moved into his new home in 1766.

Boulton's love of invention is apparent everywhere in the house: the central-heating system alone is full of ingenious details, with valves controlling warm-air ducts hidden in walls. It was in these comfortable surroundings that he and James Watt, inventor of the steam engine, formed the Lunar Society, a learned debating club. Other members included the physician Erasmus Darwin (grandfather of Charles) and the scientist and political theorist Joseph Priestley.
▶ *Soho Avenue, off Soho Road in Handsworth. 3 miles NW of Birmingham city centre, M5 Junction 1. Tues-Sun and bank hol Mon Apr-Oct.*

The Jewellery Quarter

History's hallmark on this precious reminder of Birmingham's past

Follow the signs for pedestrians, or catch a bus or Metro tram from the centre, and discover a place where echoes of 18th-century Birmingham linger – a time when the city was one vast congregation of noisy little workshops. Gold and silversmiths worked in the Hockley neighbourhood of the city. Here, in Vyse Street, Warstone Lane and other thoroughfares around the Chamberlain Clock, unveiled in 1904 in memory of the industrialist and radical politician Joseph Chamberlain, most of the jewellery made in Britain for the past 200 years has originated.

Although the city's Assay Office is still the world's busiest, hallmarking 60,000 items every day, the trade is now largely hidden behind modern shopfronts. But here and there you may spy someone working in the window of a small workshop, and in the Museum of the Jewellery Quarter, in Vyse Street, a whole factory, little changed since 1900, is preserved.
▶ *1¼ miles NW of city centre. No. 101 bus from centre. Metro tram from Snow Hill terminus. Tues-Sun and bank hol Mon Easter-Oct; Tues-Sat Nov-Easter.*

Cuts through the heart of the city

Waterways that served 'the workshop of the world' have surged back to life

1 Birmingham's canals

Forty years ago they were regarded as an anachronism. People said they should be filled in. Who needed them any more? Today **Birmingham's canals** are not only still there, but flourishing. Everywhere you go in the city you come across small oval signs announcing canalside walks. From Sherborne Wharf at the rear of the International Convention Centre in Centenary Square, for instance, it is a short walk along a towpath to crowded, colourful **Gas Street Basin**, to **Old Turn Junction** – where the Birmingham & Fazeley, Worcester & Birmingham, and Birmingham Main Line meet – and to **Brindley Place**, with its lively nightlife. Farther out, at that confluence of motorways known as Spaghetti Junction, you may glimpse, far below, green trees and the glint of water, for it is also a meeting of canals, known to boating people as **Salford Junction**.

There are eight canals within the city's boundaries, adding up to 32 miles of waterways. They were vital to its industrial expansion: when the pioneering canal builder James Brindley cut the Old Main Line between Birmingham and the Black Country in 1769 the price of coal was cut by half. The city lies on a plateau between the rivers Severn and Trent, and early canals meandered along the contours of the land. But by the time the Birmingham & Fazeley Canal was opened in 1783 the need to shorten journey times had spurred technology: the waterway climbed 25m (81ft) into the centre of

Birmingham, up two flights of locks called the **Old Thirteen**. Today their cobbled towpath contrasts with the BT tower and National Indoor Arena that soar above, but 200 years ago this was the busiest stretch of waterway in town – jammed with narrowboats and barge horses queuing to go through. As well as locks, the topography demanded embankments, cuttings and aqueducts.

Rescued from the verge of extinction

The first half of the 19th century was the golden age of canal building. One company after another floated on the stock exchange as investors sunk funds into the transport system that was fuelling industrial growth. Rivalry between the various companies grew as the number of waterways multiplied. At the junction of the Stratford & Worcester and Birmingham canals there is a rare guillotine lock that maintained a 15cm (6in) difference in water level between the two waterways until 1948, when the system was nationalised. By then the canals were in a state of decline that reached its lowest point in the disuse and dereliction of the 1960s.

It looked like the end, but in the 1970s enthusiasts helped to transform the image of the canals from grimy leftovers of the Industrial Revolution to the clean, serene arteries of tourism that they are today. Maps and information about Birmingham's canals are available from The Rotunda Tourism Centre, New Street (Tel 0870 225 0127).

CENTRAL ENGLAND

187

WARWICKSHIRE & WEST MIDLANDS

Thinktank
Bringing science to life

If you thought that science was a dry, academic subject, Birmingham's Museum of Science will change your mind. This award-winning museum, housed at Millennium Point, combines entertainment, history and technology in ten galleries. Using the past, present and future as a storyboard, more than 200 interactive and innovative exhibits explore how science has shaped our lives. Learn about aircrafts and intestines, see Birmingham as it was at the time of the Domesday book and visit the IMAX cinema – you can even meet eMo the emotional robot who learns human expressions as it interacts with visitors. This museum really will open up your eyes.
▶ *Millennium Point, Birmingham city centre, off Curzon Street. Daily.*

The Barber Institute of Fine Arts
Culture on the campus, courtesy of a rich and caring couple

Dame Martha Constance Hattie Barber did not live to see the realisation of the dream that she and her property-developer husband shared of a grand public building housing a world-class art collection and concert hall. She died in 1932, a few months after bequeathing the family fortune to the institute and seven years before the austerely elegant, stone-and-brick Art Deco building in the grounds of Birmingham University opened.

The interior is laid out around the ground-floor concert auditorium, with the galleries approached by a magnificent marble staircase.

They contain a fabulous collection of paintings, from Renaissance masterpieces by Bellini, Botticelli and Veronese, to Impressionist works by Degas, Monet and van Gogh, and 20th-century pieces by Picasso, Magritte and Schiele. There are also sculptures and miniatures, and a collection of old coins, seals and weights, chiefly from Rome, Byzantium and the Middle East.
▶ *3 miles SW of city centre off A38 Bristol road. University Station from Birmingham New Street. Nos. 61, 62, 63 buses from centre. Daily.*

Bournville
A luxurious assortment for the workers to choose from

Neat cottages in tree-shaded avenues, a village green and a brook called the Bourn running through grassy dells. It sounds like a dream of Olde England, but it is real: the garden suburb that the Quaker brothers George and Richard Cadbury created after locating their chocolate factory nearby in 1879.

They named it Bournville, after the stream. Guiding aims were homely dwellings, good sanitation (a bath in every house was one of the original specifications) and gardens. Birmingham's cramped, disease-ridden slums, just a few miles up the road, seemed a world away to the Cadbury's employees and workers from elsewhere who moved in. At its heart are half-timbered Selly Manor and Minworth Greaves – two 14th-century houses re-erected here to add veracity to the Tudor-style houses.
▶ *4 miles SW of Birmingham city centre off A38 Bristol road.*

PACKWOOD HOUSE

Packwood House

A testament in topiary to the dedication of gardeners

Graham Baron Ash, the wealthy son of a Birmingham industrialist, restored 16th-century Packwood House in the 1930s: it contains his collection of furniture, tapestries and paintings. But it was an earlier owner who created the property's most impressive feature. In the 1670s, John Fetherston, whose grandfather built Packwood, planted the Yew Garden. There are more than 100 trees, representing the Sermon on the Mount. The smallest trees, in the Multitude Walk, were planted in the 19th century and symbolise the assembled crowd. These lead to a lawn where The Apostles, a group of 12 yews, grow. Beyond them, on a hump, is The Master (Christ) – a solitary tree approached along a spiral path lined with box hedging (below). Clipping the topiary is the gardening equivalent of painting the Forth Bridge: it takes three gardeners three months to snip their way from end to end.
▶ *9 miles NW of Warwick off B4439 Hatton-Hockley Heath road. NT. Garden Wed-Sun, and bank hols, Mar-Oct. House Wed-Sun, and bank hols, pm Mar-Oct.*

Kenilworth Castle

Mellow red ramparts where the virgin queen was wined and dined

Even in its ruined state Kenilworth possesses a swaggering confidence – just like the men who shaped it. The martial John of Gaunt and Henry V, and Elizabeth I's favourite Robert Dudley, Earl of Leicester, are among those who had a hand in building and remodelling the sandstone fortress at various times between the early 12th and late 16th centuries.

Look through one of the arrow slits and you can easily imagine the fluttering pennants of Good Queen Bess's entourage appearing across the meadows. The Queen visited Kenilworth three times culminating in a stay involving

19 days of pageantry, dancing and hunting in 1575. The earl built Leicester's Gatehouse, the only part of the castle still lived in, and a luxurious tower residence to impress his monarch.
▶ *5 miles NW of Leamington Spa off A452 Castle Bromwich road. EH. Daily.*

Coventry Cathedral

Modern masters embellish the phoenix rising from a ruin

At first, the powerful works of art make a greater impact than the building as a whole. There is Jacob Epstein's bronze, *St Michael and Lucifer*, which dominates the steps by the main entrance. Once inside, the colours in John Piper's baptistery window – which curves like a screen behind the font, a huge boulder from Bethlehem – take on a dazzling vividness, concentrating to a golden colour at the centre. Yet even this is outshone by Graham Sutherland's 23m (75ft) high tapestry showing a seated Christ with piercing eyes. But the impression that lingers in the memory is the visual relationship between the old cathedral, bombed in 1940, and the new one, consecrated in 1962. Both are built of the same warm red sandstone, linked by an immense glass screen.
▶ *Coventry city centre.*

Museum of British Road Transport

Highways of dreams in motor town

Shining bodywork, dazzling chrome, stainless steel and brass – everything in this museum is polished to perfection. There are more than 500 vehicles, from early bicycles – the first one was manufactured in the city in 1868 by the Coventry Sewing Machine Company – to *Thrust SSC*, holder of the land world speed record of 633mph. There are also buses, fire engines, motorbikes and, of course, cars – from royal limousines and Princess Diana's Metro to thoroughbred roadsters and family saloons.
▶ *Coventry city centre. Daily.*

WARWICKSHIRE & WEST MIDLANDS

WARWICK CASTLE

Rugby museums

Play the game, visit the name

William Webb Ellis did the unexpected in 1823: he picked up the ball and ran with it, so originating the game named after his school, Rugby, and inspiring the statue of him which stands outside it. Inside, a museum tells the story of the game and its personalities. Employment as well as sporting renown followed young Ellis's innovative tactics: the nearby firm of James Gilbert, maker of footwear for the pupils, turned to making rugby balls in 1842, and is now a museum.

▶ *Town centre. School museum Mon-Sat pm. Webb Ellis Rugby Football Museum Mon-Sat.*

Warwick Castle

A formidable fortress where history comes to life

Few castles rival the scale and grandeur of Warwick. The original motte and bailey fort was built here by William the Conqueror. Today the castle towers over the River Avon, dominating the unspoilt town at its feet, just as the 1st Earl of Warwick dominated the kings of the 15th century. Its vast gardens and grounds were one of 'Capability' Brown's first commissions.

At Warwick you witness history in a series of brilliantly conceived tableaux, from a 14th-century dungeon to a Victorian weekend party. And this is not just the story of kings and noblemen. The 'Kingmaker' exhibition re-creates the practical preparations for a Wars of the Roses battle in 1471, when the 1st Earl, 'Warwick the Kingmaker', fought Edward IV's army at Barnet and was killed. Wheelwrights, longbowmen and seamstresses, all the ordinary people in Warwick's service, come to life here.

▶ *Warwick, off A46, 2 miles from M40 (Junction 15). Daily.*

Lord Leycester Hospital

A tranquil retreat for the military above the bustle of Warwick

Elderly gentlemen in black and blue Tudor uniforms welcome visitors at Lord Leycester Hospital. With great pride they will guide you through these timbered, gabled buildings above Warwick's west gate, showing off the Chapel and the enchanting black and white enclosed courtyard with its painted mottoes. The Great Hall, Master's House, Guildhall and Brethren's Kitchen form its square – look out for four small, carved bears, each holding a staff, which symbolise the earls of Leicester.

In the 14th century this secretive place was built by the powerful craft guilds, but after Henry VIII disbanded them in 1546 it was acquired by Robert Dudley, Earl of Leicester, as a hospital and almshouses for old or disabled soldiers and their wives. It is now home to eight ex-servicemen who live here under 'The Master' – take a moment to enjoy the peaceful seclusion of his garden.
▶ *Warwick, inside old west gate, above High Street (A429). Tues-Sun and bank hols.*

Stratford-upon-Avon

Five houses Shakespeare knew well

Surprisingly little is known about William Shakespeare, but at Stratford you can get as close as is possible to our greatest writer and gain a fascinating insight into English life at the turn of the 17th century.

The interiors of **Shakespeare's birthplace**, a house Shakespeare inherited in 1601, are alive with the bright colours and patterns of their restored late 16th-century furnishings. The playwright would also have known the finely carved timber frontage of **Harvard House** in the High Street. Built in 1596 by Thomas Rogers, grandfather of the founder of Harvard, America's oldest university, it now houses an incomparable collection of pewter. Just beyond it is **Nash's House** in Chapel Street, next to the site of New Place where Shakespeare spent his last years. New Place was demolished in 1759, but its foundations can still be seen. Nash's House is furnished as New Place might have been. Shakespeare's eldest daughter married John Hall, a physician, who built Hall's Croft in 1613. It has glorious furniture and paintings, and also offers a glimpse of 17th-century medical practices.

At Wilmcote, outside Stratford, is a hamlet of two houses where Shakespeare's mother, Mary, lived. **Mary Arden's House** was not, as once thought, the half-timbered farmhouse but its neighbour, which was faced with brick in the 18th century. They compose a charming evocation of rural life and history.
▶ *All in centre of Stratford – except Mary Arden's House, 3 miles N of Stratford, signed off A3400. Daily – except Harvard House – May-Oct. For details of Harvard House, Tel 01789 204507.*

Heritage Motor Centre

A glamorous showcase for the British motor car

Gaydon used to be a wartime airfield. Larks sing over its 26ha (65 acres) of windy downland and an old RAF watchtower still stands on the site. Crouching nearby is a huge Art Deco-style structure, rising from the ground like the low-slung bonnet of a sports car. This purpose-built museum charts the history of the British car industry over the past hundred years or so.

More than 300 British motor vehicles are garaged here: from a Wolseley Tri-Car prototype built by Herbert Austin in 1896, when he was manager of the Wolseley Sheep-Shearing company in Birmingham, to the first Range Rover of 1970, as well as the latest. You can even trace the history of your own old car in the Centre's huge archive, which includes technical information, sales material and engineering records from British car manufacturers such as Aston Martin, Lagonda, Riley and Rover. The cars are the thing, but Gaydon also offers nature trails, quad biking, off-road trekking and special events such as Austin Healey open days.
▶ *Off M40 (Junction 12) between Warwick and Banbury, or signed from A422. Daily mid Mar-Oct; Wed-Sun Nov-mid Mar.*

Edgehill

Tall trees where once Englishman turned against Englishman

Edgehill's dark ridge, about 213m (700ft) above sea level, is visible for miles across the great sweep of green and gold quilted country of Warwickshire. Today the area is covered in tall beechwoods, but in October 1642 it was open grassland. Parliamentarian troops must have felt a chill of apprehension as they approached the king's forces from Kineton village for their first encounter. Charles I gathered his equally large army of 14,500 men on the escarpment's edge and looked down at the subjects who had become his enemy.

The woods were planted in 1742 to mark the 100th anniversary of the battle, and a castellated stone tower was erected at the spot where Charles I raised his colours. It is now known as the Castle Inn and is the best place to enjoy the fantastic views. The battle itself was fought just below Edgehill – a bloody and entirely inconclusive confrontation.
▶ *Castle Inn near Ratley village on minor road linking B4086 and A422. It stands alone in a break in woods, just beyond turning to Ratley.*

CENTRAL ENGLAND

Grand settings for treacherous plots

CHARLECOTE PARK

In an age of religious hatred, there were safe houses where a Jesuit priest could hide and conspirators meet

2 Charlecote Park ▶ *5 miles E of Stratford-upon-Avon off B4086. NT. Fri-Tues early Mar-Oct; Sat-Sun Dec. (Tel 01789 470277 for gardens and grounds).*

3 Coughton Court ▶ *5 miles S of Redditch on A435 Alcester road. NT. Tel 01789 762435 for opening times.*

4 Baddesley Clinton ▶ *5 miles S of Solihull, off A4141 Warwick road. NT. Wed-Sun, bank hol Mon, pm Mar-early Nov (mid-Dec grounds).*

The pulse of history beats long and strong in these parts – the very heart of England – and nowhere more so than in the mellow brick and stone of some of the area's grand houses. Take **Charlecote Park**: the Lucys have lived in this rambling manor by the River Avon since the 12th century, and architecture, interiors and furnishings reflect family taste down the years. Pictures of the dynasty hang in the grand hall, including a striking group portrait of the third Sir Thomas Lucy, his wife, seven of their 13 children, their nurse, dogs and a hawk.

It was the same Sir Thomas before whom, reputedly, a certain William Shakespeare appeared, charged with poaching deer from the park. It was an encounter that inspired the playwright to lampoon Charlecote's master in the shape of Falstaff's acquaintance, Justice Shallow.

Beheadings and burnings

While the Lucys held their property rights dear, two other local families were motivated by the far more politically dangerous matter of religious rights. The Throckmortons, who have owned **Coughton Court** for six centuries, were one of the leading players in the tale of Roman Catholic intrigue and conspiracy that dominated domestic politics in a Protestant age. Sir George Throckmorton was advised by Henry VIII's

chancellor, Thomas Cromwell, to 'live at home and meddle little' after he criticised the king's divorce of Catherine of Aragon and marriage to Anne Boleyn. One of his sons, Francis, received more than warning words: in 1584, he was executed for his part in the Throckmorton Plot to overthrow Elizabeth I and put Mary, Queen of Scots on the English throne.

A white shift, said to have been worn by Mary to her beheading, is on display at Coughton Court, and there is also an exhibition about the most famous conspiracy of all, the Gunpowder Plot of 1605. The mother of the chief conspirator, Robert Catesby, was Anne Throckmorton, and the house was used as a meeting place by those planning to blow up the Houses of Parliament and James I. Although he went on to live into his eighties, the finger of suspicion also pointed at Henry Ferrars, lord of the manor of **Baddesley Clinton**, less than 2 hours by horse from Coughton Court. Not only did Ferrars lease a London house where Guy Fawkes stored gunpowder, he also let his moated home to the devoutly Catholic Vaux sisters, cousins of the Catesbys. They held illegal masses there, officiated by Jesuit priests, who could hide in any of three priest holes – one of them reached from the garderobe (lavatory) – if King James's soldiers came searching.

WORCESTERSHIRE

1 Stourport-on-Severn **2** Harvington Hall **3** Holly and mistletoe market, Tenbury Wells

4 Witley Court

Stourport-on-Severn

A Georgian new town that owes its fortune to a visionary canal builder

At the end of the 18th century Stourport-on-Severn was second only to Birmingham as the busiest inland port in England. Two centuries later, the canal basins under the old Clock Warehouse are still bustling with narrowboats, but today they carry holidaymakers instead of coal and carpets.

Stourport was the first industrial new town to be built in England, and it retains a brash, workmanlike, urban air alongside its elegant Georgian architecture. It came into existence with the building of the Staffordshire & Worcestershire Canal in the 1770s. James Brindley, 'the father of British canals', proposed to link the rivers Severn and Stour with the Trent & Mersey Canal, 46 miles away, by a canal climbing 104m (340ft) across the watershed of England. Yet Stourport might never have been created had not the people of Bewdley, a few miles upstream, disdained the canal. 'A stinking ditch,' they said. So Stourport-on-Severn was born and thrived, and Bewdley went into genteel decline.

▶ *Stourport, A451, 3 miles S of Kidderminster.*

Harvington Hall

Elizabethan hall of secrets and sanctuary for persecuted priests

The finest series of priests' hiding places anywhere in Britain have been revealed at Harvington Hall. In the reign of Elizabeth I at the end of the 16th century, when to be a Roman Catholic priest was to commit high treason, the clerics found refuge at this safe haven. They were secreted under the oak stairs, above a bread oven, and in the rafters and walls. Some of the priest holes are known to be the work of Nicholas ('Little John') Owen, master builder of such hiding places. In 1606 he was starved out of one of his own hides and tortured to death in the Tower of London.

The moated, russet-brick house, set among lawns with stables and a church, is an evocative fragment of Elizabethan England. Inside is a puzzle to be unravelled – an atmospheric warren of rooms, staircases and passageways intricately decorated with late 16th-century monochrome wall paintings.

▶ *3 miles SE of Kidderminster, ½ mile E of A450. Wed-Sun and bank hol Mon Apr-Sept; Sat and Sun Oct.*

Holly and mistletoe market, Tenbury Wells

Christmas decorations by the ton at a riverside market town

Buyers come from far and wide to purchase enormous bunches of plump-berried holly and mistletoe at Tenbury Wells' annual Christmas market. Every Tuesday in December the town centre is buried under a 1m (3ft) carpet of greenery.

For more than 200 years Tenbury has been known as 'The Town in the Orchard'. It stands on the banks of the fast-flowing River Teme, whose valley is still noted for its hops and cider apples. Mistletoe favours apple trees and drapes the branches with great swatches of pale green and pearl white berries every autumn, just in time for the festive season.

▶ *20 miles NW of Worcester, on A4112, off A456. Last Tues Nov, first two Tues Dec.*

Witley Court

The grandest of ruined palaces

Kings and courtiers were entertained at Witley Court in conditions of the most extravagant luxury. Today, this magnificent Palladian palace is but a ruin, destroyed by fire in 1937. Yet the first sight of what lies beyond its roofless skeleton never fails to bring a gasp of delight.

The Earl of Dudley lavished attention on the property in its heyday in the 19th century. The gardens, designed by William Nesfield around a stone fountain set in a shining lake, have been restored to their former splendour.

▶ *A433, 10 miles NW of Worcester. EH. Daily Apr-Oct; Wed-Sun Nov-Mar.*

CENTRAL ENGLAND

WORCESTERSHIRE

Great Witley church

The finest Baroque church in Britain

An astonishing white and gold papier-mâché confection in which are set ten jewel-like stained glass windows and paintings by Italian artists embellishes the interior of St Michael and All Angels, the parish church of Great and Little Witley. Originally, the ensemble decorated the Duke of Chandos's palace chapel in Edgware. They were bought by Lord Foley, owner of Witley Court, in 1747 and transported by wagons to his Georgian church to create an unparalleled baroque extravaganza.
▶ *From Witley Court or track from Great Witley, on A433, 11 miles NW of Worcester.*

Tardebigge flight of locks

Watch narrow boats negotiate Britain's longest lock staircase

One of the most demanding stretches of canal navigation in Britain is at Tardebigge, a climb of 91m (300ft) through 30 locks in just three miles to reach the summit of the Worcester & Birmingham Canal.

From the River Severn at Worcester narrow boats negotiate 58 locks, rising 130m (428ft) in 15 miles, to Top Lock at Tardebigge. Top Lock is a challenge in itself. There is barely enough space between its narrow brick walls to allow boats to squeeze through. Plunging 4.2m (14ft), it is the deepest narrow lock in Britain. Beyond lies Tardebigge Tunnel, 530m (1739ft) long, and nearby is the reservoir from which clay was dug to line the canal when it was built between 1791 and 1815.
▶ *Tardebigge, off A448 Bromsgrove-Redditch.*

Droitwich Brine Baths

How to get rid of that sinking feeling

Can't swim? Don't worry. With 2½lb of salt in every warm gallon of water – ten times the concentration in seawater – the brine baths are just the solution to buoy you up. They owe their existance to an underground lake 60m (200ft) below the town, a sort of subterranean Dead Sea. In the 1830s the original baths made the town a fashionable health resort, and their modern replacements, opened in 1985, are still a popular way to rise above life's cares.
▶ *S of town centre off A38 Worcester road. Daily. Tel 01905 793446 to book.*

Chateau Impney

A fairytale castle fit for a princess

When John Corbett, 'Salt King of Droitwich', fell in love with a beautiful young governess, Anna O'Meara, while on a trip to Paris, he did what wealthy, middle-aged men often do in such circumstances: he gave her the most expensive present money could buy. In his case it was a grand home imitating the chateaus of the Loire that his love so admired – a flourish of brick and stone, turrets and dormers.

John and Anna, by then Mrs Corbett, moved into Chateau Impney and its 49ha (120 acres) of landscaped parkland in 1875. It had taken six years to build and cost the equivalent in current terms of £7.5 million. Nine years later she left him. Today the showy mansion is a hotel.
▶ *1 mile E of Droitwich town centre on A38 Bromsgrove road (Junction 5 off M5). Tel 01905 774411.*

Worcester County Cricket Ground and Cathedral

A scene that will hit you for six

With its sheltering shimmer of willows and view across the Severn to the cathedral, this cricket ground is for many the most idyllic in the whole of England. On summer weekends you can stroll the few yards to the river and catch a ferry to the opposite bank, where a gauge beside the steps to College Green marks the height of the river when it floods.

The cathedral is a treasure-trove of church building styles down the centuries, starting with the crypt – the largest in Britain – a forest of Norman columns built in the 1080s. The west window and the pinnacles on the tower, both so apparent from the cricket ground, belong to extensive High Victorian alterations made by Sir George Gilbert Scott.

▶ *Cricket ground ¾ mile W of city centre, Tel 01905 748474. Cathedral city centre.*

Royal Worcester Porcelain

Where skill conjures exquisite china from humble materials

The transformation of a lump of wet clay into an item of fine china is fascinating. At the Royal Worcester Porcelain Works you can see all the stages – a process essentially unchanged since production started in 1751 – down to the painting by hand of detailed fruit-and-flower decorations.

Adjoining the oldest porcelain factory in England is a museum containing examples of every sort of Royal Worcester ware from earliest days to the present. There are grand coronation plates, high quality tableware, ornamental vases and porcelain figures, all beautifully crafted.

▶ *S of city centre in Severn Street.*

Bredon Hill

Muse for a poem and everyday story

Bredon Hill surges dramatically from the flat Vale of Evesham, like a whale breaching in a calm sea. The 300m (1000ft) outlier of the Cotswolds, with its drystone walls and thin soils where orchids grow, contrasts with the lush countryside below. A 2nd-century BC hill fort and the 18th-century Parson's Folly share the summit, high above encircling villages, which include Ashton under Hill, claimed as the model for Ambridge – home of *The Archers*, radio's long running soap. But Bredon Hill has higher literary credentials – most notably it inspired A.E. Housman's romantic elegy 'In Summertime on Bredon'.

▶ *6 miles S of Evesham off A44 Pershore road.*

Fleece Inn, Bretforton

Two pints of best bitter and a bundle of asparagus, please

Pubs are usually visited for their ale and good company – both of which can be found in abundance in Bretforton's Fleece Inn – but go in May or early June and you could find the bar lined with neat green bundles rather than beer glasses. This is one of the asparagus auctions – three are held over the six-week season – when shopkeepers and wholesalers bid for the crop, grown along with other vegetables, fruit and flowers in the vale's rich soils. The half-timbered inn, originally a medieval longhouse, where the farmer and his family lived at one end and livestock were penned at the other, has altered little over the centuries. In 1848 Henry Byrd, whose family had owned the property for more than 400 years, sold the land and was granted a licence to brew and sell beer and cider in the house. His great grand-daughter, Lola Taplin, ran the Fleece for 30 years until she died at the age of 83, in 1977. The building is almost exactly as she left it – with low beamed ceilings, worn flagstones scored with 'witchmarks' (said to ward off evil) and a collection of Stuart pewter reputed to have been left by Oliver Cromwell in return for booty of gold and silver plate taken to pay his troops.

▶ *3 miles E of Evesham on B4035 Weston Subedge road. NT. Tel 01386 831173.*

CENTRAL ENGLAND

195

Waters and heights that lift the spirits

Deep springs and Victorian resorts in the wild

Malvern Hills – inspiration for the music of Edward Elgar

There is something exotic about the Malvern Hills, so abruptly do they rise from the flat Severn plain, an undulating ridge of rock 9 miles long and more than 500 million years old. In winter they are snow-capped; in summer, tawny and bare. At night the glittering necklace of lights strung along the northern hills could be taken for those twinkling over a Mediterranean resort, while the elegant villas and lush gardens of **Great Malvern** have the flavour of a late 19th-century Italian spa. A wonderfully florid railway station and fully operational gas street lights add to the Victorian holiday air.

The east flanks of the Malverns descend steeply to the plain below, while on the west they fold into curves of woodland. Roads encircle them, but the hills are made for walking. From the calm sunlight of a crisp winter's day in the village of West Malvern, try the gentle climb to the bracing summit of North Hill. Directly south lies **Worcestershire Beacon**, the highest point of the Malverns at 425m (1394ft). From this exhilarating vantage point the lower but wilder southern hills descend into the remote horizons of Gloucestershire. Look west to glimpse a more rugged prospect beyond the Welsh border; while to the east is patchwork England, with villages and church spires amid woods and fields.

As you move south the hills trace a sinuous line like the spine of a slumbering animal to reach Malvern Wells, where medicinal springs were discovered in the 17th century. Malvern water is now produced commercially in Colwall, on the west slopes. Tucked into the wooded, bracken-covered slopes, and joined to a 14th-century Benedictine priory, is **Little Malvern Court**, which incorporates the Prior's Hall with its splendid smoke-blackened timber roof. At nearby Wynds Point, where the A449 cuts across the hills, you can walk up through the woods and out onto the grassy heights and intoxicating air of the British Camp, a mighty Celtic hill fort that crowns the 340m (1115ft) Herefordshire Beacon.

A place of very English muses

The composer Edward Elgar loved these hills. He was born at **Lower Broadheath**, north of Great Malvern near Worcester, in a small brick cottage that is now a shrine to his memory. The Malverns also inspired the 14th-century poet William Langland, who slept on the hills and dreamed *The Vision of William concerning Piers the Plowman*. Seven hundred years later, Evelyn Waugh used **Madresfield Court**, a delectable jumble of Elizabethan and Victorian styles for which the Malverns provide a theatrical backdrop, as the real 'Brideshead' of his novel *Brideshead Revisited*.

WORCESTERSHIRE BEACON

1 **Great Malvern** ▶ *6 miles S of Worcester on A449.*

2 **Worcestershire Beacon** ▶ *Footpaths from Great Malvern.*

3 **Little Malvern Court** ▶ *Little Malvern, off A4104. Wed and Thur pm, mid Apr-mid July. Priory daily.*

4 **Elgar Birthplace Museum** ▶ *Lower Broadheath, W of Worcester on B4204. Daily; closed Christmas-end Jan.*

5 **Madresfield Court** ▶ *Madresfield, 6 miles SW of Worcester off A449. Guided tours only, Apr-July.*
Tel 01905 830680 to book.

ISLE OF MAN
210-211

Ramsey
Douglas
Castletown

CUMBRIA
210-211

The Pennines

Carlisle

Workington
Keswick
Whitehaven
Lake District
National Park
Penrith
Brough
Windermere
Kendal
Barrow-in-Furness

LANCASHIRE,
Liverpool and
Manchester
212-217

Blackpool
Clitheroe
Preston
Blackburn
Burnley
Southport
Bury
Rochdale
Bolton
Oldham
Wigan
Manchester
St Helens
Salford
Stockport
Liverpool
Warrington
Birkenhead
Runcorn
Ellesmere Port
Wilmslow
Macclesfield
Chester
CHESHIRE
and The Wirral
200-202
Crewe

Northwest England

The pageants of city and country seem on the verge of joining ranks. Never far away from Liverpool's pierhead or Manchester's palaces of learning, sport and commerce lie coasts of gaudy seaside delights and tide-ripped sandbanks, wild Pennine hills, and the deep waters of the Lake District.

Key

1 Main entry

2 Feature entry

━━ County boundary

━━ Motorway

━━ Principal A road

(See 'Finding your way', page 7)

CHESHIRE & THE WIRRAL

Dee Estuary

Across the sands of Dee

Climb the footpath up the hill which rises behind the half-timbered, thatched cottages of Burton village and you will be rewarded with panoramic views across the vast stretches of mud flats, sand and salt marsh of the Dee Estuary. The village of Burton once served as a port for boats to and from Ireland but as the Dee silted up it lost its position on the coast, and the area became instead a port of call for a different type of visitor.

   The estuary provides a winter refuge of over 100,000 wading birds: two-thirds of Britain's over-wintering wildfowl. As the tide goes out it reveals a feeding ground for a vast array of species. October heralds the peak period for shelduck, redshank and curlew and in December ragged flocks of lapwing make spectacular patterns against the winter sky.
▶ *Burton Mill Wood, 3 miles SE of Neston off A540.*

Port Sunlight

A village fit for factory workers

The neat cottages and gardens, spacious streets and open areas of this model village have a rural serenity: a place of peace and quiet, built by William Hesketh Lever for workers at his adjoining Sunlight soap factory. The village is more than a vivid testimony of Lever's enlightened ideas as an employer; it also reflects his interests in architecture and town planning. The original layout was his, and he paid close attention to the designs of the 30 architects who worked on the 900 houses – most of which were completed during the 1890s and early years of the 20th century, although some of them date from the 1930s.

   On The Diamond, in the village centre, Lord Leverhulme, as he became, built the Lady Lever Art Gallery in memory of his wife. Behind its classically styled walls are almost 2000 works of art, including pre-Raphaelite paintings, Chinese porcelain and French sculptor Maurice Ferrary's *Salambo*, inspired by Gustave Flaubert's novel.
▶ *2½ miles SE of Birkenhead centre off A41 Chester road. Gallery daily.*

Ness Botanic Gardens

Plants from the roof of the world

Arthur Bulley made a fortune as a cotton broker, and ploughed much of it into the gardens he created from 1898 at Mickwell Brow – a sandstone outcrop above the Dee estuary where he built his house. Bulley's special interest was plants from the Himalayas and mountains of China. He sponsored several plant-hunting expeditions to the region, cultivating at Ness the rhododendrons, azaleas, camelias, pieris and other species brought back, and laying the foundation for today's gardens. But this wealthy Liverpudlian was no amateur: under his expert guidance many new varieties were created – work which led to the establishment of his plant and seed company, Bees.
▶ *8 miles N of Chester off A540 Neston road. Daily.*

The Rows, Chester

The origins seem black and white, but it is easy to be deceived

The city-centre streets with their black-and-white, half-timbered galleries (the Rows), reached up a few steps from the pavement – with a lower crypt-like storey at the level of a semi-basement – give Chester the appearance of a medieval city, but it is largely Victorian: more fantastic fake than perfect preservation. To spot the differences, walk up Watergate Street towards the centre, carrying straight on at The Cross, into Eastgate Street.

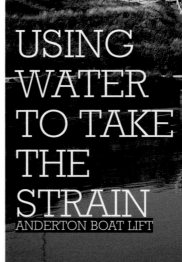

USING WATER TO TAKE THE STRAIN
ANDERTON BOAT LIFT

Watergate's Rows are mostly the genuine article, built between the 13th and 17th centuries. Among them is Bishop Lloyd's House, the finest medieval building in the city, with a richly carved façade. By contrast, Eastgate's 19th-century Rows, whether original or replacements of medieval ones, are larger, and the timber framing more complicated and decorated with carvings.
▶ *Chester city centre.*

Beeston Castle
As seen on the road to Damascus

When Ranulf, Earl of Chester, built it in 1225, Beeston Castle was at the cutting edge of fortress technology, incorporating features from strongholds in the Holy Land observed by the earl during the Crusades. Four centuries later, it remained formidable enough to withstand a year-long siege by Parliamentarian forces.

History marches on: the castle is now a ruin, but time cannot steal its commanding location. From the ramparts, perched on an isolated craggy 150m (500ft) summit, eight counties can be seen, in a great sweep of land from the Pennines to the Welsh mountains.
▶ *12 miles N of Whitchurch off A49 Tarporley road. EH. Daily Apr-Sept; Thurs-Mon Oct-Mar.*

The Boat Museum
Voyage into the canal age

The great basin at the junction of the Shropshire Union and Manchester Ship canals contains the world's largest collection of inland waterways craft, from coracles to narrow boats. Among the more unusual vessels is an ice boat, with a handrail stretching centrally from bow to stern that those on board would grasp as they rocked the hull to break frozen water. Old warehouses and dock workers' cottages line the sides of the basin.
▶ *1 mile E of Ellesmere Port town centre. Junction 9 off M53. Daily.*

Anderton Boat Lift
Using water to take the strain

A bewildering array of pillars, pulleys and pistons is an ingenious solution to a complex problem: how to lift canal boats 15m (50ft) from the River Weaver to the Trent and Mersey Canal. Two enormous boat-carrying tanks, or caissons, are used in the operation. Each weighs 252 tonnes when full of water and 80 tonnes when empty. At rest, one tank is level with the canal and the other with the river. To move the tanks, a small amount of water is removed from the bottom tank. As the heavier top tank descends, it forces hydraulic fluid into a connected cylinder on the lighter tank, pushing it upwards. Built in 1875, this was the world's first boat lift and is the only one of its kind in Britain.
▶ *In Anderton off A533. Signed for 2½ miles from centre of Northwich.*

Alderley Edge
Listen for snoozing knights and enjoy a panoramic view

The oak-clad escarpment of Alderley Edge rises sharply to 198m (650ft) above the Cheshire Plain, coming to an abrupt end at Castle Rock. A far-reaching view through the trees extends to the northern edges of the Peak District and as far as the Pennines. Stone and Bronze Age people took refuge in caves along the Edge, and copper, cobalt and lead were mined here from before the Romans came to Britain until the mid 19th century.

Legend has it that King Arthur's knights sleep beneath the rocks of Alderley Edge and will ride out again in England's hour of greatest need. A bearded face, said to be that of Merlin, is carved above the Wizard's Well, with an inscription reading: 'Drink of this and take thy fill, For the water falls by the wizard's will.'
▶ *Signed from B5087, SE of Alderley Edge town. NT.*

NORTH WEST ENGLAND

CHESHIRE & THE WIRRAL

9 Quarry Bank Mill **10** Maggotty's Grave **11** Little Moreton Hall

12 Jodrell Bank

Quarry Bank Mill

A Georgian mill where raw cotton is still transformed into fine fabric

Britain's largest working waterwheel drives the machinery at Quarry Bank Mill. It measures more than 7m (24ft) in diameter, but is smaller than the original wheel, installed in 1818, which was nearly 10m (32ft) across. Founded in 1784, Quarry Bank is a perfectly preserved Georgian cotton mill. Many original features, including power looms, carding machines (to remove impurities and knots from raw cotton) and a full-length spinning mule (to spin thread), have been returned to working order. They now produce more than 9000m (9800yd) of cloth each year.

As Quarry Bank flourished in the early 19th century, a large working community with a shop, school, cottages, terraced housing and two chapels was established. Orphans who had been drafted in from workhouses around England to provide cheap labour lived in Apprentice House, built in 1790 and now restored. Try out the straw-filled mattresses here and then stroll in the garden, where the same varieties of fruit and vegetables that fed the apprentices are grown today.
▶ *Styal village, 2½ miles N of Wilmslow on B5166. NT. For opening times, Tel 01625 527468.*

Maggotty's Grave

The ghost of England's last court jester

Wander through the leafy shade of Maggotty's Wood's northern edge and you will stumble across two huge inscribed slabs, dappled in sunlight – you may even glimpse a spectral figure riding a white horse. The stones mark the final resting place of Samuel Johnson, England's last paid jester.

The eccentric Johnson, also known as Lord Flame, lived at nearby Gawsworth Hall, a 15th-century manor house, until his death in 1773. He wanted to become a ghost, so he asked to be buried in unconsecrated ground and chose this small area of beech and ash woodland. Johnson is said to ride out from this quiet coppice to haunt Gawsworth village.
▶ *3 miles SW of Macclesfield off A536. Maggotty's Wood lies between Gawsworth village and Gawsworth Hall.*

Little Moreton Hall

Crazy angles stand the test of time

Lopsided windows, imperfect right-angles and a carp-crowded moat all contribute to Little Moreton Hall's bizarre architectural charm. It is one of the finest examples of a timber-framed, moated building in England, and it seems miraculous that its three storeys, with their bulging walls, are still standing. The earliest sections of the hall, including the porch, parlour and great hall, were built in 1450-80. In the 1560s, the 21m (68ft) long gallery was added, causing the walls of the south wing to bend and bow outwards under its weight.

Look above the doorways for exquisite wood carvings, early attempts at Renaissance design, and – above a window – the inscription of Richard Dale, a carpenter who worked here in the 1550s.
▶ *4 miles SW of Congleton on A34. NT. Wed-Sun Mar-Oct; Sat and Sun Nov-Dec.*

Jodrell Bank

Explore the final frontier

A 76m (250ft) dish, weighing 3200 tonnes, towers above the Cheshire Plain. This is the Lovell Telescope at Jodrell Bank – the world's second-largest fully steerable telescope. Radio waves emitted by objects in space are collected by the dish and converted into signals that are used to map distant stars and galaxies. The telescope is capable of recording Cosmic Microwave Background radiation, the oldest type detected by any radio telescope, originating 300,000 years (a mere split second in evolutionary terms) after the 'Big Bang'.

Completed in 1957, the Lovell Telescope has discovered quasars (intense, star-like sources of radio waves) and researched pulsars (the collapsed cores of supergiant stars). Its visitor centre will take you on a tour of outer space.
▶ *Signed from the M6, Junction 18. Daily mid Mar-Oct; Tues-Sun Nov-mid Mar.*

CUMBRIA

1 Birdoswald **2** St Michael's, Burgh-by-Sands **3** Cars of the Stars

4 Long Meg and Her Daughters

Birdoswald

In the footsteps of the Roman army with fabulous countryside views

Hard-bitten Roman legionaries must have been impressed by the view from Birdoswald fort, even if their priority was to protect the nearby river crossing and look out for barbarians. Birdoswald, built around AD 125, overlooks Irthling Gorge – a steep, wooded hillside where the river snakes its way into the northern wilds. The gorge is reputed to be the site of Arthur's death during a battle between Britons and Saxon invaders.

Birdoswald fort has been excavated to reveal Roman towers, gates and walls. The site would once have been guarded by 500 foot soldiers or 300 cavalry. A timber hall dated to around AD 500 suggests it was also inhabited during the Dark Ages. Walk less than half a mile east to see the remains of Roman bridges that were built at Willowford. Cross the River Irthing on a new steel footbridge nearby to view the most extensive surviving stretches of Hadrian's Wall.
▶ *On minor road, 1 mile E of Gilsland on B6318. EH. Daily Apr-Oct.*

St Michael's, Burgh-by-Sands

Warlike church architecture tells of border conflict

The walls of Burgh church's 14th-century tower are 1.5m (5ft) thick, with slits for windows and no door. Such fortification is evidence of the violent border disputes between the Scots and English. The only entrance to the tower is within the church through a yett (a heavy iron gate). Inside, you find yourself in a gloomy little cavity, where locals once huddled in fear, overlooked by shadowy stone carvings of mysterious beasts. Unnerving carvings that lurk above the lintel have been interpreted as a hippopotamus and elephant, but whoever shaped the stones could not have seen such exotic animals. Perhaps the carver dreamt of them – they certainly possess an other-worldly quality.

St Michael's stands squarely within the bounds of a Roman fort and is built entirely of its stone. Edward I's body was brought here for temporary safe-keeping in 1307 after he died leading his troops to do battle with the Scots in one last weary campaign across the Solway Firth. In the years that followed, villagers built the strong belltower to protect themselves from the Scottish enemy.
▶ *1½ miles N of Moorhouse off B5307.*

Cars of the Stars

See automobile heroes of the big and small screen in close up

Whatever happened to the ramshackle Reliant van used in *Only Fools and Horses* or FAB1 from *Thunderbirds*? Where do the sleek Aston Martins retire to when 007 has run them in and just how comfortable was the Batmobile? The answers are found tucked away in the heart of Lakeland. The motor museum is home to many of the original vehicles used in films and television classics, from *Mr Bean* and the *The Pink Panther* to *All Creatures Great and Small* and *Chitty Chitty Bang Bang*.
▶ *Standish Street, Keswick town centre. Daily Easter-Nov. For other times, Tel 017687 73757.*

Long Meg and Her Daughters

Enduring enigma of standing stones

Mystery surrounds Long Meg, a rugged slab of red sandstone that stands nearly 3.5m (12ft) tall. Her surface is carved with spirals and lines that are now almost weathered away. According to local tradition, she is a witch turned to stone for dancing on the Sabbath.

A few yards away, forming a ring around her, are the 59 stones called her daughters – their purpose is unknown. At midwinter sunset Long Meg's shadow aligns with those of the other stones to mark the solstice, the turning point of the pagan year. The stones are thought to date from the late Neolithic period, more than 4000 years ago. Around Long Meg the countryside is unspoilt: a mix of pastures and tree-lined hedges, and small farms in the aptly named Eden Valley.
▶ *Follow track from minor road NE of Little Salkeld, 5 miles NE of Penrith on A686.*

NORTH WEST ENGLAND

CUMBRIA

High Cup Nick

An inspirational panorama for the determined walker

Nothing prepares you for the moment you find yourself at the 'nick' (head) of High Cup Gill on the brow of the Pennine moors. It is one of the pivotal points on the spine of England, overlooking the finest views and set in the wildest landscape. If you have any breath left, it is taken away. A chasm opens out below you and great curved faces of rock sweep away to create a deep amphitheatre-like bowl. A tiny stream jinks into the distance and disappears into the verdant Eden Valley. Beyond is the grandeur of the Lakeland fells.

To reach High Cup requires some effort. It is on the route of the Pennine Way, which is well signed from Teesdale. For a really enjoyable walk, take a friend, choose a clear day and arrange for someone to collect you so that you can cover the whole section one way – a distance of just over 13 miles.

▶ *Forest-in-Teesdale, on B6277 between Middleton and Alston. Dufton, signed from B6542 2½ miles N of Appleby.*

Appleby Horse Fair

The ultimate equine bazaar

Caravans and cars line the byways for miles as gypsies and tourists from all over Britain converge on Fair Hill in Appleby on the second Wednesday in June. They come for the final day of the annual Horse Fair, first held in 1685. Horse-trading is the essential business of the week-long event, but other activities from farriery (shoeing horses) to harness racing have grown up around it.

Visitors flock to the little town to see horses being washed in the River Eden, buy lucky charms, have their fortunes told and wander among some of the 200 stalls. But the fair has not turned into a commercial show – everyone gets caught up in the romance of the occasion.

▶ *On B6542, S of A66 between Penrith and Brough.*

Great Asby Scar

Water-worn rocks conceal a secret garden of rare plants

Long, broad sweeps of grey rock lend an almost surreal quality to the tops of several of the fells visible from the M6 between Kirkby Stephen and Shap. One of the most dramatic stretches of this 'limestone pavement' is at Great Asby Scar. From a distance the huge rocky slabs appear to

be featureless and smooth, but closer inspection shows clearly where water has carved out a honeycombe of hard blocks, known as clints, separated by deep channels, called grikes. It is in these grikes that a hidden world of rare trees and alpine flowers is left to flourish, safe from grazing animals.

▶ *Footpath from minor road S of Great Asby village, 6 miles S of Appleby off B6260.*

Castlerigg Stone Circle
Bronze-Age megaliths ringed by mountains

On days of dank mist the standing stones of Castlerigg Circle (below) seem to brood and loom large, while on crisp bright mornings of scudding cloud they shiver and dance. Level ground is a rarity in the Lake District, so the people who chose this spot for their ritual site made the most of it and created a monument to last. That was three to four thousand years ago. The wide circle comprises 38 roughly hewn standing stones, the tallest of which is over 2m (7ft). All around are high fells and mountains. The effect is to turn the sky into a hemisphere, with you and the stones at its centre. The time of day, time of year, winds and weather all change the look and feel of the place. What it all meant in the Bronze Age remains a mystery but it is hard now not to make up your own magic.

▶ *2 miles E of Keswick, via layby on minor road to Naddle Bridge. NT/EH.*

Langdale Pikes
A challenging ascent to reach fine views

The steepest and highest Lake District mountains crowd the flanks of the valley of Great Langdale. This walk will reward you with some of the most far-reaching views in the area. Look down from the mat-grass and heather of the high fells to the green oasis below and a clue is revealed to a slice of history. A cascade of rocky debris, the Langdale Screes, sweeps down to the foot of the fells. It may look natural, but it is actually the waste chippings from a Neolithic axe factory. Stone axe-heads were roughly fashioned here, and then sent to the coast to be polished and traded.

▶ *NT car park at Stickle Ghyll on B5343 from Skelwith Bridge, W of Ambleside on A593.*

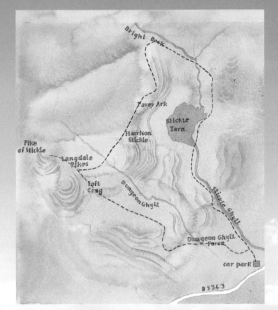

Top of the world *From car park, take steep path to the plateau around Loft Crag – a sanctuary for rare mountain ringlet butterflies. Then, wander on a circuit of the peaks, known locally as Pikes, from Pike of Stickle, via Harrison Stickle to Pavey Ark. The walk is only 4 miles but with steep climbs.*

CASTLERIGG STONE CIRCLE

Sweet muses of the lakes and fells

The awesome beauty of Lakeland has fired the imagination of creative spirits for more than two centuries

1 Claife **2** Dove Cottage **3** White Moss Common **4** Derwentwater **5** Brantwood **6** Hill Top

The Lake District was just another place of work for woodsmen, miners, bobbin-makers and shepherds until the late 18th century, when the travel writer Thomas West published *Guide to the Lakes* (1778). All at once it became fashionable for the cultured classes to venture into this wild terrain to visit viewpoints or 'stations', where the formal qualities of the landscape could be appreciated.

One of West's stations survives as a substantial ruin at **Claife** on the fellside above Lake Windermere (access from Ash Landing car park). In the heyday of this strange building in the 1830s, the drawing room had coloured windows representing different lighting effects – yellow for summer, blue for moonlight, lilac for thunder. People learned to respond to the picturesque in a prescribed way.

Such 'ordered rationality, shared standards and conventions' was rejected by the Romantic movement in the early 19th century. At the forefront of this rebellion was William Wordsworth. He had been born in Cumbria and made his mark as a poet while living at Rydal and Grasmere (where one of his homes, **Dove Cottage**, is now a museum; open daily, closed early Jan-early Feb). At the time, his poetry achieved something quite new: a personal response to things seen, experienced and felt, full of emotional intensity. Soon, other writers such as Thomas De Quincey and Samuel Taylor Coleridge took up residence.

Invasion of the art set

What the local farmworkers thought of the Romantic poets can only be imagined. They were not keen to write about real people and places; the Lakeland landscape was an inspiration rather than a subject. It was left to Wordsworth's sister Dorothy to tell us through her journal about workaday people and the places she and William went for walks. **White Moss Common** (access from NT car park off A591 Grasmere-Rydal) was one of their favourite strolls: a place of 'fairy valleys and fairy tarns, miniature mountains, alps above alps'. Here, William would pace to and fro reciting poems loudly to himself.

In the early days of the Romantic movement, painters found the Lake District a daunting subject and provided their clients with grotesque representations of awesome cliffs, chasms and waterfalls. The painter who captured the

... THE INTENSE JOY, MINGLED WITH AWE, THAT I HAD LOOKING THROUGH THE MOSSY ROOTS, OVER THE CRAG, INTO THE LAKE.

JOHN RUSKIN ON SEEING DERWENTWATER FROM FRIAR'S CRAG

untamed landscape best of all was J.M.W. Turner (1775-1851). His greatest champion was John Ruskin (1819-1900), the foremost art critic of the Victorian age, who had an abiding passion for the Lake District.

Ruskin had fallen in love with the area as a small boy when he first set eyes on **Derwentwater** from Friar's Crag (a short walk from Keswick). In the 1860s he bought a house on the shores of Coniston Water from William James Linton, a wood engraver and illustrator. The latter part of his brilliant but tragic life – he died insane, his marriage an unconsummated disaster – was played out at **Brantwood** (Coniston Water; daily, except Mon and Tues in winter), his home from 1872 and still full of his drawings, watercolours, books and furniture.

In the 20th century, Lakeland inspired some of Britain's best-loved children's books. Arthur Ransome located his *Swallows and Amazons* on Coniston and Windermere, and Beatrix Potter based many stories at **Hill Top** (Near Sawrey, Sat-Wed, Apr-Oct; also Thur Jun-Aug, NT). Melvyn Bragg, Margaret Forster and other writers have continued the literary tradition in the 'agreeable wilderness'. But it was Wordsworth who gave the place its sinews and soul.

CUMBRIA

10 Buttermere **11** Whitehaven

Buttermere

Hard rock meets still waters

Like a glittering jewel, gripped in the steel and gold setting of the rocky fells that surround it, Buttermere is seductively beautiful. It is also one of the few Cumbrian lakes with a path all the way round it, offering a feature-packed walk that can be covered easily in about two hours. Sheer cliffs of green slate tower on either side, broken up at intervals by cascading waterfalls. Flocks of long-haired Herdwick sheep, a rare local breed, graze in the pastures beside the lake.

Buttermere village, based on farms and mills where Norse settlers once scratched a living, was home to the Maid of Buttermere, whose story of love, elopement, deception and shame created a Victorian scandal. It inspired the novel of the same name by Melvyn Bragg.
▶ *S and W from Keswick on B5289 via Honister Pass; or E from Cockermouth on B5292/B5289.*

Whitehaven

Where American revolutionaries struck at the heart of British trade

On 22 April, 1778, the last invasion of the British mainland took place at Whitehaven, when American revolutionaries led by John Paul Jones tried, and failed, to strike at the heart of the British economy by attacking the merchant fleet docked in the harbour. At the time, Whitehaven was the most important British port after London, its wealth reflected in its elegant Georgian buildings. Finding such fine architecture, still largely intact, in such an out-of-the-way location, can be surprising.

Shipbuilding boosted the town's fortunes well into the 19th century. By then merchant vessels had become too large to enter the harbour. Whitehaven was then obliged to settle for a comfortable but rapidly diminishing prosperity, exporting coal from nearby mines, and trading in rum, spices, tobacco and slaves.

This colourful past is commemorated in The Beacon, the town's museum. On the top floor there is a weather centre, where visitors can use computers to view the latest satellite weather pictures from anywhere in the world.
▶ *SW from Cockermouth on A66, then S from Bridgefoot on A595. Tel 01946 592302 for Beacon opening times.*

NORTHWEST ENGLAND

CUMBRIA

Sellafield Nuclear Power Station
Stepping out of this world

Whatever your views on nuclear power, the Visitor Centre at Sellafield will deliver a thought provoking experience. This is the site of the world's first commercial nuclear power station and although it is no longer possible to tour the power station, the Centre explores the ways in which electricity can be generated.

The aim of the facility is to provoke debate about power generation and not to champion nuclear energy. Go to Europe's first Immersion Cinema and you can join in the action through your own touch screen. But it is the view from the observatory that is most impressive, as you gaze out over a vast panorama of reprocessing plants and nuclear reactors. Like Alice in Wonderland you will suddenly feel very small.
▶*Signed off A595 S of Egremont.*
Tel 01946 727027 for visitor and tour details.

Wastwater and the Screes
Vast chutes of rubble tower above the deep cold waters

The pretty little road from Nether Wasdale does not prepare you for the marked contrast of the austere, savage landscape that confronts you on reaching Wastwater, the deepest lake in England at 78m (256ft). Stand on a grassy bank among the oak trees to look out over the cold and lifeless crystal clear water. An awesome 400m (1300ft) high curtain of scree, or ice-shattered rubble, flanks the southwest shore, opposite. Very little grows on these unstable slopes. In the distance, at the head of the lake, are the peaks of Great Gable, flanked by Yewbarrow and Lingmell. If the view seems familiar, it is because its stylised image forms the Lake District National Park emblem.
▶*S of Egremont on A595, then E at Gosforth on minor road to Nether Wasdale.*

Sandscale Haws
Serenaded by a chorus of toads

On late spring and early summer evenings, the 'song' of the rare natterjack toad floats across the marram-covered dunes of Sandscale Haws. The common toad and frog, and the smooth, palmate and great-crested newts, are also found here, making it one of the few places in Britain where all six native amphibians live.

Wild flowers are a bonus in summer. Drifts of marsh orchids turn the damp hollows, known as slacks, pink and purple, while rest harrow and dune pansy cover the baking sand, and sea holly and sea rocket crowd the upper beach. Burnet roses, edging the pathways, fill the air with a heady scent.
▶*Duddon estuary, off A590, W of Dalton-in-Furness. NT.*

Roa and Piel islands
A haunt for smugglers, clerics, pirates and a would-be king

The seascape around Barrow-in-Furness has a pedigree. Stand at the little harbour on Roa Island and look from Barrow, where the Vickers shipyard has been building warships since 1896, across the deepwater channel to Walney Island, Piel Bar and the ruins of Piel Castle. Pirate-ships once plied these waters and nuclear-powered submarines still do.

Medieval monks at nearby Furness Abbey were among those who profitted from the flow of contraband across these waters. In the 14th century, the monks built a castle on Piel Island to guard the entrance of Barrow harbour and so protect their investment. It is now an imposing ruin. The island is also where Lambert Simnel, a pretender to Henry VII's throne, landed, before marching south to defeat at the Battle of Stoke in 1487.

To reach Piel Island take a ferry across the half-mile of water from Roa, where you can also visit the Barrow Lifeboat station at weekends and in the school holidays.
▶*Roa Island, off A5087, S of Barrow;*
Tel 01229 820941 for lifeboat details. Piel Island, Tel 01229 475770 for boat from Roa. Piel Castle, daily; EH.

Arnside Knott

Butterflies from the good old days

Choose a summer afternoon and settle down in the dappled sunshine of Arnside Knott. Its flower-strewn verges should be abuzz with bees. Soon a butterfly or two will join you.

North meets south at this wooded limestone knoll. The Duke of Burgundy rubs shoulders with the Scotch argus, the former at its northern limit, the latter as far south as it chooses to go. On a good day you are also likely to see a brimstone, mountain argus, purple hairstreak and small pearl-bordered fritillary. You may even glimpse the rare brown fritillary. A mix of coppiced woodland, scrub and open grassland probably draws the unusually large number of insects.

▶ *At end of B5282, near Milnthorpe on A6. NT.*

Levens Hall

Step back into a 17th-century garden

Blocks, cylinders and cones of green foliage, balanced one on another, lie scattered around the grounds here like a giant Chinese puzzle, waiting to be fitted together. The topiary that Guillaume Beaumont designed in 1694 as the centrepiece of the gardens at Levens Hall has been preserved with little change for over 300 years. For a vivid sense of life back then, meander among the fanciful shapes of yew and box, along the beech alleys and past the flower beds glowing with seasonal colour. Also admire the pannelling inside the stately Elizabethan hall, which is still a family home.

▶ *S of Kendal off A590; or from Junction 36 on M6. Sun-Thur Apr-mid Oct.*

Blackwell

An Arts and Crafts masterpiece

Blackwell's stark, rather austere clifftop presence above Lake Windermere gives little clue to the wealth of finely crafted detail and glowing jewel-like colour to be found inside. All of the original Arts and Crafts features of Blackwell, created by architect M.H. Baillie in 1897-1900 as a retreat for a Manchester brewer, have survived remarkably intact. For nearly 50 years, while the building served first as a school, then as offices, the décor was boarded over or hidden behind filing cabinets. Then in 1999 all was revealed, and the restored rooms are again free to dazzle and delight.

▶ *1½ miles S of Bowness-on-Windermere, on B5360, off A5074. Tel 015394 46139 for details.*

AN ARTS AND CRAFTS MASTERPIECE
STAINED GLASS WINDOW AT BLACKWELL

NORTHWEST ENGLAND

ISLE OF MAN

1 Calf of Man **2** TT races **3** Laxey Wheel

4 Kirk Maughold **5** Manx railways

6 The Ballaugh Curraghs

MOTORBIKE ROAD RACING CAPITAL OF THE WORLD
TT RACES

Calf of Man
A living legacy from the days of the Norse invaders

You may come face to face with a six-horned ram on the craggy Calf of Man. Meet the last of the Vikings. The flock of Manx Loghtan sheep, which lives on the 243ha (600 acre) island off the southern tip of the mainland, is thought to be descended from stock introduced by raiding Norsemen a thousand years ago. Today, the Calf is managed as a wildlife sanctuary, and is renowned for its bird life, which includes a large breeding population of the dashing, red-legged chough – 'king of the crows' – and the mysterious, burrow-nesting, night-flying Manx shearwater.

▶ *Calf of Man can be reached in summer by regular boat trips from Port Erin. MNH.*

TT races
Motorbike road racing capital of the world

The roar of motorbikes careering around the normally quiet roads of the Isle of Man at speeds of more than 120mph is a thrilling annual experience. The island's population expands by more than half each June and July as 40,000 biking enthusiasts arrive to witness the famous TT races. They take place on a twisting, tortuous 38 mile route that encircles the island and winds high over a shoulder of Snaefell mountain using public roads. When the first Tourist Trophy races for motorbikes were organised in 1907 the winners averaged less than 40mph.

The story of the TT races is described in the Manx Museum in Douglas.

▶ *TT course marked by orange signs. Manx Museum, Mon-Sat.*

Laxey Wheel

The watery wheel that keeps on turning

The world's largest working water wheel continues to function long after the mine it served closed down. Engineer Robert Casement was employed by Captain Richard Rowe to construct the 22m (72ft) diameter wheel to pump water from Rowe's profitable Great Laxey lead mine in the hills above. Casement then applied his architectural skills to embellish and transform the functional nature of the wheel into a popular and much-admired monument of Victorian engineering.

The great, white-painted circular tower, complete with a 95 step spiral staircase leading to a dizzily exposed viewing platform over the top of the wheel, serves no practical purpose. But ever since its opening in 1854 it has attracted thousands of visitors who have a head for heights. The row of lead miners' cottages that leads up from the Manx Electric Railway became known as 'Ham and Eggs Terrace' because of the refreshments its residents provided for visitors. The wheel is named Lady Isabella, after the wife of the island's governor Charles Hope, who set it in motion at its inauguration.
▶ *Laxey can be reached by Manx Electric Railway from Douglas or Ramsey, or by minor road off A2 Ramsey-Douglas road. Daily Apr-Oct.*

Kirk Maughold

'Three Legs of Man' find their way into an ancient parish church

The earliest representation of the Three Legs of Man – the Isle of Man's symbol – can be found inside the tiny, cliff-top church of Kirk Maughold. It appears on a shield on the 14th-century Maughold Parish Cross.

Maughold has been a religious centre since the 5th century when St Maughold came to Man after his banishment from Ireland by St Patrick. The present 11th to 12th-century parish church stands inside an embanked enclosure, which includes the remains of three *keeills* – small, oblong Celtic churches. A fine collection of 44 mostly Celtic carved crosses is displayed in the churchyard's cross shelter, along with the work of Norse sculptors, some of the Vikings who settled on the island.
▶ *3 miles S of Ramsey off A15. MNH.*

Manx railways

A train enthusiast's dream

The Isle of Man has more preserved rail track a square mile than anywhere else in Britain. The 18 mile, 0.9m (3ft) gauge **Manx Electric Railway** opened in 1893. Original tramcars – the world's oldest still in operation – ply the scenic east coast route from Douglas to Ramsey. It connects with the 5 mile long **Snaefell Mountain Railway** at Laxey.

The **Isle of Man Steam Railway** runs locomotives dating from 1874 south from Douglas for 15 miles to Port Erin, where there is a railway museum. Volunteers operate the **Groudle Glen Railway**, a 0.6m (2ft) narrow-gauge line that takes passengers the short distance to the coast at Sea Lion Rocks, where, when the line opened in 1896, holidaymakers could view sea lions and polar bears in a zoo.
▶ *Manx Electric Railway operates all year. Other railways, summer only. For details Tel 01624 663366 (Isle of Man Transport).*

The Ballaugh Curraghs

The Manx mangroves – home of a ghostly wetland hunter

Following the boggy trails that wind through the strange, wet wilderness of the Ballaugh Curraghs is like walking through a fairy-tale landscape. Lichens drip from the branches of twisted and gnarled willows, which dip their fronds in the secret, still pools of the 81ha (200 acres) of waterlogged former peat cuttings. Then, overhead, a wraith-like shape hovers over the reed beds. This is the elegant marshland raptor, the hen harrier. Up to a hundred pairs roost here in winter – the largest number in Western Europe.

The Curraghs are also home to many other birds, including the peregrine falcon, merlin, grasshopper warbler and greylag goose.
▶ *Off A3 Ramsey-Kirk Michael Road near Ballaugh. Curraghs Wildlife Park daily Easter-Oct; weekends in winter.*

NORTHWEST ENGLAND

LANCASHIRE, LIVERPOOL & MANCHESTER

1 Leighton Moss **2** Morecambe Bay **3** Ashton Memorial **4** Trough of Bowland

5 Blackpool **6** Wycoller **7** National Football Museum

Leighton Moss

A waterside haven for the shy heron of the reed beds

The 79ha (195 acres) of rippling reed beds at Leighton Moss are home to Britain's largest concentration of breeding bitterns. In summer, the rare bittern's 'booming' call is a familiar sound across the Moss, which it shares with the bearded tit and marsh harrier, two other almost equally endangered birds. The bittern disappeared from Britain in the 19th century but began to breed again in the last century.

A causeway at the Moss leads to a public hide from where water rail, reed, sedge and grasshopper warblers, shoveler, teal, pochard and tufted duck can also be seen.

▶ *4 miles NW of Carnforth off A6 or M6 (Junction 35A). Close to Silverdale rail station. RSPB. Daily.*

Morecambe Bay

Vast sands that only the pilot knows

To stand in the middle of the 10-mile-wide expanse of Morecambe Bay is an unforgettable experience. Up to 120 square miles of glistening sand laced with pools extends far and wide, hugely empty and lonely save for thousands of wading birds. Only the foolhardy would risk the tide and attempt alone the ancient right of way across the Kent Channel from Morecambe to Kents Bank in Cumbria. Instead, Cedric Robinson, the official Queen's Guide and so-called 'Sand Pilot of Morecambe Bay', leads walkers safely to Kents Bank from Hest Bank or, more usually, Arnside.

▶ *W of M6 (Junction 34/35A) or A6. Hest Bank, 2 miles N of Morecambe on A5105. Arnside, 10 miles N of Morecambe on B5282, off A6. To contact Queen's Guide, Tel 01539 532165.*

SCARE YOURSELF SILLY IN THE LAS VEGAS OF THE NORTH
BLACKPOOL

Ashton Memorial

Sweeping views from a familiar Lancashire landmark

From Lancaster it is possible to glimpse the Isle of Man across the sea, the distant hills of North Wales beyond Liverpool Bay and, closer to home, Morecambe Bay and the Lakeland fells, all from the upper balcony of the Ashton Memorial. The ornate domed folly, perched at the highest point of Williamson Park, dominates the city. Opened in 1909, the memorial and palm house (now a butterfly house) was built to commemorate his family by Lancaster born industrialist Lord Ashton, a millionaire producer of oil cloth and linoleum.
▶ *Signed in Lancaster centre and from M6 (Junctions 33 and 34). Daily.*

Trough of Bowland

An eerie highway over moors forever associated with witchcraft

Bleak, windswept moorland ripples outwards from the Trough of Bowland, a high pass across the Forest of Bowland moors between Dunsop Bridge and Marshaw. The Grey Stone of Trough, at the top of the pass, today simply marks the boundary between Lancashire and North Yorkshire. But for the Pendle Witches who travelled through the Trough in 1612, bound for trial and execution at Lancaster, the pass must have seemed like a point of no return. Accusations of witchcraft were rife in these remote parts of Lancashire in the early 17th century and many alleged witches were brought to trial and hanged.
▶ *7 miles E of M6 (Junction 33) or A6, via Dolphinholme, Abbeystead and Marshaw.*

Blackpool

Scare yourself silly in the Las Vegas of the north

With ten white-knuckle rides, including the original 1923 'Big Dipper', Blackpool is Britain's roller coaster capital. At 72m (235ft) high and just over a mile in length, the Pepsi Max Big One is Europe's tallest and fastest roller coaster, reaching speeds of 87mph. For a high-speed careering ride through water, fire, mist, blizzards, flaming arrows, spooky forests and an icy graveyard take the Valhalla.

The railway brought the first trippers to Blackpool in 1846. Now for more than 16 million people each year the Pleasure Beach, the 158m (518ft) high Tower built in 1894 to imitate the Eiffel in Paris, the spectacular illuminations (from September to November) and the piers make Blackpool Britain's gaudiest, craziest seaside resort.
▶ *M6 (Junction 32), then M55. Rail access to Blackpool via Preston.*

Wycoller

In the footsteps of a Brontë

Wycoller Hall, now an evocative ruin, is said to have inspired 'Ferndean Manor' in Charlotte Brontë's novel *Jane Eyre*. Built in the 16th century, the hall was extended by Squire Cunliffe in a scheme to attract a wealthy wife.

The nearby leafy dene of Wycoller has an unusually large concentration of bridges. One of the seven crossings, in the centre of the hamlet, is a twin-arched packhorse bridge from the 13th century. At least 200 years older is the clam bridge – a single huge slab of gritstone spanning a beck.
▶ *6 miles NE of Burnley off A56. Wycoller Country Park signed from Trawden on B6250.*

National Football Museum

Preston scores a home win with fixture about the 'beautiful game'

A door shaped like a fan's rattle, a lift inspired by a referee's whistle and windows that look like goal nets are just a few of the features in the museum at Deepdale Road – home of Preston North End, first champions of the Football League in 1889.

Among the 20,000 items displayed are the shirt worn by the Scottish player Arnold Kirke-Smith for the first international match, between England and Scotland in 1872, the neck brace worn by Manchester City goalkeeper Bert Trautman following injury in the 1956 FA Cup Final, and the crossbar struck by Geoff Hurst during the 1966 World Cup final. Other exhibits reveal just how far back football's origins go: a 2000-year-old ball game played in the court of Chinese emperors and a violent, 16th-century Italian team sport contained elements of the modern game. In the art gallery, there are hilarious blow-ups of pre-First World War cigarette cards featuring the fictional Nobby Bottomshuffle in voluminous shorts and photo portraits of real-life current stars such as David Beckham.
▶ *Preston town centre. Tues-Sun. For details, Tel 01772 908442.*

LANCASHIRE, LIVERPOOL & MANCHESTER

Darwen Tower

Symbol of victory in a fight for the right to walk the moor

On a clear day, it is possible to see from Cumbria to the Welsh hills from the top of the 26m (86ft) high monument. But Darwen Tower was not built for the distant view. It was over the surrounding moor that local people secured the right to roam after the first mass trespass and a subsequent successful court case against the landowner in 1896.

The tower, started in the following year and opened in 1898, commemorates both this historic victory and Queen Victoria's Diamond Jubilee. With its porticoed base (the fins) and domed top (nose cone), the tower looks like an old-fashioned idea of a space rocket. This contrasts with the 92m (300ft) high chimney at Darwen's India Mill down in the town, completed in 1868 and inspired by the campanile in St Mark's Square, Venice.

▶ *1 mile W of Darwen (9 miles N of Bolton on A666 Blackburn road). Daily.*

Formby Hills

Dune-backed hunting ground of Stone Age man

As the tide goes out over the hard flats, it sometimes scours out the fossilised footprints of Neolithic man and the hoofprints of the animals that he hunted 5000 or more years ago – deer and auroch, an extinct, bison-like creature. More than 160 human trails have been recorded here, many disappearing into the 'hills', a belt of sand dunes planted with stabilising Scots Pine in the late 19th century and now a nature reserve and home to a thriving colony of red squirrels and the rare natterjack toad. There are several public footpaths through the dunes, and the Sefton Coastal Path runs north to Southport, six miles away.

▶ *¾ mile W of Formby. NT. Daily.*

Wigan Pier

The waterway of memories

The original pier of music hall jokes, built to load coal into barges on the Leeds and Liverpool Canal, was demolished many years ago. But there is a replica, and there is a music hall – part of the theatre group's repertoire. It puts on performances in The Way We Were, an exhibition about Victorian life and times. Also housed at the pier is the Trencherfield Mill Engine, the world's largest original working mill steam engine with an accompanying audio-visual show. Work will continue over the next few years to transform Wigan Pier into a vibrant cultural centre.

▶ *Wigan town centre. Sun-Thur.*

Albert Dock

Sip coffee on the quays where cargoes of empire were landed

Everything about Albert Dock, one of the most impressive pieces of commercial building of its time (it was completed in 1845), is on a heroic scale. The water covers an area of 3ha (7 acres), big enough to accommodate the biggest merchantmen of the day, and the five-storey warehouses surrounding it are Britain's largest group of Grade I listed buildings.

In the 1980s, the disused dock was given a new lease of life. There are restaurants and shops in the quayside colonnades and on floors above, and the city's Tate Gallery, the Merseyside Maritime Museum and The Beatles Story, an exhibition about the 'fab four', are located here. The Museum of Liverpool will open in a landmark new building in 2010.

▶ *¼ mile SW of Liverpool centre. Museums and exhibition daily.*

Philharmonic Dining Rooms

Raise a glass in vintage surroundings

This elegant late-Victorian gin palace – built by craftsmen from the Mersey shipyards and reminiscent of the grand interior of a transatlantic liner of the era – possesses opulence appropriate to the interval mood during a classical music concert. Carved and glazed mahogany partitions radiate from the mosaic-faced bar, while the high ceiling, suppported on semi-nude caryatids, is covered in decorative moulded plasterwork. Instruments once used in the orchestra and copper relief panels of musicians are a constant reminder that the Liverpool Royal Philharmonic has its home just across the street. And if toilets indicate a pub's pedigree, then the gents – all fancy tilework and red marble fittings – puts this one in a class of its own.
▶ *Hope Street, Liverpool city centre.*

Metropolitan Cathedral of Christ the King

Worship with a dazzling light show

The drama of entering Liverpool's Roman Catholic Cathedral through the main porch into a space bathed blue and red by sunlight streaming through stained-glass windows is unequalled in a British church. Gradually, your eye is drawn from the altar – a huge raised slab of white Yugoslavian marble in the centre of the circular nave – to the thorn-like canopy that covers and protects it, and then up to the 2000-tonne Lantern Tower, floating high above the sanctuary. The glass of the tower shows all the colours of the rainbow, interspersed with bursts of white to represent the Holy Trinity.

The cathedral was designed by Sir Frederick Gibberd and consecrated in 1967. It soars from a piazza above a vast crypt, which is all that was built of the original 1930s design by Sir Edwin Lutyens. The crypt's mighty brick vaults and concrete pillars are a sharp contrast to the light and delicacy of the windows, metalwork and tapestries above.
▶ *Mount Pleasant, Liverpool. Cathedral well signposted from city centre.*

Mersey Ferry

Watch Liverpool's waterfront unfold aboard Europe's oldest ferry service

After more than 800 years the Mersey Ferry – propelled to fame by the 1960s pop song *Ferry 'Cross the Mersey* – continues to ply the broad river and offer the best way to see the sights of Liverpool. For thousands of emigrants bound for America in the late 19th century, when the port of Liverpool was second only to London in size and importance, this was their last view of England.

Among the prominent features of today's skyline are the Anglican Cathedral – Britain's biggest – and majestic waterfront edifices such as the Liver Building of 1911, topped by the city's symbol: two 5.5m (18ft) tall copper Liver Birds, half cormorant, half eagle. Its clocks, each 8m (25ft) in diameter, are the largest in Britain and said to be correct to within 30 seconds a year.
▶ *Liverpool city centre. Tel 0151 330 1444.*

Chetham's Library

The oldest public library in the English-speaking world

Since it was founded in 1653 by Humphrey Chetham, a wealthy Manchester businessman, 'to cure poverty by curing ignorance', Chetham's Library has been in constant use. For the social, political and economic theorist Karl Marx it was a place to study and to meet and share ideas with Frederick Engels, founder of 'scientific socialism'. The simple desk that they used can still be seen. Today the library holds more than 100,000 volumes, of which some 60,000 are more than 150 years old.
▶ *Long Millgate, Manchester. Mon-Fri by appointment.*

Museum of Science and Industry in Manchester

A one-stop encyclopedia of science

The sights, sounds and oily smells of working gas, diesel and steam engines fill the Power Hall of the magnificent Museum of Science and Industry, built on the site of the first passenger railway station. These engines – the largest collection in the world – once powered the mills of Lancashire and Yorkshire. For smells and sounds of a different nature, venture into the reconstructed Victorian sewer, or let your imagination take flight in the Air and Space Hall.
▶ *Liverpool Road, Castlefield. Daily.*

NORTHWEST ENGLAND

From rats to riches for derelict docks

The fortunes of a once-thriving hub on the Manchester Ship Canal have been revived by futuristic projects

1 **Manchester Ship Canal** ▶ *Runs from Eastham, NW of Ellesmere Port, to Salford Quays.*

2 **Lowry Centre** ▶ *Pier 8, Salford Quays. Daily.*

3 **Imperial War Museum – North** ▶ *Trafford, Manchester. Tel 0161 836 4000 for details.*

On New Year's Day, 1894, the huge gates at Eastham locks on the Mersey estuary swung open to allow the first vessels to enter the **Manchester Ship Canal**. A convoy of 71 ships led by a steam yacht, *The Norseman*, made the inaugural 36 mile voyage inland to the terminal docks of the Port of Manchester at Salford. The idea of improvements to the rivers Irwell and Mersey to make them more navigable was first mooted in the 17th century, but it was not until 1882 that a Bill was placed before Parliament to provide the necessary powers. At the height of construction, 16,000 navvies were employed on the canal, along with stonemasons, carpenters and bricklayers. When it was officially opened by Queen Victoria, the Manchester Ship Canal was one of the world's greatest engineering achievements.

The waterway led to a rapid growth in trade and the development of Trafford Park in Manchester, Britain's first purpose-built industrial estate. Cargo-handling facilities along the canal's length brought prosperity also to Ellesmere Port and Runcorn in Cheshire. A switch to container transport and the use of increasingly larger ships in the mid 20th century led to a decline in the fortunes of the Port of Manchester, and in the 1970s the Salford docks closed. Much of the canal, however, is still in use, with docks at Runcorn, Ellesmere Port and Eastham dealing with some 3000 ships, carrying around 8 million tonnes of cargo each year.

Down but not out

The Manchester docks became perhaps the most derelict, vermin-infested corner of northwest England. But in 1985 work began on transforming them into an area for residential, commercial and leisure use. A rejuvenated landscape of glass and steel now covers the former dockland, re-named the Salford Quays, combining bold architecture with open spaces and waterways, and providing jobs for 10,000 people. Two major projects have played a key role in this startling resurrection: the Lowry Centre and the Imperial War Museum – North.

The Lowry Centre opened in April 2000 on what was once Pier 8 of the docks. Inside its spectacular glass and steel structures (below) are galleries, theatres, shops and restaurants covering an area larger than five football pitches. The galleries overflow with contemporary art exhibitions and the works of the painter associated more than any other with industrial landscapes – Manchester-born, Salford-raised L.S. Lowry (1887-1976), who gained his inspiration from the working towns of the northwest.

A footbridge over the canal connects the Centre to Trafford Wharfside, a short walk from Old Trafford, Manchester United's football ground (see right), and the **Imperial War Museum – North**, opened in summer 2002. The museum was designed by the Polish architect Daniel

BRAVE NEW WORLD
THE LOWRY CENTRE

Libeskind as a globe, shattered then reassembled into a new, angular form. Three giant 'shards' of concrete and aluminium represent earth, air and water as the three theatres of war. The Air Shard juts 55m (180ft) above the ground, the floor of the Earth Shard drops 2m (6ft) to match the curvature of the earth, and the Water Shard sweeps out over the canal waters. As a breathtaking climax to displays on themes such as 'women and conflict' and 'science and war', you are plunged into sudden darkness as 72 projectors direct real-life war-time footage onto the entire exhibition space, including visitors.

Peace reigns outside the museum, where the clean-up of the canal basin has been so successful that each evening brings in more than a thousand pochard and tufted ducks. These birds usually breed in Russia but have flown west and adopted the calmer, warmer waters at the head of the Manchester Ship Canal – nature's endorsement of an outstanding conservation achievement.

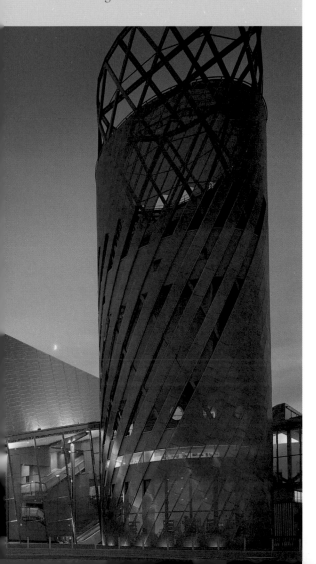

LANCASHIRE, LIVERPOOL & MANCHESTER

17 John Rylands Library **18** Old Trafford football ground

John Rylands Library
The university of Manchester's 'cathedral' to the printed word

Completed in 1899 at a cost of £500,000 (£50 million at today's prices), the John Rylands Library is one of Europe's finest examples of neo-Gothic architecture. Its outstanding feature is the sumptuous vaulted ceiling in the Reading Room.

The library was built as a memorial to the cotton magnate John Rylands by the architect Basil Champneys. It was one of the first buildings in Manchester to have electricity and was fitted with an early air-conditioning system. Its collections today exceed 750,000 printed volumes and more than a million manuscripts in 50 languages dating from the third millennium BC.
▶ *150 Deansgate, Manchester. Mon-Sat.*

Old Trafford football ground
Walk in the steps of Manchester United's footballing legends

A dazzling display of trophies of all shapes and sizes sets the scene for the enthusiasts' tour of Old Trafford, home to Manchester United, the richest club in the world and England's most successful in recent years.

A trip around the biggest all-seater club stadium in Britain – with a capacity of 67,700 – takes in the players' changing rooms, their lounges, the press rooms and the final, awe-inspiring walk out to the pitch. Learn about pre-match tactics and sit in the manager's hot-seat. The museum follows the history of the club from 1878.
▶ *Sir Matt Busby Way, Old Trafford. Museum and tours daily except home match days.*
Tel 0870 442 1994.

Key

1 **Main entry**
2 **Feature entry**
── **County boundary**
── **Motorway**
── **Principal A road**

(See 'Finding your way',
page 7)

Northeast England

Echoes of imperial Rome, monastic chant, border conflict and Victorian civic pride resonate through the swathe of land north of the Humber and south of Hadrian's Wall. Here are steel and mill towns that burst onto the industrial stage, secluded dales, remote moors, formidable castles and slabs of rocky coast.

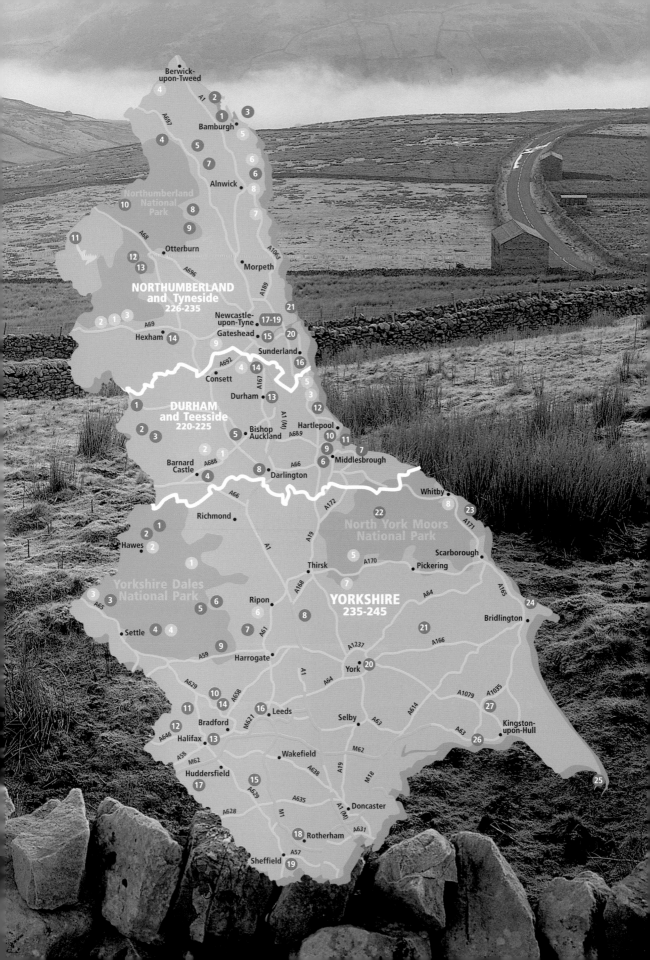

Berwick-
upon-Tweed

4

2

1

3

Bamburgh

5

4

5

6

7

6

Alnwick

8

Northumberland
National
Park

10

8

7

9

11

Otterburn

12

13

A68

A696

Morpeth

A189

NORTHUMBERLAND
and Tyneside
226-235

A1068

21

17-19

Newcastle-
upon-Tyne

2

1

3

A69

Hexham

14

Gateshead

15

20

9

Sunderland

4

14

16

Consett

A167

5

A692

Durham

13

5

12

1

Bishop
Auckland

A1 (M)

Hartlepool

9

2

DURHAM
and Teesside
220-225

3

5

A689

10

11

2

1

7

Barnard
Castle

A688

6

Middlesbrough

4

8

A66

Darlington

A66

A172

Whitby

8

23

Richmond

22

North York Moors
National Park

A171

1

A19

A19

2

Hawes

2

Thirsk

5

A170

Scarborough

Pickering

1

A168

7

Yorkshire Dales
National Park

3

3

6

Ripon

A65

5

6

YORKSHIRE
235-245

A64

A165

24

Settle

4

4

7

A61

8

Bridlington

9

A1237

A166

21

Harrogate

A59

A1

A64

York

20

A1079

A1035

27

A629

10

14

A658

York

A614

Selby

Kingston-
upon-Hull

11

16

Leeds

M621

A63

26

12

Bradford

A63

A646

13

Halifax

M62

A58

Wakefield

M62

M62

A638

A19

M18

25

Huddersfield

15

17

A629

A635

A1 (M)

Doncaster

A628

M1

A631

18

Rotherham

Sheffield

19

A57

DURHAM & TEESIDE

1 Killhope Lead Mining Museum **2** Teesdale haymeadows **3** High Force **4** Bowes Museum
5 Escomb Saxon church **6** Transporter Bridge, Middlesbrough **7** Saltburn Inclined Tramway

Killhope Lead Mining Museum
Descent into a dangerous world

High in Weardale, the waterwheel at Killhope Mine is turning again. Squeeze yourself into the miners' cramped living quarters, then have a go at operating the washing rake to separate the metal out from the stony rubble. A successful mine in the late 19th century, the place has been restored to full working order. Groups are taken down about 120m (395ft) into the mine – wellies and helmets provided – to experience the dank atmosphere and see how the ore was worked from the rock.

Lead was a flash-in-the-pan industry, but it has made a big impact on the local landscape. Heather-covered hummocks and hollows, pack-horse trails, shafts and chimneys crop up all over the north Pennine moors.
▶ *Weardale, on A689 between Stanhope and Alston. Daily Apr-Oct.*

Teesdale haymeadows
Where flowers carpet the valley

Walk through Upper Teesdale in late June, and feast your eyes on what has become a rare sight – traditional haymeadows, thick with swathes of colourful honey-scented flowers and abuzz with bees. Old-style haymaking is a slow, risky business, so few farmers bother with it these days. But here it is encouraged by subsidies, which means the meadows are cut late and have plenty of time to bloom.

Paths from Forest-in-Teesdale will lead you through oceans of eyebright, meadow saxifrage and yellow rattle, and beside drifts of cranesbill and globeflower. Then continue up through juniper-scented woodland to Cronkley and Widdybank fell, both awash with rockrose and Teesdale violet.
▶ *Forest-in-Teesdale, on B6277, between Alston and Middleton-in-Teesdale.*

High Force
Roaring little Niagara of the North Pennines

Whisky-coloured water from peat-capped moors is tossed and buffeted down the river Tees in a succession of pretty cascades. Then, suddenly, rushing over bare, craggy cliffs, it plunges 22m (70ft) – the longest single water drop in England. This fierce and noisy waterfall is High Force.

There are two ways to view the falls. The quickest, and the easiest, is to pay a small fee at the car park next to the High Force Hotel, then take the 10-minute signposted walk down the track to the foot of the falls. From here, steps lead steeply to the top, where you can pause for breath, enjoy the cooling caress of spray, and gaze on the foamy, swirling water as it thunders into the shadowy plunge pool in the gorge below. For a more picturesque route, through grassy fields and woodland, you can park at Bowlees Picnic Area and stroll upstream beside the Tees. This should take about 1½ hours, there and back (see right).
▶ *Tel 01833 641001 (Teesdale tourist office) for details of walk from High Force Hotel. Bowlees Picnic Area just off B6277, NW of Middleton-in-Teesdale.*

Bowes Museum
A grand French chateau crammed with fine art treasures

Coming across a flamboyant French chateau in deepest Durham is enough to make you gasp in disbelief. The scope of the art inside will make you think you have been transported to a major gallery in some great metropolis. John Bowes was passionate about all things French, including his wife, Josephine. Hence the style of the building that he erected on his Durham estate to house his vast collection of fine art and crafts. Sadly, the chateau, completed in 1892, took 23 years to build, by which time both John and Josephine were dead.

The Bowes' obsession with collecting is reflected in the diversity of works that are found here. French decorative art dominates, with a musical automaton of a life-sized silver swan taking centre stage. But there are also tapestries and paintings by Tiepolo and El Greco, dolls' houses, toy cars and even swords dating from the Bronze Age.
▶ *Off A688 in Barnard Castle, W of Darlington, on A67. Daily.*

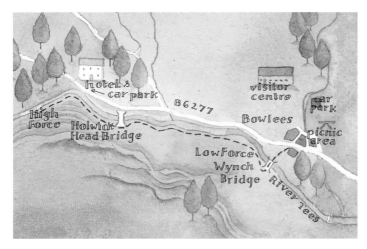

To see a river leap *Cross the stile opposite Bowlees car park, and take the path through two fields to a wall stile, then down to the Tees. Cross Wynch Bridge, turn right, and continue past Holwick Head Bridge into the nature reserve. The path leads into woods, opening out to reveal High Force. For a view from the top of the falls, continue ahead.*

Escomb Saxon church
The little church that time forgot

The weathered walls of Escomb's tiny Saxon church taper slightly towards the top, which distorts the perspective both inside and out. The masonry, much of it Roman in origin, is dark and gloomy, blackened by ingrained soot from the factory chimneys that once darkened the landscape here.

Many more celebrated Saxon buildings have been remolded and 'improved' by everyone from the Normans to the Victorians, but Escomb, now oddly encircled by a ribbon of council houses, lies like a forgotten gem among cinders. It was built some time before 675 and its main features are Celtic. However, you will also find the odd Roman inscription, the fragmented remains of a 12th-century fresco on the chancel arch, and a sundial that dates from the 16th century.
▶*W of Bishop Auckland on A689 and B6282, then N on minor road at Etherley Grange.*

Transporter Bridge, Middlesbrough

A river crossing in the air from an age of ingenuity

The biggest transporter bridge in the world operates across the River Tees between Middlesbrough and Port Clarence. It was devised in 1911 as an ingenious alternative to a drawbridge, to allow the passage of tall-masted ships. A gondola, which can carry nine cars and up to 100 people, is suspended below a high cantilever structure and winched across the water every 15 minutes. The bridge is 259m (851ft) long, and the height from low-water level to the girders is about 54m (177ft).
▶*Between Stockton-on-Tees and Middlesbrough off A66 and A1046.*

Saltburn Inclined Tramway
Scaling the heights without wasting a breath

Every few minutes a gurgle and a rush of water is followed by a gentle lurch. Then the red 10-seater tram cars glide silently past each other on their brief but inexorable journey up and down the cliff face at Saltburn-by-the-Sea. Some things around Saltburn have changed over the past century, but the Cliff Lift looks as stylish and sedate today as it did when it opened in 1884 – and it is still going strong.

Until the mid 19th century Saltburn had been a fishing and smuggling village, but the entrepreneur Henry Pease saw an opportunity to develop it into an upmarket seaside town. The Stockton-Darlington Railway was extended from Redcar in 1861, and Saltburn soon had its own promenade and pier, croquet lawn, Italian gardens and spa fountain.

Huffing and puffing up and down a cliff path between the pier and the seafront hotels was beneath the dignity of Victorian gentry. The solution for the newly invented holiday resort was the building of a hydraulic tramway, 36m (120ft) long, powered by a gas pump and 91,000 litres (20,000 gallons) of water.
▶*Opposite Saltburn pier, 4 miles S of Redcar on A174. Daily Easter-Sept; Sat-Sun and school hols Oct. For opening times of tramway, Tel 01287 622528.*

DURHAM & TEESIDE

Train, Darlington

Steaming to nowhere, a locomotive made out of bricks

Speeding forward billowing steam, David Mach's sleek, 46m (150ft) long, life-sized locomotive – *Train* – bursts out from the grassy hillside next to a supermarket at Darlington's Morton Park Industrial Estate. It runs along land that was part of the original Stockton to Darlington Railway – the world's first steam-powered public rail service. Of its 185,000 bricks, 20 are designed to encourage bats to make a home there, and the hollow centre contains a number of 'time capsules', created by children at local schools.
▶*Darlington, off A1 (M), 6 miles N of Scotch Corner.*

Billingham International Folklore Festival

Exotic dancers, strange sounds and bizarre costumes

Like most good traditions, the annual Billingham International Folklore Festival started by accident when a local folk dance team was invited to perform in the town centre to brighten up a summer weekend. That was nearly 40 years ago and today the event involves a dozen groups and some 400 artists from all over the world, who perform to enthusiastic audiences at several venues around the town every August. Colourful and lively, with obscure rituals, incomprehensible rhythms and unpronounceable languages, the event never fails to delight and surprise.
▶*Billingham, N outskirts of Middlesbrough, off A19 or A689. One week, mid summer. Tel 01642 553220 for details.*

Hartlepool Historic Quay

Press gangs, rat-catchers and the gory glory days of the British Navy

The elegant centrepiece of Hartlepool's Historic Quay is the HMS *Trincomalee*, a grand frigate with towering masts and a pedigree dating back to 1817. The quay re-creates the heyday of a Napoleonic seaport, complete with chandlers, gunsmiths and other buildings, including a jail and an admiral's house. It all comes vividly to life with dramatic re-enactments, a ghost's tour of a sea battle and virtual reality exhibits. Watch a press gang in action, or play traditional games in Skittle Square. For a taste of the real seafaring life, climb aboard the *Trincomalee*, the oldest British warship afloat. It was brought to Hartlepool in 1987 and restored with great care and attention to detail by local craftsmen.

The adjacent museum and adventure centre allow you to walk the lower decks of a blood-and-thunder warship in battle, or to test your reflexes at rat-catching duties.
▶*Hartlepool town centre, off A689, 8 miles NE of Stockton-on-Tees. Daily.*

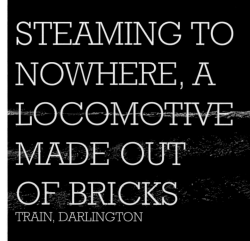

STEAMING TO NOWHERE, A LOCOMOTIVE MADE OUT OF BRICKS
TRAIN, DARLINGTON

Seal Sands

A feast for birdwatchers at the edge of industrial Teesside

There is an awesome grace about the vast chemical works of Teesside, and they provide an unusual backdrop – of steel chimneys, silos, tanks and towers – to the wide open mud flats and marshes of Seal Sands on the south side of the Tees estuary. Because of the lack of suitable muddy intertidal habitats anywhere else on the northeast coast between Holy Island and the Humber, Teesmouth attracts large numbers of winter wildfowl and wading birds. Shelduck, cormorants, godwits and curlews favour this watery landscape, as well as predators such as peregrines and merlins.

▶ *For best view use Cowper Marsh Car Park on A178, between Middlesbrough and Hartlepool, on S side of River Tees; walk E (downstream) to bird hide. Nature reserve, daily.*

Castle Eden Dene

A slippery-sloped, tree-covered cleft conceals a precious wildlife habitat

In an open landscape shaped by two centuries of industry, the primeval forest and flower-studded banks of this deep valley are an escape into a lost world. Magnesian limestone, a cream-coloured, lumpy-looking rock, outcrops more in County Durham than anywhere else in Britain. It produces wonderful wildlife sites, of which the most dramatic is the ravine of Castle Eden Dene.

Ancient woods of yew, oak, ash and elm cover the steep slopes of the dene. Ferns and mosses thrive, as do unusual plants such as herb Paris and lily of the valley. This is also a home of the rare red squirrel.

▶ *2 miles S of Peterlee off A19, signed from town centre.*

Where rich, dark seams ran deep

Mining for lead and coal changed the face of County Durham's landscape and the history of its people

1 Raby Castle **2** Cockfield Fell **3** Easington **4** Beamish North of England Open Air Museum
5 Seaham

People have been digging up County Durham for at least eight centuries. Mining for lead in the north Pennines reached its peak from the late 18th to late 19th century when dozens of productive mines, supporting communities of miners and their families, were scattered through Upper Weardale and Teesdale.

Drive through Middleton (along B6277) or Stanhope (along A689) and the number of pubs and Methodist chapels suggest that this was once Durham's Wild West. A patchwork of smallholdings farther along the dales from the towns and villages shows how mining families attempted to supplement their meagre incomes, and a lattice of footpaths reveals the route of packhorse trails that once linked mines with smelt mills. Large houses were formerly the homes of mine managers while grand mansions and estates like **Raby Castle** (near Staindrop on A688, Tel 01833 660202 for opening times) were where landowners – made wealthier by mines – lived.

An industrial harvest

Little remains of the lead mines except mazes of perilous shafts and adits (horizontal passages), riverside mill ruins and spoil-heaps of worked-out galena (lead ore). To experience life in and around a mine, visit the Killhope Lead Mining Museum (see page 220), where you can enter a mine and visit miners' cottages.

Coal began to make what would be a profound impact on County Durham in the 14th century. At first, operations were concentrated in the middle of the county where seams were close to the surface. Drift mines could be worked from hillsides and bell pits were dug a few feet from the surface. Pockmarks and dimples from these small-scale workings can be seen at places like **Cockfield Fell** (near Cockfield, NE of Barnard Castle).

Rich, deep seams were found much later towards the North Sea coast, and by the turn of the 20th century new technology had made it possible to exploit them. Fuel to power steam engines and steel furnaces was made by coking the coal – heating it to drive off any impurities like tar and sulphur. Primitive beehive coke ovens can be seen along country paths at places like Butterknowle (7½ miles W of Bishop Auckland off B6282) and Tow Law (4 miles NW of Crook on A68). But the scale of these operations rapidly grew to consume the landscape. One Victorian account recalls how

'The traveller is most strikingly arrested by the appearance of numerous collieries, blast furnaces, coke ovens, from which at night the sky is irradiated with a ruddy glow visible for miles'.

Collieries created new mining communities at places such as Blackhall, Horden, Seaham and Shotton. The region's reputation for pottery, glass, carpets, linen and leather vanished overnight: it comes as a welcome surprise in post-industrial Durham to see some of these traditions being revived. Coal's heyday was in the early 20th century. Its rise was spectacular and its fall devastating. There are no deep mines left, nor are there many places where you can see the machinery. Today, museums display the union banners, and the pithead ballads are sung only on CDs. At **Easington** (8 miles south of Sunderland off A19), the colliery's site is marked by a memorial garden to the 83 men killed in the explosion of 1951.

Visit the **Beamish North of England Open Air Museum** (signed from A1(M) junction 63, Tel 0191 370 4000 for opening times) to understand what coal mining was really like. An entire colliery village has been re-created and you can go underground into a drift mine or sit around a fire in a pitman's cottage. But this glimpse of the past should be tempered by a look at how much things have changed and what the future holds. The Durham coast, once blackened by colliery waste, has been the subject of a £10 million 'Turning the Tide' clean-up. Pick up a black shiny pebble on the **Seaham** shore (4 miles S of Sunderland off A1018) – it is the closest to coal you are likely to get.

ROOKHOPE BURN

DURHAM & TEESIDE

13 Durham Cathedral **14** Durham County Cricket Ground

Durham Cathedral
The Normans' architectural tribute to an Anglo-Saxon saint

The Normans built their greatest cathedral as a resting place for St Cuthbert, the North's most influential and best-loved saint. They believed in big buildings, but at Durham they combined their monumental, solid style of architecture with an Anglo-Saxon love of decoration and detail. The result is an inspiration.

Built between 1093 and 1133, the cathedral today is substantially unaltered. The extraordinary Galilee Chapel, built in the style of a Moorish mosque, contains the tomb of the historian and monk, the Venerable Bede. Double bays and thick, fluted, highly patterned columns support the 22m (72ft) high nave. Walk beyond the crossing and rib-vaulted transepts to the choir, the tomb of St Cuthbert and the Chapel of Nine Altars, a Gothic masterpiece. An undercroft just off the cloister contains St Cuthbert's Treasures – among the golden chalices and seals is the saint's original 7th-century coffin, a jigsaw of oak fragments with a tracery of incised figures of apostles, angels and the Virgin and Child. The contrast between the fragile remains of the saint's coffin and the power and permanence of its setting is profound.
▶ *Durham city centre. Daily. Tel 0191 386 4266 for information.*

Durham County Cricket Ground
Take your eye off the match to enjoy the fabulous scenery all around

Imagine a perfect picture of rural England and you might well conjure up the scene at Durham County Cricket Club's Chester-le-Street ground. From the pavilion there is an inspiring view across the pitch to a distant church spire, wooded hillsides and a medieval castle – all wrapped in a breathless hush on match days.

Far from being an age-old institution, the club was only granted first-class status in 1991 when the idyllic ground was planned. It hosted its first county championship match in 1995. Australia played a World Cup match here in 1998 and since 2003 it has been a venue for Test matches.
▶ *Off A1(M) junction 63, signed Chester-le-Street. Tel 0191 387 1717 for match details.*

NORTHEAST ENGLAND

NORTHUMBERLAND & TYNESIDE

Ross Back Sands

A glorious beach on a wild and windswept coast

A sweep of golden sand stretches as far as the eye can see but, unlike most beautiful beaches, Ross Back Sands is often deserted. To the south across Budle Bay stands the imposing mass of Bamburgh Castle, and to the north across Fenham Flats, on a pinnacle of rock, perches Lindisfarne Castle. The only way to reach the Sands is to park just before the road ends at Ross and walk along the marked path over the links. Take a coat whatever the weather – bitter winds can blow here.
▶*Footpath from Ross, 3 miles NE of Belford, off A1.*

Holy Island

The early Christian epicentre of the North

The thick walls, tall columns and flowing arches of the 12th-century Lindisfarne Priory on Holy Island mark the spot where, in AD 635, St Aidan founded a Christian settlement that grew in size and status to become a focal point for Anglo-Saxon art and learning. The monastery also became a target for Viking raids and was destroyed in 793. A 9th or 10th-century gravestone in the little visitor centre depicts Doomsday as a gang of Vikings.

Holy Island is so steeped in historical significance that it is easy to miss its unspoilt shoreline and rich wildlife. It is best taken at an easy stroll, around the harbour to Castle Point and back to the village and the ruins of the monastic buildings.
▶*7 miles S of Berwick-upon-Tweed off A1. Causeway impassable at high tide. Priory, EH. Daily Feb-Oct; Sat-Mon Nov-Jan.*

Farne Islands

A close encounter with sea birds, seals and the spirit of the saints

Being dive-bombed by an Arctic tern and cuddling up to a cuddy, or eider, duck are among the highlights of a boat trip to the Farne Islands. The search for peace and solitude brought a succession of early Christian hermits to these tiny islands off the northeast coast. Nowadays they are not so remote – boats regularly make the crossing from Seahouses in spring and summer. Inner Farne has a lighthouse and a chapel, and flocks of terns, puffins and shags. Staple Island is the best place to see guillemots crowded onto rock stacks. Longstone is good for grey seals.
▶*Seahouses, B1340, 14 miles NE of Alnwick. NT. Boat trips daily Apr-Sept, if weather fine.*

Yeavering Bell

A goat's-eye view of the Cheviot Hills

The distinctive dome of Yeavering Bell in the northern Cheviot Hills can be seen for many miles. From its steep slopes and double summit there are views to the coast and the Scottish lowlands. With such an advantageous position, Yeavering made the ideal site for what was the biggest Iron Age hill-fort in Northumbria – 120 hut foundations have been found there.

Both the names Yeavering Bell and Ad Gefrin – the 8th-century palace of the Northumbrian kings once sited nearby – translate as Goat Hill. Wild goats still roam the Cheviots and were probably regarded as a magical totem or mascot.
▶*4 miles W of Wooler on B6351.*

Chillingham Park

Unruly animals from medieval times in a quiet corner of the Borders

For more than 800 years the herd of wild cattle at Chillingham Park has survived famine, drought and foot-and-mouth disease. These small white cattle with black muzzles and brown ears are descendants of wild ox or aurocks. No one knows where they came from; they were enclosed with the park in the 12th century but have remained completely wild. They are never handled or helped and can be very temperamental. The only way to see them is to go on an organised visit with the warden.
▶*5 miles SE of Wooler off A697 or B6348. Mon, Wed-Sun Apr-Oct. Tel 01668 215250.*

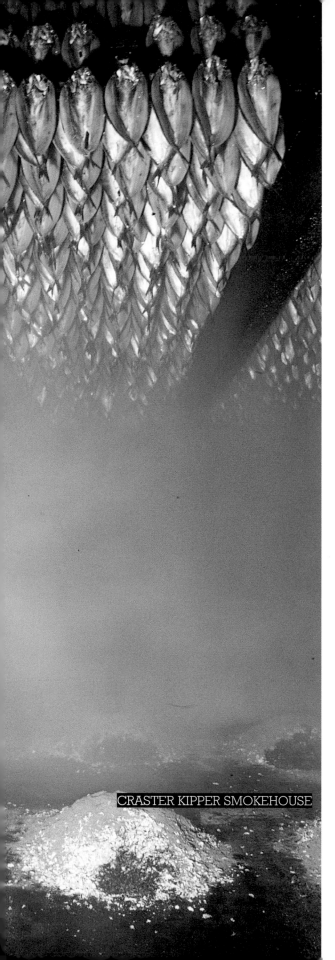

CRASTER KIPPER SMOKEHOUSE

Craster

Kippers, kittiwakes and a castle from the Wars of the Roses

Aromatic smoke from the kippering sheds fills the air around Craster, a perfect fishing village with a tiny harbour and a scatter of cobles, a type of inshore fishing boat. With the mighty Lancastrian stronghold of Dunstanburgh Castle (see page 234) in your sight to the north, stoke up on a kipper and then take the grassy coast path towards Castle Point. Built in the early 14th century, Dunstanburgh has been a ruin since Tudor times, but the keep and Lilburn Tower are substantial. The northwest wall tops a 36m (120ft) cliff face, on which nest kittiwakes and fulmars. Beyond is sandy Embleton Bay.
▶ *5 miles NE of Denwick off A1/B1340.*

Old Bewick Hill

A hilltop summit embellished with 3500-year-old rock carvings

Early Bronze Age artists have left their mark on Bewick Hill. Two huge slabs of sandstone top the summit, each deeply carved by cup and ring marks, concentric circles, grooves and channels. The carvings are thought to represent a tribal record or a map, or were part of a religious ceremony. Nearby, the ramparts of an Iron Age hill-fort on the moor indicate the presence of later inhabitants.

To reach the hilltop, park near the farmstead of Old Bewick and follow the track (bridleway) just north of the farm buildings. Turn right (south) off the track and climb a steep path to the summit, with the hill-fort to the left and the incised rocks to the right.
▶ *2 miles E of Wooperton off A697.*

NORTHEAST ENGLAND

NORTHUMBERLAND & TYNESIDE

8 Cragside House 9 Simonside 10 Chew Green 11 Kielder Skyspace

Cragside House

The showcase of an idiosyncratic Victorian inventor

Sir William Armstrong's 'country lodge', Cragside, was the first house in the world to be lit by electricity derived from water power. Armstrong was a brilliant Victorian inventor who made a fortune as an engineer. He invested both capital and ingenuity in Cragside, transforming a bare hillside into giant rock gardens and planting swathes of trees. By creating lakes and harnessing their power to drive hydraulic rams, he was able to produce electricity for the house.

As his architect, Norman Shaw, set to work in the 1870s, Armstrong was forever adding and improving things. The result was typically Victorian: bold, vivid but not entirely graceful. The house is surrounded by a vast estate of 688ha (1700 acres) filled with wildlife – roe deer and red squirrel are common. In summer magnificent rhododendrons are a highlight.
▶ *2 miles E of Rothbury, on B6341, 4 miles from A697. NT. For house and estate opening details, Tel 01669 620333.*

Simonside

Braving ancient myths to walk the rugged ridge

Beware misty evenings on Simonside ridge. According to local legends strange lights appear to lure people astray, and evil dwarfs trick the unwary into over-stepping the edge. But these tales do little to deter walkers from exploring the mysterious sandstone ridge, an eye-catching landmark, especially when it glows purple with heather in late summer.

Generations of hunter–gatherers and Stone Age farmers worked the land around Simonside. Walk a few paces from Lordenshaws car park and you are transported back and forth through pre-history, with evidence of Bronze Age field systems, burial mounds and cists, incised rocks and an Iron Age hill-fort. Beacon cairns cap the summits, where there are excellent views to the coast and the Cheviots.
▶ *Lordenshaws car park, S of Rothbury off B6342, 6 miles W of A697.*

Chew Green

The windswept edge of a lost empire

Where now there is a rippling sea of mat-grass, there was once a parade ground and the marching feet of Roman legions. Few places in Britain create such an impression of wildness as the Border Ridge. The views embrace Melrose and the Eildon Hills, where Iron Age chiefs watched the Roman advance.

The point before the Romans crossed the ridge is called Chew Green. Shadows in the sloping pasture at the head of Coquetdale – best seen in low winter sunshine – mark the position of their marching camps. The public road ends here: most of the land in this area is controlled by the Ministry of Defence. However, you can follow the Pennine Way for a few hundred metres to Brownhart Law and the site of a Roman signal station.
▶ *9 miles W of Alwinton off B6341, accessible from A696 at Otterburn.*

Kielder Skyspace

Light encounter in a hilltop chamber

Colours and tones drift almost imperceptibly; at dawn or dusk the quality of light in the landscape changes second by second. American artist James Turrel's 'Skyspace' is intended to make us look at something we do not usually pay much attention to: light.

The installation is a half-buried cylindrical chamber on a hilltop in Kielder Forest. You sit on concrete seats to appreciate the visual effects from a 3m (10ft) wide hole in the roof. After a few minutes the smooth walls of the chamber become part of the experience; there is a balance between interior and exterior light and the perfect disc of sky seems to turn to ice, pearl or steel, washed by subtle shades and unusual colours. Out onto the hilltop again and the sky may look completely different. The spell is broken as you stumble back down the track in the twilight.
▶ *Access by 1 mile uphill track from car park signed to left off Kielder Water, 15 miles W of Bellingham off B6320 and 2 miles SE of Kielder.*

At the frontier with 'wretched Britons'

Letters home and ladies' shoes, jewels and invitations tell of hard life in the Roman forts along Hadrian's Wall

1 Vindolanda Fort ▶ *Off A69, 1 mile N of Bardon Mill, or 1 mile S off B6318 (Military Road) at Once Brewed. Daily.*

2 Cawfields Roman Wall ▶ *Off B6318, 2 miles N of Haltwhistle on A69. EH. Daily.*

3 Housesteads Fort ▶ *Steep track from National Trust visitor centre on B6318, 2 miles N of Bardon Mill off A69. NT/EH. Daily.*

HADRIAN'S WALL AT CAWFIELDS

Shopping lists and worn-out sandals have an unexpected magic when they are nearly 2000 years old. They are among the many everyday objects to have been discovered in digs at **Vindolanda**, a Roman fort that pre-dates Hadrian's Wall just a mile to its north.

Vindolanda was built by Agricola, governor of Britain between AD 78 and 85. A civilian settlement soon grew up around the fort and the remains of stone statues, pots, jewels and bric-a-brac, fragments of cloth and fashionable ladies' shoes bear witness to the lives of its citizens. Most fascinating of all the finds are the hundreds of wooden writing tablets, including a letter home asking for socks and underpants, a birthday invitation and a military report that tells us for the first time that the Romans called us 'Brittunculi', or 'wretched Britons'.

To protect this northerly frontier of Roman Britain, in AD 122 Emperor Hadrian built a 75 mile long wall from Wallsend on the River Tyne to Bowness on the Solway Firth. It stood over 6m (20ft) high and 3m (10ft) wide. One of the finest stretches of the wall is at **Cawfields**, where the old whinstone quarry reveals a dramatic cross-section of the dolerite ridge. From here a milecastle (one of the small forts erected every mile), a military road and the vallum, or ditch system, can be explored east along the rolling switchback Whin Sill ridge.

Hadrian built 17 larger forts along the wall to house his soldiers of which **Housesteads Fort** is the best preserved. Standing on the crest of the Whin Sill, it was the billet for 800 men in the 2nd and 3rd centuries. Viewed from the north, the sheer grey face of the Sill would have been a daunting prospect to a potential invader: the wall on top was more than 6m (21ft) tall and may have been plastered or painted white. Within the fort, foundations remain of the barracks and baths, the commandant's house and a hospital. There are spectacular views across the marshes, loughs and forests, and the wall can be seen winding along the hills to east and west.

A MIGHTY SPIRIT OF CHANGE AT
THE GATEWAY TO TYNESIDE
ANGEL OF THE NORTH

NORTHUMBERLAND & TYNESIDE

Sidwood Bastles

Fortified farmhouses from the dark days of the Border reivers

Law and order was a makeshift institution in the borders before the union of the English and Scottish crowns in 1603. Farmers with anything worth stealing built fortified bastles: solid square buildings with tiny slit windows and thick oak doors. When bands of reiving Scots threatened, the farmer and his family would drive their livestock to the lower room, climb a ladder into the room above, shut the trapdoor and hope for the best.

Several ruined bastles survive along the Tarset Burn. This was a notorious area for rustlers and thieves, and all these bastles were plundered at some time. A trail from Sidwood links the ruin at Black Middens with the more atmospheric remains of Woodhouse, Waterhead, Shilla Hill and Bog Head bastles.

▶ *Signed from Gatehouse, along side-road from Greenhaugh, 6 miles NW of Bellingham off B6320. Walking trail is 4 miles long. Black Middens has its own car park. EH. Daily.*

Hareshaw Linn

Up the burn to a raucous waterfall

When the Hareshaw Burn is in spate it runs peat-brown and fierce, cascading noisily over a band of sandstone into an amphitheatre of oak, ash and wych elm trees. Dippers and grey wagtails fly up and downstream. To reach the waterfall, take the path north from the car park, through a gate with the burn to your left. Continue uphill by old iron workings, through a gate into mossy oak woods. The path climbs to the linn via several footbridges. The walk, there and back, is about 2½ miles.

▶ *Take Redesmouth road from Bellingham, on B6320, cross bridge and turn left to National Park car park.*

Hexham Abbey

Sanctuary on St Wilfrid's throne

Through centuries of border conflict anyone who sat in the Frith Stool in Hexham Abbey could claim sanctuary and expect a fair trial, a luxury during the Anglo-Scottish wars. The stool, a broad sandstone block, began life as the throne of St Wilfrid, who in the 7th century built the first monastic church at Hexham. It was one of Britain's earliest stone churches, said to have had no equal this side of the Alps.

Scottish raids put paid to the monastery, but the present abbey is full of fine carved stone, including the tombstone of Flavinus, a Roman soldier who died at 25 after 7 years' service in Britain. Beneath the nave is the well-preserved crypt to St Wilfrid's tiny church. Ask a steward and you can take the steep steps into the dimly lit chamber. The stonework was taken from Corstopitum Roman Fort nearby and bears sculpted designs and inscriptions.

▶ *Market Square, Hexham, off A69.*

Angel of the North

A mighty spirit of change at the gateway to Tyneside

Antony Gormley's colossal angel (left) is etched into the psyche of northeast England. It stands immutable, 20m (65ft) tall and with a 54m (177ft) wingspan, on a ridge close to the A1 and the East Coast railway line at Gateshead. More than 30 million people are thought to see it every year.

On its grassy knoll, the angel looks poised for take-off. Walk up to the ridged iron feet and you are standing over cleared mine workings, atop a plinth capping the steel piles that bond the statue to the bedrock.

▶ *Leave A1 at Gateshead South/Birtley exit onto A167 and park in layby.*

NORTHEAST ENGLAND

NORTHUMBERLAND & TYNESIDE

16 National Glass Centre **17** Tyne bridges

18 Gateshead Quays **19** Segedunum

Roman Fort **20** Bede's World

21 St Mary's Lighthouse and Island

National Glass Centre

Walking on a see-through ceiling

Walls become windows, floors and ceilings merge or disappear so that the roof refracts blues and greys from the changing skies. Children walk overhead and squeal when they realise that they are standing on glass and can see through the floor.

The National Glass Centre is terraced into the north bank of the River Wear. Its roof angles down to the level of the car park so that its structure is entirely hidden from the approach road. The deception is deliberate and the steel-framed building is big and airy.

Glass, made in Sunderland since the 7th century, is the main theme for the displays and galleries, from free-standing artworks to glass-blowing. But it is the way glass is used in the fabric of the building that is so unusual. It is hard to resist an exhilarating walk across the the roof, made from 6cm (2⅓in) thick panels.
▶*Liberty Way, Sunderland, off A1(M) (Junctions 62 or 65). Daily.*

Tyne bridges

Classic and modern river crossings

At night, as you glide over King Edward Bridge into Newcastle Station after a long train journey from the south, the shimmering lights, shapes and shadows of the River Tyne's bridges make an abiding impression.

Newcastle has seven bridges of which the double-decked High Level Bridge is the oldest (1849) and the Tyne Bridge, with its parabolic arch of steel, is the most instantly recognisable (right). Tucked between the two is the little Swing Bridge, built on the site of the Roman river crossing. Downstream is the Millennium Bridge, the 'Blinking Eye', which allows cyclists and walkers to cross from Sandgate to Gateshead and the new 'cultural quarter', but can rotate up and down to let ships through. It moves gracefully, too, pivoting its arches on two concrete islands, while its computer-controlled lights cast a glow into the indigo Tyne.
▶*Newcastle and Gateshead quaysides; easy walk from city centre car parks.*

Gateshead Quays

Old quays have new creative energy breathed into them

On the south bank of the River Tyne, next to the Millennium Bridge, is the newly revitalised area of Gateshead Quays. Once a bustling heartland of industry it has been turned into an impressive arts and cultural space that once again teems with life.

A magnificent 1950s grain warehouse houses BALTIC Centre for Contemporary Art, the biggest centre of its kind in Europe. An art factory more than a gallery, it is an innovative and provocative world where visual art is created as well as viewed. Ever-changing displays and activities in the four galleries aim to deepen the visitor's understanding and appreciation of contemporary art whilst pushing the boundaries of the medium.

In great contrast architecturally is Sage Gateshead, a striking building of steel and glass with a spectacular curved roof. This enormous venue, designed by Foster and Partners, is the new home for live music in the North of England, with performance spaces, rehearsal rooms, teaching areas, studios and an educational centre. But more than that, it offers the chance to discover and be thrilled by all the different kinds of music that are played within its walls.
▶*Newcastle Gateshead Quays. BALTIC Tel 0191 478 1810 Daily. Sage Gateshead Tel 0191 443 4661.*

Segedunum Roman Fort

Wallsend and the Tyne as seen from a Roman outpost

A 35m (115ft) high tower, built in the image of a futuristic battleship bridge, looks out over the bones of Segedunum – the Roman fort at the eastern end of Hadrian's Wall. From the top of the viewing tower, the outline of the fort with a reconstructed bath-house and a section of the wall are clearly visible.

Looking farther afield, a dramatic panorama extends across Swan Hunter's shipyards – the birthplace of luxury liners, submarines and supertankers. Giant cranes brood along the banks of the Tyne, dwarfing the old mining settlement of Wallsend and the Roman remains. The £9 million development of Segedunum spotlights empires old and new.
▶*Buddle Street, Wallsend, accessible from A187 and Tyne Tunnel. Daily.*

THE TYNE BRIDGE

Bede's World

Experimental Anglo-Saxon farming with an early Christian twist

The dedication stone in the 7th-century St Paul's church at Jarrow tells you that the church was founded 'on the ninth of Kalends of May in the fifteenth year of King Ecgfrith and the fourth year of Ceolfrith'. To read the stone you follow in the footsteps of the Venerable Bede, said to be the first person to write an honest history book.

For a few decades in the Dark Ages, before the place was sacked by Vikings in 794, the monks of Jarrow illuminated manuscripts, decorated their new church with sculpture and stained glass, and toiled on the land. Bede's World captures the past with a modern visitor centre built in Romanesque style next to a working Anglo-Saxon farm.
▶ *Jarrow, off A185 near A19 Tyne Tunnel S entrance and Bede Metro Station. Daily.*

St Mary's Lighthouse and Island

Tall stories, derring-do and a lighthouse lookout

Climbing the 137 steps to the top of St Mary's Lighthouse may make you puff, but on a sunny morning the coastal view is dazzling. The little island lies just 183m (600ft) offshore from Curry's Point – which commemorates a murderer gibbeted here in 1739 – and was remote enough to attract medieval hermits.

The lighthouse, opened in 1898, has always been a popular seaside stroll from Whitley Bay. And the traditional thrill of waiting until the last minute to beat the tide back over the causeway remains undiminished.
▶ *1 mile N of Whitley Bay off A193.*

Great fortresses of the borders

Castles in the lawless wilds of Northumberland were built to inspire fear in enemies, and loyalty in friends

4 Norham **5** Bamburgh **6** Dunstanburgh **7** Warkworth **8** Alnwick **9** Prudhoe

Centuries of conflict meant that no one trusted anybody else in the border country of the Middle Ages. Well-to-do people built tower houses, farmers aspired to bastles – fortified farmhouses – and even priests lived in defensible pele towers. Ordinary people coped as best they could in wooden shacks as raiders burnt and looted their way to and fro. On the front line was the castle at **Norham** (off B6470 SW of Berwick; EH; Tel 01289 304493), erected by the bishops of Durham on the banks of the Tweed in the 12th century. Clearly a castle built to impress, the remains of the sturdy Norman keep still rise to more than 27m (90ft) in places.

The landscape of the border hills owes its austere beauty to these troubled times. The lack of trees, the wide open spaces and the slow pace of farming developments have lent the uplands a flavour of wilderness. The more fertile river valleys and safer coastal lowlands, however, offered rich pickings for ambitious barons. Vast estates and grandiose castles were created here by those handsomely rewarded by English kings for defending the realm.

Noble power houses of the north

A castle that must have struck fear and awe in those approaching by sea is **Bamburgh** (N of Seahouses on B1340; daily Mar–Oct), on the rocky outcrop where the Anglo-Saxon Kingdom of Northumbria was founded in 547 by King Ida. One king or noble after another added to its defences until it was an almost impregnable

DUNSTANBURGH CASTLE

fortress. Yet, in the Wars of the Roses, it became the first English castle to fall to artillery bombardment, when, in 1464, the Lancastrian garrison was pounded into submission by the 1st Earl of Warwick – 'the Kingmaker'. Today's colossal restored pile makes a wonderfully romantic backdrop, best viewed from across the dunes towards Harkess Rocks.

Along the coast to the south lie the more skeletal but equally commanding remains of **Dunstanburgh** (paths from Craster or Embleton, off B1339; EH; daily Apr–Oct, Thur–Mon Nov–Mar). It is the county's most ethereal and enigmatic castle, the 14th-century stronghold of John of Gaunt, the most powerful man in England at one time, and still the haunt of a ghost called Sir Guy the Seeker. Farther south again were the awesome castles of the Percys – the mightiest of all the border barons. The ruins of **Warkworth** (on A1068, N of Amble; EH; daily Apr–Oct; Sat–Mon Nov–Mar) still seem to rule the surrounding countryside. The castle started as a Norman motte and bailey, but grew into a massive fortress. Parts of the chapel, stables and guardrooms, along with the largely intact eight-towered keep, were added by the Percys after they were granted the castle by Edward III in 1332.

The Percys' main seat of power, **Alnwick**, lies 7 miles to the northwest on the banks of the River Aln (off A1; daily Apr–Oct). In the 1760s, long after its heyday as a fortress, the castle was rebuilt in Gothic style, and then substantially altered in the 1850s. Now it is every inch the 'Windsor of the North', a suitable seat for the present Duke of Northumberland. The best way to appreciate the sheer grandeur of Alnwick, set like a jewel in the 'Capability' Brown landscape, is to view it from the sweep of pasture called the Park. Inside the castle, a grand marble staircase carries you up to lavish state rooms and an art collection that includes works by Gainsborough, Canaletto, Reynolds, Tintoretto, Titian and Turner.

Tucked along the Tyne valley west of Newcastle are the ruins of another Percy castle, **Prudhoe** (on A695; EH; Thur–Mon Apr–Sept). Its formidable Norman towers and curtain walls proved too much for the Scots in 1173 and 1174, when after two sieges they failed to take the castle.

YORKSHIRE

1 Lead mining remains, Swaledale

2 Buttertubs Pass

Lead mining remains, Swaledale
The legacy of Yorkshire's 'lead rush'

Ghostly industrial ruins haunt one of the wildest Yorkshire Dales. In the 18th and 19th centuries, the peaceful setting of Swaledale was the bustling centre of the lead mining industry. The region's past echoes through the spoil and deserted buildings littering the course of Gunnerside Gill. Follow the Gill for two miles to reach Bunton Mine. Shells of outbuildings cluster around 'hushes', or gullies, where streams were dammed to scour out lead ore. Farther east in Swaledale are remnants of workshops and stores at the Old Gang mines. The stone columns of its large peat store rise like ancient monuments in the rugged valley.
▶ *Gunnerside, 15 miles W of Richmond on B6270; Gill, 2 miles N of village. Hard Level Gill, 4½ miles E of Gunnerside on B6270.*

Buttertubs Pass
Natural phenomenon not for the faint-hearted

Strange circular fissures punctuate the rock high on the remote fells between Wensleydale and Swaledale. Peering into their 30m (100ft) depths may cause knees to tremble. These are the Buttertubs, so-called because of their resemblance to the wooden tubs once used to store butter. The fissures are young potholes, formed by the rushing waters of Cliff Beck, a tributary of the River Swale. Five deep Buttertubs and many smaller ones stand at over 518m (1700ft) on grassy pasture at the head of the pass.
▶ *On minor road linking Hawes in Wensleydale to Thwaite in Swaledale.*

NORTHEAST ENGLAND

YORKSHIRE

Gaping Gill

A capacious cavern that could accommodate York Minster

A great chasm opens wide on the slopes of the 723m (2372ft) Ingleborough mountain. Take care when approaching its awesome entrance, a depression in the moorland that leads into the 20m by 10m (65ft by 32ft) 'gape'.

Here, Fell Beck plunges 111m (365ft) into Britain's largest underground chamber, scoured out when the beck was swelled by Ice Age meltwater. Only experienced cavers dare to plumb Gaping Gill's depths, but local caving clubs take visitors down in a bosun's chair on summer bank holiday weekends. They joke that the trip down is free, but you have to pay to return to the surface.
▶ *3 mile walk from Clapham village off A65. Follow trail from village along Clapham Beck, through Ingleborough Estate to open moor.*

Malham Cove and Tarn

A natural crescent of stone

The 88m (290ft) high limestone amphitheatre of Malham Cove is spectacular enough, but thousands of years ago a cascade higher than the Niagara Falls plunged over its edge. The water, Malham Beck, now flows underground and emerges from its base. Above it, acres of crazy-paving limestone pavement with grykes (deep clefts in the limestone) and clints (level pieces of limestone between them) lead to the dry valley of Watlowes.

Malham Tarn, half a mile away, is the highest lake in the Pennines and a geological oddity: it is a natural lake sitting on a bed of impervious slate in an area of soft, porous limestone. Charles Kingsley set his children's novel *The Water Babies* here.
▶ *5 miles E of Settle. Take minor road off A65 at Coniston Cold. Follow Pennine Way signs from Malham village centre to cove and tarn.*

Kilnsey Crag

Artistic sculptings left by the Ice Age

The overhanging cowl of Kilnsey Crag, in upper Wharfedale, marks the course of Ice Age glaciers that swept through the valley 12,000 years ago. As the glaciers retreated, they sliced off a spur of limestone projecting into the dale at Kilnsey, leaving behind a huge lake, which flattened the valley below.

The dale is dominated by the 43m (140ft) crag. Occasionally, rock climbers are seen hanging upside down as they attempt the fearsome 9m (30ft) overhang, one of Britain's toughest climbs. Another peculiar rock formation is found in the picturesque village of Conistone, one mile away. It is known as **Conistone Pie** – a limestone outcrop that resembles a crusty pie with a pastry funnel rising from the centre.
▶ *4 miles N of Grassington on B6160.*

How Stean Gorge

A landscape stranger than fiction

Raised walkways and footbridges on three different levels take you above the rushing waters of How Stean Beck, and through a world of 24m (80ft) high overhanging cliffs, dark caves and dripping vegetation. The narrow, twisting gorge feels so otherworldly that it has been chosen as the setting for science fiction dramas, including *Doctor Who* and *Blake's Seven*. If you feel daring, descend the narrow wooden steps into Tom Taylor's Cave, and scramble out into Cat Hole field at the other end. The Gorge was formed by the erosive effects of melting Ice Age glaciers. Unequal erosion between harder and softer limestone created the caves and odd rock formations seen inside them.
▶ *7 miles NW of Pateley Bridge on minor road to Lofthouse. Daily.*

Brimham Rocks

Dramatic forms in rock shaped by centuries of wild weather

The first visitors to Brimham Rocks found it hard to believe that this fantastic collection of gritstone tors was not the work of an ancient civilisation. Their astonishing shapes were attributed by 18th-century historians to the Druids, and many of the rocks acquired fanciful names. The Druid's Idol is a deeply eroded boulder weighing 203 tonnes that perches precariously on a tiny 30cm (12in) wide pedestal; the flat-topped Druid's Writing Desk overlooks Nidderdale; and the Druid's Coffin, a sinister, body-shaped crevice, is tucked away among the rocks.

Brimham Rocks are the work of aeons of frost, wind and rain, which first exposed and then patiently worked on weaknesses in the millstone grit to create a curious natural sculpture park. It is a great place for children, who can enjoy games of hide-and-seek among the rocks, heather and bilberries.
▶ *4 miles E of Pateley Bridge, off B6165 or B6265. NT. Daily.*

Devil's Arrows

Old Nick's stony missiles

Three gritstone columns, fluted and grooved by centuries of erosion, stand like bizarre, prehistoric scarecrows in arable fields to the north of Boroughbridge village. The purpose of these strange and eerie monoliths, set in a straight line running east to west, is not known. Nor is it known who erected them, although legend says they were the result of target practice by the devil.

Weighing approximately 36 tonnes each, the two highest stones are 7m (22ft) tall with a circumference of 5.5m (18ft). They are thought to date from the Bronze Age and may have been part of a larger Neolithic or Bronze Age complex. How they were transported from Abbey Plain, seven miles away, where they were probably quarried, is a mystery.
▶ *On private land but visible from A1(M), N of junction 48, or from minor road leaving Boroughbridge that passes under motorway.*

The Strid

A doomed river crossing

No one has survived a fall into the notoriously fearsome rapids known as The Strid, on the River Wharfe. A narrow channel, only 2m (6ft) across, forces the rushing waters of the river between slippery gritstone buttresses. Its hazardous reputation was enhanced by Sir Walter Scott. In his epic poem *The Boy of Egremond* the fated hero drowns while attempting to leap across the chasm during a deer hunt.

The Strid is screened by the wooded Wharfe valley, just upstream from the romantic ruins of Bolton Abbey. A set of stepping stones downstream provides a safer and easier way of traversing the river.
▶ *Follow footpath N from Bolton Abbey, 6 miles N of Ilkley on B6160 to Grassington.*

Five Rise Locks

An astonishing and awe-inspiring feat of Georgian engineering

An impressive staircase of locks on the Leeds and Liverpool Canal is one of the wonders of the British canal system. With a steep rise of 18m (60ft) in five stages, it is a complex and – to inexperienced boat-handlers – daunting obstacle to negotiate. Each lock is 20m (66ft) long and 4.4m (14ft 4in) wide, with the top gate acting as the bottom gate of the next, so it is impossible to empty a lock unless the one below is empty. The whole system holds 409,000 litres (90,000 gallons) of water.

The 127 mile long Leeds and Liverpool Canal, proposed by a group of Bradford businessmen keen to transport their wares to the seaport of Liverpool, was built between 1770 and 1816. Until 2001, and the reopening of the Huddersfield Narrow Canal, it was the only waterway to cross the Pennines. Walk along the towpath to the west for wonderful views of the mills and surrounding hills, including Rombalds and Ilkley Moor.
▶ *5 miles E of Keighley. Signed from centre of Bingley off A650.*

Where tiny streams make mighty falls

Water has forced its way through the rocks of the Yorkshire Dales creating a series of spectacular cascades

1 **Aysgarth Falls** ▶ *Signed from Aysgarth village, 11 miles SW of Richmond on A684. Tel 01969 662910 for visitor centre opening.*

2 **Hardraw Force** ▶ *Behind Green Dragon Inn in Hardraw village, 1 mile NE of Hawes, off A684.*

3 **Thornton Force** ▶ *Signed from Ingleton, off A65 between Newby and Westhouse Craswall on Monnow valley road.*

4 **Gordale Scar** ▶ *1 mile N of Malham off A65 at Coniston Cold.*

Thundering collections of waterfalls punctuate the wildest rivers of the Yorkshire Dales National Park, bringing movement and energy to its stunning landscape. They form when rivers crash over beds of rock with differing levels of resistance to their erosive waters.

Clouds of spray swirl around the **Aysgarth Falls** in Wensleydale, which rush noisily over several broad terraces in the River Ure's limestone bed. An easy walk through the tree-lined gorge leads you to the Upper, Middle and Lower Falls, with viewing platforms above each one. The Falls are always spectacular, but visit after a heavy downpour to witness the most dramatic effects.

Head farther east in Wensleydale to see the highest waterfall in the Dales. **Hardraw Force** (right, in winter) plunges 30m (100ft) into a secluded amphitheatre, ringed by crags and trees. On your way to it, look out for the bandstand where brass band concerts, amplified by the rocky acoustic, are occasionally held in the summer.

The Ingleton Waterfalls in Ribblesdale have been popular since Victorian times. A two-mile stroll through the wooded valley of the River Twiss takes you past their series of tumbling waterfalls, to the grand sight of a 14m (45ft) drop made by **Thornton Force**. The river roars over a lip of limestone that sits above beds of slates formed more than 500 million years ago. The walk continues to Ingleton down the valley of the River Doe, with its own sequence of smaller falls.

The deep gorge of **Gordale Scar**, near Malham, leads through overhanging 100m (330ft) high limestone walls into a peaceful inner sanctum, where a waterfall spouts powerfully from the rock. Cross the road through Gordale to reach Janet's Foss, a waterfall encircled by trees. Folklore says that Janet, the queen of the local fairies, lived in a cave behind the graceful screen of water.

HARDRAW FORCE

YORKSHIRE

Haworth and Top Withins
Desolate moors that sparked creative minds

Charlotte, Emily and Anne Brontë found the inspiration for their great Victorian novels in the windswept Pennine moorland that surrounded their sombre home. The Georgian parsonage is now the Brontë Museum where one poignant exhibit among many reminders of their lives and troubled times is the black horsehair sofa in the dining room. It was here that Emily died of tuberculosis in 1848 when she was only 30. The table where the Brontës wrote stands nearby.

Follow a well-signposted walk that takes you for 3 miles from the village to the farmhouse at Top Withins, believed to have been the model for Heathcliff's farm in Emily Brontë's *Wuthering Heights*. The evocative but now roofless farmhouse is situated near the Pennine Way and commands extensive views across the moors. The walk passes the Brontë Falls, a favourite picnic site for the sisters and their brother, Branwell.
▶ *3 miles S of Keighley off A629. Brontë Parsonage Museum daily Feb-Dec.*

Hardcastle Crags
A natural landscape revived after the ravages of industry

The transformation of many Pennine valleys from hives of industry into havens of quietude is exemplified by Hardcastle Crags. The green, wooded valleys of Crimsworth Dean and Hebden Dale descend from Heptonstall Moors past abandoned mills and mill ponds. Now home to woodpeckers, flycatchers, dippers and a colony of hairy wood ants, the valleys once rang with industrial noise as cotton mills provided work for local families. Gibson Mill, which closed at the end of the 19th century, became a Victorian pleasure park, with swing boats and a 500 seat restaurant.
▶ *NW of Hebden Bridge off A6033. NT. Daily.*

Piece Hall
An Italian piazza in central Halifax

Three storeys of colonnaded balconies and curving archways form the impressive square of Piece Hall. It opened in 1779 as a place where handloom weavers could sell 'pieces' of cloth. It was the venue for the first balloon ascent made from Halifax in 1824 and in 1861 a tightrope walker, Charles Blondin, crossed the quadrangle 18m (60ft) above the ground.

When the textile industry was mechanised, trade fell and in 1868 the hall became a fish, fruit and vegetable market. A single vote saved the grand structure from demolition in 1972 and it has been restored – the only cloth hall to survive in Britain. Galleries and shops now occupy its interior, and markets and special events are held in the vast cobbled courtyard.
▶ *Halifax town centre. Daily.*

Saltaire
Where a textile magnate realised his industrial and architectural dreams

As you wander around Saltaire you might believe you are in Bologna, not Bradford. This complete Italianate model township was the creation of Sir Titus Salt, a local wool-stapler. Salt earned a vast fortune by importing alpaca wool from South America to create a more lustrous cloth, which became hugely popular, especially when Queen Victoria began to wear it. Salt combined his name with that of the local River Aire to create a title for the town that he built between 1853 and 1876 for his factories, workers and their families.

The first building to be constructed was a magnificent, mansion-like mill that could produce 27,000m (30,000yd) of cloth a day. It now houses shops and galleries, including the 1853 Gallery, which has Europe's largest collection of work by the Bradford-born artist David Hockney. Near it is the sumptuous Congregational Church, completed in 1859, which has a fine entrance portico with six Corinthian columns and an octagonal tower. Nearly 800 workers' houses, a hospital and public baths were built at Saltaire. Look out for images of llamas (or alpacas) – part of Salt's coat of arms – which adorn many buildings.
▶ *4 miles NW of Bradford off A650. Gallery daily.*

NORTHEAST ENGLAND

YORKSHIRE

15 Yorkshire Sculpture Park

16 Briggate Arcades

Yorkshire Sculpture Park

Britain's greatest modern sculptors get a breath of fresh air

To see sheep rubbing up against his monolithic sculptures would have delighted Henry Moore, a native of Yorkshire, who always believed his work should be viewed in the open. At the Yorkshire Sculpture Park, 202ha (500 acres) of landscaped grounds surrounding the 18th-century Bretton Hall form a fitting backdrop to remarkable pieces by Moore, Antony Gormley, Barbara Hepworth and others in what was the first permanent outdoor sculpture park in Britain.
▶ *West Bretton, 5 miles S of Wakefield, signed from M1 (Junction 38). Daily.*

Briggate Arcades

Shop till you drop in the lavish malls of Leeds

For England's most spectacular shopping experience forget London or Bath and head for the extravagant Victorian and Edwardian arcades off Briggate in Leeds. They are a vivid expression of the wealth generated in the 19th century by the wool and textile industries.

The oldest is Thornton's Arcade, built in 1877-8 in Gothic Revival style and reminiscent of a French cathedral, its roof set off by florid capitals and griffin heads. The highlight is a colourful mechanical clock featuring characters from Sir Walter Scott's novel *Ivanhoe*, such as Robin Hood and Friar Tuck. The newest arcade, Queen Victoria Street, was converted from an open street in 1990 but retains its ornate Edwardian frontages. The modern stained glasswork in the roof throws a dazzling kaleidoscope of colours on the cafés beneath.

Other shopping marvels include the glazed faience entrance to the Grand Arcade; the restored Victoria Quarter; Kirkgate Markets, with cast iron stalls and balconies supported by red dragons; and the Colosseum-like Corn Exchange, built in the early 1860s.
▶ *Leeds city centre, between Merrion Street and The Calls.*

Romantic settings for a life of peace

The rugged beauty of the dales and moors of Yorkshire is the backdrop to Britain's most atmospheric abbeys

5 **Rievaulx Abbey** ▶ *Rievaulx, on minor road off B1257, 2 miles W of Helmsley. EH. Daily Apr-Sept; Thur-Mon Oct-Mar. Terrace (NT) daily Apr-Oct.*

6 **Fountains Abbey** ▶ *4 miles W of Ripon off B6265. EH/NT. Daily.*

7 **Byland Abbey** ▶ *Near Coxwold and Wass, off A170 Thirsk-Helmsley road. EH. Thur-Mon Apr-Jul and Sept; daily Aug.*

8 **Whitby Abbey** ▶ *Clifftop, Whitby, off A171. EH. Daily Apr-Oct; Thur-Mon Nov-Mar.*

The influence of medieval monks can still be felt in the Yorkshire landscape through the moodily impressive remains of their great abbeys. Many were established by Cistercians, who were attracted to the tranquillity and remoteness of the untamed wilderness of north Yorkshire nearly 900 years ago. To St Ailred, a Cistercian abbot at Rievaulx Abbey in the 12th century, this was perfect country for a life of contemplation: 'Everywhere peace, everywhere serenity, and a marvellous freedom from the tumult of the world.'

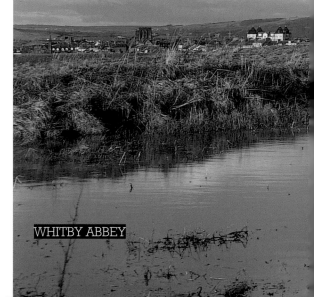

WHITBY ABBEY

The Cistercian Order evolved in the 11th century after a group of monks broke away from the Benedictine Order, which they believed had strayed too far from the original ascetic Rule of St Benedict. They vowed to follow a life of poverty and hard work 'not in towns or around fortified places or in villages, but in places far from the concourse of men'. So the Cistercians sought out what they called 'deserts', remote places in which to establish their new monasteries. Here they built trading empires founded on wealth from vast sheep farms, eventually surpassing the riches of the Benedictines.

It was this success that was to be the Cistercians' downfall. During the Dissolution, Henry VIII, keen to replenish his depleted treasury and establish himself as the head of the English Church, stripped the Yorkshire monasteries of their rich furnishings and rare manuscripts, and seized their estates. The monks were pensioned off or became secular clergy, and the abandoned abbeys fell into ruin and decay.

Glorious reminders of monastic power

The Cistercians' first permanent, stone-built monastery in the north was at **Rievaulx Abbey**, founded in 1131 in the then-secluded valley of the River Rye near Helmsley. Rievaulx is one of the most complete British abbeys, with the great eastern range, nave and choir of the church still standing almost to their original height. The best place to view it is from the Rievaulx Terrace,

high on the wooded hill above, which was built specifically for that purpose in the mid 18th century.

No abbey was more powerful than **Fountains**, whose majestic 14th-century ruins, among the largest in Europe, stand in the Skell valley near Ripley. It was founded by Thurstan, Archbishop of York, in 1132, in a place 'more fit for wild beasts than men to inhabit'. Here the monks quickly constructed the first of a series of huge buildings in the quiet valley, culminating in Abbot Huby's magnificent Perpendicular tower, which greets visitors today as they descend into the valley. To the east are the 18th-century water gardens of Studley Royal.

Not far from Rievaulx, near the market town of Helmsley, are the ruins of **Byland Abbey**, set in peaceful meadows in the shadow of the Hambleton Hills. Byland does not have the height of wall of Rievaulx or Fountains but the substantial remains, including the superb western wheel window and the glazed tiles in the chancel chapels, give some indication that, when founded in 1134, this was one of the largest Cistercian churches in England.

It was the Benedictines who enjoyed the finest setting of all – on the clifftop above Whitby. They re-founded **Whitby Abbey** (below) in the 11th century, after 9th-century Vikings had destroyed the original church, established by St Hilda in 680. The stark, brooding ruins inspired Bram Stoker to make Whitby the landing place for his fiendish vampire in the novel *Dracula*.

GARGANTUAN STEELWORKS REBORN FOR ADVENTURES IN SCIENCE

MAGNA

ELECTRODES LIVE

YORKSHIRE

17 Standedge Tunnel **18** Magna

Standedge Tunnel

Test your nerves in Britain's longest underground waterway

It took 16 years to build Britain's longest canal tunnel – completed in 1811 – and cost 50 men their lives. At 196m (645ft) above sea level, it is also Britain's highest. The Standedge Tunnel was a vital part of the Huddersfield Narrow Canal, which linked Ashton-under-Lyne and Manchester with Huddersfield. It allowed raw materials and finished products to be transported across the Pennines between mills, factories and markets.

As there was no room for a towpath for horses, pilots lay on their backs, pushing their feet against the tunnel walls, to move the boats along its 3¼ mile length (the horses had to take a 6 mile route over the moors). This was called 'legging' and the record time through the tunnel was set at 1 hour and 25 minutes in 1914 (it usually took 4 hours). In the visitor centre at Marsden, you can have a go at 'legging' a narrowboat.

▶ *Visitor centre in Waters Road, Marsden, on A62. Tues-Sun and bank hol Mon Apr-Oct. Tel 01484 844298.*

Magna

Gargantuan steelworks reborn for adventures in science

Feel the heat of a tornado of fire; cross a bridge through a space that changes with the weather; and take flight like a bird – just some of the mind-blowing experiences at Magna (left), near Rotherham. The science adventure centre has been planted with spectacular effect into the two cathedral-like 350m (1148ft) long bays of the former Templeborough Steel Works of 1915 – once Europe's largest steel melting shop.

Magna explores the four 'elements' required for steel-making – Earth, Air, Fire and Water – through dramatic interpretations and interactive challenges. Each element has its own themed pavilions linked by bridges. The transformation of the steelworks so impressed the judges of Britain's top award for architecture that it won the 2001 RIBA Stirling Prize.

▶ *M1 (Junctions 33/34), off A6178, 1 mile E of Meadowhall Shopping Centre, Sheffield. Daily, closed some Mondays in winter. Tel 01709 720002.*

NORTHEAST ENGLAND

YORKSHIRE

Millennium Galleries

A tribute to fine art and metalwork in the city of steel

Bold plans to regenerate the centre of Sheffield were given their most dramatic boost by the rise in 2001 of the glistening glass and white concrete Millennium Galleries. Light floods into a central 'avenue' through a vaulted roof of transluscent glass blocks.

Pride of place goes to the Metalwork Gallery, which displays the city's fabulous collection of more than 1000 pieces of silverware and cutlery from the 14th century to the present. In the Ruskin Gallery, drawings, paintings, illuminated manuscripts, rocks and minerals collected by the art critic John Ruskin in the 1870s are on show.
▶ *Arundel Gate, Sheffield. Daily.*

York Minster

A mighty cathedral that dominates the medieval walled city of York

The biggest Gothic cathedral in northern Europe, York Minster impresses not only with its sheer size and magnificence, but in its detail. From the glory of its medieval stained glass windows – the largest collection in Britain – to the bright new modern bosses in the roof of the south transept, reconstructed after a disastrous fire in 1984, the Minster is a remarkable example of 13th and 14th-century architecture painstakingly preserved.

A walk around the 13th-century city walls reveals York's Roman and Viking past, while the overhanging eaves of streets such as The Shambles give a taste of medieval times.
▶ *York Minster, High Petergate. Daily.*

Wharram Percy

A vanished village in the Wolds

A few ghostly farm cottages and the gaunt tower and roofless nave of Wharram Percy's parish church of St Martin's are all that is left of a once prosperous village.

In the 15th century the lord of the manor decided to convert the land from arable crops to sheep pasture and the villagers were driven out. Their cottages had thatched roofs and walls of wattle-and-daub, so little remains of them now.

Mysterious bumps and hollows in the pastures show where medieval oxen teams ploughed the land. The evocative site has also revealed evidence of Bronze Age settlement, Roman farms and a Saxon estate.
▶ *6 miles SE of Malton off B1248, ½ mile S of Wharram-le-Street.*

Farndale daffodils

Stroll along the valley where spring paints the fields yellow

Spring arrives with a bang in this remote valley on the edge of the North York Moors. One moment, everything is winter drab, the next a great sweep of yellow as countless wild daffodils burst into bloom. The 1½ mile walk from the car park in Low Mill to the neighbouring hamlet of Church Houses, where there is an inn, takes about an hour. The public footpath follows the bank of the River Dove upstream, between the steep slopes of Blakey Ridge and Horn Ridge, past a spot where, legend says, two lovers drowned themselves. Return by the same route.
▶ *5 miles N of Kirkbymoorside on A170 Pickering-Helmsley road.*

Robin Hood's Bay

A rocky reef and maze of passages make a perfect smugglers' haunt

The wide bay is a geologist's wonderland. As the tide drops, broad rock platforms stretching 550m (500yd) out to sea are exposed. This great reef is ribbed with hard, fossil-filled limestone strata, called 'scars' locally, which are all that remains of an eroded dome.

When the tide starts to come in, retreat to the village – a picturesque mixture of steep streets, labyrinthine alleyways and tight clusters of houses. In the 18th and 19th centuries the place was notorious for smuggling, and it was said a bale of silk could be carried by secret passages from the beach to the top of the town without seeing daylight. The Old Coastguard Station is an information centre.
▶ *5 miles S of Whitby off A171 Scarborough road. Tel 01947 885900 for details of information centre opening times.*

Bempton Cliffs

Feathery, raucous high-rise world

The setting is dramatic – an RSPB visitor centre and viewpoints perched at the top of 122m (400ft) cliffs, with lighthouse-topped Flamborough Head nearby. The sound is deafening – thousands of noisy sea birds flying to and from their nests. It adds up to one of the most memorable wildlife experiences in Britain.

Thirty-three species of sea bird breed at the reserve, including fulmars, gannets, guillemots, kittiwakes, puffins and razorbills. April to July, when they are raising their chicks, is the best time to come. Puffins are the most endearing of the cliffs' residents, but gannets, which have their only mainland colony at Bempton, put on the best display: gleaming white darts of swept-back wing and spear-like beak as they plunge-dive to catch fish.

▶ *1 mile NE of Bempton on B1229. RSPB. Visitor centre daily.*

Spurn Head

See it while you can – the days of the spit are numbered

The narrow 3 mile long hook of sand and shingle, scoured from the coast of Holderness to the north (the fastest-eroding coastline in Europe), is a shifting no-man's-land on the verge of destruction.

Some time in the next few years, storms will breach the narrow neck linking spit and mainland, sweeping aside the already abandoned sea defences. Water pouring through the gap will then destroy the rest of Spurn Head – and with it the lighthouse, and lifeboat and pilot's stations. Then the whole process of spit formation will start again, a cycle lasting about 250 years. For now, though, it is still possible to drive or walk to the end, where there are hides from which to watch the thousands of migrant birds for which this is a first and last stop on their annual flights.

▶ *2 miles SE of Easington at end of B1445, off A1033 Hull-Withernsea road.*

Humber Bridge

High-wire act of major dimensions

The statistics alone are amazing: 44,120 miles of wire for the cables; 480,000 tonnes of concrete for the two towers and roadway. At 1410m (4626ft), it was the longest single-span suspension bridge in the world when it opened in 1981. But this masterpiece of civil engineering is far more than a list of big numbers. The latticework of cables and the tall ladder-like towers add up to a strikingly graceful as well as monumental structure. And there are impressive small numbers too: the towers are 36mm (1½in) further apart at their tops than their bases – compensation for the curvature of the Earth.

▶ *A15, 5 miles E of Hull centre.*

Beverley churches

Top of the medieval pops

Judging by the host of carvings with a musical theme, Beverley was a medieval Tin Pan Alley. In the Minster there are about 70 carvings of musicians, and 34 in St Mary's Church, including the bagpipes player and a group of five brightly painted minstrels looking like a 14th-century boy band. The vibrant stone and wood carvings – both places of worship also contain an exceptional number of exuberant misericords – are only one of many features of these two fine churches. The Minster, the best non-cathedral church in the land, also contains the highly decorated mid-14th-century Percy Tomb; St Mary's has splendid painted ceilings.

▶ *10 miles N of Hull off A1079 Market Weighton road.*

NORTH EAST ENGLAND

NORTH and MID WALES
248-257

SOUTH WALES
258-267

Snowdonia
National
Park

Cambrian
Mountains

Pembrokeshire Coast
National Park

Brecon
Beacons
National Park

Black
Mountains

Anglesey

Holyhead

Llandudno
Rhyl
A55
Bangor
Mold
Caernarfon
Betws-y-coed
A5
A494
Wrexham
Porthmadog
Llangollen
Bala
Dolgellau
A494
A458
Welshpool
Machynlleth
Newtown
Aberystwyth
A44
LLangurig
Llandrindod
Wells
A44
Cardigan
Builth
Wells
A485
A483
A470
A438
Fishguard
Llandovery
Brecon
A40
Abergavenny
Haverfordwest
Carmarthen
Llandeilo
Monmouth
A40
A477
A48
Milford
Haven
A4076
A465
Merthyr
Tydfil
Tenby
Llanelli
A470
A449
Chepstow
Swansea
Neath
M48
Port
Talbot
Newport
M4
Bridgend
Cardiff

Wales

Rock is the heart and soul of Wales: piled up into rugged summits for castle walls to imitate; laid bare in slate quarries and mines of coal, copper and gold; stretching below becalmed chapels on oceans of moor; expiring in cliffs ringing to the cries of sea birds and seals.

Key

1 Main entry

2 Feature entry

━━ Regional boundary

Motorway

Principal A road

(See 'Finding your way', page 7)

NORTH & MID WALES

Beaumaris Castle

Multi-shelled nut too hard to crack

Its squat walls, mirrored in the moat, give the fortress an almost welcoming demeanour. But appearances are deceptive, for this is the most technically perfect medieval castle in Britain.

Begun in 1295, it was the last link in the iron ring of strongholds built by Edward I to crush the Welsh. Although funds ran out before it could be completed, the concentric system of defences (over four miles long) were state of the art. The inner boundary of the moat is lined by the low outer wall with its 16 projecting towers, or bastions. Beyond this lies a narrow courtyard, overshadowed by the inner main walls, every inch of which is covered by their massive projecting bastions and the two formidable, towered gatehouses, which lie at opposite ends of the castle.

▶ *Beaumaris, 4 miles NE of Menai Bridge on A545. Cadw. Daily.*

Parys Mountain

Post-mortem on a copper bonanza

This is a mutilated corpse of a mountain, sacrificed for the copper it contained, mined to sheath the hulls of Nelson's fleet.

It is gouged by immense pits – biggest of which is the Great Opencast, a rough-sided scoop into its heart – pierced by underground shafts and scarred with spoilheaps. Across everything lies the vivid staining of leached minerals – bruised magentas and yellows, blood-like reds and russets. An old engine house and a windmill, built to assist a steam-driven beam engine that pumped water from the workings, lie beside the two-mile-long trail that winds through this ravaged landscape: reminders of the late 18th century when Parys Mountain was the world's leading copper-producing area and 1500 miners toiled in its workings.

▶ *2 miles S of Amlwch on B5111 to Llangefni.*

Newborough Beach

A glittering bay of long strands and a rocky 'island'

A vast stretch of sand with magnificent views of Snowdonia and the serrated spine of the Lleyn Peninsula lies just a dune's width from the car park at the end of the toll road from the village of Newborough to the beach. Turn left, and there is a three-mile walk to the Menai Strait, flanked all the way by the unforested dunes of Newborough Warren, a nature reserve. The other way lies Llanddwyn Island – a cove-etched isthmus occasionally cut off by a spring tide. At the island's heart lie the remains of a 16th-century church dedicated to St Dwynwen, patron saint of lovers, and at its end two lighthouses and a terrace of pilots' cottages.

▶ *2 miles SW of Newborough off A4080 Llanfair PG-Rhosneigr road.*

Rex Whistler mural, Plas Newydd

A scene on the wall more arresting than the one through the window

When the artist Rex Whistler volunteered for the Welsh Guards in 1940 he wrote to Lord Anglesey promising to return and 'dot the anchors and cross the masts' on his mural at Plas Newydd. He never did, being killed in action four years later. But, despite its unfinished state, the 18m (58ft) long work in the dining room is spellbinding – a landscape of the imagination that borrows from and beats the one outside the 18th-century house.

Here is a romanticised vision of the Mediterranean with a touch of Snowdonia: a seductive coastline backed by plunging mountains under a theatrical sky. But what captivates most are the details – such as the Italianate town, where the arcade sweeper is the artist himself, and a little beach, like the one beside the nearby Menai Strait.

▶ *2 miles SW of Llanfair PG on A4080 Newborough road. NT. Sat-Wed pm Apr-Oct.*

Penrhyn Castle

A brash but charming fantasy fortress

Lord Penrhyn was owner of the vast slate quarries up the road at Bethesda, and made a fortune by roofing Britain's burgeoning cities. He spent it on this neo-Norman 'castle', designed by Thomas Hopper and constructed between 1820 and 1847. Through the main doors lie 150 rooms, starting off with the most visually arresting of them all, the Grand Hall, the soaring spaces of which have been likened to a grand railway terminus.

Yet Penrhyn Castle lives up to its stunning setting between Snowdonia and the waters of the Menai Strait by being romantic as well as ostentatious, fabulous as well as vulgar. The domestic scale of the kitchen and scullery contrasts with the grandeur of the apartments, and a collection of fine paintings, including works by Rembrandt, Gainsborough and Canaletto, counterbalance the elaborate carvings and plasterwork.

▶ *1 mile E of Bangor off A5. NT. Daily, except Tues, Apr-Oct.*

Great Orme Mines

Miles of passages hacked through the rock by Bronze Age people

For the last decade or so, the Great Orme headland that looms above the seaside resort of Llandudno has been yielding up an ancient secret: a maze of mines hewn by Bronze Age man between 3000 and 4000 years ago. Since excavation began in 1987, tonnes of spoil dumped by miners in the 18th and 19th centuries has been stripped away to reveal a growing labyrinth of tunnels – five miles of them so far, making this the most extensive mine discovered from the ancient world.

The scale of the workings is breathtaking, especially because the Bronze Age miners had nothing but stone and bone tools with which to extract the copper ore. The remains of these tools have been discovered in large numbers, along with charcoal, which suggests they weakened the mine face by first lighting fires against it. The highlight of the underground tour is a gallery in the limestone, 12m (40ft) high and 21m (70ft) wide.

▶ *¾ mile NW of Llandudno off minor road, or tramway to Orme summit. Daily mid Mar-Oct.*

Bodnant Garden

Wild heart behind a smooth exterior

The grounds around Lord Aberconway's house introduce themselves in a series of elegant formal terraces – wide balconies with classically regular lily ponds and flawless lawns that seem to curtsey before the panoramic view of Snowdonia. But step beyond their sedateness and the formalities suddenly end.

Bodnant's unexpected wild side is The Dell, a shady cleft carved by the Hiraethlyn stream, a tributary of the Conwy. Wider views sink behind steep rugged slopes streaked with miniature torrents and zigzag paths, and clung to by trees and shrubs. From deep below, on the floor of the ravine, giant redwoods soar upwards towards the light.

▶ *7 miles S of Llandudno Junction off A470 Llanrwst road. NT. Daily mid Mar-Oct.*

Dinorwig – slate and power

A mountain modelled by old industry and modern technology

The shining rock faces, blasted and hacked like a colossal staircase up Elidir Fawr, the brooding mountain facing Llanberis across the twin lakes of Padarn and Peris, shout the history: the Dinorwig slate quarry was once the world's biggest.

The National Slate Museum, housed in former quarry workshops, tells the story in detail. Festooned with drive belts, and running the length of these old machine shops and foundry, is the shaft of the waterwheel that powered them. Follow the shaft to find the wheel – a giant measuring 15.5m (50ft 8in) in diameter. A row of tiny cottages vividly illustrates the hard life of a quarryman and his family, and you can watch the old skill of slates being split by hand.

While the mountain wears its past on its sleeve, it keeps its present hidden in its heart – though not closed to public gaze. Twenty years ago, slate mountain was turned into Electric Mountain. Deep underground, a manmade cavern was created to house a power station with a machine hall 51m (167ft) high. When there is a surge in electricity demand, response is instantaneous: giant pipes are opened, allowing water from Llyn Marchyn Mawr, on top of the mountain, to hurtle down them and turn the turbines. Seconds later, enough power is being produced to light several small cities. At night, when power demand is low, the water, which ended up at the foot of the mountain in Llyn Peris, is pumped back to the top lake – an endlessly reusable resource.

▶ *¾ mile E of Llanberis off A4086. Museum daily Easter-Oct, Sun-Fri Nov-Easter. Power station, Tel 01286 870636 for details.*

SEASHELLS
ABOVE
THE CLOUDS
SUMMIT OF SNOWDON

Summit of Snowdon
Seashells above the clouds

The rocks at the top of the highest peak in Wales illustrate the almost inconceivable length of geological time. They contain the fossils of seashells, scattered over an ocean floor 500 million years ago, buried under volcanic ash, lifted by mountain-building forces and now exposed after aeons of erosion by water and ice. Ancient and worn down though it is, the 1085m (3560ft) summit is still a spectacular vantage point, with views south to Cadair Idris and west to Ireland.

Trains on the narrow-gauge, rack-and-pinion railway, which runs from Llanberis, make light work of the ascent, but there are several footpaths to the top. Best of these for seasoned walkers is the Watkin Path from the south (start from the Nantgwynant car park, 4 miles northeast of Beddgelert on the A498).

12 miles SE of Caernarfon off A4086. NT. Trains to summit daily late Mar-Oct.

Portmeirion
Coloratura in the land of choirs

Portmeirion has been described as the village where Wales becomes Italy, where the Mediterranean mixes with medieval Britain and the Orient. But words can't quite capture the dazzling personality of this surreal little world full of architectural jokes and influences.

The architect Sir Clough Williams-Ellis created the village between 1925 and 1972, taking a 'gay, light-opera sort of approach' to the design. Pastel-coloured buildings of all shapes and sizes are scattered around a central piazza and ornamental gardens, and every turning reveals a fake façade.

3 miles E of Porthmadog off A487 Penrhyndeudraeth road. Daily all year.

Braich y Pwll
A final trial of whirlpools and white water on the pilgrims' trail

Land meets sea in spectacular fashion on this high rocky headland at the tip of the Lleyn Peninsula. Offshore, across 2 miles of tide-ripped water, is Bardsey Island, three pilgrimages to which, in medieval times, was judged the equivalent of one to Rome. Much farther over the water lies Ireland, its mountains visible on clear days. The pilgrims prayed for safe passage at St Mary's Church, the ruins of which can still be made out on steep, bracken-covered slopes. At the foot of the cliff there is a holy well, fed by a freshwater spring, which is covered at high tide by the sea.

▶ *2 miles W of Aberdaron on minor road (car park at road end). NT.*

Roman Steps
Tread a rocky staircase into a mountain wilderness

After less than a mile the path emerges from a mossy woodland of oak, beech and hawthorn into a cleft, squeezed between craggy slopes. Here the Roman Steps begin – a broad rock pavement, with steps on the steeper sections.

The ancient packhorse trail probably dates from after the Roman occupation, although its exact origin is unknown. The path is a delight to walk on. Follow it for an hour into the lonely Rhinogs – a rumpled, broad, bare tableland of summits – before turning around and returning to the lake-head car park.

▶ *5 miles NE of Llanbedr off A496 Harlech-Barmouth road. Car park at end of lane.*

Barmouth Bridge
Woodland-skirted summits rising from a rivermouth of golden sands

Forget about the 500 timber piles that support the rail bridge across the mile-wide river mouth: look at the fabulous view. The Afon Mawddach possesses the loveliest estuary of all the rivers in Wales.

Along both shores, golden sand sweeps up to marshy pockets and woodland-stuffed valleys. Bare slopes emerge beyond these, and higher up again lie the rugged mountains of Snowdonia – the Rhinogs to the north, Cadair Idris to the south. Trains on the Cambrian Coaster railway stop on both sides of the bridge – at Morfa Mawddach Station and in Barmouth. Alternatively, payment of a small toll gives access to the footpath beside the track – part of the Mawddach Trail, which follows the route of a dismantled rail line inland along the southern shore of the estuary.

▶ *1 mile NE of Fairbourne off A493 Dolgellau-Tywyn road (S side); E edge of Barmouth, off A496 Dolgellau-Harlech road (N side).*

Wales

Cefn Coch gold mine

Follow in the footsteps of miners to reminders of a gold rush

Cefn Coch gold mine produced 1390oz (39.4kg) of the precious metal between about 1840 and 1912, when it closed. It was the third richest of more than 20 workings that sprang up in the mountains around Dolgellau, which became known as 'New California'.

The path to the mine starts from Ganllwyd on the main road and leads through woodland to open hillside on the National Trust's Dolmelynllyn Estate. Here the ruins of buildings, including an assay office, workers' barracks and a powder hut where explosives were stored, lie among the old workings.
▶ *Path starts at Ganllwyd on the A470 4 miles N of Dolgellau.*

Pontcysyllte Aqueduct

Take the tiller for a canal cruise in the sky

Those with a head for heights can take a trip on a narrowboat or walk along a towpath 39m (128ft) above ground by crossing the Pontcysyllte Aqueduct. Thomas Telford built the imposing structure in 1805 to carry the Llangollen Canal across the valley of the Dee and link it with the rest of the Shropshire Union. The civil engineer used long cast-iron troughs to hold the water, supporting them on masonry piers so slimly elegant that his doubters thought the edifice would collapse. Nearly two centuries later, it still transports boats for a dizzying 305m (1000ft) between one side of the valley and the other.
▶ *4 miles E of Llangollen, off A5 Chirk road at Froncysyllte.*

Pistyll Rhaeadr

A silvery plunge off the mountainside

This spectacular waterfall – the highest in Wales – billows like a long silver streamer thrown over the southern edge of the Berwyn mountains. From the dark, wooded hollow at the base of the falls, you can look up through spray-laden air to the distant rim, 73m (240ft) above. A footpath zigzags up the bluffs beside the water, past a rocky cauldron spanned by a natural stone arch. Here the cascade is caught mid-plummet in a deep, foaming pool before plunging on its way.
▶ *14 miles W of Oswestry, off B4580 at Llanrhaeadr-ym-Mochnant on dead-end lane.*

Birds' Rock

Cormorants' cliff rising above a calm green sea of meadows

Birds' Rock – in Welsh, Craig yr Aderyn – rears up from the tabletop-flat floor of the Dysynni valley. The sea is 6 miles away at the resort of Tywyn on Cardigan Bay, yet cormorants wheel overhead and nest on its cliffs, a link with the time when the valley was a long inlet of the sea and Birds' Rock itself was lapped by the waves. Over the centuries, the valley silted up, leaving this geographical and ornithological oddity marooned high and dry. The 232m (760ft) high rock is the farthest place from the sea in Britain where cormorants nest. It is also home to a herd of wild goats.
▶ *6 miles NE of Tywyn, off A493 Llwyngwril road at Bryncrug.*

Centre for Alternative Technology

Tomorrow's world in an old quarry

If you want to see how people might live in a future, environmentally friendly world, visit the old slate quarry where the centre (CAT, for short) is located. Windmills, solar panels, photovoltaic tiles, straw-bale building, organic gardening, self-composting toilets and other inventions and ideas show how it is possible to maintain living standards without ruining the planet: 90 per cent of the energy needs at CAT come from renewable resources – water, wind and sun.

When it began nearly 40 years ago, the centre was tolerated as a somewhat ramshackle experimental community; now its expertise is highly respected. Visitor access, appropriately, is by water-balanced cliff railway: two carriages connected by a cable, with the extra weight provided by water pumped into a tank on the descending one contributing the motive power for the carriage going up the incline.

▶ *3 miles N of Machynlleth on A487 Dolgellau road. Daily mid Jan-Dec.*

Clive Museum, Powis Castle

Memories of Madras in the marches

An alabaster Buddha with fingers and toes all of equal length to symbolise the need for equality, a hugga (a pipe for smoking tobacco through water), ceremonial swords and armour, jewellery and other artefacts, all from India – it is not what you expect to find behind the terraced gardens and red battlements of Powis Castle. This exotic collection of mementos, displayed in the old ballroom, came to the Welsh border fortress when Edward Clive, the governor of Madras and son of Robert Clive (1725-74), married into the Herbert family, owners of the castle.

▶ *1 mile S of Welshpool off A483 Newtown road. NT. Thur-Mon pm Apr-June, Sept-Oct; Wed-Mon pm July-Aug.*

TAKE THE TILLER FOR A CANAL CRUISE IN THE SKY
PONTCYSYLLTE AQUEDUCT

Conwy, cradled in a stony embrace

Walk the ramparts of Britain's finest medieval walled town

1 Conwy

Castle and walls ▶ *Daily. Cadw.*

Plas Mawr ▶ *Tues-Sun, and bank hol Mon, Apr-Oct.*
Cadw.

The Smallest House ▶ *Daily Apr-Oct.*

There is no need to read the history books to get a feel for the medieval might of **Conwy**. Instead, go to Upper Gate, the gateway that controlled the western approach to the town, and climb the steps onto the **town walls**. From here the ramparts slope up steeply to their highest point, the tower at the northwest corner, the views from which instantly justify Conwy's reputation as the best-preserved medieval walled town in Britain.

Ahead and behind, the walls march away in a line interrupted by 21 jutting bastions – one every 46m (50yd) and each a mini-fortress. Half-a-mile away across the rooftops and narrow streets is **Conwy Castle** itself: a looming eight-towered stronghold rooted on a natural crag rising out of the estuary. Here was one of the mightiest links in Edward I's 'iron chain' of castles to control the Welsh: a walled town, built to accommodate the colonising English, and a citadel that no rebel could hope to take.

In time, the defenceworks became an anachronistic reminder of the past – architectural markers that the 19th-century engineers Thomas Telford and Robert Stephenson would take for their mock-military bridges over the river. But the town changed as the barriers between the English and Welsh came down. Robert Wynn was among the locals who prospered: an Elizabethan squire whose home, **Plas Mawr** (the 'Great Mansion'), noted for its superb ornamental plasterwork, towers over its humbler neighbours in High Street.

From the grand to the diminutive: down on the quay is **The Smallest House**, a 16th-century 'dwelling' measuring 3m (10ft) high by 3m deep by 1.8m (6ft) wide, which is reputed to have once been the home of a 1.8m (6ft) tall fisherman, Robert Jones.

NORTH & MID WALES

Strata Florida Abbey

Hints of ecclesiastical splendours near the headwaters of the Teifi

The richly carved Norman west door, a grand frame for the ruins beyond, and the surviving sections of richly decorated tiled floor hint at the majesty of this 12th-century Cistercian monastery – the 'Westminster Abbey of Wales'.

An ancient yew is said to mark the burial place of Dafydd ap Gwilym, a contemporary of Chaucer and perhaps the most celebrated Welsh poet of all. A neat row of slabs and decorated headstones mark the graves of Welsh princes, and there is also the grave of one Henry Hughes Cooper – or at least that of his leg: 'The left leg and part of the thigh of Henry Hughes Cooper was cut off and intern'd here June 18th 1756', the headstone intriguingly reads. And beyond and around all this lies an upland valley of serene beauty.

▶ *7 miles NE of Tregaron off B4343 Ysbyty Ystwyth road. Cadw. Daily.*

Capel Soar

Lonely place of worship in the hills

In a country famous for its chapels, Capel Soar ranks as one of the most remarkable. The solitary whitewashed building, which dates from 1822, lies deep in the Cambrian Mountains: a beacon for the devout sheep-farming communities of these remote uplands.

With the decline of the rural population in the past 50 years or so, the chapel's future looked grim, but its doors have remained open thanks to the efforts of local people. Regular services are held during the summer months. Its reputation as a place of simple devotion set in an elemental landscape has also spread: where once a surrounding congregation would arrive on foot and by horse, visitors from as far afield as America, Argentina and Australia now draw up in cars. Inside, rows of plain wooden pews overlooked by a small pulpit match the exterior simplicity.

▶ *12 miles SE of Tregaron on minor road to Llandovery. Fork right at phone box to Soar y Mynydd, where chapel is located.*

Abergwesyn Pass

Take a big-dipper ride to the 'roof of Wales', then a thrilling descent

The 14 mile trip from Tregaron to the hamlet of Abergwesyn follows an ancient drovers' road and provides one of Britain's most memorable motoring experiences.

After reaching the head of the narrow valley cut by the Afon Berwyn, the road climbs through pine trees before emerging on the 'Roof of Wales' – a stretch of high moorland where a single red telephone box is one of the few signs of civilisation. Overhead, look out for red kites; this rare bird of prey, with its distinctive forked tail and lazy swooping flight, has made a comeback in these hills in recent years.

Soon the ridge of the 'roof' lies behind and the road runs downhill through the Tywi Forest and over a bridge spanning the river from which the dark plantation gets its name. The most spectacular section of the journey lies in the last 4 miles as the road plunges down the one-in-three 'Devil's Staircase' into the rock and oakwood-flanked gorge of the Irfon river.

▶ *E of Tregaron off A485 Lampeter-Lledrod road. Alternatively, NW of Llanwrtyd Wells off A483 Llandovery-Beulah road.*

Llanthony Priory

Sacred ruins in a remote valley

Giraldus Cambrensis (Gerald of Wales) wrote that Llanthony Priory was a place 'truly calculated for religion'. Even in the priory's ruined state, it is plain to see why the 12th-century historian and cleric was so moved. Substantial parts of the grand church still stand, including eight bays of an arcade, two sides of the tower and the west end. Beyond the large window openings with their pointed, Early English arches lie the meadows of the Vale of Ewyas and the valley's steep, green sides: still 'a wilderness far removed from the bustle of mankind', as Giraldus described it.

▶ *On minor road 5 miles N of Llanfihangel Crucorney on A465 Abergavenny-Hereford road. Cadw. Daily.*

wales

All aboard the little locomotives

For some of the best views in Wales, take a thrilling ride into the mountains by narrow-gauge train

2 Snowdon Mountain Railway ▶ *Tel 01286 870223.*
3 Vale of Rheidol Railway ▶ *Tel 01970 625819.*
4 Llanberis Lake Railway ▶ *Tel 01286 870549.*
5 Welsh Highland Railway ▶ *Tel 01766 516000.*
6 Ffestiniog Railway ▶ *Tel 01766 516000.*
7 Talyllyn Railway ▶ *Tel 01654 710472.*
8 Brecon Mountain Railway ▶ *Tel 01685 722988.*
9 Bala Lake Railway ▶ *Tel 01678 540666.*

They transport holidaymakers on a blend of sight–seeing trip and nostalgic journey back in time: a clutch of sparkling little locomotives. All shining brass and paintwork, shrill whistles and hissing steam, they chuff up and down narrow-gauge lines squeezed along ledges cut into hillsides and wound around sharp mountain bends.

Although some, such as the **Snowdon Mountain Railway**, were tourist ventures from the start, the majority of the lines and the trains that run on them originally served mountain quarries and mines. In the case of the **Vale of Rheidol Railway**, which runs between Aberystwyth and Devil's Bridge, lead and zinc ore was the cargo. But most of the lines, including the **Llanberis Lake Railway**, with its wonderful view of Snowdon across Llyn Padarn, and the **Welsh Highland Railway** from Caernarfon to Waunfawr, were built to haul slates from the huge quarries that roofed Britain.

The **Ffestiniog Railway** is the best known of the slate lines. The first steam locomotives ran on the 60cm (1ft 11½in) gauge line in 1863, and continued to trundle the 13 miles between Blaenau Ffestiniog's quarries and Porthmadog wharf until the line closed in 1946.

The railway reopens in stages

Its fortunes were not long in reviving: in 1955 volunteer enthusiasts reopened the stretch of line across the Cob at Porthmadog, from which there are wide views of mountains and coast. In following years, sections through the Vale of Ffestiniog's oak woods were brought back into service and in 1982 the last stretch of track across rugged terrain to Blaenau Ffestiniog (left) was reinstated.

The 7¼ mile long **Talyllyn Railway** between Nant Gwernol, near the head of the verdant Fathew valley, where slates from the Bryn Eglwys quarries were loaded, and Tywyn on the coast, was also rescued by enthusiasts. The route, below the craggy foothills of Cadair Idris and past the Dolgoch waterfalls (where there is a halt), posed fewer engineering problems than the Ffestiniog Railway and allowed a 69cm (2ft 3in) wide track to be laid.

The narrow-gauge **Brecon Mountain Railway** and **Bala Lake Railway** share a different history. Both are tourist ventures created on the route of standard-gauge lines closed in the 1960s. Little locos from Europe and North America are used on the Brecon Mountain line, stretching from Pant, near Merthyr Tydfil, to the lakeside halt of Dolygaer, with a further section of track under construction. Former slate quarry engines pull carriages along Bala Lake's eastern shore, giving passengers a view across the water of the Arenig mountains.

NORTH & MID WALES

24 Ynys Lochtyn 25 Twin lakes of The Black Mountain 26 Ystradfellte

Ynys Lochtyn
High lookout over Cardigan Bay

The sandy beach below the little village of Llangrannog is the starting point for this breathtaking walk. Follow the path northeast that climbs onto the cliffs. The view across Cardigan Bay is spectacular enough from here, but it gets even better from Ynys Lochtyn, half-a-mile farther on. The narrow promontory is capped by an 'islet' – accessible at low tide, cut off when the sea rises and when storms batter the coast.
▶ *Take B4334 off A487 Cardigan-Aberaeron road at Brynhoffnant. NT.*

Twin lakes of The Black Mountain
Dark waters below a rocky scarp

A primeval quality clings to Llyn y Fan Fawr and Llyn y Fan Fach, especially when mists spill down the rock faces behind and roll across their inky, icy waters. This western side of the Brecon Beacons National Park, called The Black Mountain, remains relatively unknown: a stretch of moody, high country strewn with rocky outcrops, which many visitors do not venture into, and not to be confused with the Black Mountains, which lie 15 or 20 miles to the east, above Crickhowell. The twin lakes, scooped out by glaciers during the last Ice Age, lie below the mountain's great north-facing escarpment.
▶ *2 hour walk from end of lane at Llanddeusant, off A4069 Llangadog-Brynamman road at Pont-ar-llechau.*

Ystradfellte
Silvery necklace of waterfalls

Along the southern rim of the Brecon Beacons National Park a band of limestone creates a world of caves, wooded gorges and waterfalls. Just south of the hamlet of Ystradfellte, the Afon Mellte is momentarily swallowed at the Porth yr Ogof cave entrance before emerging to cascade down a trio of spectacular falls. The most famous waterfall of all, though, is Sgwd yr Eira (The Fall of Snow) on the Hepste, a tributary of the Mellte. The overhang is so pronounced that walkers can follow a footpath behind the veil of cascading water without getting wet.
▶ *12 miles NE of Neath on minor road off A465 Merthyr Tydfil road at Glynneath.*

wales

SOUTH WALES

St David's Cathedral and Bishop's Palace

The most splendid church in Wales

St David's is Britain's smallest city, and its 91m (298ft) long cathedral is the largest in Wales. There is glorious craftsmanship in the Tudor oak roof and the intricate 14th-century rood screen. Pilgrims no longer flock to the shrine of St David, patron saint of Wales, but flowers always decorate his statue.

A rose window survives in the ruins of the 13th-century Bishop's Palace, in the Cathedral Close. None of the Palace roofs remains – they were stripped for the value of their lead in the 16th century on the orders of Bishop Barlow. He needed to raise cash for the dowries of his five daughters, and he was successful – each girl married a bishop.

▶ *14 miles NW of Haverfordwest, in Cathedral Close. Cathedral daily. Palace (Cadw) daily.*

St David's Head and Arthur's Quoit

Rugged headland that reveals remnants of people and times past

The rocky promontory of St David's Head is remarkably rich in prehistoric remains. Here, above rugged 30m (100ft) cliffs, are the circular foundations of the huts of Iron Age farmers, the raised seams of their field boundaries and the line of a double wall known as the Warrior's Dyke with which they sealed off their dwellings from the world.

Less than a mile away is Arthur's Quoit. Locals say it was thrown here from a nearby hill by the legendary hero Arthur. However, archaeologists believe that the enormous slab of stone is the capstone of a burial chamber some 5500 years old. All that prevents it from slamming to earth is one slim, upright stone.

▶ *Drive to end of B4583, park at Whitesands Bay car park. St David's Head, 1 mile walk along Pembrokeshire Coast Path. Arthur's Quoit, ⅓ mile NE of Head.*

Carreg Samson

A prehistoric grave with a giant lid

Magnificently framed by the headlands and cliffs of Abercastle Bay, Carreg Samson is a most impressive 'cromlech' or stone tomb, 4500 years old. A 5m (16ft) long capstone, shaggy with green lichen and studded with fat nuggets of quartz, is poised on three of the seven upright stones. The tomb seems solemn, weighty and curiously graceful, with the glittering sea seen shining between the stones.

▶ *Signed from road at Longhouse, ½ mile SW of Abercastle off A487.*

Dinas Island

Saints, sea birds and stunning views

When St Brynach was hungry he plucked loaves out of the oak trees, and when he built a house, stags willingly hauled the timber for him. No wonder the locals were in awe of this 6th-century Irish missionary who founded his monastery on Dinas Island on the north coast of Pembrokeshire.

Dinas is not a separate island, but a bulbous promontory, cut off from the mainland coast by a deep, marshy gully carved by Ice Age meltwaters 10,000 years ago. From the ruin of St Brynach's Church at the channel's eastern end you can walk a 3 mile circuit of the cliffs of Dinas Island. Look out for great black-backed gulls, peregrines, seals and dolphins, and enjoy the panoramic coastal views that stretch 9 miles east to Cemaes Head and 6 miles west to Strumble Head.

▶ *At Dinas Cross, 4 miles E of Fishguard on A487, take unsigned road on left by chapel and follow signs to Pwllgwaelod and car park.*

Stack Rocks, Flimston

Dramatic pillars rise out of the sea

The limestone towers of the Stack Rocks rise like steps out of the sea towards the cliffs, the tallest climbing over 46m (150ft) high. Shrieking kittiwakes, seagulls, razorbills and fulmars inhabit their ledges and crannies. Locally, the rocks are called Elegug – Welsh for 'guillemot' – Stacks. A short walk west brings you to the 'Green Bridge of Wales', a wave-beaten limestone arch. These are wildly beautiful natural formations.

▶ *Access from S end of lane (follow Stack Rocks sign) from B4319, W of Merrion. Lane and path open after 5pm Mon-Fri, all day Sat-Sun. To confirm, Tel 01646 662367.*

Milford Haven

A seagull's-eye view over southwest Wales's great natural harbour

From the middle of Cleddau Bridge, high above the brawling tides of the Daugleddau River, you can enjoy a grandstand panorama of a great commercial river. The view over Milford Haven is made up of big ships, yachts and speedboats cutting the mile-wide estuary to the west, the silhouettes of oil refinery chimneys, silos and pipework springing skywards from the cliffs, and the colour-washed houses of Neyland and Pembroke Dock framed by steep green fields. This blend of marine, industrial, domestic and pastoral – and of the small-scale and the gigantic – is truly memorable.

▶ *Views from Cleddau Toll Bridge, on A477 between Neyland and Pembroke Dock. Park in Burton picnic site at N end of bridge and walk to middle.*

St Govan's Chapel walk

Fabulous flora on the way to the rocky refuge of a hermit

A tiny 13th-century church, crammed into a crack in the cliffs on the south Pembrokeshire coast, makes for an impossibly romantic and breathtaking sight. To find it, take the marked path from the car park below Bosherston church, past the snowy blooms of the village lily ponds (in flower from June to September), to Broad Haven. Follow the Coast Path west to the car park on Trevallen Downs. Steep steps lead from here to St Govan's Chapel, camouflaged in the cliffside. A narrow recess behind its simple altar is probably the original cell of St Govan, a 6th-century monk.

▶ *Bosherston, signed from B4319, 3 miles S of Pembroke. St Govan's is near a firing range, Tel 01646 662367 for firing times.*

Barafundle Bay

Incomparable coastline

Barafundle is the perfect beach. It has rock pools, a clean sweep of sand reaching out to crystal clear waters, high sand dunes, cliffs and rock stacks – and none of the things that spoil beaches: roads, car parks, arcades or electronic noise. Barafundle has no access for vehicles, no toilets or café. It is an isolated place, reached by a grassy footpath, unsullied and unrivalled.

▶ *½ mile walk from Stackpole Quay car park. Signed from Stackpole off B4319. NT.*

Worms Head and Rhossili Bay

An exhilarating walk on the spine of a wave-battered headland

From the south end of Rhossili Bay, the three green humps of Inner Head, Low Neck and Outer Head snake seawards to form a mile-long promontory. The Vikings called it 'wurm', meaning dragon, because of its beast-like shape. The 2 mile walk to its seabird-haunted tip starts at the National Trust centre in Rhossili. Cross a green down, with views over the creamy sands of Rhossili Bay. Descend from here to hop and stumble over the rocky causeway – a 15-minute scramble. Dylan Thomas was once cut off by the tide and marooned on Outer Head. Make sure it does not happen to you.

▶ *At end of B4247, signed from Scurlage. Tel 01792 366534 to check tides. Outer Head closed Mar-Aug (nesting season).*

Paxton's Tower

A rich Londoner's sweet revenge

A triangular folly with castellated drum towers stands proudly on its headland like a castle in a dream. This dramatic landmark is Paxton's Tower and from it there are tremendous views over the Tywi Valley.

A prosperous London banker, Sir William Paxton, built the tower in 1811, ostensibly to honour Lord Nelson, England's greatest fighting admiral. In fact, Paxton was smarting at his recent rejection by the Carmarthen voters, in spite of his offer to build them a bridge across the River Tywi if they chose him as their Member of Parliament. Constructing the tower, which overlooked the site of the bridge that Paxton would never build, was the banker's way of thumbing his nose at the electorate who turned him down. The bridge was erected eventually anyway.

▶ *6 miles W of Llandeilo, signed off B4300 at Llanarthney. NT. Daily.*

RAMSEY ISLAND

Afloat in the Atlantic

Remote islands anchored off the coast of southwest Wales have become an idyllic retreat for man, bird and beast

1 Caldey Island ▶ *Crossings from Tenby (harbour at high tide, Castle Beach at low tide), 9 miles E of Pembroke on A4139. Mon-Fri Easter-Oct, also Sat mid May-Sept.*

2 Skokholm Island ▶ *Crossings from Martinshaven, signed from B4327 via Marloes. Residents – Tel 01239 621212 (Wildlife Trust of South & West Wales) for times, pre-booking essential. No day visits possible.*

3 Skomer Island ▶ *Crossings from Martinshaven (directions as above) – no booking. Tues-Sun and bank hol Mon, Apr-Oct. For information, Tel 01239 621212 (Wildlife Trust of South & West Wales).*

4 Ramsey Island ▶ *Crossings from St Justinian's, signed from St David's on A487. RSPB. Daily Apr-Oct – visitor numbers limited, booking essential. Tel 01437 721721 for times.*

5 Grassholm Island ▶ *Crossings from Martinshaven (directions as above) but no landings. RSPB. Apr-Aug. For information, Tel 01646 603110.*

Of the five accessible islands off the Pembrokeshire coast, four are run as nature reserves and on the fifth is a monastery. When you circle them in a cruise boat or step ashore onto their jetties, you are acutely aware of having slipped ties with the mainland – a spine-tinglingly exhilarating sensation.

The most easterly is **Caldey Island**, south of the seaside resort of Tenby. Caldey is the most tamed and civilised of the islands. But it possesses its full share of magic. The Reformed Cistercian Order of monks owns and runs the island, and their black-habited figures are often seen walking among the spring and summer visitors often stopping for a chat. The monks make and sell perfume, chocolate and other delights, and rely heavily on the seasonal tourism that shores up their precarious economy. Beyond the monastery are sandy beaches, farmlands, woods and clifftop paths.

Home making on wave-washed shores

Skokholm Island (pronounced 'Skoe-k'm'), a mile or so long, was made famous in 1930 when naturalist and adventurer Ronald Lockley published *Dream Island*, a best-selling account of the life he and his wife Doris led as sole occupants. Small numbers of visitors are allowed onto the island to see the farmhouse that Lockley renovated with driftwood, and to explore the cliffs and paths. Today, the island's turf is pierced by an estimated 86,000 burrows made by puffins, rabbits and Manx shearwaters. About 150,000 Manx shearwaters – half the world population – nest and breed on Skokholm and its sister island Skomer. They are extraordinary birds that spend the winter at sea off the Brazilian coast, then find their way to the islands each spring. At night tens of thousands of shearwaters skim in from their day roosts at sea to their chicks in the turf burrows, seeming to plaintively call 'Poppa's – *here*! Poppa's – *here*!'. It is an unearthly sound – powerful magic by the light of moon, stars or a lighthouse beam.

Sharing the narrow ocean channel of Broad Sound with Skokholm is **Skomer Island**. It plays host to the majority of the shearwaters and also has a population of up to 25,000 rabbits, an incredible abundance on an island that measures only a mile and a half across. Its cliffs are alive with kittiwakes screaming raucously. Fulmars ride the thermals on slim pointed wings, and puffins blink at their burrow entrances. Seals bob their heads in the tide races between the island and its offshore rocks.

Ramsey Island is 8 miles north of Skomer. Only 2 miles long, it rises to two hills and falls from superb cliffs to beaches where the seal cows give birth in late summer. The island is now run as an RSPB reserve, and nature trails allow you to explore its striking landscape. You might even spot the very rare chough, with its brilliant scarlet beak and legs, which has re-established itself on the 120m (394ft) high cliffs.

Tiny **Grassholm Island**, 7 miles west of Skomer, is another RSPB reserve – a stronghold of the gannet. Eighty thousand of these big white fishing birds nest there. You cannot land on the island (the gannets have taken over the viewing platform), but the stench, noise and sight from the cruise boat are overwhelming enough. Ronald and Doris Lockley spent their honeymoon here in the 1920s – today they would not find space enough between the gannets to put down a sleeping bag.

SOUTH WALES

GIANT SYMBOL OF NATIONAL PRIDE
CARDIFF MILLENNIUM STADIUM

Dolaucothi Gold Mines

Join a 2000-year-old search for gold above and below ground

At Dolaucothi Gold Mines you can pan the sluice in the hope of washing out real gold. Then, equipped with a helmet and lamp, go underground to view adits (horizontal passages) and shafts worked intermittently by generations of gold miners from Roman times until the 1930s.

The Dolaucothi mines are the oldest gold workings in Britain. You catch a sense of its history as you look up from a Victorian mine-shaft into roughly roofed Roman workings. It is all too easy to imagine the terror of the eight-year-old children who were employed in Victorian times to shovel shale and quartz into trucks in the pitch dark. The scramble out at the end, up a rough, rocky staircase to a high-perched cave mouth set in the cliff face, finishes your visit in dramatic style.

▶ *7 miles NW of Llanwrda, signed off A482 at Pumsaint. NT. Daily late Mar–Oct.*

Carreg Cennen Castle

A mysterious tunnel deep in the rock beneath a lofty stronghold

When the Welsh Prince of Deheubarth, Lord Rhys, built a stronghold on the rock of Carreg Cennen, he knew exactly what he wanted – an eyrie with an uninterrupted view over the surrounding country. English conquerors also saw its value. When they captured it in the late 13th century they continued to strengthen its walls and towers.

Today, Carreg Cennen stands a shattered but eye-catching ruin on its dramatic 91m (300ft) high peak. Steps in the inner ward lead steeply down to a window-lit tunnel and then to a dark passage that burrows into the heart of the rock. Is it a dovecote, a reservoir or a secret, last-resort refuge from attackers? Your guess is as good as those of the experts.

▶ *3 miles SE of Llandeilo, signed from A483 near Ffairfach. Cadw. Daily. Hire torch for tunnel exploration at farm near car park.*

St Illtud's, Llantwit Major

Fifteen hundred years of Christianity in one extraordinary church

St Illtud's Church is an 11th-century building bursting with character and interest. The whole of the west end is a museum of Christian art, from very early Celtic crosses, intricately carved, to the monuments of Elizabethan dignitaries.

And the theme is continued in the east end, which is still used for worship. Here you will find notable medieval wall paintings – a 14th-century Mary Magdalene anointing the feet of Christ, a 15th-century St Christopher hefting the Christ child on his shoulder. The symbol of the cross appears in many guises, too, from primitive gouges to highly elaborate Georgian designs. St Illtud's, founded by a Celtic scholar in the 6th century, offers a lesson in art history, a reflection on religious development, and an affirmation of a tough and long-lasting faith.

▶ *Centre of Llantwit Major, off B4265 between Barry and Bridgend.*

Majestas, Llandaff Cathedral

Dramatic 20th-century church sculpture

'If the Majestas were the last work I were ever to make,' said Sir Jacob Epstein of his modern masterpiece, 'I would be content.' Installed in 1957, the Majestas immediately draws the eye of those who enter Llandaff Cathedral. The 4.8m (16ft) figure of Christ in Majesty, cast in unpolished aluminium, is fixed to the cylindrical organ case, itself a bold design, and hoisted on a concrete arch 15m (50ft) over the nave. Christ faces the west door and appears to be soaring upwards – an inspired idea that enhances the ancient stonework around the sculpture.

▶ *Llandaff Cathedral, off A4119, 2 miles NW of Cardiff centre.*

Cardiff Millennium Stadium

Giant symbol of national pride

Imagine the roar of 72,500 Welshmen and women singing 'Bread of Heaven' at the tops of their voices as their 15 rugby heroes in red shirts run onto the pitch. That is the sound that shakes the awesome Millennium Stadium on match days when the Welsh team comes out to play.

The stadium, which was opened just in time to host the 1999 Rugby World Cup, has a palletised pitch – just lift out the damaged section and drop a new one in – and a giant retractable roof, 111m X 76m (365ft X 250ft). It cost £114 million to build and most Welshmen reckon it was worth the money.

▶ *Cardiff Arms Park, beside River Taff in city centre. Tours daily (except match or event days), Tel 029 2082 2228.*

wales

Romance of a lord's bizarre castles

Gothic fantasy was brought to South Wales by the fevered imaginations of two extraordinary Victorians

MEDIEVAL FANTASY
CASTELL COCH

6 Cardiff Castle ▶ *Castle Street, Cardiff city centre. Daily.*

7 Castell Coch ▶ *Signed off A470 Merthyr Tydfil road (M4, Junction 32). Cadw. Daily (closed early Jan-mid Feb).*

The 3rd Marquess of Bute, John Patrick Crichton Stuart (1847-1900), was a serious-minded, intense youth of 18, immensely rich with inherited industrial wealth, when in 1865 he met the remarkable William Burges (1827-81). Burges was a flamboyant, laddish figure, a great drinker and socialiser, given to working with a parrot on his shoulder. He was also a brilliant architect, who shared his employer's obsession with the extravagance and nostalgia of the high Gothic fashion. Together they utterly transformed the neglected Cardiff Castle in the city centre, and the tumbledown Castell Coch 5 miles away on the northern outskirts of town.

A Victorian take on ancient styles
At **Cardiff Castle** no expense was spared and no romantic mock-medieval idea left unexplored. The Banqueting Hall under its tremendous wooden roof is the centrepiece, with reliefs, murals and stained-glass windows telling the story of the castle. There is a Winter Smoking Room inside the Clock Tower, with figures of ladies and gentlemen hunting and skating, and a corresponding Summer Smoking Room at the top of the tower, where summery courting couples disport themselves between the starry domed ceiling and the zodiac tiled floor. Lord Bute's bedroom has biblical scenes based around St John the Evangelist (and a mirrored ceiling), while there is a lighter touch in the Nursery with its tiled scenes from nursery tales. The arcaded and buttressed ceiling in the Arab Room is a marvel of gilt elaboration.

Castell Coch (left) has fewer rooms, but the high Gothic drama is pursued here too. There are panels of hand-painted flora, fleets of butterflies and flights of parakeets across the walls of the Dining Room. Murals of early Christian martyrs being picturesquely done to death adorn the Dining Hall. The tremendous over-elaboration and obsessive space-filling in both castles would seem grotesquely excessive if carried out today, but more than a century's distance has lent warmth and charm to the visions of Bute and Burges.

SOUTH WALES
16 Cwm **17** Blaenavon Ironworks

Cwm
Clear vision of the valley's past

Like a life-size demonstration of perspective, the two ruler-straight, mile-long rows of terraced housing each side of the approach road up Ebbw Vale appear to converge at the far end of the village of Cwm.

The Marine Colliery that once employed the coal miners of Cwm has shut, like all but one of the dozens of pits in the Valleys district of South Wales; the buildings and machinery at the pitheads have been demolished and dismantled. But the architecture of the pit villages persists right across the old coalfield, and nowhere more strikingly than at Cwm. At any moment, you expect the doors to open, disgorging hundreds of miners.
▶ *3 miles S of Ebbw Vale on A4046 Aberbeeg road.*

Blaenavon Ironworks
White-hot birth of the industrial age

When Blaenavon Ironworks were at full production, roaring and blazing night and day, a hydraulic lift would raise wagons full of pig-iron up the water-balance tower, the tallest remaining building at the works, while others filled with casting sand made the descent. The sight of the counterbalanced wagons sliding past the arched openings earned the tower the nickname of 'the guillotine'.

The blast furnaces that melted iron out of ore, and the casting houses where the molten metal was poured into moulds to harden into 'pigs', have been restored, along with the workers' houses of Stack Square. The last are cramped and insanitary, but luxurious compared with the hovels in which many of the workers' families lived.
▶ *Blaenavon centre. Cadw. Daily Apr-Oct.*

wales

SOUTH WALES

18 Big Pit National Coal Museum 19 Tintern Abbey 20 Chepstow Castle

21 Caerwent

Big Pit National Coal Museum

Ride the cage down to the stygian world of the miner

'Just imagine how those ponies felt,' says guide and former miner Colin as he switches out the lamps on the visitors' helmets. He pauses before continuing: 'One week's holiday up at the surface every year; other than that, down here in the dark all their working lives.' At 90m (300ft) underground, Big Pit certainly is dark – the epitome of pitch-blackness. And it is draughty too, thanks to air blowing down the ventilation shafts and whistling between the galleries.

When the 120-year-old pit closed in 1980, the miners restored the workings – from which no coal had been extracted for a number of years – and opened the colliery as a visitor attraction, staffed and maintained by themselves and former mining colleagues. Big Pit stands on the edge of Blaenavon Industrial Landscape, now a World Heritage Site.

▶ ¾ mile W of Blaenavon town centre. Daily. Tel 01495 790311.

Tintern Abbey

Soaring stonework to stir souls

Walking between the columns of the roofless abbey church, it is easy to see why the place inspired the painter J.M.W. Turner and the poet William Wordsworth. The dove-grey ruins are intensely romantic: grass underfoot, the sky above, and beyond the great windows at either end of the nave, views of the Wye Valley.

Little is left of the first Cistercian church, which was founded in 1131; the remains that stand today date mostly from the last 30 years of the 13th century.

▶ 5 miles N of Chepstow on A466 Monmouth road. Cadw. Daily.

Chepstow Castle

Warlord's stronghold over the river

Like one cliff piled on top of another, the formidable fortress rises from a bluff-bound spur in a bend of the Wye. William fitz Osbern, brother-in-arms and powerful ally of William the Conqueror, began construction in 1067, within a year of the Battle of Hastings, and his yellow-stone Great Keep is the oldest surviving Norman fortification work in Britain. The following centuries saw walls, towers, bastions and the magnificent 13th-century gatehouse marching along and around the castle's precarious perch above the river.

▶ Chepstow town centre. Cadw. Daily.

Caerwent

Walled capital west of the Severn

In the 4th century, Venta Silurum (the Roman name for Caerwent) had around 3000 inhabitants – a number not exceeded by any other town in Wales for another 1500 years. This was no mere garrisoned outpost of empire, but a self-governing civitas or regional capital with all the trappings of Roman civilisation. There are knee-high remains of the shops, forges and houses of the Romanised Silures tribe, along with a temple, forum and great basilica. And around all this are the best-preserved Roman town walls in Britain, still 5m (16ft) high in places.

▶ 5 miles W of Chepstow off A48 Newport road. Cadw. Daily.

SOARING STONEWORK
TO STIR SOULS
TINTERN ABBEY

Scotland

Past border keep and over heathery hill are vibrant cities of industry and culture. A breathtaking wilderness lies beyond, where mountain, sea loch and scattered isle cradle dramatic prehistoric sites: Scotland's scale and swagger set it apart.

Key

1 Main entry

2 Feature entry

Regional boundary

Motorway

Principal A road

(See 'Finding your way', page 7)

Durness **13** **7**

Thurso **6**

Wick

A99

11

**NORTH HIGHLANDS
AND ISLANDS**
294-303

Lairg

A9

8

Ullapool

11

9 A835

23

25

24 Skye

14

Portree **13**

14

Kyle of Lochalsh **15**

12 Loch
Ness

A87

16

16

22

Mallaig
A830

21

18 **19** **17**

20

Fort
William **15**

16 A82

28

Mull

Oban **17**

Crianlarich
A85

A82
Loch Lomond
& The Trossachs
National Park

24

A816

25

Loch
Lomond

Lochgilphead

2

13

Dumbarton

A78

Glasgow **14-19**

1

East
Kilbride **11**

Irvine

Kilmarnock

A70

26

6

7

Ayr

A76 **8**

A77

SOUTHWEST
270-276

5

Dumfries

Stranraer **1**

2

A75

4 **3**

A75

Moffat

A701

M74

A7

A75

Hawick

Jedburgh **21**

25

A68

Orkney Islands

3 **9**

1-5 Kirkwall

4 **7**

17

5

6

**Shetland
Islands**

1 Lerwick

8

2

A96

Elgin **9**

4 Nairn

Inverness **1**

5 **7**

9

10

2 **3**

5 **1**

6 **8**

4

Fraserburgh

A952

Peterhead

A90

Aberdeen **9**

A96

A93

6 Cairngorms
National Park

Newtonmore

7

Braemar

8

10

A9

**CENTRAL
AND NORTHEAST**
286-293

Pitlochry

A90

11

21

20

18 **13** Forfar

12

19 Dundee

14

Perth

1 St Andrews

2

Grampian Mountains

A9

A811 Stirling

22

A91

M90

A9

A84

Kirkcaldy

4 **5**

8 **7** **6** **3** Edinburgh

16

15

A1

9-13

1

14

17

18

19

**FIFE AND
SOUTHEAST**
277-285

12

9

10

M8

A70

A702

20 Peebles

Coldstream **23**

22

24

M74

A7

SOUTHWEST SCOTLAND

1 Logan Botanic Garden 2 Whithorn 3 Caerlaverock Castle and Wildlife Centre

4 Sweetheart Abbey 5 Glenkiln Reservoir sculptures 6 Electric Brae 7 Culzean Castle

8 Sanquhar Post Office 9 New Lanark and the Falls of Clyde

Logan Botanic Garden

A touch of the tropics in a surprising setting

New Zealand cabbage palms and Brazilian gunneras with 2m (7ft) long leaves are not expected discoveries in the Scottish landscape, but at Logan they thrive. Situated on a peninsula jutting into the Irish Sea, Logan benefits from the warming effects of the Gulf Stream passing less than a mile offshore. An almost sub-tropical climate supports exotic plants from temperate regions around the world. Delicate species are protected by 12ha (30 acres) of woodland, tree ferns and richly colourful rhododendrons.

The botanic garden was developed in the late 19th century by Agnes Buchan-Hepburn and her husband James McDouall. In 1969 it was gifted to the Royal Botanic Garden of Edinburgh, and plantings are used as biological standards for research and conservation.

▶ *14 miles S of Stranraer off B7065, 1 mile from Port Logan. Daily Mar-Oct.*

Whithorn

From Rome to the Solway Firth with a mission and some masons

Scotland's earliest recorded Christian settlement has been uncovered at the mouth of the Solway Firth. It owes its origin to St Ninian, a locally born missionary who, in the late 4th century, travelled to Rome. He was ordained bishop by the pope and given the task of spreading Christianity to western Britain. On his journey home to Scotland, St Ninian acquired masons from St Martin of Tours who were to help him build his first church and priory in AD 397. The 'Candida Casa' or White House, as it became known, was translated by the Picts as 'Hwit Aerne', hence the village name of Whithorn.

The present priory ruins date from the 12th century, but archaeological digs have revealed the existence of several churches in the area from between 500 and 1500, and fragments of stained glass show that Whithorn was one of the most significant places of pilgrimage on the British mainland. Irish, Northumbrians, Vikings, Anglo–Normans and Scottish settlers all followed St Ninian here.

▶ *16 miles S of Newton Stewart off A75. HS. Whithorn visitor centre, George Street; daily Apr-Oct.*

Caerlaverock Castle and Wildlife Centre

Safe landings on the Solway Firth

The 5500ha (13,600 acres) of salt marsh and sand on the Solway Firth's northern shore are the favourite winter retreat for up to 24,000 barnacle geese, who descend from Svalbard, north of Norway in the Arctic.

Brooding over the watery wilderness, where the tide is said to 'ebb at the speed of a galloping horse', is the ruined, 13th-century moated stronghold of Caerlaverock Castle, home of the once-powerful Maxwell family.

From the nearby Wildfowl & Wetlands Trust centre at Eastpark, a dazzling array of wildlife can be seen, including Whooper and Bewick's swans, pink-footed geese from Iceland and Greenland, wigeon, shovelers, teals, peregrine falcons, otters and badgers. To get the best out of the fauna, you can stay overnight at the centre.

▶ *8 miles SE of Dumfries on B725. Castle daily; HS. WWT centre daily, Tel 01387 770200.*

Sweetheart Abbey

A 13th-century love story enshrined in a casket

Red sandstone ruins in a serene setting survive to commemorate the enduring relationship between Lady Devorgilla of Galloway and her husband, John Balliol. Together they had founded the college named after them at Oxford, and their son, also John Balliol, became King of Scotland in 1292. After Balliol's death, Devorgilla built the Cisterian abbey in memory of her husband, and carried his embalmed heart with her in a casket wherever she travelled. When Lady Devorgilla died and her body was interred before the high altar, the casket containing the heart was placed beside her. In recognition of this, the monks named their abbey 'Dulce Cor' or 'Sweetheart' in her memory.

▶ *8 miles SW of Dumfries on A710. HS. Daily Apr-Sept; Sat-Wed Oct-Mar.*

Glenkiln Reservoir sculptures
Strange figures in the wilderness

Travelling the lonely roads into the hills west of Dumfries you might be forgiven for thinking you were seeing things when out of the mist appears a Henry Moore sculpture – and then more. There is Moore's *Standing Figure*; on Bennan Hill is his *Glenkiln Cross*; and overlooking Glenkiln Reservoir sits his *King and Queen. John the Baptist* by Auguste Rodin proclaims from a rock. Other works include pieces by the environmental sculptor Andy Goldsworthy.

When a local landowner, the late Sir Henry Keswick, had the idea of placing contemporary art on a roadside in the 1950s he caused controversy. Now the sculptures are integral to the landscape.
▶ *9 miles W of Dumfries off A75. Turn N to Shawhead and Glenkiln Reservoir.*

Electric Brae
An optical illusion to confuse even the most experienced of drivers

The mind plays tricks on those travelling along the Ayrshire coast on the A719 north of Girvan. It is possible to stop the car, leave the brake off, and very slowly your vehicle will appear to roll uphill.

A roadside stone between Dunure Village and Croy Bay tells you that for a quarter of a mile from the bend overlooking Croy railway viaduct to the west, at 87m (286ft) above sea level, to the wooded Craigencroy Glen to the east, 92m (303ft) above sea level, the configuration on either side of the road makes it look as if the slope is going the other way. It was once believed that this illusion was caused by magnetic attraction, hence the name 'Electric Brae'.
▶ *4 miles S of Dunure on A719.*

Culzean Castle
A cliff-top palace for a dynamic dynasty and an American president

The oval staircase at Culzean Castle and the saloon with windows 46m (150ft) above the Firth of Clyde are among the finest achievements of the architect Robert Adam. He designed Culzean, clinging by its elegant fingernails to the top of a cliff, in the late 18th century for the all-powerful Kennedy family. For Adam it was a departure from his usual classical buildings into a more romantic style.

The Kennedys were a stormy dynasty. One led the Scots forces under Joan of Arc to relieve Orléans in 1429; another roasted alive the Commendator of nearby Crossraguel Abbey to force him to hand over abbey lands. Nowadays, you can pass the night as a paying guest in the Eisenhower Apartment, which was opened up to America's 34th president in recognition of his role as Supreme Commander of the Allied Forces in Europe during the Second World War.
▶ *12 miles S of Ayr on A719, 4 miles W of Maybole. NTS. Castle daily Apr-Oct; Country Park daily.*

Sanquhar Post Office
The post office with a world record

A postal service between Dumfries and Ayr was established at Sanquhar in 1712, which makes the bow-fronted Sanquhar Post Office building the oldest of its kind in the world. Its closest contender is the head post office in Santiago, Chile, built 70 years later.

Sanquhar Post Office Museum incorporates interactive displays, postal artefacts and an audio visual theatre, where you can watch the film *Night Mail* with words by W.H. Auden.
▶ *25 miles N of Dumfries on A76. Daily Apr-Oct; closed Sun Nov-Mar.*

New Lanark and the Falls of Clyde
Well looked-after workers in a model mill village

J.M.W. Turner was moved to paint the spectacular Falls of Clyde near Lanark in the early 19th century, but a visiting cloth merchant, David Dale, and an inventor, Richard Arkwright, had already had other ideas. Arkwright had built the spinning frame, and in 1793 Dale coupled it with the power of the falls to set up mill factories employing 2500 people. One innovation followed another and in 1800 Dale's son-in-law, Robert Owen, began to revolutionise employment by providing houses for his workers, a school, cooperative store and dance hall. Although the cotton industry has declined, the village, including its handsome mill buildings, has been restored. The surrounding area, including the waterfalls, is now a nature reserve.
▶ *1 mile S of Lanark. Village and nature reserve daily.*

Putting on the Glasgow Style

Wherever you go in his native city, there are shrines to the architect and designer Charles Rennie Mackintosh

1 **Glasgow**
2 **The Hill House** ▶ *Upper Colquhoun Street, Helensburgh. 20 miles NW of Glasgow off A814. NTS. Daily pm Easter-Oct.*

Glasgow School of Art ▶ *167 Renfrew Street. For details of tours, Tel 0141 353 4526.*

The Willow Tea Rooms ▶ *217 Sauchiehall Street. Daily (including bank hols).*

The Lighthouse ▶ *11 Mitchell Lane. Mon-Sat, Sun pm.*

The Mackintosh House ▶ *Hunterian Art Gallery, Hillhead Street, Hillhead. Mon-Sat (closed bank hols).*

House for an Art Lover ▶ *Bellahouston Park, 10 Dumbreck Road. Daily Apr-Sept; Sat and Sun Oct-Mar; also some winter weekdays, Tel 0141 353 4770 for details.*

THE HILL HOUSE

He is the man you are sure to encounter in Scotland's biggest city, **Glasgow**. Its favourite artistic son, Charles Rennie Mackintosh (1868-1928), CRM for short, is everywhere – in museums, exhibitions, and in bricks and mortar – you can even sip a cup of tea with his ghost. One man's name and works is synonymous with the revered 'Glasgow Style'.

Mackintosh was prodigiously gifted: an innovative architect who also designed the interiors, furniture and fabrics for many of his buildings; the creator of original jewellery, glass and metalwork; a talented graphic artist and a painter of exquisite watercolours. In posterity's shorthand he is often described as the finest British exponent of Art Nouveau (the 'new art') – which is true, but it does not tell the whole story.

Curved lines behind straight ones

Mackintosh's art cannot be labelled. On the outside, his buildings have strong angular lines reminiscent of the Arts and Crafts Movement; the interiors leave an impression of subtle almost sensuous curves. It is this contrast that distinguishes Mackintosh from any of his contemporaries and puts him ahead of his time. Take **The Hill House**, designed for the publisher Walter Blackie and completed in 1904: its exterior (above) is all crisp-edged gables and rectilinear chimney stacks, but inside flowing curves predominate in everything – from the furniture, light fittings and wall clocks to the fabrics created by Margaret MacDonald, Mackintosh's wife and life-long collaborator. Adding to the impact, and apparent as soon as you enter the entrance hall, is the architect's mastery of light and space – a feature that also enhances his best-known building.

In 1896 Mackintosh won a competition to design the new **Glasgow School of Art**, where he had been a student less than ten years before. For the workaholic young architect, the time required to get from drawing board to final building must have been frustrating. An eight-year delay to secure extra funding meant that he was

40 when the building was finally completed. The wait was worth it. On either side of the asymetrical central entrance – with projecting windows set to one side of a flight of steps from the pavement to main door – are two long wings, dominated by the huge but elegant windows of the studios. The central portion is Art Nouveau in style – a graceful metal light support spans the steps, and the masonry around the door and first-floor balcony is decorated with flowing motifs. By contrast, the wings are simple – all about form following function – but the two styles fuse effortlessly. Inside, a number of rooms have been set aside as a permanent display. They contain some 200 pieces of furniture and other items such as light fittings and cutlery designed by the architect. There are also about 100 works on paper – watercolours, and architectural and interior design drawings.

Some of the items donated to the art school's public collection came from tea rooms designed for Kate Cranston, owner of the city's successful 'Willow' chain. At one of these, **The Willow Tea Rooms** in Sauchiehall Street, Mackintosh was given free rein to design every detail of the premises, down to the waitresses' dresses and the tea spoons. The Mackintosh-designed façade of No. 217, now a jewellers, is still there. Inside, two of the 'rooms' have been meticulously restored, and serve teas. The Gallery – where city gents met to discuss business – has a dark, restrained character, but in the amazing Room de Luxe Mackintosh's trademark high-back chairs are finished in silver – the better to reflect in the leaded mirror friezes that line the walls.

No doubt the customers at the tea rooms read *The Glasgow Herald* (now called *The Herald*), which in 1897 had moved to a new building designed by Mackintosh. The newspaper moved offices more than 20 years ago, but the old Mitchell Lane premises has taken on new life as **The Lighthouse**, with space dedicated to the Mackintosh Interpretation Centre, which contains an exhibition and displays about his life and work. These include design drawings and plans for the Glasgow School of Art – the school can be seen from high up in the gallery, originally designed as the building's water tower.

From public commissions to domestic comforts: before 6 Florentine Terrace, the Mackintoshes' home in 1906-14, was demolished in the early 1960s the contents were saved and are now displayed in **The Mackintosh House** – a series of re-created rooms in the Hunterian Art Gallery. It is a treasure trove of original pieces, completed with reproductions based on contemporary descriptions and photographs. But CRM's legacy lies even more in inspiration than what he left behind, as the **House for an Art Lover** demonstrates. This 1996 mansion was inspired by a portfolio of Mackintosh drawings submitted to a German magazine in 1901. Its rooms have been furnished and decorated by contemporary artists and craftspeople – all emulating and perpetuating the Glasgow Style.

SOUTHWEST SCOTLAND

Little Sparta

A poetic oasis created by an artist gardener

The writer, gardener and art curator Sir Roy Strong described Little Sparta as 'The most original contemporary garden in the country. Full of classical inscriptions and images, allusions and symbols.' In this oasis of imagination in the Pentland Hills, classical columns rise triumphant beside a series of ponds, planted areas and a collection of literary inscriptions carved into stone. The sculptor Ian Hamilton Finlay began to transform his land during the 1960s, inspired by the complex relationship between the wildness of nature and the nature of revolution.
▶ *A702 to Dolphinton, 20 miles SW of Edinburgh; turn W to Dunsyre and after 1 mile W take track to Little Sparta. Fri and Sun pm mid June–mid Oct.*

Chatelherault and Hamilton Mausoleum

Exuberant follies that echo with the ghosts of a powerful family

When the dukes of Hamilton embarked on a major new project on their estates south of Glasgow, no expense was spared. In 1732, the 5th Duke, who held the French title Duc de Chatelherault, commissioned William Adam to build a sumptuous folly shaped like a hunting lodge, which the architect described as 'the dog kennels of Hamiltons'. It fell into disrepair in the 20th century after the Hamiltons' grandiose palace nearby began to sink into a coal mine. In 1987 the lodge was restored.

The 10th Duke also had grand ideas, earning him the name 'Il Magnifico'. He commissioned a family tomb in 1842 with massive bronze doors – modelled on those of the Baptistry in Florence – and an octagonal chapel guarded by stone lions. The chapel has never been used for worship as it has an echo that lasts a resounding 15 seconds.
▶ *Chatelherault, Hamilton, M74 (Junction 6)/A723; visitor centre daily, lodge daily except Fri. Hamilton Mausoleum, 9 miles SE of Glasgow, M8/A725 or M74 (Junction 5 or 6); Tel 01698 328232 for details.*

Kirk o'Shotts

'The wee kirk without a steeple, and wi' the wee doo-cote belfry'

A nameless poet once wrote that the sun hated to shine on the mining town of Shotts, but as a centre for making gas-lamp standards in the Victorian age the cry went out, 'Shotts lights the world'. Now, the floodlit Kirk o' Shotts lights up the night sky from its 274m (900ft) perch high above the M8 motorway. For centuries the church doubled as a beacon of faith and a staging post for travellers. Indeed, the town is said to be named after Bertram Shotts, a giant highwayman.
▶ *On B7066, 3 miles S of M8 (Junction 5).*

The Whangie

A giant crack in the landscape

Local legend proclaims that The Whangie came about when the devil playfully whipped his tail across Auchineden Hill. The result was a great gash through the hill 15m (50ft) deep and 91m (300ft) long. A more prosaic explanation is that the fault occurred through glacial movement in the Ice Age. Either way, The Whangie is now an irresistible draw for walkers and rock climbers.

From the car park, one path leads directly to the summit, from which there are expansive views of Loch Lomond, Ben Lomond, the Kilpatrick Hills and Burncrooks Reservoir. A second path to the right divides: the higher track goes to the summit, the lower meanders along the hillside to The Whangie itself.
▶ *4 mile walk from Queen's View car park on A809 NW of Carbeth, 8 miles N of Glasgow. Climb over stile at back of car park, go up short slope to a second stile and follow path.*

Necropolis

A final resting place for the great and the good of Glasgow

A haunting Gothic beauty surrounds the rambling burial ground on the crest of a ridge running downhill towards the River Clyde above Glasgow Cathedral. Opened in 1831, the Necropolis was conceived as an ornamental garden of the dead, modelled on the Père Lachaise cemetery in Paris. It was here that many of the city's richest families, war heroes and captains of industry and commerce – including Thomas Lipton, the tea magnate – were interred. The tombs reflect the breadth of the wealth generated in this merchant city and the lofty ambitions of its creators, so you will find a Jews' enclosure close to Egyptian vaults and Roman-style catacombs. Dominant over all stands an obelisk of more than 62m (200ft), raised in tribute to the Protestant reformer John Knox, although he is buried in the rival city of Edinburgh.

▶ *Glasgow city centre. Daily, although times vary; Tel 0141 204 4400 to check.*

Glasgow's football shrines
Fantasies of club and country

Every Glasgow boy's dream is of becoming a top footballer. Supporting a team and its colours is an essential part of the culture of a city that has three of the world's hottest cauldrons of football emotion: **Hampden Park**, the national stadium; **Ibrox**, home of Rangers; and **Celtic Park**, the stadium of Celtic.

The oval-shaped 52,500 capacity Hampden Park is home to Queen's Park Football Club (the 'Spiders') and the Scotland team. Until Brazil's Maracana Stadium was built in 1950, Hampden was the largest football stadium in the world, squeezing in 149,547 fans, most of them standing, for a game against England in 1937. Hampden also houses a museum of Scottish football history.

An 'old firm' match between Rangers and Celtic is football rivalry at its most passionate. One game in 1939 at Ibrox – 40 years after the first at the ground – attracted a crowd of 118,567, a British league record. The capacity is now 50,500. Visit the trophy room to see silverware, porcelain and crystal won by Rangers since the club's first games in 1872. At Celtic Park, the beating heart of Celtic since 1892, more than 60,500 fans can watch the famous team in green and white hoops.

▶ *Hampden Park, 3 miles from centre, off A77; museum and tours daily, except match days, Tel 0141 616 6139. Ibrox, off M8 Junction 23; stadium tours Thurs, Fri & Sun, Tel 0871 702 1972. Celtic Park, 1½ miles E of centre; museum and tours daily, Tel 0141 551 4308.*

City Chambers
A grand theatre of local politics

The politicians of the second city of the Empire certainly knew how to celebrate their self-importance. Ten million bricks went into the construction of Glasgow's City Chambers. Scottish granite and Italian marble, alabaster, glass and mosaics were lavished on this Renaissance-style palace, which is still the city council's headquarters.

The building, designed by the Glasgow-trained William Young and opened by Queen Victoria in 1888, is grand in every respect. The spectacular Carrara marble staircase – the only three-storey example in Europe – overlooks floors 55m (180ft) long. In the Council Chamber a stained-glass dome rises to 9m (30ft) and the walls are lined in Spanish mahogany. In the 34m (110ft) long Banqueting Hall huge murals represent the city's history.

▶ *George Square, Glasgow city centre. Guided tours, Mon-Fri, Tel 0141 287 4018.*

Glasgow Science Centre
All-round views from Scotland's tallest structure

The 100m (328ft) high Glasgow Tower, rising from the south bank of the River Clyde, is the world's only tall structure that can rotate 360 degrees from the ground up. From its 'cabin', spectacular views stretch over Glasgow and 40 miles across the surrounding countryside. The curved bulk of the titanium-clad Science Mall lies next to the tower like a huge beached sea-creature. Inside, there are four floors of displays and hands-on exhibits offering insights into the worlds of science, health and medicine and the environment. A further strikingly bulbous structure contains an IMAX theatre, which has Scotland's biggest cinema screen at 24m by 18m (80ft by 60ft).

▶ *Pacific Quay, S side of Kingston Bridge, opposite Scottish Exhibition Centre (see above), off M8. Daily Apr-Oct; Tues-Sun Nov-Mar.*

BOLD OFFSPRING OF THE RE-BORN CLYDE
THE ARMADILLO

The Armadillo
Bold offspring of the re-born Clyde

If you stand on the Kingston Bridge crossing over the River Clyde, it is easy to see how the silver shell-like Clyde Auditorium – clad in shiny, reflective 'scales' of aluminium – got its nickname. The building, next to the Scottish Exhibition Centre, opened in 1990 and has become a landmark for Glasgow to rival Sydney's Opera House.

▶ *Finnieston Quay, take Clydeside Expressway from Glasgow city centre.*

The Burrell Collection
A shipping tycoon's treasure trove

Sir William Burrell bequeathed an astonishing collection of 8000 treasures to the people of Glasgow in 1944. It is also remarkable that, given their priceless value now, he never paid more than £14,500 for any of the items.

The museum built to display the bequest in 1983 has high glass walls that allow light to flood in against the lush green backdrop of the Pollok Country Park beyond. The breathtaking range of exhibits embraces ancient Egyptian relics, Chinese jade and bronzes, Turkish carpets, arms and armour, silver, glass and 600 paintings, including works by Degas, Bellini, Rembrandt and Raeburn. An integral part of the museum's structure are the monumental porches and arches Burrell bought from the William Randolph Hearst Collection. Burrell stipulated that exhibits must never be loaned out, so make the most of a visit.

▶ *2060 Pollokshaws Road, 3 miles S of Glasgow centre. Daily.*

FIFE & SOUTHEAST SCOTLAND

1 The Old Course, St Andrews **2** Scotland's Secret Bunker **3** Inchcolm Island

4 The Pineapple **5** Culross

The Old Course, St Andrews

Mystique and fiendish hazards at 'the home of golf'

It is every golfer's dream to tee off on the Old Course at St Andrews, the most famous 18 holes in the world. Although 'golfe' is first mentioned in a disapproving royal decree of 1457, some version of the game is thought to have been played on the dunes at St Andrews as early as the 12th century.

The Royal and Ancient Club, the sport's governing authority, was formed in 1754. Its clubhouse overlooks the baize-smooth 18th green and the 1st tee, which leads into the links, where traps such as the Swilken Burn and notorious Hell Bunker on the 5th have evolved. With six courses, this is Europe's largest golfing complex and home to the British Golf Museum.
▶ *Off A91, 24 miles E of M90 (Jct 8). Museum daily.*

Scotland's Secret Bunker

What if the bomb had dropped?

The Soviet bombers can be seen approaching on the radar screens and their likely targets have been plotted on a map. The Tannoy calls for the secretary of state to come down to the Ops Room as clocks tick off the final minutes before nuclear annihilation.

This nightmare from the Cold War is brought to life with chilling conviction in a bunker, hidden deep beneath a field, that was designed to be a regional government headquarters in the event of an atomic war. The base was decommissioned in 1992 but its maze of concrete corridors, dormitories, communications rooms and offices remains a sinister and intriguing reminder of the nuclear fear that once gripped Britain.
▶ *SE of St Andrews off B9131. Daily Apr-Oct.*

Inchcolm Island

Wildlife and ruins on the 'Iona of the East'

Seals, gulls and puffins are now the only permanent inhabitants of this magical little island in the Firth of Forth. But its ruins tell the story of its long, tempestuous past.

Just above the beach a stone-vaulted hut is said to be the cell of a hermit who gave shelter to Alexander I when he was marooned on Inchcolm in 1123. Behind stand the remains of the abbey that the king had built in thanks for his deliverance. Despite being pillaged by the English, it is still one of Scotland's best-preserved monastic buildings. Tunnels and gun emplacements built during two world wars are the scars of more recent conflicts.
▶ *Boats from South Queensferry, S of Forth Bridge. HS. Daily Apr-Oct.*

The Pineapple

Fruit on the grand scale

Delightful and completely ludicrous, the 14m (46ft) high stone pineapple in Dunmore Park is one of Britain's most bizarre buildings. Built in 1761, it contains an elevated summerhouse from which the lairds of Dunmore could survey their walled garden and glasshouses, where they proudly cultivated the exotic fruit.

The folly was restored in 1974 and is let as holiday accommodation.
▶ *Dunmore Park, 7 miles SE of Stirling, off A905. NTS. Garden daily. To book folly, Tel 01628 825925 (Landmark Trust).*

Culross

From industrial boom town to Scotland's prettiest village

The cobbled lanes around the Mercat Cross in the centre of Culross seem frozen in a time warp of architectural perfection. The colour-washed houses with pantiled roofs and crow-step gables date from the late 16th and early 17th centuries, when the village was Scotland's wealthiest town. An enterprising laird, Sir George Bruce, was largely responsible for this prosperity.

Sir George built ironworks and salt pans and dug a coal mine that extended beneath the Firth of Forth with an off-shore shaft that was a wonder of the age. His splendid home, **Culross Palace**, was bought by the newly formed National Trust for Scotland in 1931, when the village was falling into ruin. Since then the Trust has restored many of its properties.
▶ *5 miles E of Kincardine off A985. NTS. Palace daily June-Aug; Thur-Mon Apr-May and Sept-Oct.*

SCOTLAND

Forth Rail Bridge

Victorian engineering genius at its most masterful

Best seen from the waterfront at South Queensferry, the mile-long bridge over the Firth of Forth (right), completed in 1890, is a triumphant celebration of the 19th-century's faith in industry and science.

The rail bridge's massive, double-cantilevered spans make no attempt to blend with the environment, treating nature as a challenge to be conquered by man's new world of iron and steam. The sturdy web of giant tubes and girders rejoices in its muscular development and strength, proclaiming that the railway is striding over water as it takes the march of progress to the North.

Contrast this bravado approach with the delicate appearance of the 1964 suspension bridge, tip-toeing across the Firth half a mile upstream. Each bridge is a work of art, expressive of its age.
▶*A90 at South Queensferry.*

Grangemouth

Technology as performance art

Against a backdrop of romantic hills, flares belch flames into the sky, steam swirls out of cooling towers and sunlight glitters off science-fiction-like pipework. BP's refinery and petrochemical works at Grangemouth has a strange and fearful beauty. The plant functions as a huge machine, processing 4,550,000 litres (1,001,000 gallons) of fuel a day. Take the public road running through the site for the best views.
▶*20 miles W of Edinburgh on A904.*

Falkirk Wheel

Lifting canals into the 21st century

Spectacular in scale, thrilling in design and hypnotic in its steady motion, the world's first rotating boat-lift, built in 2001, raises eight boats at a time from an 18th-century canal to a 21st-century aqueduct 33m (110ft) above. Plans to reopen the inland waterways that linked Edinburgh to Glasgow until the 1930s faced a major challenge: the difference in levels between the Forth & Clyde and the Union canals. The giant, futuristic wheel of steel and concrete, weighing 1800 tonnes when filled with water, provided the solution.
▶*2 miles W of Falkirk.*

Calton Hill

An acropolis of follies

In pursuit of the accolade 'The Athens of the North', Georgian Edinburgh acquired its own acropolis of monuments and ruins on Calton Hill, high above the New Town. A massive portico of Doric columns dominates the scene – all that was constructed of a Napoleonic war memorial intended to be a full-scale copy of the Parthenon.

Scarcely less bizarre is the telescope-shaped tower commemorating Lord Nelson. The 'time-ball' at its top was designed to drop at 1 o'clock every day as a signal to shipping on the Forth. From the hill's grassy slopes there are fine views of Edinburgh Castle, Princes Street and the red cliffs of Salisbury Crags.
▶*Central Edinburgh, off Leith Street.*

Charlotte Square

Style and wealth in Edinburgh's Georgian New Town

In the late 18th century the heart of Scotland's capital city shifted north from the medieval lanes around the Royal Mile to a modern New Town. The architectural climax of the development was Charlotte Square, designed by Robert Adam in 1791. This is one of Britain's finest Georgian squares, with a perfect composition of classical façades with richly decorated columns. The square soon became Edinburgh's most fashionable address, and the lifestyle of its first inhabitants can be seen at No. 7, the **Georgian House**, where rooms have been returned to their original appearance.
▶*Georgian House, 7 Charlotte Square. NTS. Daily Mar-Nov.*

VICTORIAN ENGINEERING GENIUS AT ITS MOST MASTERFUL

FORTH RAIL BRIDGE

FIFE & SOUTHEAST SCOTLAND

Royal Botanic Garden

Rain forest immune to a cold climate

On winter days the outside world may lie blanketed in snow, but in the Tropical Aquatic House a banana tree dangles fruit above a steamy pool in a dense rain forest. It is one of ten environments that have been created at the Botanic in conservatories dating from the 1830s to 1970s. In Britain's tallest Palm House the trees almost touch the 21m (70ft) high roof; and a summer highlight is an Amazonian water lily with pads 2m (7ft) wide that can support a weight of 75kg (11 stones 8lb).
▶*Inverleith Row, Edinburgh. Daily.*

Landform, National Gallery of Modern Art

A garden that became a sculpture

Swirling forms of grassy banks and terraces enclose crescents of water that reflect the changing skies and ripple with the breeze. Landform, created in the grounds of the National Gallery in 2001 by the American architect Charles Jencks, is a new take on the old tradition of sculpting landscapes into art. Although artworks are displayed within its green embrace, this is not a sculpture-garden but a garden that is sculpture.
▶*Belford Road, Edinburgh. Daily.*

THE FORMIDABLE FORTRESS OF A WARLORD CLAN

TANTALLON CASTLE

Royal Yacht *Britannia*

Glimpses of royal life on board ship

The distinctive lines and paintwork of the Royal Yacht stimulate a thrill of instant recognition on Leith's rejuvenated waterfront. Crewed by 244 officers and men, *Britannia* sailed more than a million miles between her launch on the River Clyde in 1953 and decommissioning in 1997.

The 125m (412ft) long ship cost more than £2 million to build. It was used not just for royal tours, but also for private holidays and honeymoons away from the world's press, a dual role that is intriguingly apparent once you are on board. The dining-room table can seat 96, there are reception rooms for up to 250, the drawing room would grace a stately home and the on-deck garage houses a Rolls-Royce. Yet the private rooms, such as the Queen's own modest bedroom, are surprisingly plain in their furnishings.

Five tonnes of luggage would accompany the Queen on board for a state visit, including her jewels and Malvern water for her tea.
▶ *Ocean Terminal, Leith. Daily.*

Rosslyn Chapel

Light and dark in a carved contest

Set above a wooded gorge with a ruined cliff-top castle, the chapel, completed in 1490, is a place of supernatural secrets, coded messages and pagan symbols. The interior is almost overwhelming, for every column, arch and vault has been richly carved with marvellous designs. Along with the expected saints and angels, there are devils, monsters and Green Men, dancers and musicians, geometric patterns and Masonic symbols. Among many oddities, avarice is illustrated as a virtue and there are carvings of cobs of maize, made before Columbus sailed to the New World. The Holy Grail is said to lie concealed in the vaults, guarded by Crusader knights.
▶ *8 miles S of Edinburgh off A701 Penicuik road. Daily.*

Museum of Flight

The conquest of the air – from the era of biplanes to the missile age

With its hangars, control tower and Nissen-hutted township still remarkably intact, East Fortune airfield is one of the best preserved wartime aerodromes in Britain and an appropriately evocative location for the Museum of Scotland's collection of historic aircraft. Exhibits range from warplanes to experimental craft, including the perilously tiny 1930s autogyros that, it was believed, might replace cars as the transport of the future. Among the more modern exhibits are a Lightning fighter, a Vulcan bomber that saw action in the Falklands and Concorde. Every July the airfield roars back into life when it hosts the three-day Festival of Flight.
▶ *3 miles E of Haddington off A1 Dunbar road. Daily Apr-Oct; Sat-Sun Nov-Mar.*

Tantallon Castle

The formidable fortress of a warlord clan

Protected on three sides by 30m (100ft) cliffs rising from the North Sea and with a curtain wall of dusky sandstone to its front, Tantallon was always an intimidating fortress. From the 14th to the 16th centuries it was the stronghold of the 'Red Douglases', a family notorious for murder, plunder and treason. The last of many sieges that the castle endured came in 1651 when 91 Royalist 'moss troopers', or guerrilla fighters, defended it against an army of 3000 Parliamentarians under the command of General Monk. After 12 days the besiegers' cannons had blown holes in the once-impregnable walls – scars that are still apparent on the ruined ramparts.
▶ *4 miles E of North Berwick on A198 Dunbar road. HS. Daily Apr-Sept; Sat-Wed Oct-Mar.*

St Abb's Head

Never mind that the chicks can't fly, their time has come to leave the nest

Between May and July, more than 70,000 sea birds nest on dramatic cliffs to the north of the pretty little fishing harbour of St Abbs. The view from the footpath that climbs and dips along this jagged shore reveals an avian metropolis in which every ledge and cranny is occupied by shrieking birds, mostly guillemots and razorbills. To the consternation of onlookers who may not be ornithologists, the chicks of both species leave the nest while still incapable of flight and make a death-defying plunge into the foaming sea 30m (100ft) below. Seals and puffins may be seen offshore, where the crystal-clear water attracts divers to explore a seabed noted for its rich, exotic fauna, making this one of the foremost marine reserves in Britain. On the headland there is a lighthouse (not open to the public) dating from 1862, and on Kirk Hill there are traces of the monastery established in 643 by St Abb, a Northumbrian princess.
▶ *15 miles N of Berwick-upon-Tweed on B6438 off A1 Dunbar road. Daily.*

EDINBURGH CASTLE

At the heart of the Scottish capital

Walk through one thousand years of Edinburgh's past when you step out along the Royal Mile

1 Edinburgh

Few streets in the world cram in as much history and legend as the long, straight stone-paved thoroughfare that cuts through the Old Town of **Edinburgh**. The Royal Mile runs from the Castle to Holyroodhouse, a distance of one Scots mile (1980yd). It is overlooked by tall stone tenements, churches and great public buildings that have defined the city's character.

The **Castle** (daily), on its high bastion of volcanic cliffs, has guarded Edinburgh for nine centuries. Mons Meg, the huge gun that was Scotland's ultimate deterrent in the 15th century, is stationed on the battlements. Its barrel weighs 5.7 tonnes and could fire a 150kg (330lb) shot two miles, but 100 men were needed to transport it.

Beyond the castle's Esplanade, where the Military Tattoo is held in August, every block has something to satisfy the curious visitor. **Gladstone's Land** (NTS, daily Easter–Oct) is a tenement restored to its original condition and provides a glimpse of life in 17th-century Edinburgh. Behind the High Street's fine façades, the old city was a labyrinth of narrow 'wynds' (alleys) that descended the slopes to either side. Their tunnel-like entrances still lead off the pavement to fragments of dwellings that have survived. **Mary King's Close** lives on as a ghostly presence and lies deep beneath the City Chambers – the walls of its houses support the Georgian building overhead. In a maze of darkened vaults, doors open into long-abandoned homes with rusty fireplaces and stencilled decorations on their walls. Some 500 people died here during an outbreak of plague in 1642 and spectral figures have been seen by a few visitors. Call 08702 430160 to book a tour of the close.

City of devoted and restless spirits

Across the street, 11th century **St Giles' Cathedral** (daily, Sun pm) is presided over by the spirit and statue of John Knox, the Protestant reformer. **John Knox House** (daily Jul-Aug; Mon-Sat Sept-Jun), farther along the High Street, is a finely restored late 15th-century house, with oak panelling and a painted ceiling. Canongate forms the last half of the Royal Mile and was a separate community that spread up the ridge from the now-ruined Abbey of Holyrood. From the early 12th century the Augustinian monastery served as a palace for Scotland's kings, who hunted on the hills of Arthur's Seat and Salisbury Crags in its park. In the adjacent **Palace of Holyroodhouse** (for opening times, Tel 020 7766 7300) Mary, Queen of Scots witnessed the murder of her lover Rizzio – a stain on the floor of her apartments is said to be his blood.

Many myths and traditions are associated with the Royal Mile. It is customary to spit when passing over the paved **Heart of Midlothian** on the site of an old prison where traitors' heads were displayed on spikes. There are tales of a ghostly piper who plays in a secret tunnel under the High Street and of haunted vaults beneath the South Bridge. Even problems encountered during construction of the new Scottish Parliament building have been blamed on spirits disturbed by the development. The latest addition to the Royal Mile is still controversial. Is it exhilarating modern architecture or an affront to good taste? A street that began beneath feudal walls and canon now ends in a democracy of furious debate.

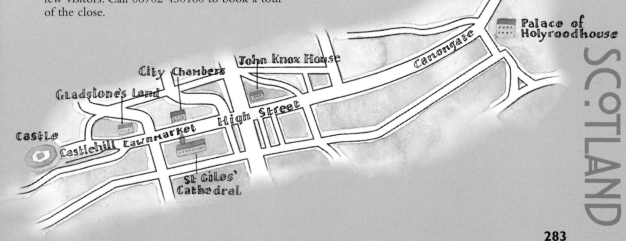

FIFE & SOUTHEAST SCOTLAND

Edin's Hall Broch
Solid protection built to shrug off the legions' siege machines

The Iron Age chieftain who built this broch or fortified tower on the slopes of Cockburn Law took no chances. In an age when the most powerful artillery piece was the catapult used by Roman armies, he built the walls 6m (19ft) thick: strong enough to take a hit from a high-explosive shell.

Still head-high, the 1st-century dry-stone work contains an entrance passage, guard chambers and the bottom steps of a staircase that led to the top of the walls. Beyond lies a space 17m (55ft) across, where the wooden structure of the chieftain's living quarters would have stood. By far the most southerly example of a broch, a type of defencework that originated in the Northern Isles (see page 299), Edin's Hall occupies a stunning site overlooking the meandering Whiteadder river.
▶ *5 miles N of Duns, off A6112 Grantshouse road, on minor road signed to village of Abbey St Bathans. Daily.*

Manderston
Best marble for the guest rooms – and the dairy, and the stables

When Sir James Miller married Eveline Curzon, the daughter of Lord Scarsdale and sister of the Viceroy of India, in 1893, wealth was matched with aristocracy. It was largely to impress her family and friends that Sir James decided to transform his relatively modest 18th-century home into Scotland's grandest country house.

'Money is of no importance whatsoever,' Sir James told the architect of Manderston, John Kinross, when work began in 1901. Reflecting this contempt for cost, the house is quite mind-boggling in its opulence. The staircase is made of silver, floors and columns of rare marble. Walls are hung with silk, pelmets coated in gold leaf. It could all be hideously vulgar, but the patina of age has burnished glitter into elegance and the quality of workmanship is so superb that the extravagance becomes a celebration of neoclassical design. Opulence extends beyond the reception rooms and apartments. The barrel-vaulted stables contain teak stalls, brass and marble fittings and tiled troughs. In the 22ha (54 acre) gardens Lady Miller and her friends would occasionally play at being dairymaids, making butter in a marble dairy modelled on medieval cloisters.
▶ *2 miles E of Duns on A6105. Thur and Sun May-Sept.*

Tweed Walk
Upstream to a borders fortress, then a return beside shaded pools

This gentle 3 mile circuit, starting and ending beside the bridge in Peebles (see map, right), explores one of the River Tweed's most beguiling stretches. The high point of the stroll is Neidpath Castle, on the north bank. In this most romantic of Borders towers dark stairways lead to rooms that have been decaying since the 18th century. The ceiling in the bedroom used by Mary, Queen of Scots has collapsed, exposing a medieval vault, and a cupboard door creaks open to reveal a hidden 'sleeping chamber'. Half a mile further on, the path crosses a disused railway viaduct to return to the town along a wooded slope overlooking salmon pools.
▶ *Peebles town centre. Tel 01721 720333 for castle opening times.*

Jedburgh Abbey
Stones that defy the ravages of time

Some ruins demand a leap of the imagination, but not Jedburgh Abbey, the largely intact shell of which instantly conveys a sense of past splendour. Founded by David I in about 1138, and still unfinished when sacked by an English army in 1544, the abbey is a mix of round and pointed arches – Romanesque and Gothic – with delicate stone carving and a stunning vista down the nave. A small museum contains a model of the church in its heyday, along with artefacts found during excavations. These include a beard comb made from walrus ivory, which possibly belonged to an Anglo-Saxon prince whose hall pre-dated the abbey.
▶ *Jedburgh town centre. HS. Daily.*

Abbotsford
Prompts for the writer's imagination

Sir Walter Scott's home has all the romance of one of his novels. He could not resist a suit of armour, broadsword or set of thumbscrews, particularly if a patriotic provenance was claimed for it. The result is a bizarre collection of historic artefacts and fakes, displayed in a house that borrows from the architecture of abbeys, castles and medieval palaces.
▶ *2 miles W of Melrose off B6360 Selkirk road. Tel 01896 752043 for opening times.*

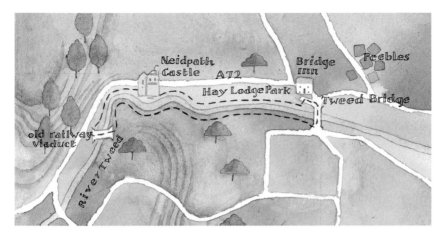

Along the riverbank to the castle's walls *From Tweed Bridge in Peebles follow the lane past the Bridge Inn to the riverside path. Walk upstream across Hay Lodge Park and continue through woodland to Neidpath Castle, which is reached by an indistinct, steep path on the right. On leaving the castle, rejoin the path and continue upstream to an old railway viaduct. Cross the viaduct to the opposite bank and return on the path signposted to Peebles.*

Scott's View
Captivating exterior of a mythical hollow kingdom

It is said that the horses pulling Sir Walter Scott's funeral cortège came to a halt, as if reined in by an unseen hand, when they reached this view of the three Eildon Hills across the Tweed gorge above Leaderfoot. The writer is far from alone in falling under their spell: the artist J.M.W. Turner made the hills the subject of a fine engraving, and folk tales claim they contain a hidden realm – the fairy queen's according to one story, that of a sleeping King Arthur says another. Such stories may originate from a time when the capital of an ancient tribe stood on one hill – of which the ramparts and foundations of some 300 dwellings are still visible.
▶ *Hills, 1 mile S of Melrose. View, 3 miles W of Melrose on B6356, signed off A68 Jedburgh-Lauder road.*

Traquair House
Slàinte! Fine flavours of history and ale, fermented by the Stuarts

The Stuart family have occupied this historic house near Innerleithen for more than 500 years and their long tenure is delightfully apparent in a home that has scarcely altered since the early 18th century. Little, it would seem, has ever been thrown out and the clutter of extraordinary possessions ranges from a cradle in which Mary, Queen of Scots rocked the infant James VI to a 400-year-old pocket calculator made from tiny wheels of bone. In 1965 the 20th laird revived a medieval brewery underneath the chapel, which now produces celebrated ales.
▶ *2 miles S of Innerleithen on B709. Daily Apr-Oct; Sat-Sun Nov.*

Carter Bar
Eyeball to eyeball, steel to steel

The most dramatic border-crossing between England and Scotland lies on the wild Cheviot escarpment, 418m (1371ft) above sea level. To the south lie miles of rugged moorland; to the north the land drops steeply to a gentler Borders landscape. One of the oldest national frontiers in the world, established in 1018, passes through this spot, and for centuries Scots and English clashed in these debated lands: the last official skirmish, Redeswire fray, was fought nearby in 1575 and resulted in the deaths of 20 or more English yeomen.
▶ *10 miles S of Jedburgh on A68.*

CENTRAL & NORTHEAST SCOTLAND

1 Fort George 2 Culloden 3 Clava Cairns 4 Findhorn

Fort George

A massive fortress built to control the Highlands

Constructed in response to the Jacobite uprising of 1745, and still serving as a military garrison, Fort George is the finest example of Georgian military architecture in Britain. Covering some 6.5ha (16 acres) and designed to house 2000 troops, the fort's most formidable defences are, significantly, on the landward side, where an outer bastion, a moat with a drawbridge, inner ramparts and artillery batteries were intended to deter any further thoughts of Highland insurrection.

Restored interiors of barrack-rooms bring to life the tough existence of 18th and 19th-century soldiers, and the former magazine houses the Seafield Collection of Georgian weaponry. On a more pacific note, walk along the ramparts to try to spot dolphins in the Moray Firth.
▶ *11 miles NE of Inverness off A96. HS. Daily.*

Culloden

Haunting atmosphere at the site of a grim moorland battle

On April 16, 1746, more than 5500 Highland clansmen who had risen to the standard of Prince Charles Edward Stuart (Bonnie Prince Charlie) made ready for battle. They met the full might of the British army – 9000 soldiers commanded by the Duke of Cumberland – on a bleak expanse of moorland above Inverness.

Demoralised by a long retreat, outnumbered and out-gunned, the Jacobites were slaughtered by their Hanoverian opponents and their cause became a lost romantic dream. The battlefield remains a desolate and haunted spot. Just a few hundred yards of scrub and bog separate flags that mark the Jacobites' front line from the cairns and hummocks of clan graves at the limit of their last charge. At least a thousand men died in that final hail of musket-fire and grape-shot. Even now, heather will not grow on these grassy mounds. Some clan chiefs were subsequently executed for high treason and the Highland way of life was brutally suppressed, but the Prince evaded capture for five months before escaping into exile.
▶ *5 miles E of Inverness on B9006. NTS. Daily. Visitor centre daily.*

Clava Cairns

A meticulously constructed trio of prehistoric mausoleums

Sheltered in a copse of beech trees, the cemetery of Bronze Age tombs at Balnuaran of Clava is known traditionally as 'The Good Stones'. Formed in a style only found in this area, each of the three cairns is edged with a stone kerb and surrounded by a circle of standing stones. The cairns have chambers at their hearts, which, although hidden from the outside world, are open to the sky. Recent experiments suggest that their architecture possesses a curious acoustic quality that distorts and muffles sound. People still leave offerings of flowers, gems and shells at this intriguing burial site, just as prehistoric visitors did, judging from deposits discovered here.
▶ *5½ miles E of Inverness, signed from B9006. HS. Daily.*

Findhorn

New-age village where you can experience the good life

The village that has grown over the past 30 years on a spit of sand and woods by Burghead Bay is unlike any other community in Britain. From a car park at the entrance, quiet lanes wind beneath the trees past caravans and tents, modest shacks and large, sophisticated 'eco-homes' with roofs of living turf.

Findhorn was founded in the 1960s as a self-sustaining commune and is now a thriving centre of New Age enterprise with around 80 full-time residents. Some visitors are attracted by a range of courses and a lively programme of music and performing arts. Others come to shop for organic food and craft-works, or just to absorb Findhorn's unique, idealistic spirit.
▶ *5 miles N of Forres on B9011. Visitor centre Tel 01309 690311.*

Wee dram of the national drink

Some of the finest whiskies are produced in distilleries around the fast-flowing waters of the River Spey

1 Craigellachie Hotel
2 Dallas Dhu
3 Benromach
4 Glenlivet
5 Cardhu
6 Glenfarclas
7 Glen Grant
8 Glenfiddich
9 Strathisla

According to tradition, whisky, like the Gaelic language, was introduced to Scotland by Irish settlers during the 6th century AD. By 1500 it was being drunk by James IV at Holyrood and in the 18th century it was illicitly distilled in most Highland glens. Now *uisge beatha*, the water of life, is consumed throughout the world.

Most whisky is blended, but connoisseurs prefer a single malt, the distinctive product of a single distillery. Almost every glen above the Spey has a distillery, producing the traditionally smooth and mild malts of the area. At the **Craigellachie Hotel** (Tel 01340 881204) a customer who asks for 'Scotch' in the Craich Bar must choose between 400 different drams. At **Dallas Dhu** (HS, daily, closed Thur and Fri in winter) a 19th-century distillery has been preserved with its original equipment. From here a signposted 'Whisky Trail' leads to eight other sites where the whole process can be seen.

The magic is in the making

Distilling is more alchemy than science. The distilleries, unmistakable for their curious pagoda roofs that protect the drying-kilns from rain, use equipment and skills that have been unchanged

for generations. Wherever you go, the process has the same basic elements – malted barley steeped in water, fermenting wort foaming in wooden vats, spirit distilling in enormous bulbous copper stills. But each distillery has its secrets and traditions: the source of its water, the precise shape of its stills, the types of cask in which the whisky is matured. The character of every malt is different and cannot be mistaken for a rival's.

Most distilleries were established in the 19th century, after draconian taxes on whisky were lifted. The smallest, **Benromach** (Tel 01309 675968), was rescued in recent years, reopening in 1999, a century after its foundation. **Glenlivet** (Tel 01340 821720) and **Cardhu** (Tel 01340 872555) both date from 1824 – two of the earliest distilleries. At **Glenfarclas** (Tel 01807 500257) the Grant family have made their malts since 1836. Other Grants established **Glen Grant** (Tel 01340 832118) in 1840 and **Glenfiddich** (Tel 01340 820373) in the 1880s. To visit the oldest distillery, **Strathisla** (Tel 01542 783044), founded in 1786, head for Keith where you can take a nip of a 12-year-old single malt in the Victorian opulence of the Dram Room.

CENTRAL & NORTHEAST SCOTLAND

Sueno's Stone

Images from the front line inscribed in sandstone

Overlooked by trim suburban houses, this thousand-year-old monolith bears a message from the dawn of Scotland's history. Intricately carved depictions of scenes from an unknown battle cover the 6.5m (21ft) high stone. Dating from around AD 900, it may record a Dark Ages victory by the Scots over the tribe of the northern Picts. The conflict is recorded chronologically, starting at the top with cavalry, archers and foot-soldiers facing up to fight and ending at the base with an illustration of decapitated prisoners. A cross on the western face is inscribed above a panel that may depict the coronation of a king to rule both the victorious and defeated sides.
► *1 mile E of Forres centre, signed off A96.*

The Osprey Centre

A rare sight in the British skies

In early summer, binocular-clad birdwatchers gather in a hide to view ospreys feeding fish to their chicks in a huge nest of twigs and branches on a nearby tree – hidden cameras also relay live pictures to the Centre. Once persecuted as a pest, the birds disappeared from Britain from 1916 until 1954, when a pair was spotted nesting by Loch Garten. Their descendants still return here each year.

The ospreys arrive in spring and stay to hatch and rear their young until mid August, when they begin their long migration back to West Africa. Early on a springtime morning, visitors may also see capercaillie (a species of grouse the size of a turkey) performing their dramatic 'lek', or mating dance, accompanied by raucous cries.
► *At Loch Garten, 8 miles NE of Aviemore, signed off B970. RSPB. Daily Apr-Aug.*

Rothiemurchas Forest

Primeval woods where wild cats still hunt for prey

The landscape around the shores of Loch an Eilein has hardly altered in 8000 years. Gnarled Scots pines, with an undergrowth of heather, juniper and bilberry, are remnants of the great Caledonian Forest that covered much of north Scotland after the last Ice Age and was gradually destroyed by man's demands for timber, fuel and grazing land. This surviving enclave, replanted and preserved for centuries, remains a rare and precious habitat for red squirrels, pine marten and some of Scotland's last remaining wild cats, which inhabit rocky outcrops by the loch.
► *5 miles S of Aviemore, signed off B970.*

Ben Macdui

An inhuman presence in the hills

The Cairngorm mountains form a huge, trackless wilderness of bare rock slopes and moorland around Ben Macdui, Britain's second highest peak at 1309m (4296ft). Far from any road, this can be a frightening place when clouds shroud the cliffs and cries echo unheeded through the empty corries.

Some climbers have reported meetings here with a terrifying apparition. Slow, heavy footfalls may be heard that seem to creep up ever closer from behind. Then, looming from the mist, a grey phantom appears, taller than a man, with indistinct, inhuman features. An Fear Liath Mor, the Big Grey Man of Ben Macdui, may be a figment of the imagination or a trick of the light, but it has troubled otherwise quite fearless mountaineers.
► *Cairngorms can be seen, and climbed, from Glenmore Forest Park, off A9 at Coylumbridge.*

Crathes Castle and Garden

Sculpted hedges and secret gardens of a romantic fortress home

The 300-year-old yew hedges that surround Crathes Castle's formal gardens form huge banks of greenery trimmed into fantastic shapes. Tunnels through the branches lead to a series of enclosures with colourful herbaceous borders, terraces and fountains. The castle, completed in 1596, is a fine example of a Scottish tower house, built both for comfort and security. There are colourfully painted ceilings in the bedrooms and a 17th century oak ceiling in the Long Gallery. Above the fireplace in the Great Hall hangs the legendary Horn of Leys, an ivory drinking horn given to the Burnett family by Robert the Bruce in 1323 as a token of their right to own the land.

▶ *3 miles E of Banchory on A93. NTS. Castle daily Apr-Oct, Wed-Sun Nov-Mar. Gardens daily all year.*

Dunnottar Castle
Reliving the long, bloody history of an impregnable cliff-top fortress

With battlements and towers that cling precariously to a headland rising sheer out of the sea, Dunnottar is an awe-inspiring fortress. Even now, the steep approach seems almost unassailable, climbing up through tunnels and defiles with gun ports menacing at every turn. Within the citadel itself, which lies spread across a plateau of 3.5ha (9 acres), ruined halls and towers line the courts and lawns around a deep freshwater well. There is even a lion's den, which later also housed a bear – both beasts were pets of the castle's owner in the 17th century.

Bombardment in the Civil War reduced Dunnottar to a ruin. However, in 1685, a dungeon, which can still be seen, was used to house 122 men and 45 women – Covenanters, who refused to accept the spiritual authority of the king and use the new prayer book. They were held there for ten weeks, in unspeakable conditions. Two fell to their deaths attempting to escape.

▶ *2 miles S of Stonehaven off A92. Daily Easter-Oct, Fri-Mon Nov-Easter.*

Edzell Castle
A Renaissance garden to fire the mind and stimulate the senses

The garden Sir David Lindsay laid out in 1604 at his estate at Edzell was intended as much for the cultivation of the mind as for horticultural display. The high walls that cut it off from the distractions of the outside world are decorated with stone plaques, carved with symbols of the cardinal virtues, the arts and the planetary deities, while to satisfy the senses there are recesses for scented flowers and nesting spots for songbirds. A pavilion still houses the table around which Sir David's friends gathered to contemplate nature, philosophy and art. A stroll around its geometric flowerbeds and miniature box hedging – incorporating heraldic symbols and Lindsay family mottoes – is like a tour through the spirit of the Renaissance.

▶ *6 miles N of Brechin on minor road, off B966. HS. Daily Apr-Sept; Sat-Wed Oct-Mar.*

Seaton Cliffs
Weaving through a bizarre cliffscape haunted by smugglers

Northeast of Arbroath, the steep red sandstone cliffs have been eroded by the sea into weird sculpted forms that can be viewed from the safety of a nature trail. The 3 mile walk passes the Needle E'e, a window punched through solid rock, and the sinister profile of The Deil's Heid, a weathered off-shore stack. There is also Dickmont's Den, a deep, hidden cove and secret lair of smugglers in the 18th century. At the end a natural arch, known as the Dark Cave, tunnels through the headland out into the bright bay beyond.

▶ *Signed from Victoria Park, Arbroath, NE of Dundee on A92.*

Glamis Castle
A ghost-spotting tour

Seat of the Earls of Strathmore, Glamis is a vast, fairy-tale castle bristling with towers and pointed turrets. It is said to have a secret room. Some say it is haunted by a band of fugitives who were bricked up in their hiding place; others that the 4th Earl and his cronies sit there, playing cards with the devil; and some believe it is the lair of the 'Glamis Monster', an heir to the earldom, born half-man, half-beast. There is also talk of a Grey Lady in the chapel, a tongueless woman on the lawn, and a crazed figure striding across the roof on 'The Mad Earl's Walk'.

▶ *6 miles SW of Forfar on A94. Daily Mar-Dec.*

Discovery Point
Evocative memorial to courage and endurance

Discovery, the elegant wooden ship used for Captain Scott's first expedition to Antarctica in 1901, sits by Dundee quayside, seemingly ready to set sail. On board, the crew's quarters, chart room and laboratory recall the spirit of adventure of a century ago, with the table laid for dinner in the officers' saloon and Scott's uniform hanging in his cabin. Up on deck, the crow's-nest is carved with the initials of men who spent hours on end within its cramped confines, 18m (60ft) aloft in freezing winds. The expedition endured two winters stuck in ice, before returning to Britain late in 1904.

▶ *Dundee, off A85 (Riverside Drive), near station and W of Tay Road Bridge. Daily.*

CENTRAL & NORTHEAST SCOTLAND

15 Aonach Mor **16** Glen Coe **17** The Hollow Mountain

Aonach Mor
A journey to frozen heights

Even when the glens below Aonach Mor are bathed in spring sunshine, a 15 minute ride by cable car can take winter-sports enthusiasts, climbers and sightseers to an alpine wonderland of ice and snow at an altitude of 655m (2150ft). There is a cafeteria at journey's end with colossal views across the Highlands from its windows. Chair lifts and walk routes lead still higher up the mountain and from the 1221m (4006ft) summit the notoriously

A SECRET GLEN SCARRED BY INFAMOUS KILLINGS
GLEN COE

dangerous north face of Ben Nevis – Britain's highest mountain at 1343m (4406ft) – can be seen across a deep, intimidating corrie.

▶ *4 miles NE of Fort William signed off A82. Daily except mid Nov-Christmas.*

Glen Coe
A secret glen scarred by infamous killings

A long, steep-sided pass overshadowed by ferocious mountains, Glen Coe is an intimidating place, with an atmosphere haunted by memories of massacre. On February 13, 1692, 38 Macdonalds were slaughtered here and their houses burnt by government troops under the command of Captain Campbell of Glen Lyon. For the lowland troops involved, Highland clansmen were barbarians and cattle thieves. Loyal only to their chief, the Macdonalds of Glen Coe pillaged lowland farms and drove their stolen cattle north across the wastes of Rannoch Moor. Here, above the Meeting of Three Waters, the rustled livestock were concealed in Coire Gabhail, a high, secret glen between the hills.

The glen, also called the Lost Valley, can be entered only through a narrow defile following a tree-lined gorge. Then, unexpectedly, the landscape opens up into level pastures that could hold a thousand head of stolen cattle. This is still a place apart, secretive and strange, enclosed within majestic hills. For lowlanders 300 years ago it was the fastness of a primitive and despised culture.

▶ *From car park 1 mile W of waterfall on A82, follow path down to bridge by Meeting of Three Waters. Cross River Coe and follow path that climbs beside stream up into Coire Gabhail.*

The Hollow Mountain
The secret at Ben Cruachan's heart

A tunnel more than half-a-mile long takes minibus passengers from the shore of Loch Awe to a hydroelectric power station buried 370m (1200ft) beneath Ben Cruachan. The cavernous Machine Hall – the height of a seven-storey building and the size of a football pitch – looks like a sci-fi film set. The plant is ingeniously designed to meet fluctuations in demand for electricity. If 10 million kettles are switched on during a commercial break the generators whirr instantly to life, driven by water from the reservoir above. In off-peak periods, they run in reverse – replenishing the top reservoir with water from Loch Awe.

▶ *3 miles W of Lochawe on A85 Inverlochy-Oban road. Daily Easter-Nov, winter Tel 01866 822618.*

CENTRAL & NORTHEAST SCOTLAND

Meigle Pictish stones

A new twist on King Arthur

Many locals in Meigle believe that a large earth mound in the churchyard is the grave of Queen Guinevere. They say she was abducted by a Pict, Prince Mordred, who held her captive in his fort on Barry Hill. When King Arthur rescued her, he ungallantly condemned her to be torn apart by wild beasts, perhaps suspecting that she had enjoyed some aspects of captivity. Carvings on a 9th-century cross-slab from her 'grave' are believed to illustrate this tale. Visitors can make up their own minds, for the slab, along with 33 other fascinatingly carved Pictish stones, is now on display in the nearby village museum.
▶ *5 miles N of Coupar Angus on A94. Daily Apr-Sept.*

Meikleour beech hedge

The world's tallest hedge

In the autumn of 1745 Robert Murray-Nairne had just finished planting a 530m (580yd) long beech hedge when he was swept up in the Jacobite uprising. He died at Culloden, but his saplings thrived. They are now around 30m (100ft) high and ensure that his descendants enjoy ample privacy. Once every ten years a team of four men using a hydraulic platform give the hedge a shapely trim, a job that occupies them for six weeks.
▶ *Meikleour, 12 miles N of Perth on A93.*

The Hermitage

Tall trees and tall tales by the thunder of a waterfall

Britain's tallest tree, a 64.5m (212ft) Douglas Fir, stands above waterfalls and rapids on the River Braan as it churns through a romantic wooded glen. A folly overlooks the Black Linn falls, which crash down below an open belvedere with a terrifying roar that echoes off the walls. The ornamental building was designed in 1782 for the 3rd Duke of Atholl and, like a nearby grotto in the woods, commemorates Ossian the Bard, a mythic figure from the mists of Celtic lore.
▶ *1 mile W of Dunkeld on A9. NTS. Daily.*

The Scottish Crannog Centre

An Iron Age home on the water

In a large, dimly lit roundhouse, wisps of smoke swirl up from the hearth towards the high thatched roof. Underfoot, through layers of straw and timber, the loch waters lap against wooden piles. Close by, and safe from thieves or predators on shore, are wicker pens for livestock, a loom, a quern – a hand mill for grinding corn – crude pottery and wooden implements, with a few precious tools of iron.

This is life on a crannog, an Iron Age lake dwelling. One has been reconstructed at Loch Tay, based on remains found just across the water. It is an attempt to re-create a prehistoric home and to rediscover ancient skills. Within this strangely comforting place, you feel close to the world 2000 years ago.
▶ *Off A827 8 miles W of Aberfeldy. Daily Mar-Oct, Sat-Sun Nov.*

Stirling Castle

Scotland's most historic castle

With origins that lie buried within Dark Age legends, Stirling's massively impressive fortress has played centre stage through centuries of Scotland's history. Its walls, high above the River Forth, overlook the battlefields of Stirling Bridge and Bannockburn, where Wallace and the Bruce beat the English.

The magnificent Renaissance palace that was home to Mary, Queen of Scots is being restored to its former splendour. In the Great Hall, the fresh-cut timber of 400 oak trees went into the new hammerbeam roof, the largest in Scotland. In defiance of the old saying, the roof's weight rests on a square peg jammed into a round hole, an ancient trick that allows the joint to tighten as the wood expands. The Hall's exterior is equally astonishing: as gleaming and immaculate today as it was when built 500 years ago.
▶ *Stirling, off M9. HS. Daily.*

Commando Memorial

A moving tribute to brave men

Standing tall as giants in an empty landscape, an intensely lifelike trio of young soldiers scour the hills for hidden danger, their faces frozen in eternal youth. During the Second World War the mountains of Lochaber were a training ground for the elite force of special action troops and the monument is an evocative memorial to the 1700 commandos who died on missions behind enemy lines.

▶ *Spean Bridge, 9 miles NE of Fort William on A82.*

Inveraray Castle

Clan Campbell's show of strength

The central hall, soaring the full height of the house, is decorated from floor to ceiling with guns, swords, Lochaber axes, pikes and dirks: 1350 weapons that give a taste of the power wielded by chiefs of the Clan Campbell. These ruthless and ambitious warlords rose from 14th-century obscurity to dominate Argyle by the 18th century and enjoy vast wealth as landed aristocrats. In 1745 the 3rd Duke, who opposed Bonnie Prince Charlie's uprising that year, demolished the clan fortress, together with a nearby village, and replaced it with today's turreted fantasy fortress, with its Gobelins tapestries and Georgian silver.

▶ *¾ mile N of Inveraray town centre off A819 Dalmally road. Tel 01499 302203 for details.*

Kilmartin Glen

A landscape peopled by ghosts

Kilmartin is haunted by the spirits of its early inhabitants. Stone circles and alignments, tombs and shrines stand in the fields, while rock-faces in the hills above are etched with enigmatic carvings. The oldest monuments were built by Neolithic farmers who settled here 6000 years ago. Succeeding generations down to the Bronze Age worshipped and were buried in the valley. Nearby, on Dunadd Hill, the first Gaelic-speaking Scots from Ireland built a citadel in the 5th century.

▶ *10 miles N of Lochgilphead on A816 Oban road. Village museum daily Mar-Dec.*

Mount Stuart, Bute

The Xanadu of a Victorian eccentric

The Isle of Bute in the Firth of Clyde is the setting for one of Britain's most extraordinary monuments to High Victorian extravagance and Gothic taste. Built between 1880 and 1900, Mount Stuart was the home of the 3rd Marquess of Bute, a lover of medieval architecture and of all things mystical and strange. With an income of £300,000 a year (the equivalent of £15 million today), he was said to be the richest man in Britain. His enthusiasm and fortune were devoted to the restoration of historic buildings, including Castell Coch (see page 264), but his home was his own private fantasy: a place intended to astound, which it continues to do.

▶ *5 miles S of Rothesay on A886 Kingarth road. Daily May-Sept and Easter weekend.*

Iona

Island landfall of the saint who brought christianity to Scotland

A boat-shaped mound above a lonely beach, Port na Curaich, on Iona's southern shore, is said to mark the spot where St Columba buried his skin-covered coracle when he arrived here from Ireland in 563. Despite the summer visitors, time has stood still on this idyllic bay in the intervening years, preserving the island's allure as a place of solitude and refuge. Elsewhere on Iona, the restored medieval abbey, surrounded by old ruins, Celtic crosses and the unmarked graves of Scottish kings, encourages a more communal experience of sanctity.

▶ *1 mile off SW tip of island of Mull. Ferry all year from Fionnphort, on Mull.*

Fingal's Cave

Where nature outdoes the work of man

The naturalist Sir Joseph Banks invited comparison with grand feats of architecture when, in 1772, he described Fingal's Cave as being far superior to any building of the ancient or the modern world. The great sea cave on the isle of Staffa does indeed resemble a manmade structure – a cathedral, with a 'nave' 70m (227ft) long by 13m (42ft) wide and walls some 18m (60ft) in height formed from hexagonal basalt columns. In place of organ music there is the surge and echo of the sea, a sound that inspired Felix Mendelssohn, who visited Staffa in the summer of 1829, to compose his Hebrides Overture.

▶ *8 miles N of SW tip of island of Mull. Frequent boat-trips all summer from Fionnphort, on Mull.*

NORTH HIGHLANDS & ISLANDS

1 Up Helly Aa, Lerwick 2 Jarlshof 3 Brough of Birsay 4 St Magnus Cathedral, Kirkwall

5 Italian Chapel 6 Dunnet Head 7 Smoo Cave 8 Dunrobin Castle 9 Corrieshalloch Gorge

10 Clootie Well

Up Helly Aa, Lerwick

Music, rockets and a burning ship herald the return of the sun

Skies ignite above Lerwick and the streets are set aglow when, in fiery Viking tradition, Shetlanders celebrate the rebirth of the sun after a midwinter when it has barely risen above the horizon.

In January, at the festival of Up Helly Aa, one thousand costumed 'guisers' march by torchlight through the town, dragging in their midst a 9m (30ft) Viking longship. To the thump of brass-band music and the boom of rockets fired by boats in the harbour, the sacrificial ship is laid to rest and the guisers cast their torches in its hull. As the doomed ship blazes, the song *The Norseman's Home* rises with the smoke to drift across the sea.

▶ *Lerwick, Shetland Islands. Last Tues in Jan.*

Jarlshof

Four millennia of home building on Shetland's southerly tip

A complex tapestry of grassy mounds, walls, doors, hearths and passageways is woven into the landscape at Sumburgh Head. The buildings span some 4000 years and were constructed by many different tribes and races, each one with its own idea of what a home should be. The oldest houses to survive belonged to Neolithic farmers in the 3rd millennium BC, who lived within a midden of discarded rubbish that may have been a symbol of ancestral ownership.

By the Iron Age, 2000 years later, houses had become more spacious and many were equipped with souterrains: underground passages that may have been used for storing cheese and butter. The next building to appear was the defensive broch, a round dry-stone tower dating from the 1st century BC.

Later, the Picts built wheelhouses with chambers radiating from a central hearth. They, in turn, were displaced by Vikings, whose village flourished for 400 years. Finally, Scots warlords built a series of great mansions, the last of which remained inhabited until the 17th century.

▶ *22 miles S of Lerwick. HS. Daily Apr-Sept.*

Brough of Birsay

Viking comforts on a tidal island

The beautiful small island of Brough of Birsay, which can be reached dry-shod only at low tide, was for centuries the power centre of the Orkneys, under both Picts and Vikings. Little has survived of the Pictish settlement, which was destroyed by the Vikings in the 9th century. They then established the sprawling township that remains substantially intact, albeit in ruins. The buildings include impressive halls, smaller dwellings and a bath-house or sauna with benches, hearth and drains. The church dates from the 12th century, shortly before the island was abandoned to rabbits and puffins.

▶ *20 miles NW of Kirkwall, Orkney Islands, on A966. HS visitor centre June-Sept.*

St Magnus Cathedral, Kirkwall

A Norse cathedral that survived the ravages of the Reformation

Kirkwall's magnificent Romanesque cathedral retains the aura of medieval faith. It was founded by a Norseman, Rognald Earl of Orkney, in 1137. In the cavernous and shadowy nave, shafts of sunlight spill through heavy Norman arches to illuminate old tombs and shrines. The rich, red-stone walls, offset with blocks of pale gold, glow with warmth and colour. High overhead, carved corbels represent Vikings from 900 years ago.

▶ *Kirkwall centre. Daily.*

Italian Chapel

An eccentric labour of love on the coast of Scapa Flow

On a windswept shore 1500 miles from Rome stands a Nissen hut with a theatrically Italianate façade of columns, pinnacles and belfry. Inside this far-flung outpost of the Roman Church, the 'barrel-vaulted' roof is painted to resemble stone, and a vibrant mural decorates the sacristy.

The chapel was created by Italian prisoners of war who were helping to construct the Churchill Barriers around Scapa Flow during the Second World War. Using scrap and waste for their materials, they worked in their free time to create a building that reminded them of home and still exemplifies the triumph of their spirit in adversity.

▶ *8 miles SE of Kirkwall on A961. Daily.*

Dunnet Head

Most northerly headland pits its face against the elements

Eerie sea mists creep in without warning and windows in the lighthouse, although 105m (345ft) above sea level, are sometimes smashed by stones thrown up by gale-whipped waves. Dunnet Head is a place of wild extremes, with weather that can seldom be predicted. The cliff-girt headland rightfully claims the title as the most northerly point of mainland Britain over John o'Groats, 12 miles to the southeast. From this rocky outpost, Second World War gun emplacements scan the full length of Scotland's north coast to the cliffs of Cape Wrath, 58 miles away, and across to the Old Man of Hoy (see page 300) poking up above the skyline of its Orkney isle.
▶ *B855 from Dunnet, signed off A836 between Thurso and John o'Groats.*

Smoo Cave

A boat trip through a strange prehistoric underworld

Viking raiders used Scotland's largest natural cavern as a secret base for their longships when launching raids along the northern coast, but they were far from being its first occupants. The outer chamber is a huge sea cave, more than 30m (100ft) deep and 15m (49ft) high, with a floor of debris left by its prehistoric inhabitants. In the area beyond this lies a lake, fed by a waterfall that thunders from a sink-hole in the roof. During the summer, you can hire a ferryman to take you from here deep into an underworld of narrow passages, where strange rocky formations loom out of the darkness, glistening with moisture. Geologically, the system was created by a fault in limestone layers deposited around 500 million years ago, but exploration of its inner reaches seems akin to the experience of Jonah, after he had been swallowed by a whale.
▶ *2 miles E of Durness on A838.*

Dunrobin Castle

The Loire-style chateau where political correctness is ignored

A vast baronial pile, the seat of the Dukes of Sutherland, remodelled in the 19th century by Sir Charles Barry, exemplifies the wealth and privilege of aristocracy. This is in sharp contrast to the living conditions of the 5000 tenants the 1st Duke evicted during the Highland clearances. The colossal statue of him on a mountain above the nearby town of Golspie is still a source of outrage to some. But to most modern eyes the greatest shock here is the family museum. It contains some fascinating artefacts, including early Pictish symbol stones, but these are overshadowed by the trophies brought back by the 5th Duke and his wife from big-game hunting trips all over the world. They clearly shot anything that moved, for the room is filled from floor to ceiling with stuffed wildlife, from giraffe and elephant to porcupine and iguana.
▶ *2 miles N of Golspie on A9. Daily Apr–Oct.*

Corrieshalloch Gorge

A bridge with views of a lost world

For those with a good head for heights, the footbridge over Corrieshalloch Gorge is one of Britain's most thrilling river crossings. The Victorian suspension bridge, built in 1867 by Sir John Fowler, joint designer of the Forth Railway Bridge (see page 279), sways gently underfoot as it spans a sheer canyon just 18m (60ft) wide and 61m (200ft) deep. To one side are the Falls of Measach, thundering down 46m (150ft). To the other there is vertigo: a chasm that defies all sense of scale, with ferns and mosses growing from its dripping granite walls. Far below lies a world of rare plants created just after the last Ice Age, which has remained inviolate ever since.
▶ *S of Braemore on A832, off A835. NTS. Daily.*

Clootie Well

A sacred spring where torn clothes recall ancient Celtic rituals

Above a roadside spring that spills into a basin of time-worn stone, branches of overhanging trees are draped with clothes and odd scraps of cloth. This strange display, which dates back many generations, is a rare survival from old folklore. The waters from such sacred wells are said to cure illness and other afflictions, but in return their guardian spirits must be offered some item that has been worn by the supplicant, as a token of his or her soul.
▶ *1 mile W of Munlochy on A832.*

NORTH HIGHLANDS & ISLANDS

11 Inverewe Garden 12 Urquhart Castle 13 Bealach na Ba 14 Plockton

Inverewe Garden

A sub-tropical Eden on a windswept shoreline, at a more northerly latitude than Moscow

On the wild, craggy banks of Loch Ewe, tall Scots pines screen a lush garden oasis that is gently brushed by the warming waters of the Gulf Stream. Here you will find the unlikely sight of tall Australian gum trees growing happily alongside richly scented Chinese rhododendrons and Blue Nile lillies.

In 1861, when Osgood Mackenzie inherited this estate, there was only one dwarf willow growing on the whole peninsula. Beginning with the planting of shelter-belts of trees, he patiently set about its cultivation. By the time of his death, in 1922, Inverewe was internationally renowned for its rare plants and shrubs, gathered from the remotest corners of the world.

The gardens are most colourful in spring and early summer, when the rhododendrons and azaleas are in flower, although, since this is essentially a woodland garden, autumn often brings an equally dazzling display. The setting contributes to the magic, with glimpses of the sea shimmering through eucalyptus leaves, lily ponds in hidden glades, and rocky glens that have been transformed into exotic Himalayan valleys.

▶ *6 miles N of Gairloch on A832. NTS. Daily Jan-Oct; additional winter opening Tel 0844 4932225.*

Urquhart Castle

Waiting for Nessie

Visitors who linger on what remains of the 16th-century battlements of Urquhart Castle might claim to be admiring the views along Loch Ness. But most also harbour a hope of spotting a dark hump, or long prehensile neck, emerge out of the waters far below. Legend states that St Columba was threatened by a 'water beast' here in the 6th century. It then kept a low profile until the 1930s. Since then countless sightings of Nessie have been reported, and more occur each year.

▶ *15 miles SW of Inverness on A82. HS. Daily.*

Bealach na Ba

Nerves of steel are required to tackle Britain's highest road

A sign at the foot of Britain's highest and most intimidating road-pass warns learner drivers to proceed no further. This is sound advice, for within a mile the narrow road is snaking up and around hairpin bends with gradients of 1:5 in a remorseless ascent to 626m (2053ft). The views are spectacular, with Loch Kishorn sparkling silver far below.

Even in fine weather this is an adrenaline-pumping drive. Ferocious torrents and a lunar landscape contribute to the drama. If clouds descend there may be blizzards at the summit in mid June. The Gaelic name translates as both 'Pass of the Cattle' and 'Pass of the Fool'.

▶ *6 miles W of Lochcarron, on unclassified road signed to Applecross off A896.*

Plockton

Riviera living in a West Coast haven

Gaily painted cottages, lines of palm trees on the waterfront and a backdrop of stupendous wooded crags lend Plockton an exotic charm that is rarely found in Highland villages. Sheltered by a headland from the winds and open sea, the small community is located at the mouth of Loch Carron.

There are unspoilt sandy beaches on the seaward shore, reached only by footpaths, and a maze of narrow lanes explores the hinterland of forests, lochs and mountain moors. Plockton developed as a herring port in the early 19th century, but the local economy now depends on summer visitors, including artists, naturalists and yachtsmen.

▶ *5 miles NE of Kyle of Lochalsh, signed along minor roads. NTS.*

Time travel among ancient Orcadians

Scratch the surface of Orkney and a 5000-year-old realm, mysterious yet amazingly sophisticated, is revealed

1 Maeshowe **2** Stones of Stenness **3** Barnhouse **4** Ring of Brodgar **5** Skara Brae
6 The Tomb of the Eagles **7** Minehowe

They lie on the margin of today's world – beyond Cape Wrath, a ferry voyage or flight away. Yet 5000 years ago Orkney was at the centre of things, a crossing of sea routes, with sheltered havens, lush pastures, good building stone, rich fishing and a milder climate than now. Orkney then was in a golden age, one of the most advanced regions in Europe. We know because those ancient Orcadians bequeathed an archaeological landscape that challenges our perceptions of human progress.

Megalithic building boom

Head west from Kirkwall on the Stromness road and you soon reach one such thought-provoking place. In the parish of Stenness, where the B9055 peels off to the right, a narrow strip of land scarcely wider than the road stretches northwards. On one side lie the unchanging, dark waters of Loch of Harray; on the other is Loch of Stenness – an inlet of the sea, forever changing with the tide. Nearby four astounding monuments reflect a spate of megalithic construction.

The tomb of **Maeshowe** (daily, except Sun mornings, HS) is reached along a passage aligned exactly on midwinter sunset. The walls of its interior are so precisely constructed that you cannot slip a sheet of paper between the stones. Half-a-mile away stand the **Stones of Stenness** – four thin shapely slabs, the tallest 5m (17ft) high. Almost in their shadow is the Neolithic village of **Barnhouse**, where the porch of the largest house, aligned on the midsummer sunrise, had a fireplace set in its floor. A short distance farther north lies the **Ring of Brodgar**, where a

henge of 27 stones is surrounded by a ditch cut into the rock. There is unlimited public access to all three of these sites (HS).

Follow the B road across the serene Orkney landscape for 6 miles and you reach the Bay of Skaill, and one of the most remarkable prehistoric sites in Europe. **Skara Brae** (daily, all year) is unique: a preserved Neolithic village uncovered by a storm in 1850. The houses contain stone beds and other furniture, storage tanks and hearths; there are even what appear to have been lavatories. Built 5000 years ago, the village was home to people whose way of life was more sophisticated than that of many 19th-century crofters.

It was the local laird who initially excavated Skara Brae and, unsurprisingly in a place so rich in prehistoric remains, landowners continue to play a major role in their discovery and investigation. The **Tomb of the Eagles**, at the end of the B9041 near the southern tip of South Ronaldsay, which is connected to the principal island of Mainland by causeways, was found in 1958 by Ronald Simison, a local farmer. He also excavated the tomb, finding the remains of more than 300 humans, mingled with the bones and talons of sea eagles. More recently **Minehowe** (Tel 01856 861209 for opening times) at Tankerness, east of Kirkwall, was opened by farmer Douglas Paterson and excavated with help from Channel 4's *Time Team* in 1999. Its stone staircases descend 6.5m (21ft) below ground, but whether it was a tomb or place of ritual remains a mystery.

STONES OF STENNESS

NORTH HIGHLANDS & ISLANDS

15 Eilean Donan Castle **16** Inverie, Knoydart **17** Neptune's Staircase

18 Glenfinnan Monument

Eilean Donan Castle

Inspirational dreams and a magical renovation

Superbly situated on a rocky islet at a point where three deep sea lochs meet, the seat of the Macraes appears unaltered by the centuries. But Eilean Donan's extraordinary secret is its youth. The 13th-century castle was reduced to utter ruin after a Jacobite uprising in 1719. It was rebuilt as a private home between 1912 and 1932 by John MacRae-Gilstrap, a wealthy descendant of the clan. Farquhar MacRae, his clerk of works, claimed to be guided by visionary dreams as he re-created its medieval halls, passages and turrets without any records to refer to or experts to advise him. When old plans were discovered in a vault in Edinburgh, the accuracy of his second sight was confirmed. Historic character and detail blend with the sophisticated needs of a prewar millionaire, and his dream castle became one of the 20th century's most romantic homes.

▶ *10 miles E of Kyle of Lochalsh on A87. Daily Apr-Oct. Tel 01599 555202.*

Inverie, Knoydart

By boat or wilderness walk to mainland Britain's most remote pub

With the exception of the 80 people who live on the remote Knoydart peninsula, customers at the Old Forge Inn in the village of Inverie arrive by one of two memorable ways. Most catch the mail boat from Mallaig, which makes a spectacular passage across a sound overlooked by the mountains of Skye and the mainland.

More adventurous souls walk in from Glenfinnan, on the Fort William to Mallaig road – a stunning, two-day trek across 30 miles of mountains, glens and bogs. Whether you arrive by boat or on foot, the destination is a place apart. Children play hopscotch on the little-used road behind Inverie Bay – a single-track lane starting here and ending a few miles west, on the coast at Airor – and tide tables are more important than clocks.

▶ *10 miles NE of Mallaig, across Loch Nevis. Tel 01687 462320 for boat service details.*

Neptune's Staircase

Carrying ships between sea and glens on a voyage from coast to coast

From the basin at the top, there is a long view down this flight of locks to Loch Linnhe, 19.5m (64ft) below, and if they are in use the sight is even more arresting. Like all parts of the Caledonian Canal, the eight locks are capable of taking ocean-going ships, and to view a merchantman or tall ship up to 46m (150ft) long ascending or descending the slope is a surreal experience.

Thomas Telford designed the 60 mile long waterway between Fort William and Inverness, an engineering triumph of which the evocatively named flight of locks is the high point. Begun in 1803, the canal opened to shipping 19 years later, but it was another 25 years before it was fully complete – all at a total cost of £1.3 million.

▶ *2 miles N of Fort William off A830 road to Mallaig.*

Glenfinnan Monument

Flawed tribute, flawless setting

It would be hard to find a place more calculated to appeal to a Highlander. In morning light, Loch Shiel is a gleaming silver ribbon between a narrowing perspective of high peaks. Glens cut through the hills.

Bonnie Prince Charlie, if good at little else, knew how to tug at heartstrings, for this is where he raised his standard and launched the 1745 rebellion. Within months many of the clansmen who gathered at Glenfinnan lay dead on Culloden Moor. It seems appropriate, then, that the 20m (65ft) high monument to their impetuous leader leans slightly out of true and is not located exactly where he made his call to arms. Furthermore, the statue at its top bears no likeness to the Prince, since the sculptor copied the wrong portrait from a group of paintings hanging on a wall.

▶ *16 miles W of Fort William off A830 Mallaig road. NTS. Daily; visitor centre Easter-Oct.*

Fortresses of a forgotten race

Defensive strongholds or eccentric dwellings? We may never know the real purpose of the Scottish brochs

Massive, circular stone towers known collectively as brochs are among the most impressive prehistoric monuments in Britain. Found throughout the northern islands of Scotland and along the Highland coast, brochs first appeared in the 1st century BC and continued to be built, in a virtually unaltered style, for 200 years. Abandoned long before the birth of Pictish culture, they are the work of people who left no trace of their way of life apart from this extraordinary architecture.

Mousa Broch is stunningly located on the shoreline of a long-deserted Shetland island. It stands 13m (43ft) high, having lost only the top courses of its dry-stone walling in 2000 years. Its design is typical of brochs: a colossal cylinder of stone with a curving outer surface, rather like a cooling tower. A narrow entrance passage leads to a central yard overlooked by galleries and stairways built into the hollow walls. The yard may once have had a roof, or been partially protected by overhanging eaves. With timber platforms rising several storeys high above a central hearth, there would have been space for a chieftain and his entourage.

The **Broch of Gurness**, in Orkney, was discovered in 1929 when an artist sketching from the top of a grassy mound felt his stool subside beneath him. Excavations revealed the broch, with 3.5m (12ft) high walls, and also a settlement of houses, workshops, passages and lanes.

Although more than 500 brochs have been identified, most have been so plundered for their stone that only heaps of rubble remain. **Dun Carloway** and **Dun Dornaigil** still stand to just over half their full height. The two **Glenelg brochs** – Dun Telve and Dun Troddan – are well preserved and especially enigmatic. They stand just a small distance apart in wild country that was sparsely populated when they were built. Their owners were on good terms, presumably, but how was the land divided? And what threat could justify the construction of such well-defended towers? After a century of scientific archaeology, the brochs are still a mystery.

DUN CARLOWAY BROCH

War zone where rock and surf clash

The cliffscapes of Scotland's far north and west bear rugged witness to an elemental power struggle

NEIST

Every coast is a battle line between land and sea, but the northern shores of Scotland carry the scars of an all-out war between the elements. Here the pitching of ferocious North Atlantic gales against rocks formed and shaped by mighty tectonic forces, vulcanism and Ice Age glaciers has shaped wild, majestic cliffs, full of extravagant sculptural gestures.

To complete the drama, westerly winds and the warm Gulf Stream ocean current bring weather that can switch between all four seasons in a single day. The clarity of the air creates an extraordinarily sharp light, bringing distant islands into close-up, while scudding clouds and the reflective sea contribute to kaleidoscopic sunsets.

Britain's highest cliffs are found around the desolate wild headland of **Cape Wrath**, where Clo Mor rises 280m (920ft) from the boiling ocean. In the islands of the Hebrides the headland at **Neist** and **Butt of Lewis** are equally exposed to the unleashed power of the waves.

The evidence of a violent past

The Isle of Skye, although relatively sheltered from the ocean's full fury, has one of the most dramatic landscapes on the west coast, the legacy of volcanic upheavals in the relatively recent geological past of 50 million years ago. Glaciers smoothed the lava flows into rounded hills, while the harder and more brittle rocks were shattered by the ice to form jagged mountain ridges, pinnacles and cliffs. The whole geological story is laid out in the view from **Elgol** where rolling slopes crown contorted cliffs, while on the far side of Loch Scavaig the serrated Cuillin Hills rise steeply to over 900m (3000ft).

For passengers on ferries between the Orkneys port of Stromness, and Thurso or Aberdeen on the mainland, the **Old Man of Hoy** is a sight that never fails to astonish. With surf sweeping around its base and its top leaning at an angle, the towering 135m (445ft) rock pillar seems to be looking towards the island cliffs, of which it was once a part, for support. Like a slice of layer cake, the Old Man displays its geological origins: lower seams of basalt, a volcanic rock, are topped by bands of sandstone formed about 350 million years ago, when what is now Scotland lay close to the Equator.

NORTH HIGHLANDS & ISLANDS

19 West Highland Line **20** Ardnamurchan Point **21** Sgurr of Eigg

22 Kinloch Castle **23** The Quiraing

West Highland Line
Carried on mighty hollow legs

The line from Fort William to Mallaig is one of the most scenic railways in Britain, with many of the finest views from the viaducts that carry it across glens and rivers. Built between 1897 and 1901 by 'Concrete Bob' McAlpine, founder of the large construction company, they were innovative structures, utilising hollow concrete piers rather than solid masonry. While the Borrodale Viaduct, near Arisaig, was being built a horse and cart plummeted 25m (80ft) into an open pier and remains there to this day; an enigma that may puzzle archaeologists in the distant future. But the most impressive feature on the line is the 380m (1248ft) long, 30m (100ft) high Glenfinnan Viaduct.
▶ *Tel 08457 550033 to book.*

Ardnamurchan Point
Historic lighthouse on a wild shore

The most westerly point of mainland Britain is a lonely headland of ferocious beauty; a place of rugged, storm-lashed cliffs and sandy coves, with stunning views of the Hebrides. The lighthouse, built in 1849, was designed by Alan Stevenson, an uncle of the novelist Robert Louis Stevenson. Over a period of half a century, two generations of the family were responsible for constructing some 60 lighthouses around Britain's coast and overseas, transforming safety at sea. Although no longer manned, the 55m (180ft) granite tower still beams its light across the waters of The Minch and is open to the public.
▶ *80 miles W of Fort William at end of B8007 road, off A861. Daily Apr-Oct.*

Sgurr of Eigg
Over volcanic rock to an island view

High cliffs and the towering 'sgurr' – a massive fist of bare volcanic rock – give the Isle of Eigg a distinctive profile when seen from the mainland. The climb to the 393m (1290ft) summit of An Sgurr is far less challenging than it looks, though memorable nonetheless.

From the harbour – the focus for the small community who own and manage Eigg – a lane winds up through woods and meadows. The upper path is steeper, climbing through a landscape of lava flows and precipices lined with dark columns of glassy rock. Huge tumbled walls above a natural 'staircase' on the upper slopes are remnants of an Iron Age citadel. Perhaps it was a temple in the sky rather than a refuge for people and livestock – a more likely explanation, given the remote setting. An epic Hebridean panorama reveals itself at the summit: Rum, Canna and Skye to the north, Coll, Tiree and Mull to the south.
▶ *10 miles off coast at Arisaig on A830 Fort William-Mallaig road. Tel 01687 450224 (Arisaig) or 01687 462403 (Mallaig) for boats.*

Kinloch Castle
Waltz to the music of time

In the hall, which seems to await the return of tweed-suited hunters, an 'orchestrion' booms out jolly waltzes that echo down deserted corridors. A mechanical construction of pipes, drums and brass, it was in its time the ultimate home-entertainment system.

The clocks seem to have stopped in 1914 in this mansion where, nearly a century ago, the only visitors allowed were guests of George Bullough, laird and heir to a textiles fortune. Now the deserted isle of Rum is a nature reserve and lesser mortals can enjoy the faded glamour of a house that was extravagant even by the standards of its age.
▶ *Sailings all year from Mallaig and Arisaig. SNH. Tel 01687 462037 for opening times.*

The Quiraing
Fearsome mountain hideout of the cattle raiders

This jagged ridge on north Skye's Trotternish peninsula inspires a sense of awe. Pinnacles of rock with names such as The Needle and The Prison rise like broken fangs from a monstrous jaw of cliffs and plunging chasms. In the days, up to three centuries ago, when feuding clans rustled each other's cattle, the chaotically confusing labyrinth of the Quiraing was the perfect place to conceal stolen livestock. Those unfamiliar with the paths should treat this place, where mountain mists can suddenly sweep in to shroud precipices in a deadly veil, with profound respect.
▶ *Skye, 18 miles N of Portree on minor road from Staffin to Uig.*

SCOTLAND

Dunvegan Castle

A fortress surrendered to the forces of fiction and romance

A frail, faded scrap of ancient fabric hangs in pride of place in the elegantly furnished drawing room of this ancient castle on Skye. Of all the fine possessions that the chiefs of Clan MacLeod have accumulated over the past 800 years, this is the most priceless. According to some experts, it was manufactured in the Middle East 1500 years ago and may have been a holy relic. Others claim that it is a Norse battle standard. But, as is frequently the case in Scotland, the facts soon become entangled and obscured by legend, with clan storytellers insisting that this is the Fairy Flag, woven by fairies and guaranteeing the protection of the MacLeods from disaster.

The urge for theatrical effect embellishes the castle in other ways: defences have been built to increase the romantic appeal of the fortress rather than its military strength, and dirks are displayed alongside Georgian silver.

▶ *Dunvegan, Skye, 22 miles NW of Portree off A850. Daily.*

Fairy Glen

Play Gulliver in a miniature kingdom

Stumble across this scaled-down landscape and you could believe yourself to be in a land of illusion. Pinnacles of rock and conical 'mountains' scarcely 20m (60ft) in height soar above tiny lochs and rivulets, hidden caves and secret paths in a landscape where a child becomes a giant. This unexpected glen is said by some to be a homeland of the 'Little People' – a borderland between real life and the realm of dreams. In reality it was created 10,000 years ago by landslips and erosion after the last Ice Age retreated from Skye.

▶ *Skye, 1 mile S of Uig off A855 on minor road to hamlet of Sheader.*

THE LILT OF GAELIC AND THE DIP OF A MEDIEVAL WARSHIP'S OARS

ISLE OF BARRA

Isle of Barra

The lilt of Gaelic and the dip of a medieval warship's oars

The strange charm of Hebridean life strikes visitors who fly to Barra from the moment the plane touches down, not on a runway, but on a mile-wide beach of firm white sand set against a landscape of bare hills and fields brilliant with wild flowers. Tides and weather dictate life on this remote outpost of the British Isles, where Gaelic is still spoken among the population of some 1500 fishermen and crofters. Offshore from Castlebay, the island's tiny 'capital', Kisimul Castle rises picturesquely from the waters of the harbour, and age-old folksongs tell of mythical days when MacNeil chiefs and Kisimul's galley were feared throughout the Hebridean seas.

▶ *Regular sailings from Oban on mainland and Lochboisdale on South Uist. Castle daily in summer. HS. Tel 01871 810313 for opening times.*

Calanais Standing Stones

Don't ask why, just stand and stare at the prehistoric sentinels by the sea

Casual visitors gaze at the stones with wonder, archaeologists can do little more. The dozens of great megaliths – some as tall as 5.5m (17ft) – are arranged in a cross with a circle of 13 stones at its centre, and at the heart of the circle is a small tomb dating from about 2700 BC.

When the stones were erected and for what purpose remain mysteries. Experts suggest that they may be spaced out in megalithic yards, a unit of measurement used throughout Neolithic Britain – but that sheds no light on the enigma. Some astronomers claim that the stones are aligned with the Moon at certain times of year, and folklore has it that a spring spirit dances here when the cuckoo arrives on the isle of Lewis. Study such ideas at leisure: when you visit, reserve your attention for the sheer drama of this far-northern Stonehenge and its setting overlooking a sea loch.

▶ *Isle of Lewis, 12 miles W of Stornoway off A858. HS. Daily. Visitor centre daily except Sun.*

SCOTLAND

Key

1 Main entry

2 Feature entry

Motorway

Principal A road

(See 'Finding your way', page 7)

The province seems to hold up a watery mirror to its beauty: the glint of lough, whether salty inlet like Strangford, or silvery-fresh ribbon like Erne, is never far away, while along the coast reflections of strand, rock and island are caught in the ocean's swell.

Northern Ireland

Rathlin Island

16

17

15 Ballycastle

Portrush

18

Coleraine

A2

A37

Glens of Antrim

A43

14

A44

A26

A42

A6

Sperrin
Mountains

5

A42

Ballymena

A36

Larne

A31

A6

M2

A57

Carrickfergus

A505

6

M22

Antrim

NORTHERN IRELAND
304-311

Cookstown

Lough
Neagh

M5

Belfast

Bangor

11-13

A29

Strangford
Lough

10

Dungannon

Lisburn

A20

A4

M1

A7

A22

Craigavon

A24

Armagh

A3

A1

Downpatrick

9

A29

A25

A25

Newry

8

Mourne
Mountains

7

A29

A2

NORTHERN IRELAND

1 Belleek Pottery **2** Lough Erne **3** Devenish Island **4** Florence Court and Castle Coole

Belleek Pottery

Craftspeople weave porcelain wonders from a handful of clay

The craftsman's fingers tease and roll the strip of clay, laying it delicately into its appointed place in the latticework he is painstakingly constructing. One careless slip with the homemade tool − a 5 inch long nail with its point flattened − would destroy the day's work; but Michael has been making Belleek pottery baskets for 15 years − there will not be a slip.

Tomorrow he will fashion a number of minute flowers to embellish the piece. Then, hand-painter Maureen will use her talents to colour it. Fired and finished to a gleaming glaze, the fragile piece of Parian ware will sell in the pottery's gift shop for around £400. Visitors to Belleek Pottery, which was founded in 1857, can view the whole process, from a lump of Cornish china clay and powdered glass to an exquisite porcelain ornament. Before modelling begins, the clay mixture is mechanically kneaded like dough to remove any air, then put in a machine and extruded in the spaghetti-like strands needed to make the baskets.

▶ *5 miles E of Ballyshannon on A47. For details of opening times and tours, Tel 028 6865 9300.*

Lough Erne

Islands and shore dissolving into legend-filled watery expanses

Some say Lough Erne was formed when a pair of careless lovers took the lid off a magic well and allowed its contents to spill across the landscape. Others will tell you that Jeremiah, the prophet of doom, lies buried beneath its surface. It is scarcely surprising that legends cling to its waters as readily as morning mists: Lough Erne is an extraordinary feature − two great expanses of water joined by channels that meander around Enniskillen and for several miles south of the town. On a map, Lower Lough Erne − an island-spattered sheet of water 26 miles long and up to 5 miles wide − resembles a leaping dolphin. Upper Lough Erne, with its maze of islands (there are around 160 in the two parts of the lake), looks like the 16 mile long splash left in the dolphin's wake − a great arc where land and water craze into hundreds of creeks, peninsulas and islets.

▶ *22 miles SW of Omagh on A32 Enniskillen road.*

Devenish Island

By boat to haunting monastic remains and a view from a tower

Little green Devenish Island lies at the southern end of Lower Lough Erne, a marvellously peaceful spot even though the mainland is only a short distance off. The island is filled with a remarkable collection of monastic monuments − a medieval church and priory ruins, ancient gravestones, an elaborately carved high cross, and a 12th-century round tower 25m (82ft) high − not the tallest in Ireland, but one of the most complete. Four carved heads stare down from the cornice. A series of wooden ladders leads to the top level, from which there are spectacular views over Lower Lough Erne.

▶ *Ferries from Enniskillen and Trory jetty, 3 miles N of Enniskillen off A32. Daily Apr-Sept.*

Florence Court and Castle Coole

Grand residences of Anglo-Irish landowners

Florence Court and Castle Coole, 7 miles apart, are the best examples of 18th-century 'Big Houses' in Fermanagh. Florence Court was built by the Cole family, later earls of Enniskillen. Superb rococo plasterwork inside seethes with foliage, fruit and figures, watched over from their portrait frames by the hawk-nosed and red-haired earls. Look out for a Belleek china chamberpot with a portrait of Gladstone in the bottom − a measure of his increasing unpopularity when he supported Home Rule.

Castle Coole, just outside Enniskillen, is the finest example of a neoclassical house in Ireland. It was designed by the architect James Wyatt for the 1st Earl of Belmore. Much of Wyatt's interior design survives, along with wonderful regency furniture. It was not a happy home for the first earl − his wife caused great local scandal when she left him.

▶ *Florence Court, 6 miles S of Enniskillen, signed off A32; NT; for opening times Tel 028 6634 8249. Castle Coole, 2 miles SE of Enniskillen, signed off A4; NT; for opening times Tel 028 6632 2690.*

The enigma of the lough's statues

Ancient stone figures on islands in Lough Erne speak of the dawn of Christianity and earlier, pagan times

1 Boa Island ▶ *10 miles E of Belleek on A47. Statues are signposted off road 1 mile beyond bridge leading to island.*

2 White Island ▶ *Ferry from Castle Archdale, off B82 3 miles S of Kesh. Daily July-Aug, Sat Sun and bank hols Apr-June*

Two of the 97 isles of Lower Lough Erne contain remarkable stone statues: **Boa Island**, which lies at the northernmost point of the lake, and **White Island**, off the eastern shore. Experts cannot agree on the meaning of these ancient figures, perhaps 2000 years old, so you are free to make what you will of them.

Carved to hold the blood of sacrifices

In picturesquely overgrown Caldragh graveyard on Boa Island stands the waist-high Janus Man, so-called because, like the ancient Roman god of gates and doorways after which it is named, the statue has two faces – carved on opposite sides of the stone. The state of phallic upswing depicted on one of the figures indicates that it is assertively male; the one on the reverse may be female.

Where the heads join on the crown of the stone, a deep hollow has been carved – a libation bowl in the view of some, a receptacle for the blood of sacrificial victims according to others. Next to Janus Man is the smaller, more worn statue known as Lusty Man – named after its original location of nearby Lustymore Island, from which it was brought to this spot, rather than because of any anatomical features.

While the two Boa Island statues are pagan, the caryatids mounted on a wall on White Island (below) are later and mix primitive religion and early Christianity. The smallest of the figures (farthest left, below) is a sheela-na-gig, a grinning woman in a sexually provocative pose; next to her is a figure holding what might be a book. Then comes a monk, perhaps St Patrick, a youth pointing to his mouth, a curly haired figure, perhaps Christ, and a man with a shield. The seventh carving is unfinished. At the end is a single, staring head.

WHITE ISLAND

NORTHERN IRELAND

5 Sperrin Hills **6** Bog archaeology **7** Slieve Gullion **8** Mourne Wall **9** Struell Wells

10 Strangford Lough **11** Samson and Goliath **12** Tropical Ravine, Belfast Botanic Gardens

Sperrin Hills

Wild moorland hills, perfect for seekers of solitude

Tyrone is Northern Ireland's least-known and most sparsely populated county, so it is hardly surprising that the Sperrin Hills have remained something of a secret – quiet and uncrowded. Sawel, the highest of the Sperrin summits, is only 678m (2224ft) high so these are not formidable mountains. Walking here, you have time and space to enjoy mountain hares, hen harriers and buzzards, springy turf underfoot and an abundance of extensive views.

The Sperrins stretch for 40 miles along the Tyrone-Londonderry border. The secluded green valleys of the Glenelly and Owenkillew rivers cut through the range from east to west.
▶ *Sperrin Heritage Centre at Cranagh on B47 in Glenelly Valley, 17 miles E of Strabane.*

Bog archaeology

Protective quagmire that covered a prehistoric landscape

Under the thick blanket bog that is found across the middle of County Tyrone lies one of Europe's most important archaeological finds. The treasures that have been unearthed at sites near Creggan, most of them accidentally by the spades of turf cutters, are outstanding. They include the connecting stone circles and avenues at Beaghmore, and neolithic tombs at Cregganconroe and Creggandevesky. The latter is an astonishing structure 15m (50ft) long with pincer-shaped ceremonial court and stone interment chambers, perfectly preserved in a beautiful site overlooking Lough Mallon.
▶ *An Creagán Visitor Centre at Creggan, 12 miles E of Omagh on A505. Daily.*

A MONUMENT TO HARD WORK AND HARDER TIMES
MOURNE WALL

Slieve Gullion

Legends of a bewitching landscape

At the lofty 575m (1886ft) summit of Slieve Gullion is a 5000-year-old passage grave. Crawl into it to find a domed stone chamber, a highly atmospheric spot associated with legend. It was on this mountain that the Irish hero Fionn MacCumhaill (Finn McCool) was instantly transformed into an old man when he was tricked by a witch into diving into her enchanted lake near the peak. His companions dragged the spiteful sorceress from her lair – the passage grave – and forced her to restore Fionn's strength. Some locals will still advise you not to touch the water of Calliagh Bernas Lough, the witch's lake.

▶ *5 miles SW of Newry on B113. Slieve Gullion Forest Visitor Centre daily Easter–end summer.*

Mourne Wall

A monument to hard work and harder times

The early 20th century was a lean time in poverty-stricken County Down. Thousands of local men earned their bread between 1910 and 1922 by helping to build the Mourne Wall – 22 miles of stone wall up to 1.5m (5ft) high, that enclosed the catchment area of a reservoir in the Silent Valley of the beautiful Mountains of Mourne. As you walk the Mourne Wall, a tremendous circuit of the main Mourne peaks, spare a thought for its creators' impoverishment and hunger, to which every yard of wall bears witness.

▶ *On B27 just S of Spelga Reservoir or from minor road S of Silent Valley reservoir.*

Struell Wells

Ancient spa where St Patrick took an ice-cold bath

Holy and curative wells in Ireland are usually simple stone enclosures standing on their own, but Struell Wells is a complete spa, thousands of years old. In a craggy green field are several separate springs and runs of water, including a well to cure eye diseases, a medieval bathhouse for men and another for women.

It is said that the indomitable St Patrick spent a great part of the night immersed in one of the wells, stark naked, singing psalms and spiritual songs. The saint must have been an incredibly resilient man, since the well's water is deathly cold.

▶ *2 miles SE of Downpatrick, signed off B1 Ardglass road.*

Strangford Lough

A great tidal inlet, home to migrant birds and wealthy eccentrics

East of Belfast the Ards Peninsula hangs down from the shoulder of County Down, sheltering the 20 mile long inlet of Strangford Lough and its thousands of overwintering birds.

Two grand houses, each with a strong whiff of eccentricity, overlook the lough. **Mount Stewart** has splendid gardens, which contain grotesque statuary and a terrace dedicated to the dodo. They were created in the early 20th century by Edith, Lady Londonderry, whose flamboyance extended to having snakes tattooed on her legs.

At 18th-century **Castle Ward**, Bernard and Anne Ward could not agree on a design. He went ahead with a Palladian style at the front, while she ordered exuberant Moorish-Gothic at the back. The two blend surprisingly well – unlike the Wards, who separated.

▶ *Mount Stewart, 6 miles SE of Newtownards on A20 Portaferry road; NT; Tel 028 4278 8387. Castle Ward, 7 miles NE of Downpatrick off A25 Strangford road; NT; Tel 028 4488 1204.*

Samson and Goliath

Twin symbols of shipbuilding

The twin cranes known as Samson and Goliath tower 100m (330ft) above Harland & Wolff's shipyard in canary-yellow majesty, a landmark from many parts of Belfast. Each capable of lifting 840 tonnes, they stand like heroic sculptures, reminders of great vessels built by the yard – liners such as *Titanic* and *Canberra*, and warships, including the aircraft carrier HMS *Eagle*.

▶ *¾ mile N of city centre on E bank of River Lagan.*

Tropical Ravine, Belfast Botanic Gardens

Vision of an equatorial world

Shadowy fish and terrapins make ripples in the water below the dripping foliage of avocado, cinnamon, loquat, banana and sugar-cane plants. The air below the glazed roof is a warm, wet blanket. Gazing down on this lush green profusion from the gallery, you realise that Cornwall's Eden Project (see page 15) is far from the first re-creation of the tropics. Back in 1887, Charles McKinnon, curator of the gardens, set up a fernery here, and a dozen years later a furnace was added to create the steamy heat. The exotic jungly ravine, 9m (30ft) deep, still flourishes.

▶ *South Belfast, off Stranmillis Road. Daily.*

NORTHERN IRELAND

Art of The Troubles

Ulster's divisions splashed across the walls of houses

The four men in black hoods point their automatic rifles threateningly from the house wall on the loyalist Shankill Road in Belfast. 'For God And Ulster' trumpets the slogan, with the words 'Red Hand Commando' underneath. Shankill citizens pass by without a glance; 30 years of The Troubles have inured them to mural polemic. Political and paramilitary allegiances are dramatically spelled out in the huge, crude and colourful wall art of Ulster. Down the nationalist Springfield and Falls roads the slogans change: 'Free the PoWs', 'Slán – Goodbye, Soldier', they read. One of the city's cabbies will take you on a tour of the best of this populist street art.
▶ *Various areas around Belfast city centre.*

Glens of Antrim

Spectacular realm of rivers, waterfalls and rock

The Antrim coast is a geological confusion of granite, limestone, sandstone and basalt. Rivers flowing northeast to the sea have wriggled round harder obstacles and cut down through soft rock to create nine spectacular glens. The A2 coast road skirts their seaward ends and side roads thread their lengths. Glenariff is the most eyecatching and popular, with woodland and waterfall trails based on the Visitor Centre, off the A43 high in the glen. Waterfalls coursing over black basalt sills under the trees make walking here a memorable experience.
▶ *Follow A2 Larne-Ballycastle coast road.*

Carrick-a-Rede rope bridge

Swaying high above the beach on a crossing between cliffs

It looks too flimsy to support anyone, and it sways and lurches alarmingly under the walker. The bridge – a cat's cradle of rope and planks suspended over a 24m (80ft) deep chasm – seems a horribly precarious way of reaching the great rock stack separated from the mainland. But the design has stood the test of 350 years, ever since salmon fishermen first slung their homemade bridge across the gap to set nets for fish from the base of the rock. Tourists as well as fishermen use the bridge these days – the former with squeals of fear, the latter with admirable sang-froid.
▶ *½ mile walk from car park off B15 Ballintoy road, 3 miles NW of Ballycastle. NT. Daily Mar-Oct.*

Rathlin Island

Come on along and listen to the loudest band in bird land

You round a corner on the descent to the RSPB reserve viewpoint and there they are – 250,000 shrieking, wheeling, quarrelling and cooing seabirds. The sight, sound and smell are enough to knock you down the cliff steps. It is an overwhelming experience, this first encounter with the multitudes of birds nesting each spring and summer on the Cliffs of Kebble at the western end of Rathlin Island. Fulmars, guillemots, razorbills, cormorants, puffins, kittiwakes and gannets, along with wheeling buzzards and stooping peregrine falcons, can all be seen on a visit.

The human inhabitants of this 5 mile long, L-shaped island off the north Antrim coast are rather fewer in number – about 70 farmers, fishermen and caterers to the island's skimpy tourist trade. These are laid-back folk, happy to chat and to point you towards the birds, the beaches and orchid meadows of their island.
▶ *6 miles off N coast of Antrim. Daily ferries from Ballycastle. Reserve viewpoint open Apr-mid Sept; Tel 028 2076 3948 to confirm.*

Giant's Causeway

How amorous Fionn kept his feet dry

The giant was Fionn MacCumhaill (or Finn McCool); the causeway, chunks of cliff he hurled out to sea to act as stepping stones when he visited a giantess girlfriend far to the north on the Hebridean isle of Staffa. In reality, the great geometric groyne spilling out into the sea is made up of some 37,000 basalt columns, created by the cooling of lava after a volcanic eruption some 60 million years ago. In the cliffs behind are more huge, pipe-like basalt hexagons known as the Giant's Organ. A visitor centre explains the geology and mythology of this World Heritage Site.
▶ *12 miles NE of Coleraine, on B146 coast road off A2 Ballycastle-Bushmills road. NT. Daily.*

Mussenden Temple

A clifftop rendezvous for trysts and secret masses

The folly, built in 1785, perches on the edge of cliffs, a classical rotunda in an attention-grabbing if risky position. In that, it mirrors the lifestyle and demeanour of its builder, the highly idiosyncratic Frederick Hervey, 4th Earl of Bristol and Protestant Bishop of Londonderry. He named the little domed building after a cousin, Mrs Frideswide Mussenden, who died before it was finished. Hervey, owner of the surrounding Downhill Estate, was an eccentric and spendthrift, who may well have housed one or more of his mistresses in the folly and is also said to have organised horse races on the sands below in which clergy jockeys rode for the prize of a parish in his diocese. He was also a compassionate and ecumenically minded man who allowed Mass to be said in the isolated building at a time when Roman Catholic priests were being persecuted in Ireland.
▶ *1 mile W of Castlerock on A2 Coleraine-Limavady road. NT. Grounds daily; Tel 028 2073 1582 for Temple opening arrangements.*

March with history along the walls

The defenceworks that ring Ulster's second city supply powerful insights into the province's past

3 City walls

Abandon any misconceptions fostered by headlines: Londonderry or Derry, according to whether you talk to a member of the unionist or nationalist community, is a magnificent city. The mile-round **City Walls** offer an hour-long stroll past bastions and gates, above a gridiron of streets.

From Shipquay Gate – one of the main gateways in the walls – climb the steps onto the ramparts and set out in an anti-clockwise direction, with the city centre on your left. Built between 1613 and 1618 to protect a plantation of English Protestants from the Catholic locals, the walls, which are up to 8m (25ft) high and 6m (18ft) thick, were planned and built by the wealthy Corporation of London guilds – hence the change of name from Derry to Londonderry.

Past bastions and rows of cannon

The severest test for the walls began in April 1689, when the deposed James II arrived below them with an army. Four months earlier, the city keys had been seized by 13 Protestant Apprentice Boys, who locked the gates against the threat of attack by forces loyal to the former Catholic sovereign. Now, the defenders, shouting 'No surrender', battened down for a 105-day-long siege. At the **Tower Museum** (Tues-Sat), situated in O'Doherty's Fort, a short distance into the walk, you can discover how the siege failed, as well as gain an overview of the city's history.

From the walls by the museum you can see the spire of **St Columb's Cathedral** (Mon-Sat), which lies about 20 minutes' walk away, past rows of cannon used in the siege. Their muzzles symbolically point over the Bogside, the Catholic area where the events of Bloody Sunday in 1972, now commemorated in a memorial, contributed to The Troubles of the past three decades. The cathedral itself, completed in 1633, contains a fine reredos, stained glass depicting the siege and the city keys seized by the Apprentice Boys.

Continue along the walls towards the starting point and one final destination. The late-Victorian **Guildhall** (open Mon-Fri), which lies outside the walls near Shipquay Gate, is a tribute to the restorer's art. Destroyed by fire and bombs, it has on each occasion been painstakingly rebuilt – down to the fine stained-glass windows depicting scenes of the siege.

NORTHERN IRELAND

INDEX